THE SUPREME COURT AND THE PRESS

WITHDRAWN

Medill School of Journalism
VISIONS *of the* AMERICAN PRESS

─────────◇─────────

GENERAL EDITOR
David Abrahamson

Selected titles in this series

THE SUPREME COURT
AND THE PRESS
THE INDISPENSABLE CONFLICT

Joe Mathewson

Foreword by Fred Graham

MEDILL SCHOOL OF JOURNALISM

Northwestern University Press
Evanston, Illinois

Northwestern University Press
www.nupress.northwestern.edu

Copyright © 2011 by Joe Mathewson. Foreword copyright © 2011 by Fred Graham.
Published 2011 by Northwestern University Press. All rights reserved.

Printed in the United States of America

10 9 8 7 6 5 4 3 2 1

Library of Congress Cataloging-in-Publication Data

Mathewson, Joe, 1933–
    The Supreme Court and the press : the indispensable conflict / Joe Mathewson ;
foreword by Fred Graham.
        p. cm. — (Visions of the American Press)
    "Medill School of Journalism."
    Includes bibliographical references and index.
    ISBN 978-0-8101-2621-3 (pbk. : alk. paper)
    1. Freedom of the press—United States. 2. Mass media—Law and legislation—
United States. 3. Government and the press—United States. 4. United States.
Supreme Court. 5. United States. Supreme Court—Press coverage. I. Medill School
of Journalism. II. Title. III. Series: Visions of the American press.
KF4772.M38 2010
342.7308′53—dc22

                                                                2010028930

To the truth seekers of the world

CONTENTS

◈

Part Four
Closing Arguments

FOREWORD

◈

Fred Graham

Based solely on logic and the law, it is difficult to say what the relationship between the Supreme Court and the press should be. There is no statute, such as the Freedom of Information Act which governs the executive branch, that lays out how transparent the judiciary must be. And logically speaking, an argument can be made that a Court that has been historically free of scandal and corruption doesn't much need the presence of the watchdog press. Plus—let's face it—the justices have lifetime tenure, and they can theoretically do what they want to do.

Indeed, some of the justices seem to feel that reporters should be free to attend the courtroom arguments and read the issued opinions—and that's about it. Over the years, because the Court had no articulated policy encouraging openness, practices that needlessly made the journalist's job more difficult remained in effect. For years the Court's official transcripts of its hearings identified the members of the Court only as "Justice," so it was impossible to tell which justice asked what questions. Until relatively recently the Court stuck with its tradition of issuing opinions only on Mondays, even though that meant an unmanageable outpouring of jurisprudence would be dumped on the press on some Mondays. The Court had no policy controlling what to disclose if a justice fell ill. For example, Chief Justice Rehnquist once called a roomful of reporters "a bunch of vultures" for asking about his health problems. Other instances abound of abrasive points between the Court and the media, and there have been scant broad principles to apply to reduce the friction.

What seems to have happened in recent years is that the justices have realized that, given the growing importance of the Court's work, the Court needed to become more transparent in its dealings with the outside world. The result has been an evolution in the relationship between the Court and the media toward more openness. Interestingly, the innovative force behind this process was Chief Justice Warren Burger, after the liberal and supposedly more enlightened Earl Warren did little about it. In a series of small changes the Court has transformed its anachronistic media practices into a modern communications operation. But the process has certainly been piecemeal and erratic, as Joe Mathewson documents in this wonderfully comprehensive volume.

For the most part, this evolutionary process described by Mathewson has run its course. Many of the friction points between the journalists and the justices have been resolved. The Court's Public Information office, under Kathy Arberg, has become a helpful and professional media operation. All this is admirable, but with regard to the Court's media relations, the end of history, as they say, has not quite been reached. Most particularly, the Supreme Court has yet to come to terms with the fact that it can accomplish an enormously educational public service by opening its sessions to television coverage—and the justices stubbornly refuse to do so.

There are many reasons why members of the public should be able to watch the Court's proceedings on television and on the Internet. Like it or not, these days most people get most of their news from television. Ban TV, and you have lost them. Currently, controversial decisions often hit the public like a confusing bolt out of the blue, because the public has not previously been exposed to discussions of the issues. As a matter of principle, people should be able to watch the Supreme Court when it is conducting business in public, unless this causes a problem.

The justices' hostility to television coverage has a curious history. Chief Justice Burger was an "over-my-dead-body" opponent. He said that TV lights hurt his eyes (but also rejected radio coverage), and after his retirement there were rumors that the Court was ready to consider allowing television coverage. Justice Lewis Powell told me that, after Burger left, the sentiment on the Court was virtually unanimous that they would wait a while, so as not to make a change that might seem to be a slap in the face to Burger—but then they would move toward allowing television coverage. Justice Powell said two events soured this feeling among the justices. One was the raucous televised Senate confirmation hearings on the Supreme Court nomination of Robert Bork, and the other was the chaotic televised murder trial of O. J. Simpson. After that, the sentiment on the Court toward television seems to have turned steadily negative.

Different members of the Court have given different reasons for opposing TV, and they offer a window on how the Court sees itself. The reasons include fears of showboating, concern that the presence of a camera will upset the natural chemistry of the hearings, and worries that the justices will become recognizable and therefore less secure in public. But the most substantial concern may be one that the justices don't mention in public: that the Court enjoys a favorable mystique that might be eroded if the justices were seen doing their work from day to day, warts and all. Before President Obama took office, one member of the current Court expressed it to me this way: "Polls show that Congress and the president are low in public esteem. They are both on television. We [the Court] are not on television, and we score pretty high with the public." The Court can hardly base its case on the argument that, if it is seen as it actually is, its reputation will suffer. But until the justices become comfortable with the idea that the Court's high public image will not be undermined by TV coverage, they seem unlikely to admit cameras.

Eventually, as Mathewson puts it, the Supreme Court will open up to the public because "it is *their* Court, *their* Constitution." And in doing so, not only will the public be well served, but it will also remove one of the few lingering friction points between the Supreme Court and the press.

PREFACE

◈

Why the Supreme Court? Of all the governmental entities covered by American journalists, it is the strangest. While presidents and governors and legislators hold news conferences and "town hall" meetings and appear on talk shows, the justices of the Supreme Court hide behind a red velvet curtain. While both elected and appointed officials seek publicity, the justices shun it. Unless they have just published a book, they do not sit for interviews. They may occasionally speak at a law school or in a limited public forum, but only in a general fashion about the law, never to discuss cases, even old ones, and no television, please. Yet these nine women and men are the ultimate power in our democracy, making decisions of immense importance, on one memorable occasion even deciding a disputed presidential election—by one vote. They are the modern embodiment of Theodore Roosevelt's credo: "Speak softly and carry a big stick."

One might ask, where is that stick? For in fact the Supreme Court commands no battalions. Still, its word is law, and in our law-abiding society, the law must be observed. The Supreme Court has achieved this pinnacle of authority not from the Constitution, which merely created the Court, but from its own carefully crafted decisions and their relentless, persuasive logic. This is the way the Court speaks, not through news conferences. It is the silent branch of government.

That, of course, is not the end of it. When the Court speaks, who listens? Who transmits each new rule of law to the citizenry? Even in the Internet era, when the Court posts its opinions promptly on its own Web site, both justices and citizens still depend on journalists to get the word out to the broad public. It is still reporters who immediately read the often challenging legal language and reasoning and make sense of it for lay understanding (and in this book the terms "Negro" and "colored" appear where historically appropriate). The justices give them no coaching, no off-the-record briefings, no time to read the opinions before release. Nor do they point out to reporters later any errors in their stories to help them deepen their understanding of the law and the Court. So, if knowledge is power, journalists at the Supreme Court wield a lot of it.

At the same time, the Supreme Court has power over the news media. The Court is the ultimate interpreter of the First Amendment's free speech and free press clauses, and of the Federal Communications Act and other statutes that regulate the media.

Having one foot in journalism and one in law, and having covered the Court for a time, I find this interdependence a fascinating and singular aspect of our democracy. If the relationship were political, compromise and horse-trading would be in order. But there is none of that. Justices and journalists may circle warily around each other, but they strive to accomplish their respective missions in the finest way without overtly relying on the other side or seeking its forbearance.

So the dynamics of this two-century-long relationship, so essential to the workings of our democracy, are worth pondering. I believe this assessment makes a worthy addition to the Visions of the American Press series published by Northwestern University and its Medill School, long a respected training ground for journalists around the world.

Credit for instigating this book belongs to the general editor of the series, David Abrahamson. His dedication to this excellent project, his patience, and his wisdom are inordinate. I am especially grateful to him. I also thank my very capable researchers Leslie Patton, Becca Milfeld, and Shannon Donohoe. With the guidance of research librarians at the Northwestern University Library, they provided invaluable assistance while earning their master's degrees in journalism. Kathy Arberg, the press officer at the Supreme Court, and her staff welcomed me back to the pressroom I once frequented and answered countless queries about today's Court. Tom Goldstein, Lyle Denniston, and their associates at Scotusblog .com contributed important background and case statistics. The completion of this book was pleasantly facilitated by John Fraser, Mary Graham, Sheila Robinson, and their colleagues at Massey College of the University of Toronto, who provided quiet writing space and access to the fine libraries of the university. My heartfelt thanks to all!

Needless to say, any errors herein are my responsibility. I trust they are few and will not impair the message of this book, a story I have greatly enjoyed reporting and writing.

JOE MATHEWSON

THE SUPREME COURT AND THE PRESS

PART ONE
OYEZ! OYEZ!

ONE

THE ESSENTIAL INTERDEPENDENCE

Tensions erupted early between the Supreme Court and the press. It was very personal. John Marshall, the great nineteenth-century chief justice who built both a Court and a nation over thirty-five years, handed down an audacious assertion of federal preeminence that invalidated a state tax on the Second Bank of the United States.[1] Thomas Ritchie took it hard. Ritchie was the editor of Virginia's most influential newspaper, the *Enquirer.* That he had known Marshall for thirty years and lived only a block away in Richmond did not undermine his ferocious opposition to the unanimous decision, which he saw as threatening state sovereignty and perhaps even, one day, slavery, the backbone of Virginia's way of life.[2]

Ritchie launched in the *Enquirer* a campaign to defend the states against federal domination and provided space in the paper for others to carry it on. One of the writers was another Marshall neighbor, William Brockenbrough, a Virginia judge who lived two blocks away. He wrote two long essays for the *Enquirer* attacking the Court's holding that the powers of the federal government should be construed liberally, an interpretation that upheld the congressional charter of the Second Bank. Then still another neighbor piled on. Spencer Roane, a federal appellate judge whose property adjoined Marshall's, protested in the *Enquirer* that Marshall's opinion augured a strong central government that would override the Constitution and the states.

Marshall was incensed. Signing himself "A Friend of the Constitution," he responded in the Alexandria *Gazette,* defending the Court's holding that the Constitution was the act of the people, not the separate states, and that "the power to tax involves the power to destroy."[3]

The fact that the chief justice resorted to the press reflected the relative stature of the two institutions. Newspapers had been influential in America since the early eighteenth century. By exchanging and circulating essays and news of events in the colonies and in England, they fomented the notions of a new nation, of independence, and, eventually, of revolution. They nourished, and sometimes resented, the new government and its leaders. The Supreme Court, by contrast, was just barely created by the Constitution, with no clear definition of duties or powers.[4] Its role in the government was so uncertain, so anomalous, that outstanding lawyers shunned appointment to it. Then, providentially, along came John Marshall, one of Virginia's most respected advocates and a believer in the Federalist creed of a strong central government. His Court, squeezed as an afterthought into an obscure meeting room in the new Capitol building, in 1803 claimed for itself the unstated and indeed unimagined authority to hold acts of Congress unconstitutional.[5] Despite alarm, the ruling stood. But still, some sixteen years later, Marshall was so nettled by newspaper attacks on another nation-building ruling that he, too, reached out to the newspapers for legitimacy.

Today the tables are turned. Housed since the 1930s in a majestic

Greek temple whose marble grandeur bespeaks its omnipotence, the Supreme Court has wrought for itself an unanticipated but accepted major role in American government and life. The press, now better called the news media, has flourished too, but today it casts itself merely as reporter and interpreter of the doings of this highest tribunal. Still, there is an unspoken relationship, truly an interdependence, between the two. To do their job well, the media must cover the Court, because its decisions are always significant and often momentous. As Linda Greenhouse, who retired in 2008 after twenty-seven years as the Supreme Court reporter for the *New York Times,* observes,

> Especially in an era when the political system has ceded to the courts many of society's most difficult questions, it is sobering to acknowledge the extent to which the courts and the country depend on the press for the public understanding that is necessary for the health and, ultimately, the legitimacy of any institution in a democratic society.[6]

Further leavening the relationship between Court and press, and sometimes straining it, the Court makes the final call on the reach of the First Amendment, the guarantor of freedom of expression: "Congress shall make no law ... abridging the freedom of speech, or of the press...." The Court also determines the scope of statutes like the Freedom of Information Act and the Federal Communications Act that empower as well as limit the media. On the other side of the relationship, the Court relies on the media to inform the nation of its decisions.

To the eye of any journalist, William J. Brennan, Jr., who served on the Court from 1956 to 1990, was absolutely correct when he wrote in 1980 that there exists a fundamental and necessary interdependence of the Court and the press. The press needs the Court, if only for the simple reason that the Court is the ultimate guardian of the constitutional rights that support the press. And the Court has a concomitant need for the press, because through the press the Court receives the tacit and accumulated experience of the nation, and—because the judgments of the Court ought also to instruct and to inspire—the Court needs the medium of the press to fulfill this task.[7]

Linda Greenhouse sees the Court and the media as

partners in a mutual democratic enterprise to which both must acknowledge responsibility. The responsibility of the press is to commit the resources necessary to give the public the most accurate and contextual reporting possible about the Court, its work, its members, and its relationship with other branches of government. The Court's responsibility is to remove unnecessary obstacles to accomplishing that task.[8]

However, William Rehnquist, chief justice from 1986 to 2005, saw the relationship very differently. He once told a social gathering of Supreme Court reporters, "The difference between us and the other branches of government is that we don't need you people of the press."[9] On occasion other justices have publicly berated the media. Speaking to a meeting of the National Italian American Foundation in Washington, Justice Antonin Scalia, a member of the Court since 1986, "expressed disdain for the news media and the general reading public, and suggested that together they condone inaccurate portrayals of federal judges and courts." The report by the Associated Press (AP) went on:

"The press is never going to report judicial opinions accurately," he said. "They're just going to report, who is the plaintiff? Was that a nice little old lady? And who is the defendant? Was this, you know, some scuzzy guy? And who won? Was it the good guy that won or the bad guy? And that's all you're going to get in a press report, and you can't blame them, you can't blame them. Because nobody would read it if you went into the details of the law that the court has to resolve."

At the same meeting, according to the AP, Justice Samuel Alito, then newly appointed to the Court, "complained that people understand the courts through a news media that typically oversimplifies and sensationalizes."[10]

Dismaying as these harsh judgments may be, the very journalists who cover the Court agree that the media could do a better job of conveying an understanding of its work to the public. Veteran Supreme Court reporter Tony Mauro writes almost apologetically: "I am deeply aware of the media's inadequacies in the enterprise of covering courts. For the most part, we are untrained and deadline crazed, with short attention spans and an inbred preference for heat over light and simplicity over nuance."[11]

At the same time, the insiders feel the Court itself could contribute to improving journalists' products. As Linda Greenhouse puts it, there are "conventions and habits both within the press and within the Supreme Court itself that create obstacles to producing the best possible journalism about the Court, journalism that would provide the timely, sophisticated, and contextual information necessary for public understanding of the Court."[12] From its beginning, in fact, the Court has lagged far behind the public's need to know what the Court is up to. Greenhouse characterizes the situation this way: "I see a Court that is quite blithely oblivious to the needs of those who convey its work to the outside world, and a press corps that is often groping along in the dark, trying to make sense out of the shadows on the cave wall."[13] For more than a century the Court failed to deliver printed copies of its opinions to the press on the same day that the justices announced their rulings from the bench. The *Atlanta Constitution* reported in 1906:

> WASHINGTON, May 28—The case of Reuben Hodges and others v. the United States was decided by the supreme court of the United Sates today, which refused to take jurisdiction in the matter. The decision was announced by Justice Brewer, but owing to the fact that the dissenting opinion in the case was not ready for filing, the controlling opinion also was withheld.

And, underscoring the risks created by such dilatory practices, the paper got the story wrong. The Court did not deny jurisdiction; it accepted the case and reversed the decision of the lower court.[14]

In the last century the Court has grudgingly, little by little, made minor adjustments in its practices to facilitate press coverage and thus public understanding, such as spreading out its barrage of end-of-term decision announcements over more days in May and June, and just recently beginning to release its transcripts of oral arguments immediately after each hearing. But the Court still generally declines, with only rare exceptions (just one case in the 2008–09 term), to release its audiotapes of arguments, and it steadfastly refuses to admit cameras to the courtroom despite great evidence from other courts that they do not disrupt decorum or encourage histrionics.

Fred Graham, who covered the Supreme Court for both the *New York Times* and later CBS, found inherent disadvantages on the beat. He writes in an entertaining but incisive memoir:

> Covering the Supreme Court was like being assigned to report on the Pope. Both the justices and the Pope issue infallible statements, draw their authority from a mystical higher source, conceal their humanity in flowing robes, and—because they seek to present a saintly face to the world—are inherently boring. They also both have life tenure, which implies a license to thumb their noses at the news media.[15]

This book will sample coverage of the Court over the past two centuries, both to call attention to inadequate reporting and to celebrate good journalism that does justice to the important work of the Court. We will concentrate on coverage of what makes the Court important: its decisions. What constitutes a good story about a Supreme Court decision? Most important, the story should state and explain the decision itself, including the legal basis for it and the justices' reasoning. This seems obvious, but, as we shall see, much of Supreme Court journalism in fact is reaction and commentary, easier quarry for most journalists than the justices' thinking. Two-thirds of Supreme Court decisions reverse the lower court ruling. The public is entitled to know why. What was the constitutional or statutory question at issue? What about legal precedents, earlier decisions by the Court itself, that influenced the decision? Then, looking forward, what are the legal implications for future cases, especially those already in the courts?

This focus is not to deny the importance of other stories about the Court and the justices, such as the Senate Judiciary Committee's 2009 hearings on President Obama's nomination of Sonia Sotomayor to the Court. Such a public event gives the media running room, the freedom and opportunity to present substantive stories about the nominee, the history and members of the Court, important decisions from the past that may be cited to the nominee for comment, and the confirmation process itself. The nomination of Sotomayor prompted the *New York Times* to turn out ten stories overnight, including a front-page mini-biography that jumped to two full pages inside, the work of no fewer than fourteen reporters and three researchers;[16] a searching analysis by *Times* Supreme Court reporter Adam Liptak of her court of appeals opinions ("usually models of modern judicial craftsmanship");[17] a story in the sports section about how Sotomayor, when a trial judge, ended the baseball strike of 1995;[18] and even a story on type 1 diabetes, "the disease she has lived with for more than 45 years."[19] The *Times* also editorialized that Sotomayor "could become an extraordinary Supreme Court justice."[20] In all the *Times* printed literally dozens of stories about her and the Court over the several weeks between the president's announcement in late May and the Senate hearings in mid-July, which of course prompted more stories. Then came the Judiciary Committee approval and the Senate confirmation, played prominently by all the media. Several *Times* stories were op-eds by outsiders, including one by Harvard law professor Noah Feldman, who observed that while many Sotomayor-related stories suggested that "the most successful Supreme Court justices had been warm, collegial consensus-builders," in fact,

> measured by their lasting impact on Constitution and country, many of the greatest justices have been irascible, socially distant, personally isolated, arrogant or even downright mean. Stephen J. Field, appointed by Lincoln, once insulted a woman's romantic past so outrageously from the bench that her husband later attacked him on a train—and was shot dead by Field's bodyguard.[21]

Another worthwhile Supreme Court story is the coverage of oral arguments before the justices, in which they typically ply the lawyers with quick, penetrating, provocative questions, and drop in their own comments about the weaknesses of a particular line of reasoning presented to them. We will not undertake to include oral argument coverage in this book, so let us pause here to note that one of the most capable reporters currently covering the Supreme Court, Nina Totenberg of National Public Radio, has raised such stories to a new journalistic art form. She weaves together succinct paraphrases of the colloquy with staccato quotations of justices and lawyers, capturing the crux of the legal argument while simulating effectively the actual give-and-take in the courtroom. For instance, in covering a 2009 oral argument about whether a felon convicted years earlier had a constitutional right to a new, more definitive test of his DNA that could, in her words, "definitively prove his innocence,"[22] Totenberg reported that the Alaska assistant attorney general Ken Rosenstein "immediately faced skeptical questions, mainly from the Court's liberals." An excerpt:

> Justice Breyer: He's willing to pay for it. Why don't you want to give it to him?
>
> Answer: Because if he doesn't allege actual innocence this is a meaningless exercise.
>
> Well, then, the Justices wanted to know, if he actually filed a sworn innocence claim, as the state now suggests he should, would the state agree to give him access to the DNA?
>
> It's conceivable, said Assistant Attorney General Rosenstein.
>
> Justice Kennedy: All you can say is, it's conceivable?
>
> Justice Souter: If he walks into court and says, I'm innocent, subject to the penalties of perjury, you will not let him look at the DNA?
>
> Answer: I cannot say we actually would.[23]

In the end, the decision went against the inmate in a familiar split, with the dominant conservatives—Chief Justice John Roberts and Justices Scalia, Alito, Arthur Kennedy, and Clarence Thomas—finding no constitutional right to a test, and the four liberals—Justices John Paul Stevens, Stephen Breyer, David Souter, and Ruth Bader Ginsburg—arguing for it.

Oral arguments occasionally give rise to insights about the justices themselves. The United Press wrote this tantalizing story in 1948:

> WASHINGTON, May 4 (U.P.)—Feuding Supreme Court Justices Hugo L. Black and Robert H. Jackson put on another wrangle today.
>
> The Justices, who have been at odds since they got into a dispute over a coal mine case many years ago, disagreed this time on what to do with ex-Nazis who are still in this country.
>
> They were hearing an appeal by a German-born Nazi against a government deportation order. . . .
>
> Black snapped at [Justice Department attorney Stanley] Silverberg that the plain intent of the law was to get rid of dangerous people in time of war, not to punish them.
>
> Jackson interrupted to comment that Black's views might permit "the whole fifth column" to stay in this country indefinitely.[24]

Fred Graham feels that oral-argument stories alert the public about significant pending cases so they will not come as total surprises when they are decided. But he had to forgo oral arguments when he switched from the *Times* to CBS, as he explains in his memoir:

> Stories about Court arguments can't compete for television time because TV executives hate to leaden their screens with color-pencil sketches and secondhand recitations of what happened inside. The result is that there has been inadequate coverage of the Supreme Court, because television reporters have been restricted to the video equivalent of communicating with a quill pen.[25]

This handicapping of the nation's most popular news medium seriously limits what the public learns about the Court and its decisions. Inexplicably, this is the way the justices want it. They say they would lose personal privacy, and television might have an adverse impact on oral arguments. But this disregards the long experience of two U.S. courts of appeals and two-thirds of the state supreme courts. We will explore this issue further in the last chapter. But for the present, network television reports of Supreme Court decisions, always constrained by time limitations, typically are characterized by brief, often oversimplified statements of the ruling, minimal if any explanation of the legal basis and the justices' reasoning, short and preferably punchy quotations from the majority and dissenting opinions, and then instant comments, reactions, and predictions of future impact, sometimes from persons unconnected to the case and whose opinions are highly predictable. When the Court struck down a minority set-aside system of city contracting in Richmond, Virginia,[26] how was it edifying for CBS to interview civil rights advocate Jesse Jackson for his opinion?[27] Such stories too much resemble the superficial coverage—who won, who lost?—berated by Justice Scalia. As a result, they often sound more like legislative actions or political pronouncements than reasoned conclusions of law.

Striving to "make the best of the situation," Fred Graham in the 1970s created television stories about important cases before they were decided:

> My approach was to go to the community where each dispute arose, take pictures of the scene, interview the people involved, and present the legal question through the stories of the people who raised it. This seems obvious now, as it is the way all the networks do it. We pioneered it at CBS, and while it was TV legal journalism at its best, as long as we were excluded from the courtroom it was not good enough.[28]

On occasion there are other types of Supreme Court stories, more human interest than important, but good reading. A 1908 report from Boston quoted a prominent physician's "startling statement" at a legislative hearing considering a bill to require "ten distinct tests for life in every case of reported death before a burial certificate be given," intended to preclude live burial. According to the story, Dr. John Dixwell declared, "This horror exists as a fact and cannot be denied. I have two judges of the United States Supreme Court, whom I have promised I would see should never be buried alive. They are friends of mine and I know they live in deadly fear of being buried alive." He did not name the justices, but "it is believed he meant Justices Holmes and Moody," the story stated. Oliver Wendell Holmes and William Henry Moody were from the Boston area.[29]

With all due respect for such melodrama, we will confine ourselves to coverage of Supreme Court decisions, especially newspaper stories. This is partly because newspapers existed long before broadcasting, but it also is a recognition of the fact that newspapers, if they choose to, can devote considerably more attention to a Court story, and experience shows that they do. However, at the outset of the republic it was only occasionally that newspapers sent reporters or correspondents to actually cover the Court; papers outside Washington commonly reprinted stories from the few that did. With the advent of the telegraph and the news wire services like the Associated Press and United Press in the second half of the nineteenth century, most papers had access to Court decision stories, but how they placed the stories and wrote the headlines, and indeed whether they ran the stories at all, remained matters of local editorial judgment. That is still true today. In part 3 of this book we will sample stories that did appear, in five major categories: building the new nation and federalism, slavery and civil rights, regulating business and labor, voting rights and election law, and the more modern, often inflammatory social controversies such as abortion, school prayer, flag burning, and affirmative action. Our objective is to judge how well the media covered important decisions in each of these areas. In other words, how well did the media do by the Court?

However, because the Supreme Court is the custodian of the First Amendment and its rights of free expression, we will first examine in part 2 of this book the Court's decisions affecting the media, in these categories: the right to publish, libel and privacy, the rights of persons accused of crime, the application of statutes such as the Federal Communications Act and the Freedom of Information Act that both empower and limit the media, and the legal protection of confidential sources. In other words, how well did the Court do by the media?

In recent decades the Court's interpretation of the First Amendment has become increasingly consistent with the original, pre-Independence free press principles set forth in the constitutions of the first states. This trend has benefited both the media and the public. However, the remaining legal restrictions on the media, notably the potential legal liability of confidential sources and the journalists who tapped their knowledge, put newspapers and broadcasters in the occasional role of pleader before the Court, an awkward but inevitable aspect of this curious interdependence. For the most part this book does not undertake to evaluate the media coverage of media cases, for, not surprisingly, all media hands—reporters, editors, producers, publishers, and networks—consider them highly important and report them assiduously. It would not be instructive to document this truth.

We essay to look at the whole history of the Supreme Court, more than 200 years in all, so necessarily we will be selective. Many cases considered will be of historical importance. Others are not but are included because they commanded considerable public attention at the time, for instance, the Court's 1895 ruling on the constitutionality of the post–Civil War income tax, a case called *Pollock. v. Farmers' Loan & Trust Co.*[30] We separate the cases by chief justice, more for convenience in following the trends than to characterize each administration, though now and then such labeling is inescapable.

This is a tale of two fundamental institutions, both constitutional, how well they serve each other and the American democracy, and how they can do it better. Let us begin.

PART TWO
THE SUPREME COURT'S EFFECTS ON THE PRESS

TWO

A RIGHT TO PUBLISH

The nineteenth century was not a good time for U.S. constitutional freedoms. So it was that, more than three decades after the Fourteenth Amendment barred the states from denying their citizens due process of law or equal protection of the laws, the Supreme Court in 1896 emasculated these protections to affirm the conviction of a New Orleans shoemaker named Homer Plessy (his first name was never stated in the opinion, though the respondent's was). Plessy appeared white but carried one-eighth African blood. With due notice to the railroad, he deliberately defied Louisiana law by sitting in a whites-only railcar, obtaining an arrest, a conviction, and a place in American history.[1]

Two years later a life was at stake, and the Fourteenth Amendment was again at issue. Henry Williams, an African American, sought reversal of his murder conviction and death sentence by an all-white jury comprising only registered voters who, as required by local law, had paid their taxes and were subjected to individual, sworn examination as to their qualifications to vote. Unanimously the Supreme Court affirmed Williams's conviction and sentence, concluding enigmatically that the Mississippi laws he challenged "do not on their face discriminate between the races, and it has not been shown that their actual administration was evil, only that evil was possible under them."[2]

Similarly, in 1899 the Court agreed with a Georgia ruling that a school board could levy taxes for the support of a whites-only public high school after closing the county's only high school for blacks.[3] A few years later the Court upheld the conviction of a private Christian institution, Berea College, for admitting both white and Negro students in violation of a Kentucky law.[4]

The chief justice at this time was a former Chicago business lawyer and an experienced Supreme Court advocate named Melville Fuller (1888–1910), appointed by President Grover Cleveland in an effort to shore up his midwestern strength as he sought reelection. Fuller's principal interests were property and corporations, and he carried the Court's indifference to individual rights well into the twentieth century.

So there was a certain consistency in the Court's affirmations of contempt-of-court convictions of a Colorado publisher (a former U.S. senator) and later of an Ohio editor for publishing criticisms of state judges. In the Colorado case the eloquent and persuasive Justice Oliver Wendell Holmes, in the early years of a distinguished three-decade run on the Court, wrote for a seven-judge majority and summarily dismissed the First Amendment.[5] In the Ohio case the Court at least acknowledged "the assuredly secured freedom of the press," but found it "subject to the restraints which separate right from wrong-doing."[6]

In the same vein, the Supreme Court saw no First Amendment barrier to a publisher's indictment in Alabama for mailing a newspaper containing an advertisement for a legal lottery in Louisiana, finding it a violation of a federal statute prohibiting mail distribution of lottery ads and the deposit of such materials into the mail.[7] The Court also upheld the postmaster general's denial of low-cost, second-class mailing privileges to newspapers that failed to provide certain information required by law. Their publishers, in New York City, balked at answering questions about their editors, stockholders, creditors, and circulation. One appellant's lawyer called this requirement "inquisitorial" and a means to enforce "censorship of the press," but Chief Justice Edward Douglass White held it appropriate to the enjoyment of "great privileges and advantages at the public expense."[8] White, who served as chief justice from 1910 to 1921, had been appointed by President William Howard Taft to succeed Melville Fuller. Sixty-five years old at the time, White had served sixteen years as an associate justice, and was the first sitting justice promoted to chief. He was a former U.S. senator from Louisiana, and best known then for his steadfast support of the state's sugar industry.

The Supreme Court's longtime, cramped view of freedom of the press, and of speech, was more famously set forth in the Court's several post–World War I affirmations of convictions under both federal and state laws for wartime speeches and for the distribution, however modest, of leaflets and newspapers critical of the war and sometimes the draft.

In a case characterized by constitutional scholar Geoffrey R. Stone as "the Supreme Court's first significant decision interpreting the First Amendment,"[9] Justice Oliver Wendell Holmes, then seventy-eight years old, who had been thrice wounded as a Union Army volunteer in the Civil War, wrote a unanimous opinion affirming the convictions of Charles Schenck and others. They were charged under the 1917 Espionage Act, which prohibited the obstruction of military recruiting, for circulating an antiwar pamphlet to men called for military service. In his opinion Holmes fashioned two immortal phrases limiting the First Amendment. He declared: "The most stringent protection of free speech would not protect a man in falsely shouting fire in a theater, and causing a panic." And, "The question in every case is whether the words used are used in such circumstances and are of such a nature as to create a clear and present danger that they will bring about the substantive evils that Congress has a right to prevent."[10] Thus "falsely shouting fire in a theater" (often misquoted as "a crowded theater"), illustrating a reasonable limitation of everyday speech, and "clear and present danger," later adopted by the Supreme Court as an appropriate test of speech limitations for national security reasons, entered the American lexicon.[11]

However, it is strange that only one week after handing down *Schenck,* a unanimous Court, with Holmes again writing the opinions, affirmed two similar convictions without mentioning its new "clear and present danger" standard. Jacob Frohwerk, an editor of the German-language *Missouri Staats Zeitung,* was convicted and sentenced to ten years' imprisonment under the Espionage Act for helping to publish a series of twelve antiwar, antidraft articles that proposed no specific acts of opposition. However, Holmes, again brushing aside the First Amendment, wrote that "a conspiracy to obstruct recruiting would be criminal even if no means were agreed upon specifically by which to accomplish the intent."[12] On the same day, affirming the conviction and ten-year sentence of Socialist leader Eugene Debs for a speech praising three Socialists jailed for opposing the war, Holmes easily dismissed the First Amendment defense as having been settled by *Schenck.* He declared that the jury was justified in finding that "one purpose of the speech, whether incidental or not does not matter, was to oppose not only war in general but this war, and that the opposition was so expressed that its natural and intended effect would be to obstruct recruiting."[13]

Despite their own dependence on the First Amendment, newspapers were remarkably indifferent to these cursory dismissals of it. Neither did they take note that *Schenck*'s "clear and present danger" standard, which would have been difficult to satisfy in *Frohwerk* and *Debs,* was not even mentioned in those opinions. Major papers used an Associated Press story on *Frohwerk* and *Debs* that stated simply, in the second paragraph: "While not passing directly on the constitutionality of the [Espionage] act, the court in effect did declare valid the so-called enlistment section and reaffirmed its opinion that the espionage law is not an interference with the constitutional right of free speech."[14] The story did not explain how Holmes subordinated the First Amendment, but that dark hole in the AP's report was an accurate reflection of those opinions.

In fact, the *New York Times,* the *Chicago Daily Tribune,* and the *Washington Post* editorially applauded the *Frohwerk* and *Debs* decisions. The *Times* saw Eugene Debs not as a champion of the Constitution but as "its enemy. . . . His theory amounted simply to the impossible doctrine that he had full liberty to overturn the Constitution, but that the Government had no power to stay him."[15] The *Tribune* rejoiced: "The government, as well as all loyal citizens, have denied political animus but insisted that freedom of speech does not constitute license to arouse hatred of national duty."[16] The *Post* proclaimed that *Debs* "serves notice upon propagandists of radicalism that, even though they may masquerade under the cloak of a political party and claim the privilege of free speech guaranteed by the Constitution, they nevertheless are responsible for their utterances and their deeds and can be held to a strict accounting."[17]

WHENCE CAME THIS FREEDOM?

So, one might ask, what was this freedom of expression that the Founding Fathers so readily adopted, yet was so long belittled, even ignored, by the Supreme Court? Indeed, in its origin and in its scope, it was far more than the First Amendment.

The First Amendment, ratified in 1791 as part of the Bill of Rights, states that "Congress shall make no law . . . abridging the freedom . . . of the Press. . . ." This language, restraining just one branch of the federal government and not the states (inclusion of the states was considered by Congress but rejected), was in fact a comparatively faint shadow of strong, positive guarantees of the right to publish already embedded in constitutions enacted even before Independence by 9 of the 13 original states; only 2 adopted early constitutions without such a guarantee, and only one of the 11 also guaranteed freedom of speech, indicating the primacy attached to a free press. "Freedom of the Press is one of the great bulwarks of Liberty and can never be restrained but by Despotick governments," boldly stated the Virginia Declaration of Rights, part of the state's constitution, the first to be enacted.[18] The wording in the Massachusetts constitution, written by John Adams, was typical of several others: "The liberty of the press is essential to the security of freedom in a state: it ought not, therefore, to be restrained in this Commonwealth."[19]

The revolutionary leaders advocated and cherished freedom of the press, an entirely new concept in the history of the world. They were reacting to the Crown's control of the press in England and its governors' attempts to quash critical newspapers in the colonies. But the colonists, believing that a free press was essential to their own freedom, fought back, refusing to indict or convict newspaper editors charged with seditious libel, or criticism of the government. Famously, a jury of New Yorkers in 1732 acquitted immigrant printer John Peter Zenger of libeling the governor of New York, accepting defense lawyer Andrew Hamilton's argument that truth should be recognized as a defense to a libel accusation, a concept unknown in English law but later adopted in all of the United States.[20]

The centrality of press freedom to democracy was aptly stated by Thomas Jefferson, who, despite his own numerous differences with the press, declared: "These formidable censors of the public functionaries, by arranging them at the tribunal of public opinion, produce reform peaceably, which must otherwise be done by revolution."[21]

Scholars still debate whether the Founders intended the First Amendment to abolish seditious libel, a common (judge-made) criminal law prohibiting criticism of the government. This English import lived on for a time in both federal and state courts. But no one doubted, then or now, that the amendment prohibited the government from interfering with the right to publish, in preemptive actions termed prior restraint. In Jefferson's words: "Freedom of the press means freedom from prior restraint and not at all to the matter, whether good or bad."[22] Yes, libel law meant there could be consequences for false or irresponsible publication that wrongly sullied someone's reputation, but publication itself was to be uninhibited, particularly as to information and commentary about government.

While adoption of the First Amendment's free press clause was noncontroversial, for everyone believed in it, enforcement was another matter. Just seven years after its approval by Congress and the states, the First Amendment was ignored by Congress in its passage of the Sedition Act of 1798, signed by President Adams, which forbade press criticism of the president and other senior government officials (but not the vice president, then Thomas Jefferson, of the opposition party). The act was enforced against editors (and even a congressman) who had criticized the administration, and several were jailed, all in direct contradiction of the press clause of the First Amendment, which was never invoked in the act's brief three-year history.

The Supreme Court's priorities in the nineteenth century were nation-building, papering over issues of slavery and race, and then bolstering the authority of state governments and the rights of business and property owners. The promises of the Bill of Rights and the Fourteenth Amendment languished. The contempt-of-court rulings against newspaper executives in the early twentieth century clearly provided greater protection for one aspect of government, the judicial process, than for the press. Similarly, the antiwar cases of 1919 and the 1920s were not treated primarily as First Amendment questions, but rather as questions of government power and authority. Authority won.

Then, slowly, things began to change at the Supreme Court. As to the First Amendment, no transformation was more dramatic than that of Justice Holmes, the author of the *Schenck, Frohwerk,* and *Debs* opinions and a stout supporter of most legislative enactments, both state and federal. Holmes had always been, by any definition, a conservative, a defender of the status quo. But just months after *Schenck, Frohwerk,* and *Debs,* Holmes dissented when the Court affirmed the convictions and twenty-year sentences under the Sedition Act of 1918 of Jacob Abrams and four other Russian-Jewish immigrants who had distributed antigovernment leaflets calling for a general strike. His dissenting opinion, joined by Justice Louis Brandeis, was truly remarkable.[23] Majorities may persecute dissident voices, Holmes stated, but when men have realized that time has upset many fighting faiths, they may come to believe even more than they believe the very foundations of their own conduct that the ultimate good desired is better reached by free trade in ideas—that the best test of truth is the power of the thought to get itself accepted in the competition of the market, and that truth is the only ground upon which their wishes safely can be carried out. . . . [I]n their conviction upon this indictment the defendants were deprived of their rights under the Constitution of the United States.[24]

Holmes's central concept, often misquoted as "the free marketplace of ideas," has rung through First Amendment cases ever since, indelibly stamping him as a historical leader in the cause of free expression, despite his record of suppressing it.

It is worth noting that in his *Abrams* dissent Justice Holmes wrote, for the first time in a Supreme Court free press case, the phrase "right to publish." He did not proclaim it as a general proposition, however, merely referring to the publications for which the defendants were convicted: "In this case sentences of twenty years imprisonment have been imposed for the publishing of two leaflets that I believe the defendants had as much right to publish as the Government has to publish the Constitution of the United States now vainly invoked by them."[25] It would be many years before the Court enshrined this right as law.

Two years later, in 1921, Holmes and Brandeis again dissented when the Court upheld the postmaster general's revocation, under the Espionage Act, of the second-class mailing privilege of the *Milwaukee Leader* for publishing allegedly false articles designed to undermine the war effort, to obstruct recruiting, and to encourage the success of the enemy. Holmes pithily observed that "the use of the mails is almost as much a part of free speech as the right to use our tongues and it would take very strong language to convince me that Congress ever intended to give such a practically despotic power to any one man. There is no pretence that it has done so."[26]

Change was in the air, but the news-publishing business could not command a Supreme Court majority until another decade passed, and then only barely. Curiously, the First Amendment was hardly mentioned. The case was the first of several, spread over many years, that dealt with the issue of prior restraint, a basic foundation of the press clause.

THE OLD ORDER CHANGETH

The turning point was a case called *Near v. Minnesota,* decided in 1931.[27] The Court was divided, with the majority opinion written by Chief Justice Charles Evans Hughes (1930–41), then sixty-nine years old, a former Republican governor of New York who had served several years as an associate justice, then resigned to run for the presidency in 1918. He had been secretary of state under Presidents Warren G. Harding and Calvin Coolidge, and was appointed chief justice by President Herbert Hoover. The case arose under Minnesota law and involved partners named Near and Guilford who published a Minneapolis weekly newspaper called the *Saturday Press.* In the fall of 1927, during Prohibition, the paper ran several articles alleging that the city's mayor, the chief of police, and the county attorney were derelict in not cracking down on "a Jewish gangster . . . in control of gambling, bootlegging and racketeering in Minneapolis." The police chief also was accused by the paper of taking graft from gangsters. One of the *Saturday Press* partners, Guilford, was shot after the first issue was published, and made no further appearance in the dispute. The county attorney, acting under a law that authorized enjoining the publication of any "malicious, scandalous and defamatory newspaper," sued to shut the paper down, and obtained a court order to that effect. The Minnesota Supreme Court affirmed.

Colonel Robert R. McCormick, the strong-willed, conservative publisher of the *Chicago Daily Tribune* and a leader in the American Newspaper Publishers Association, was alarmed by this latter-day invocation of prior restraint, despite the unsavory reputation of owner J. M. Near, who was deemed anti-Semitic, anti-black, anti-Catholic, and anti-labor. McCormick mobilized his fellow publishers and put his own lawyers on the case, asking the U.S. Supreme Court to review it.

The Court did, and by a slim majority of 5-4, found for the newspaper and Near. In his opinion Chief Justice Hughes fervently supported freedom of the press and roundly criticized the prior restraint, upholding in particular "the immunity of the press from previous restraint in dealing with official misconduct." He declared: "The fact that for approximately 150 years there has been almost an entire absence of attempts to impose previous restraints upon publications relating to the malfeasance of public officers is significant of the deep-seated conviction that such restraints would violate constitutional right." Hughes noted approvingly that such suppressions had been struck down in "many decisions under the provisions of state constitutions."[28]

Still, with little explanation, the chief justice based his ruling not on the First Amendment but on the Fourteenth Amendment's guarantee of due process of law. He noted that the Minnesota court had declared, "There is no constitutional right to publish a fact merely because it is true," and he took no issue with that holding.[29]

In fact, just six years earlier the Supreme Court, in *Gitlow v. New York,* had held that the Fourteenth Amendment made the First Amendment applicable to the states.[30] But Hughes's opinion made no mention of that, either. Justice Pierce Butler, a Minnesotan, wrote a sharp dissent, which three other justices joined. Clearly, the First Amendment, after 140 years, still had little traction at the Supreme Court, even on such a fundamental reason for the First Amendment as prior restraint.

Even three decades later, though the Court ruled more forcefully against prior restraint, it was still not under the First Amendment. In the center chair sat Earl Warren, a popular three-term Republican governor of California who had supported General Dwight D. Eisenhower for the presidency in 1952 and in turn been appointed chief justice by Eisenhower. Warren's tenure (1953–69) would prove to be of monumental import to both the law and the nation. In a 1963 case, two book publishers and a Rhode Island distributor of books and magazines challenged the constitutionality of the Rhode Island Commission to Encourage Morality in Youth, whose statutory mission was to combat juvenile delinquency by identifying publications containing obscene material or "manifestly tending to the corruption" of those under eighteen. The commission would notify distributors of such publications and call at their offices to urge them to remove them from sale. *Peyton Place,* by Grace Metalious, *The Bramble Bush,* by Charles Mergendahl, and magazines such as *Playboy* and *Rogue* were listed. Police visits to the distributor and to stores followed, and prosecution for obscenity violations was explicitly threatened in the event any proscribed publications were found.

By 8-1 the Supreme Court ruled the system unconstitutional under the Fourteenth Amendment.[31] Justice William J. Brennan, Jr., a consistent proponent of freedom of the press, wrote that "the Commission deliberately set about to achieve the suppression of publications deemed 'objectionable' and succeeded in its aim." The Court deemed this "a system of prior administrative restraints" without judicial supervision or findings. Justice William O. Douglas, in a concurrence, added: "This is censorship in the raw."[32] Through a record-long tenure on the Court (1939–75), Douglas stood firmly on the side of the news media.

THE FIRST AMENDMENT LIVES

Under Chief Justice Warren the Supreme Court strengthened the guarantees of the Bill of Rights in many ways, including a marked expansion of the reach of the First Amendment's press clause. The decision in *New York Times Co. v. Sullivan,* a 1964 Alabama libel case we will consider more fully in chapter 3, was arguably the most important enhancement of freedom of the press ever handed down by the Supreme Court.[33] Once more the phrase "right to publish" crept in. It was in a concurring opinion by Justice Hugo Black, a former Democratic U.S. senator from Alabama and an ardent supporter of President Franklin D. Roosevelt's anti-Depression New Deal, appointed in 1937 by Roosevelt as he sought to revamp the Court that had serially held unconstitutional several of his New Deal measures.[34] As with Justice Holmes's mention of a "right to publish" in *Abrams,* Black's usage referred only to the controversy at hand: "Unlike the Court, therefore, I vote to reverse exclusively on the ground that the Times and the individual defendants had an absolute, unconditional constitutional right to publish in the Times advertisement their criticism of the Montgomery agencies and officials."[35] Black's use of "unconditional" meant just that, for he believed that the First Amendment's

"Congress shall make no law" permitted absolutely no legal restraints on the press.

It was not until 1971 that the Supreme Court came down hard on prior restraint of the press in a decision based on the First Amendment, but even then the Court was divided. Unique in the nation's history, the case was an explosive confrontation between a president of the United States, Richard M. Nixon, and two of the country's leading newspapers.[36] Presiding was Chief Justice Warren E. Burger (1969–86), sixty-three years old, of Minnesota, a former circuit court of appeals judge appointed only two years earlier by President Nixon. Fred Graham, then the Supreme Court reporter for the *New York Times,* wrote later that Burger, as a "lonely right-wing voice" on the liberal U.S. Court of Appeals in Washington, had caught White House attention by occasionally "sending copies of his dissents to Richard Nixon, and . . . that persuaded Nixon to make Burger chief justice."[37]

A classified Defense Department study entitled "History of U.S. Decision-Making Process on Viet Nam Policy" was leaked by one of its authors, Daniel Ellsberg, to the *New York Times* and then to the *Washington Post.* After three months of study and deliberation, in June 1971 the *Times* began to print excerpts of the so-called Pentagon Papers. But the Nixon administration immediately sought injunctions to prevent both papers from publishing, and the twin cases moved with lightning rapidity through the New York and Washington U.S. district courts and the respective courts of appeals to the Supreme Court.

The Court heard oral argument on June 26, and only four days later (on the traditional last day of its term), by a vote of 6-3, held for the newspapers. It was a curious opinion, just three paragraphs long, "per curiam" or by the Court. But each of the nine justices appended a personal opinion, six concurring, three dissenting.

Justice Black, invoking his absolutist interpretation of the First Amendment's press clause, wrote sharply in concurrence:

> Both the history and language of the First Amendment support the view that the press must be left free to publish news, whatever the source, without censorship, injunctions, or prior restraints. In the First Amendment the Founding Fathers gave the free press the protection it must have to fulfill its essential role in our democracy. The press was to serve the governed, not the governors. The Government's power to censor the press was abolished so that the press would remain forever free to censure the Government. The press was protected so that it could bare the secrets of government and inform the people. Only a free and unrestrained press can effectively expose deception in government. And paramount among the responsibilities of a free press is the duty to prevent any part of the government from deceiving the people and sending them off to distant lands to die of foreign fevers and foreign shot and shell.[38]

Justice Douglas joined Justice Black's opinion, and appended his own, which Black joined. Quoting the relevant portion of the First Amendment, Douglas wrote: "That leaves, in my view, no room for governmental restraint on the press."[39] Justices William Brennan, Potter Stewart, Byron White, and Thurgood Marshall wrote their own concurrences, but they were less absolute, some suggesting that in the case of a dire threat to the nation's security a prior restraint might indeed be lawful.

Dissenting were Chief Justice Burger, Justice Harry Blackmun, also a Nixon appointee, and Justice John Marshall Harlan. However, they objected more to the haste with which the courts, including their own, had considered and decided the case, than to the outcome, and all voiced respect for the First Amendment's prohibition of prior restraint. It had taken 180 years, but the Supreme Court at last explicitly recognized what the authors of the press clause intended.

Soon the Court supplied reinforcement. In midsummer 1974, when the Court was in recess, the publisher of the *Times-Picayune,* of New Orleans, asked Justice Lewis Powell, as circuit justice for the Fifth Circuit, to stay a local court's order restricting news coverage of the separate trials of two suspects in a widely publicized rape-murder. The court had banned reporting of testimony in hearings on pretrial motions and had placed other restrictions on reporting before and during the trials, including bans on publishing interviews with subpoenaed witnesses, the defendants' criminal records, or confessions unless entered into evidence during the trial, and editorial comments tending to influence the trial court, the jury, or witnesses.

Justice Powell granted the stay, pending an application by the newspaper publisher for a writ of certiorari requesting review by the full Court. "On the record before me," Powell wrote, "I cannot say that the order of the state court would withstand the limitations that this Court has applied in determining the propriety of prior restraints on publication. . . . Moreover, the court has available alternative means for protecting the defendants' rights to fair trial."[40]

About then, the phrase "right to publish" again appeared, this time in a dissenting opinion by Justice Potter Stewart. He wrote: "[W]e have held that the right to publish is central to the First Amendment and basic to the existence of constitutional democracy," citing *New York Times Co. v. United States* (the Pentagon Papers decision) and *Grosjean v. American Press Company,*[41] a 1936 tax case decided in favor of several Louisiana newspapers. In fact, neither opinion had used the "right to publish" phrase, but the Court was building, ever so slowly, toward embracing it.[42]

GAGGED BUT NOT SILENCED

Especially important to the news media was a 1976 Supreme Court ruling that invalidated a prior restraint by a Nebraska trial judge.[43] The judge had ordered the news media not to publish accounts of confessions made by an accused murderer as well as facts implicating him in the notorious killings of six persons in one family. The crime, which received widespread publicity, occurred in a small town of 800 residents, but the media were alarmed by the judge's order, even though it applied only to pretrial coverage and was intended to preserve the defendant's Sixth Amendment right to an unbiased jury and a fair trial. The Nebraska Press Association brought the legal challenge, supported by a number of amicus curiae ("friend of the court") briefs from the likes of the National Broadcasting Co., American Newspaper Publishers Association, Reporters Committee for Freedom of the Press, Tribune Co., and Washington Post Co.

The Supreme Court, reversing the Nebraska Supreme Court, held unanimously for the press, though with many voices. Chief Justice Burger wrote for a majority of five. He delved deeply into the history of freedom of the press, as well as the right to a fair trial. He quoted Jefferson declaring that "[o]ur liberty depends on the freedom of the press." He recalled the unfortunate "carnival" atmosphere surrounding the trial of Bruno Hauptmann for the Lindbergh kidnap-murder in the 1930s. He cited the Supreme

Court's rulings in *Near v. Minnesota* and *New York Times Co. v. United States.* The chief justice concluded that prior restraint was not necessary to a fair trial:

> [O]n the record now before us it is not clear that further publicity, unchecked, would so distort the views of potential jurors that 12 could not be found who would, under proper instructions, fulfill their sworn duty to render a just verdict exclusively on the evidence presented in open court. . . . We reaffirm that the guarantees of freedom of expression are not an absolute prohibition under all circumstances, but the barriers to prior restraint remain high and the presumption against its use continues intact.[44]

Justice William Brennan, by now well established as the Court's most passionate defender of the press clause, did not join the majority opinion but concurred in the judgment with a long opinion joined by Justices Potter Stewart and Thurgood Marshall. Justice Brennan noted that during jury selection a trial judge can weed out prospective jurors who have been influenced by any pretrial news, but he put his faith in the press to determine what to write even about such sensitive matters: "[T]he press may be arrogant, tyrannical, abusive, and sensationalist, just as it may be incisive, probing, and informative. But at least in the context of prior restraints on publications, the decision of what, when, and how to publish is for editors, not judges."[45]

In a separate concurrence, Justice John Paul Stevens, while hesitating to totally embrace Brennan's opinion, declared: "I do, however, subscribe to most of what Mr. Justice Brennan says and, if ever required to face the issue squarely, may well accept his ultimate conclusion."[46]

Was that final? Not quite. With the authority that only the

Supreme Court can assume unto itself, the Court a few years later carved out two exceptions to its anti–prior restraint position. William Rehnquist, sixty-two years old, of Arizona, with a fourteen-year record as the Court's most conservative member, had been promoted to chief justice by President Ronald Reagan in 1986. In the following year a federal court in New York, trying U.S. Representative Mario Biaggi and the former Bronx borough president Stanley Simon on racketeering charges involving a military contractor, imposed a gag order on prosecutors, defendants, and defense counsel, ordering them not to talk to the press. Although the court subsequently relaxed the order to allow explanations of motions or other aspects of the trial, Dow Jones & Company, Inc., publisher of the *Wall Street Journal,* challenged it as an unconstitutional prior restraint. Nevertheless, the Second Circuit Court of Appeals affirmed the order, finding no prior restraint because it was directed at trial participants and not the news media. Dow Jones asked the Supreme Court to grant a writ of certiorari, a consent to review the case, but the Court, as it does with most such requests, denied certiorari, letting the order stand.

Registering an unusual objection to such a denial, Justice Byron White, joined by Justices Brennan and Marshall, contrasted the Second Circuit's holding with that of the Sixth Circuit Court of Appeals in a similar case, *CBS Inc. v. Young,*[47] and stated: "Because of the importance of this issue and conflicting resolutions given it by the courts of appeals, I would grant the petition for certiorari."[48] For reasons unstated, Justice Stevens, the author of one of the concurrences in *Nebraska Press Association,* did not participate in the consideration of the case. His vote could have been the fourth needed to grant certiorari.

Two years later, in another high-profile prosecution, a federal court in Florida ordered the Cable News Network (CNN) not to broadcast taped conversations between former Panama president Manuel Noriega, in jail facing trial for alleged drug trafficking offenses, and his lawyer. The trial judge said he would first need to review the tapes to determine if they would prejudice Noriega's trial, but CNN declined to submit them. The Eleventh Circuit Court of Appeals affirmed the order, and the Supreme Court (including Justices Stevens and White) again denied certiorari, this time over the dissents of Justices Marshall and Sandra Day O'Connor. Marshall wrote, "In my view, this case is of extraordinary consequence for freedom of the press." Pointing to *Nebraska Press Association* and *New York Times,* he declared, "I do not see how the prior restraint imposed in this case can be reconciled with these teachings." He noted further: "The court entered this order without any finding that suppression of the broadcast was necessary to protect Noriega's right to a fair trial."[49]

So, very slowly, and with continuing reservations, the Supreme Court energized the Founders' aversion to prior restraint of the press and their belief in the desirability of, and indeed the need for, press monitoring and criticism of government.

STATE SHACKLES NO, DISTRIBUTION YES

During the same decades, commencing in the 1930s, the Court further strengthened the press clause, ruling against discriminatory state taxation and other restrictive state laws, and encouraging the distribution of newspapers through the mails and the sidewalk boxes called newsracks.

In fact, it was the tax case mentioned earlier in which the Court first based a pro-press ruling on the First Amendment. That came in 1936, five years after the Court had relied on the Fourteenth Amendment to strike down a prior restraint in *Near v. Minnesota*.

During the incumbency of the colorful, freewheeling U.S. senator Huey ("Kingfish") Long, who had his detractors among the press, Louisiana imposed a 2 percent gross receipts tax on the advertising revenue of any publication with a weekly circulation exceeding 20,000. Publishers of all thirteen newspapers affected by the tax sued in federal district court; it enjoined collection of the tax, declaring it in violation of the Constitution.

The Supreme Court, a conservative, anti–New Deal court, a court not enamored of constitutional liberties, a court that President Roosevelt would later confront with his "court-packing" plan to add more justices, nevertheless granted a direct appeal, inasmuch as a constitutional issue was presented. The newspapers' counsel argued that of the thirteen newspapers (out of 163 in the state) targeted by the tax, "twelve were active in their opposition to the dominant political group in the State, which group controlled the Legislature and at whose dictates the Legislature passed this law."

The Supreme Court unanimously affirmed the ruling of the trial court. Justice George Sutherland, a former U.S. senator from Utah, citing English press controls that included special taxes, as well as the First and Fourteenth Amendments, wasted no time getting to the heart of the matter:

> [S]ince informed public opinion is the most potent of all restraints upon misgovernment, the suppression or abridgement of the publicity afforded by a free press cannot be regarded otherwise than with grave concern. The [statute] . . . is seen to be a deliberate and calculated device in the guise of a tax to limit the circulation of

information to which the public is entitled in virtue of the constitutional guarantees.[50]

Years later the Supreme Court, with somewhat different reasoning, invalidated as First Amendment violations a Minnesota ink-
and-paper tax imposed on a small number of newspapers[51] and an
Arkansas sales tax exemption for religious, professional, trade, or
sports periodicals.[52] However, the Court sustained an Arkansas tax
imposed on cable television companies but not newspapers, finding no First Amendment violation because the tax did not single
out the press.[53] Notably, the Court did not find any of these three
cases clear-cut; there were dissenters from each decision.

Following its prior restraint and taxation rulings, the Supreme
Court for the first time articulated a right to publish, though it
came in an antitrust decision, *Associated Press v. United States,* which
found an unlawful restraint of trade by the news organization because nonmembers could not publish its stories.[54] Justice Black,
writing for a unanimous Court, declared, "Freedom to publish is
guaranteed by the Constitution." He added in a footnote: "The
decree does not compel AP or its members to permit publication
of anything which their 'reason' tells them should not be published."[55] "Freedom to publish" was obiter dictum, a statement not
required to resolve the case, but nevertheless a historic recognition
of a right not expressly stated in the First Amendment yet entirely
in accord with it.

Further fortifying the right to publish, in the 1960s and 1970s
several questions of who controls newspaper space were decided
in favor of the publishers, sometimes by lower courts. For instance,
in one closely watched case, the Seventh Circuit Court of Appeals in Chicago rejected a labor union's request, bottomed on the
First Amendment, to purchase advertising in the *Chicago Tribune*

to protest a store's sale of imported clothing. The Supreme Court declined to review the case, leaving the appellate decision standing.[56]

Even in the face of restrictive state statutes, a newspaper's control of its own space was affirmed. In 1966 the Supreme Court struck down an Alabama criminal statute that prohibited solicitation of votes on election day.[57] The editor of the *Birmingham Post-Herald* had been prosecuted for publishing an election-day editorial urging voters to adopt the mayor-council form of city government. Although the trial court considered the law an unconstitutional restriction of press freedom, the Alabama Supreme Court found it reasonable and affirmed the conviction.

A unanimous U.S. Supreme Court reversed. Justice Black wrote for the Court in a terse, firm opinion that a "major purpose" of the First Amendment "was to protect the free discussion of governmental affairs." He went on:

> Suppression of the right of the press to praise or criticize governmental agents and to clamor and contend for or against change, which is all that this editorial did, muzzles one of the very agencies the Framers of our Constitution thoughtfully and deliberately selected to improve our society and keep it free. . . . We hold that no test of reasonableness can save a state law from invalidation as a violation of the First Amendment when that law makes it a crime for a newspaper editor to do no more than urge people to vote one way or another in a publicly held election.[58]

In a strongly worded concurrence, Justice Douglas called the statute "a blatant violation of freedom of the press" and noted that two press associations, which had filed briefs as amici curiae, or friends of the court, "tell us that since November 1962 editorial comment on election day has been nonexistent in Alabama. The chilling effect of this prosecution is thus anything but hypothetical; it is currently being experienced by the newspapers and the people of Alabama."[59]

A restrictive Florida statute met a similar fate. Criticized by the *Miami Herald,* a legislature candidate demanded space for a rebuttal as required by a 1913 right-of-reply law. The newspaper refused, and gained a victory in the trial court, which held the law unconstitutional. But the Florida Supreme Court sided with the candidate. However, in a unanimous decision the U.S. Supreme Court held for the newspaper. Chief Justice Warren Burger wrote with understanding of the journalistic enterprise:

> The choice of material to go into a newspaper, and the decisions made as to limitations on the size and content of the paper, and treatment of public issues and public officials—whether fair or unfair—constitute the exercise of editorial control and judgment. It has yet to be demonstrated how governmental regulation of this crucial process can be exercised consistent with First Amendment guarantees of a free press as they have evolved to this time.

Concurring, Justice Byron White added: "[T]his law runs afoul of the elementary First Amendment proposition that government may not force a newspaper to print copy which, in its journalistic discretion, it chooses to leave on the newsroom floor."[60]

The Court even set aside the criminal conviction of a publisher for its newspaper's disclosure of confidential information regarding a judge's misconduct. The Norfolk *Virginian-Pilot* had accurately reported on a pending investigation by the Virginia Judicial Inquiry and Review Commission and named the state judge whose conduct was being questioned. Tried without a jury, the publisher, Landmark Communications, Inc., was found guilty of violating the confidentiality of the commission's proceedings and was fined $500 plus the costs of prosecution. The Virginia Supreme Court affirmed, but the U.S. Supreme Court unanimously reversed, Chief Justice Burger again assigning the opinion to himself. He wrote that the state high court had failed in its effort to apply the "clear and present danger" test enunciated by Justice Oliver Wendell Holmes, requiring in this case a finding of danger to the orderly administration of justice. While acknowledging "some risk of injury" to the judge, the system of justice, and the commission's operations, the chief justice went on: "but the test requires that the danger be 'clear and present' and in our view the risk here falls far short of that requirement. Moreover, much of the risk can be eliminated through careful internal procedures to protect the confidentiality of Commission proceedings."[61]

Several years later the Supreme Court again found for the press in a state criminal law matter. A reporter for the *Charlotte Herald-News* in Florida wanted to write about his experience as a witness before a grand jury investigating alleged improprieties by the offices of the Charlotte County prosecutor and sheriff. Although his intended publication would have occurred after the grand jury's term, the reporter was aware that Florida law required that grand jury witnesses remain forever silent about their testimony, so he asked a federal district court to rule that the requirement was an unconstitutional restriction on speech. The court held against him, but the U.S. Court of Appeals for the Eleventh Circuit reversed, deciding that the reporter could disclose information he had acquired before telling it to the grand jury. The Supreme Court agreed. Chief Justice William Rehnquist, the forthright conservative elevated from associate justice in 1986, wrote for a unanimous Court. He cited *Landmark Communications* as well as other cases and declared that "[t]he potential for abuse of the Florida prohibition, through its employment as a device to silence those who know of unlawful conduct or irregularities on the part of public officials, is apparent."[62]

Implicitly recognizing that the right to publish encompasses the right to distribute the publication, the Supreme Court gave further support to publishers by curtailing the postmaster general's discretion to withhold second-class mailing privileges, a discretion that, as noted above, had been upheld in 1921,[63] and by striking down city efforts to remove news racks from sidewalks.

Esquire magazine's second-class mailing privilege was removed in 1943 by the postmaster general, who pointed to a statutory requirement that the publication must be "published for the dissemination of information of a public character, or devoted to literature, the sciences, arts, or some special industry." The postmaster general's objection, according to the Supreme Court's opinion by Justice William O. Douglas, was that certain "jokes, cartoons, pictures, articles, and poems" were reflective of "the smoking-room type of humor, featuring, in the main, sex." To Douglas the decision to ban the magazine turned on "whether the contents are 'good' or 'bad.'" But, he went on, "Congress has left the Postmaster General with no power to prescribe standards for the literature or the art which a mailable periodical disseminates." The Court affirmed an appellate court ruling overturning the postmaster general's decision.[64]

When the Cleveland suburb of Lakewood required that newspaper distributors obtain an annual permit to sell papers through sidewalk news racks, the publisher of the *Cleveland Plain Dealer* challenged it as unconstitutional. The city's ordinance empowered the mayor to decide whether a news rack could be placed, and it specified no standards or criteria to be used in that decision.

Justice Brennan, writing for a Supreme Court majority of four in 1988, saw two major "First Amendment risks" in such a licensing scheme: "self-censorship by speakers in order to avoid being denied a license to speak; and the difficulty of effectively detecting, reviewing, and correcting content-based censorship 'as applied' without standards by which to measure the licensor's action." Because of the mayor's "boundless discretion," the majority found the ordinance in contravention of the First Amendment.[65]

In a similar vein but for different reasons, five years later the Court struck down a Cincinnati ordinance that banned the distribution of commercial handbills on public property, interpreted by the city to prohibit the distribution of free magazines, although not the sales of newspapers via news racks. The ordinance was challenged by two publishers of magazines that contained primarily advertising but also some information, about real estate and current events, deemed of general interest.

For the majority in a 6–3 decision, Justice John Paul Stevens mentioned the *City of Lakewood* case, but relied primarily on cases protecting "commercial speech," the First Amendment right of businesses to state their case, truthfully, to the public. He wrote: "The regulation is not a permissible regulation of commercial speech, for on this record it is clear that the interests that Cincinnati has asserted," public safety and aesthetics, "are unrelated to any distinction between 'commercial handbills' and 'newspapers.' "[66] Chief Justice Rehnquist, joined by Justices Byron White and Clarence Thomas, dissented. Noting that the decision would permit banning *all* news racks, the chief justice declared that it "places the city in the position of having to decide between restricting more speech—fully protected speech," which would include newspapers, "—and allowing the proliferation of newsracks on its street corners to continue unabated."[67]

LOSSES WITHOUT DEFEAT

As a postscript to these cases undergirding the right to publish, we must note one that went the other way, though it eventually brought about helpful protection for the press. The case emanated, surprisingly, from a college newspaper. Student papers rarely go to court except to fight for their own right to publish without faculty censorship, but in the 1970s the *Stanford Daily* initiated a federal lawsuit for a broader purpose. Palo Alto police officers, with a warrant issued on a judge's finding of probable cause that the *Daily* had photographs of demonstrators assaulting the police at a hospital, searched the paper's offices for such photos in an effort to identify perpetrators. The paper itself was suspected of no wrongdoing, and for that reason a U.S. district court found the search a violation of the First Amendment and the Fourth, which bars unreasonable searches and seizures. The Ninth Circuit Court of Appeals affirmed, but the Supreme Court, by a 5–3 vote, reversed. Justice Byron White wrote for the majority: "[W]e decline to reinterpret the [Fourth] Amendment to impose a general constitutional barrier against warrants to search newspaper premises, to require resort to subpoenas as a general rule, or to demand prior notice and hearing in connection with the issuance of search warrants."[68]

Though the *Stanford Daily* lost, the case triggered a pro-press reaction in several state legislatures and in Washington. Congress passed the Privacy Protection Act of 1980, effectively granting the press what the Supreme Court had not.[69] The act generally requires a subpoena, which takes longer and can be challenged before a judge, rather than just a warrant, to undertake newsroom searches and seizures, and then only when a journalist holding materials such as notes or first drafts or photographs is suspected of a crime, or when the materials must be seized immediately to prevent bodily harm. Photos and documents may also be seized to prevent their destruction. Thus *Zurcher v. Stanford Daily* is remembered as a net plus for the press.

It is important to note that as the Supreme Court in the twentieth century was defining and fortifying a right to publish, it was also affirming, not surprisingly, that the news business had to abide by laws of general application, the First Amendment notwithstanding. *Stanford Daily* is an illustration of that. Other decisions denied requested press exemptions from laws governing restraint of trade, labor, mail fraud, human relations, copyright, and even breach of contract.

For instance, we mentioned earlier *Associated Press v. United States,* the 1945 antitrust case in which the Court first recognized a right to publish. The AP's bylaws enabled it, the Supreme Court held by a 6–3 vote, to "block all newspaper nonmembers from any opportunity to buy news from AP or any of its publisher members" and thus constituted a restraint of trade forbidden by the Sherman Antitrust Act of 1890. While recognizing that "[f]reedom to publish is guaranteed by the Constitution," the Court rejected the AP's claim of a First Amendment exemption from the Sherman Act.[70]

In the same vein, over the following four decades the Court rejected First Amendment claims to hold that

- publishers are obliged to pay overtime as required by the Fair Labor Standards Act of 1938;[71]
- the postmaster general could halt a magazine's delivery and payment of its money orders on the grounds that a puzzle contest in the magazine was a fraud;[72]

- the *Pittsburgh Press* must comply with a local human relations ordinance prohibiting gender separation of job advertising where gender was not a bona fide occupational qualification;[73]
- the *Seattle Times* could not print information obtained through the pretrial discovery process in a lawsuit involving the newspaper itself;[74]
- a news magazine, the *Nation,* violated the Copyright Act when it used verbatim quotations from President Gerald Ford's not-yet-published memoir;[75]
- there was a breach of contract based on promissory estoppel, a general rule that a person may not benefit by breaking his own promise, when the *Minneapolis Star Tribune* and *St. Paul Pioneer Press* violated their promise of confidentiality to a news source and printed his name.[76]

Despite these unexceptionable cases requiring publishers to abide by general laws, the Supreme Court in the twentieth century greatly strengthened the First Amendment's press clause and the news publishing business by explicitly recognizing over time a constitutional right to publish. At the same time, in other cases the Court was broadening, if sometimes erratically, the definition of what the news media could constitutionally publish, balancing the First Amendment against the laws of libel and privacy and the constitutional right to a fair trial. Conversely, the Court made it difficult, indeed practically impossible, for journalists to maintain their promises of confidentiality to their sources, promises sometimes essential to good journalism, especially investigations. We shall examine these conflicting trends in the next three chapters.

THREE

FIRST AMENDMENT VERSUS LIBEL AND PRIVACY

Having begun in the 1930s to undergird the business of publishing news, though mostly by divided votes, the Supreme Court in the 1960s commenced to define what the media could rightfully publish. Its work proved breathtaking. However, like the piecemeal, attenuated recognition of the right to publish, this enlargement of the constitutional practice of journalism evinced no overarching plan or historical purpose. It was simply case by case, with inconsistencies and changes of course that arguably should not happen in a precedent-based legal system. Some cases generated as many questions as answers.

To what extent this broadening interpretation of the First Amendment was based in history rather than in law will never be known, but it must be noted that the metamorphosis emerged during the heat of the civil rights revolution, and the Court's first monumental cases of this genre related to it.

It was a time when the law of libel, the principal legal limitation of freedom of the press, was as inherited from English common law, though sometimes codified in state statutes. It generally required only proof of publication of critical words about someone plus some indication that they were defamatory, harmful to the person's reputation. No actual harm or loss had to be proved. Truth was sometimes recognized as a defense, but mostly not. Cases were tried in state courts without reference to the First Amendment, even when newspapers were the defendants.

So, when newspaper and television stories about burning civil rights controversies were rife, it was anomalous that a revolution in libel law commenced with an advertisement.[1] Its signers were Eleanor Roosevelt, labor leader A. Philip Randolph, actors Marlon Brando, Sidney Poitier, Ossie Davis, Ruby Dee, Sammy Davis, Jr., Shelley Winters, and Robert Ryan, musician Nat King Cole, singer Mahalia Jackson, baseball hero Jackie Robinson, writers Nat Hentoff and Langston Hughes, the Reverend Harry Emerson Fosdick, and a number of other prominent citizens, all putting their names to a full-page ad in the *New York Times* that cost a bit more than $4,800.[2]

"Heed Their Rising Voices," the ad proclaimed, asserting that "thousands of Southern Negro students" engaged in nonviolent demonstrations were "being met by an unprecedented wave of terror." Details of alleged confrontations in various cities were spelled out, including this:

> In Montgomery, Alabama, after students sang "My Country, 'Tis of Thee" on the State Capitol steps, their leaders were expelled from school, and truckloads of police armed with shotguns and tear-gas ringed the Alabama State College Campus. When the entire student body protested to state authorities by refusing to re-register, their dining hall was padlocked in an attempt to starve them into submission.

The ad requested donations, to a committee at a New York address, to support the "embattled students" and the legal defense of the Reverend Martin Luther King, Jr., leader of the Negro boycott of the Montgomery bus system, then awaiting trial: "They have bombed his home almost killing his wife and child. They have assaulted his person. They have arrested him seven times—for 'speeding,' 'loitering' and similar 'offenses.' And now they have charged him with 'perjury'—a *felony* under which they could imprison him for *ten years.*"[3]

L. B. Sullivan took offense. He was one of three elected commissioners of the city of Montgomery, and his responsibility was the police and fire departments. Though the police department was actually managed by its chief, and neither the chief nor Sullivan was mentioned in the advertisement, Sullivan filed a libel suit against the *Times,* contending that the ad defamed him personally because it described police action in offensive terms. Backed by the testimony of friends and colleagues, who said the ad harmed his reputation, Sullivan won a jury judgment of $500,000, the full amount he had sought and the largest libel award in Alabama history. The supreme court of Alabama upheld the verdict. Other libel suits were filed against the *Times,* also seeking big damages.

Was the cause civil rights or freedom of the press? The U.S. Supreme Court, while it had given only sporadic and usually divided support to the actual work of journalists, for a decade now had been fully immersed in the civil rights conflict, commencing with its stunning, indeed revolutionary decision in 1954 declaring segregated public schools to be unconstitutional.[4] It could hardly sidestep this case, called *New York Times Co. v. Sullivan.*[5] The justices heard oral arguments on January 6, 1964, and only two months later announced a unanimous and far-reaching decision reversing the Alabama courts. In a strong, historically grounded opinion by Justice William Brennan, the Court punctured the plaintiff's legal theory and his evidence, gave the press considerable wiggle room to excuse minor errors, interpreted the First Amendment to protect advertising as well as news, and established tough new constitutional standards for public officials to overcome in any future libel lawsuits based on press criticism of their performance in office. Furthermore, a lawsuit by a public official alleging personal defamation, Justice Brennan wrote at the end, "may not constitutionally be utilized to establish that an otherwise impersonal attack on governmental operations was a libel of an official responsible for those operations."[6] Inasmuch as the Court had already demolished Sullivan's case, this closing jab was hardly needed to finish it off, but in a broader, First Amendment sense, yes, it was needed. It clarified, or perhaps simply emphasized, that the Founders were seeking free and unrestrained criticism of government. As the opinion stated: "we consider this case against the background of a profound national commitment to the principle that debate on public issues should be uninhibited, robust, and wide-open, and that it may well include vehement, caustic, and sometimes unpleasantly sharp attacks on government and public officials."[7]

The Court's core pronouncement, adapted from the libel law of several states, was this:

> The constitutional guarantees require, we think, a federal rule that prohibits a public official from recovering damages for a defamatory falsehood relating to his official conduct unless he proves that the statement was made with "actual malice"—that is, with knowledge that it was false or with reckless disregard of whether it was false or not.[8]

In regard to the specifics of Sullivan's case, the Court found that he was not sufficiently identified to claim defamation; that he offered no proof other than witnesses' personal opinions that the ad had in fact damaged his reputation; that mistakes in the ad (the police actually were deployed *near* the college campus and did not ring it; Dr. King had been arrested *four* times rather than seven) were insignificant aspects of his claim; that the *Times*'s advertising staff could not be expected or required to check and verify every statement of an ad submitted by well-known and responsible persons; and, in sum, that he failed to prove actual malice by the *Times*. It was a historic, resounding victory for the news media.

Later the Court decided in a New Hampshire case that the term "public official" could encompass appointed officials as well those elected: "the 'public official' designation applies at the very least to those among the hierarchy of government employees who have or appear to the public to have, substantial responsibility for or control over the conduct of governmental affairs."[9]

PUBLIC FIGURES, TOO

More importantly, in two concurrent, prominent cases, one arising from the civil rights struggle, the Supreme Court added "public figures" to the category of plaintiffs who must meet a higher standard of proof to win a libel judgment. But it was done clumsily, with no clear majority agreement on what that higher standard was.

A libel suit against the Associated Press was filed by an outspoken former U.S. Army major general named Edwin Walker, who had commanded federal troops sent by President Eisenhower to enforce a school desegregation order in Little Rock in 1957. He subsequently resigned to engage in political activity, particularly to oppose such use of federal troops to force desegregation. Walker alleged that the AP incorrectly reported that he had personally led a charge of protesters against federal marshals seeking to enforce a federal court decree ordering the admission of a Negro, James Meredith, to the all-white University of Mississippi, in 1962. A Texas jury awarded Walker $300,000 in compensatory damages, recognizing actual damage to reputation. However, the Supreme Court held that Walker, although no longer in government and clearly not a public official, was nevertheless prominent enough to be deemed a "public figure" under the ordinary rules of tort, or personal injury, law. According to Justice John Marshall Harlan's opinion for a plurality of four, Walker "may have attained that status . . . by his purposeful activity amounting to a thrusting of his personality into the 'vortex' of an important public controversy, but . . . commanded sufficient continuing public interest and had sufficient access to the means of counterargument to be able" to argue publicly against any defamatory statements. Therefore, the opinion went on, he should be held to a higher standard of proof as a libel plaintiff, but the justices could not agree on what that standard should be. Justice Harlan offered this:

> We consider and would hold that a "public figure" who is not a public official may also recover damages for a defamatory falsehood whose substance makes substantial danger to reputation apparent, on a showing of highly unreasonable conduct constituting an extreme departure from the standards of investigation and reporting ordinarily adhered to by responsible publishers.[10]

Walker had proved no such "highly unreasonable conduct" by the Associated Press, the plurality concluded, noting that the AP was operating under time pressure to report the story and that the reporter, Van Savell, was seasoned and competent, his stories reflecting no animus toward Walker. Walker's libel judgment was reversed; the other five justices stated their concurrence in three separate opinions.

However, Chief Justice Earl Warren, while concurring in the result, protested that Justice Harlan's new standard was an unwarranted deviation from the *New York Times* standard of "actual malice." He stated: "I cannot believe that a standard which is based on such an unusual and uncertain formulation could either guide a jury of laymen or afford the protection for speech and debate that is fundamental to our society and guaranteed by the First Amendment."[11] The new standard had only a short life at the Supreme Court. But the "public figure" plaintiff remained in the evolving law of libel.

Who else might be a public figure? The justices classified a Maryland real estate developer, prominent in his community, as a public figure (though he was also a state legislator, the Court did not rely on that), and thus reversed his libel judgment against a community weekly newspaper that had reported the developer was accused in a public meeting of using "blackmail" to obtain city zoning variances. The Court said the offensive word was "no more than rhetorical hyperbole, a vigorous epithet" voiced by the developer's opponents and no accusation of crime.[12]

The "public official" category was stretched to include candidates for public office in a New Hampshire libel case. The Court reversed a judgment obtained by a primary election candidate for the U.S. Senate against a newspaper and a columnist who had called the candidate a "former smalltime bootlegger," based on a Prohibition-era conviction. The case was also significant because it held that critical press statements referring to a public plaintiff's private life were protected by the *New York Times v. Sullivan* decision.[13]

Continuing on its libel bent, the Court determined that the omission of just a single word, "alleged," not used in a newsmagazine story about a U.S. Commission on Civil Rights report that mentioned an act of brutality by a Chicago police officer, was not sufficient to show actual malice.[14] A newspaper in Florida was exonerated despite its error in reporting that the mayor had been indicted for perjury when in fact it was his brother.[15]

A LAWYER PLEADS, THE COURT "CLARIFIES"

Changing course, the Supreme Court attempted to alleviate the confusion in a case focusing primarily on the public-private distinction, but it took the opportunity to also address the extent of the actual malice protection of the *New York Times v. Sullivan* decision. A prominent, reputable Chicago labor and civil rights lawyer, Elmer Gertz, sued the company of Robert Welch, head of the far-right John Birch Society, which had published in its monthly magazine an article calling Gertz a "Communist-fronter" and a "Leninist." It also suggested that he had a police record and had been a member of Socialist organizations, and that he had helped arrange a "frame-up" of a Chicago police officer convicted of second-degree murder. All of this was false, all stemming from Gertz's representation of a murder victim's family in a civil suit against the policeman.

A federal district court jury awarded Gertz a judgment of $50,000, but the judge set aside the verdict on the ground that Gertz had not proved either falsity or reckless disregard for the truth, the *Times v. Sullivan* standard for a public official or a public figure. The appellate court affirmed. The Supreme Court reversed, however, declaring Gertz a private figure, at least in the context of this dispute, who needed to prove only negligence by the magazine, not actual malice. But the decision was close, 5–4.[16]

Justice Lewis Powell's plurality opinion devoted several pages to a recognition and analysis of the justices' widely varying views on how much protection the First Amendment provides to news media sued for libel, concluding that

1. a private plaintiff who proves only negligence or some such standard of proof less than actual malice is limited to damages compensating him only for actual injury, including out-of-pocket losses, personal humiliation, damage to reputation in the community, and mental anguish; and

2. any award of punitive damages, intended as punishment over and above compensation for actual injury, requires a showing of actual malice.[17]

The Supreme Court remanded the case for a new trial. Indeed, Gertz did prove actual malice and was awarded $100,000 in actual damages and $300,000 in punitive damages, affirmed by the Court of Appeals for the Seventh Circuit.[18]

The elaborate effort at libel clarification laid out in *Gertz* was simultaneously criticized by the four dissenters. Chief Justice Warren Burger wondered whether "negligence," though a common standard of responsibility, meaning careless indifference, applied in other tort, or personal damage, actions, could be applied to the news media as well; he and the other dissenters felt the original trial verdict against Gertz's claim should have prevailed. Justice William O. Douglas contended that libel law cannot limit the

First Amendment. Justice Byron White characterized the Court's several libel decisions as resting on "insufficient grounds for scuttling the libel laws of the States in such wholesale fashion, to say nothing of deprecating the reputation interest of ordinary citizens and rendering them powerless to protect themselves."[19]

CLARITY? HARDLY

Then, for a time, the pendulum swung back toward tougher libel standards for the press. Continuing to struggle with the public-private distinction, the Supreme Court declared that even some well-known persons were private plaintiffs, thus diminishing the press's protection under the First Amendment. For instance, in 1976 the Court ruled that a wealthy woman with a prominent name, Mary Alice Firestone, who was involved in a heavily covered, high-stakes divorce case, was a private plaintiff because she had not sought the spotlight.[20] Three years later the Court gave similar private status to a Michigan scientist who had received grants from the National Science Foundation and other federal agencies to investigate the behavior patterns of animals,[21] and to an immigrant Russian translator who had pleaded guilty to a contempt charge for failing to appear before a federal grand jury investigating Soviet espionage.[22]

However, a few years later the Supreme Court also limited the legal impact of the private-plaintiff status. The issue was a series of five articles in the *Philadelphia Inquirer* that described a businessman named Maurice S. Hepps, whose company operated convenience stores, as using links to organized crime to influence both legislative and administrative actions of the state government. As in so many other libel cases, the Court was divided, the majority again just the minimum five. They acknowledged that he was a private plaintiff, but nevertheless overturned a judgment Hepps had won against the newspaper.

Writing for the majority, Justice Sandra Day O'Connor reflected the concern of several justices that newspapers' fear of liability might discourage the publication of controversial stories. She declared: "Because such a 'chilling' effect would be antithetical to the first amendment's protection of true speech on matters of public concern, we believe that a private-figure plaintiff must bear the burden of showing that the speech at issue is false before recovering damages for defamation from a media defendant."[23] But Justice John Paul Stevens, a liberal on most issues, was joined by three conservative justices, Chief Justice Burger, Justice White, and Justice Rehnquist, in a spirited dissent. Stevens attacked the Court's holding as "a pernicious result" because it imposed on a private plaintiff a new burden inconsistent with most state libel laws, benefiting only publishers "who act negligently or maliciously."[24]

Must journalists render quotations exactly as they were spoken? The Supreme Court cut the press considerable slack in reversing a California libel case brought by a prominent psychoanalyst, a public figure, against a well-known author who had interviewed him extensively on tape and written two *New Yorker* magazine articles about him that were also published as a book. Dr. Jeffrey Masson had recently been dismissed as projects director of the Sigmund Freud Archives near London, after stating publicly he was disillusioned with Freudian psychology. The writer, Janet Malcolm, quoted him extensively in her articles, but six quotations challenged as false or distorted by Dr. Masson could not be found on her more than forty hours of audiotapes. He was quoted as saying that two senior colleagues considered him "an intellectual gigolo," that he deemed himself the "greatest analyst who ever lived," and as saying that he had planned to make the Freud house a place of "sex, women, fun." The trial and appellate courts had ruled that these and other quotations, although unsubstantiated, were not sufficient proof of actual malice and therefore granted summary judgment to the defendants, meaning there was no triable issue of fact to be presented to a jury.

The Supreme Court reversed, sending the case back for trial, but in so doing accommodated the press, permitting not only erroneous quotation but even deliberate change so long as it does not represent actual malice: "We conclude that a deliberate alteration of the words uttered by a plaintiff does not equate with knowledge of falsity for purposes of *New York Times Co. v. Sullivan* . . . and *Gertz v. Robert Welch, Inc.* . . . unless the alteration results in a material change in the meaning conveyed by the statement."[25] Applying this standard, a jury found no libel, and an appellate court affirmed.[26]

Given the steep burden of proof established by the Supreme Court for a public plaintiff—publishing a known falsehood or with reckless disregard for the truth—has the Court ever affirmed such a finding? Not often, but it did in the companion case to General Walker's, *Curtis Publishing Co. v. Butts,* where the *Saturday Evening Post* ran with an unsubstantiated allegation from a questionable informant about fixing a football game.[27] Two decades later the Court again found reckless disregard, on a similar showing of blatantly irresponsible journalism, in the case of Daniel Connaughton, an unsuccessful candidate for a municipal judgeship in Hamilton, Ohio, who won a substantial judgment against the local newspaper, the *Journal News.* That lawsuit grew out of a pre-election story quoting a grand jury witness who alleged that the candidate acted unethically, lied, and extorted witnesses to influence the grand jury, which was investigating bribery by an employee in the office of his opponent, the incumbent judge, whom the newspaper supported editorially for reelection. A federal jury awarded the plaintiff $5,000 in compensatory damages, for actual impairment of reputation, and $195,000 in punitive damages. An appellate court affirmed.

The Supreme Court combed through the testimony and tape-recorded conversations considered by the jury, concluding that the newspaper had failed to firmly corroborate the grand juror's allegations, and in fact had deliberately avoided talking to the grand juror's sister, whom the candidate and others had pointed to as an eyewitness who should be questioned. "[I]t is likely that the newspaper's inaction was a product of a deliberate decision not to acquire knowledge of facts that might confirm the probable falsity of Thompson's [the grand juror's] charges," Justice John Paul Stevens wrote for a unanimous Court. Calling this "purposeful avoidance of the truth," the Court ruled the evidence was "'unmistakably' sufficient to support a finding of actual malice."[28]

BEYOND FACTS: OPINION AND STATE OF MIND

Another marker for the press was established in a case dealing with defamatory opinion. Opinion, or "fair comment," was protected by the common law, at least in regard to factual matters of public concern. However, the Court made things difficult for the press in a strange case extending over fifteen years that came before the justices no fewer than three times. Sending it back for still further proceedings, the Court denied a constitutional protection for opinion but came close to providing it anyway by referring to several of the cases described above.

Michael Milkovich was the wrestling coach at Maple Heights High School in Ohio when his team became involved in an altercation during a home match; several people, including opposing wrestlers, were injured. He and the schools superintendent, H. Donald Scott, testified about the brouhaha at a hearing convened by the Ohio High School Athletic Association. The association censured Milkovich for his behavior during the incident, put his team on probation for a year, and excluded it from the state tournament. However, the actions against the team were challenged in court for lack of due process, and the court, after a hearing in which both Milkovich and the superintendent testified, overturned them. The next day the *News-Herald,* which circulates in Lake County, Ohio, published a column by J. Theodore Diadiun under the heading "TD Says," declaring that anyone who had attended the wrestling match "knows in his heart that Milkovich and Scott lied at the hearing after each having given his solemn oath to tell the truth. But they got away with it."

Milkovich sued for libel. Scott sued separately, but eventually lost, the Ohio Supreme Court holding that the column was constitutionally protected opinion.[29] That court subsequently dismissed an appeal from Milkovich, who lost his case, too. Surprisingly, after twice rejecting the case, the U.S. Supreme Court decided to hear it and reversed the Ohio court, sending the case back for further proceedings. Chief Justice William Rehnquist wrote that "the connotation that petitioner [Milkovich] committed perjury is sufficiently factual to be susceptible of being proved true or false," in part by comparing his testimony before the athletic association with his testimony before the trial court.[30] (Of course, although the Court did not say so, his testimony could have been consistent but untruthful in both hearings, so this comparison alone could not have been determinative.)

Justice Brennan, joined by Justice Marshall, dissented, noting that Diadiun, the column writer, did not purport to have attended the court hearing, did not quote directly from it, and thus, they contended, "[n]o reasonable reader could understand Diadiun to be impliedly asserting—as fact—that Milkovich had perjured himself."[31] But the Court's teaching from the protracted case was clear: a journalist's opinion should be based on provable fact.

LIKE DEFAMATION, PRIVACY

During this quarter-century when the Supreme Court was strengthening the First Amendment's protection of the news media against libel suits, it was extending much the same benefit in regard to allegations of invasion of privacy. The legal concept of a right to privacy, unlike libel, is not rooted in the English common law, but developed in American state courts and legislatures during the twentieth century. It encompasses four different torts: intrusion upon a person's seclusion or into his private affairs (typically by a reporter or photographer); disclosure of embarrassing facts; placing someone in a false light in the public's mind (but short of defamation); and appropriation, or unauthorized use, of a prominent person's name or likeness for commercial or other advantage.

The earliest, and perhaps still most striking, example of constitutionalizing the law of libel was the Court's reversal of a judgment under New York's privacy statute[32] on behalf of James Hill, whose family had been held hostage in their suburban Philadelphia house by escaped convicts but released unharmed. The drama inspired a novel and then a play, both fictionalized to include violence, but when *Life* magazine in 1955 published a story about the play linking it specifically to the Hills' ordeal, including photos of the house (though they no longer lived there), implying that the play was a factual report, Hill sued under the privacy statute. He alleged misrepresentation of the family's experience in order to boost circulation, and won a judgment of $30,000 for compensatory or actual damages that was upheld by New York's highest court, the court of appeals.

The Supreme Court heard arguments and then, not yet ready to decide, called for reargument. Still, the Court could reach no consensus, dividing 5-4. It threw out the judgment, saying that Hill was a public figure by virtue of his enforced ordeal, though he had refused to be interviewed about it afterward, and that the statute could not be applied "to redress false reports of matters of public interest in the absence of proof that the defendant published the report with knowledge of its falsity or in reckless disregard of the truth."[33] Four justices objected that this was too stringent a test. A remedy should be available under the statute, Justice John Marshall Harlan wrote, when the press violates a standard of reasonable care, or negligence, applied to physicians and other professions, creating "a severe risk of irremediable harm to individuals involuntarily exposed to it and powerless to protect themselves against it."[34] James Hill, who had been litigating the case for eleven years already, did not pursue it further.

Citing the *Hill* case as well as libel precedents, the Supreme Court several years later threw out a judgment of intentional infliction of emotional distress, a form of invasion of privacy, because the public-figure plaintiff had not shown that the publication acted with malice or recklessness. The case involved a clearly labeled though offensive advertisement parody in *Hustler* magazine representing that the outspoken conservative preacher Jerry Falwell, a public figure, experienced his "first time" in an outhouse with his mother. Writing more expansively than the case required, Chief Justice William Rehnquist celebrated political cartooning and satire, declaring that it is "often calculated to injure the feelings of the subject of the portrayal . . . is often not reasoned or evenhanded, but slashing and one-sided." He lauded in particular the "intentionally injurious speech" of Thomas Nast, "probably the greatest American cartoonist to date," who conducted in *Harper's Weekly* after the Civil War "a graphic vendetta against William M. 'Boss' Tweed and his corrupt associates in New York City's 'Tweed Ring.' "[35] Hardly constitutional reasoning.

More important to the mainstream media, the Supreme Court in the 1970s and 1980s struck down invasion-of-privacy lawsuits challenging the publication of names protected by state statutes. Although a Georgia law prohibited publishing the name of a rape victim, a reporter for WSB-TV in Atlanta found a seventeen-year-old victim's name in indictments made available for public inspection in the courtroom, and named her on the air. Reversing a civil judgment against the reporter and his employer, Justice Byron White stated for the Court:

> Public records by their very nature are of interest to those concerned with the administration of government, and a public benefit is performed by the reporting of the true contents of the records by the media. The freedom of the press to publish that information appears to us to be of critical importance to our type of government in which the citizenry is the final judge of the proper conduct of public business.[36]

Similarly, the Court upheld a newspaper's publication of the name of a fourteen-year-old arrested for the murder of a schoolmate in West Virginia, whose criminal code forbade naming juvenile offenders, because reporters had obtained the name lawfully, simply by questioning eyewitnesses, the police, and a prosecutor at the school.[37] And in the same vein, the Court reversed a judgment against a Florida newspaper for publishing the name of a rape victim in violation of state law; the source was the police department itself, which placed the crime report in its pressroom.[38]

Still, the Supreme Court found limits to its protection of the press in regard to invasion of privacy. One violation of the privacy right is the placing of a person in a "false light" before the public, a misrepresentation without the defamation necessary to libel. Five months after Melvin Cantrell and forty-three others died in an Ohio River bridge collapse, Joseph Eszterhas, the *Cleveland Plain Dealer* reporter who had covered the story, which won a journalism prize, returned to the Cantrell home to write a follow-up. He produced a Sunday magazine piece that described the family's poverty and Mrs. Cantrell's "same mask of non-expression she wore" at her husband's funeral. But in fact Mrs. Cantrell was not at home when the reporter called; he talked only to her children. Oddly, the Court likened the case to *Time, Inc. v. Hill*,[39] although that opinion did not mention false light and turned on interpretation of a New York privacy statute. The Court ruled against the public-figure plaintiff in *Time,* but this time went the other way. It found "a number of inaccuracies and false statements" in the *Plain Dealer* story, declaring, "These were 'calculated falsehoods' and the jury was plainly justified in finding that Eszterhas had portrayed the Cantrells in a false light through knowing or reckless untruth," in the words of Justice Potter Stewart.[40]

In another, though novel, case setting limits on the media, the Supreme Court found a violation of a branch of privacy law called the right of publicity. This prohibits the use of another person's name or likeness for commercial or other benefit. Ignoring the request of a "human cannonball" performing at an Ohio county fair, a television station filmed his performance, in which he was shot 200 feet into a net, and showed it in its entirety as part of a local news broadcast. The cannonball, one Hugo Zacchini, claimed the station had appropriated his professional property, violating his right of publicity. But, relying heavily on *Time, Inc. v. Hill,* the Ohio Supreme Court held that freedom of the press shielded the station from liability.

Not so, the U.S. Supreme Court ruled, though only by 5-4.[41] Justice Byron White distinguished *Time* as a false-light privacy case, not applicable here. He said the right of publicity is akin to copyright and patent law, intended to encourage creativity and protect its benefits. White noted pointedly that Ohio could choose "to protect the entertainer's incentive" without violating the First Amendment, and the case could have been decided under Ohio law, but it was not. "Petitioner [Zacchini] does not seek to enjoin the broadcast of his performance; he simply wants to be paid for it," White wrote.[42]

The Supreme Court's numerous rulings on libel and privacy in the latter decades of the twentieth century were clearly supportive of the press and of the nation's need to have open debate about public issues and public persons. But it could also be argued, as Justice Black and Justice Douglas did repeatedly, that even these rulings fell short of the absolute admonition to "make no law" guaranteed by the First Amendment. Instead, the Court balanced the First Amendment against state-law libel and privacy restrictions on publication. In the next chapter we will consider cases where such balancing is mandatory in a different constitutional setting, where the First Amendment comes up against the Sixth Amendment and the Fourteenth Amendment. These three amendments' guarantees cannot, the Court says, be absolute.

FOUR

FREE PRESS VERSUS FAIR TRIAL

In all criminal prosecutions, the accused shall enjoy the right to a speedy and public trial, by an impartial jury of the State and district wherein the crime shall have been committed, which district shall have been previously ascertained by law, and to be informed of the nature and cause of the accusation; to be confronted with the witnesses against him; to have compulsory process for obtaining witnesses in his favor, and to have the Assistance of Counsel for his defence.
—The Sixth Amendment to the Constitution

No state shall . . . deprive any person of life, liberty, or property, without due process of law. . . .
—The Fourteenth Amendment to the Constitution

Like the First Amendment, the Sixth Amendment was a breath-taking, truly revolutionary statement of individual rights at the time they both were adopted, in 1791, as parts of the Bill of Rights. No other nation made such firm promises to its citizens. The Fourteenth Amendment duplicates the guarantee of the Fifth

Amendment, which restrains the federal government, and makes it applicable to the states as well. In a criminal context, "due process of law" refers generally to the protections specified in the Sixth Amendment.

It was not clearly recognized at the outset, but there is an inherent conflict between the guarantees of free press and fair trial. That became apparent as they were interpreted and applied by the courts over the years, particularly in the mid-twentieth century. Did a "public trial" mean open to the press as well? Cameras? What about important preliminary court proceedings, like pretrial hearings on admissibility of evidence? Unlike certain challenges to common law and state law that the Supreme Court considered in the twentieth century, gradually applying the First Amendment to them, the guarantees of free press and fair trial are equal before the law. Because they are part of the Constitution, the Supreme Court must be the final arbiter of their meaning. Neither guarantee can be absolute when they are in confrontation. They must be balanced.

Such balancing questions were first faced by the Court during the influential chief justiceship of Earl Warren (1953–69), when it handed down new, broader interpretations of the rights of criminal suspects as well as the rights of the press. For instance, during the same years that it was putting muscle on the First Amendment in *New York Times Co. v. Sullivan, Associated Press v. Walker,* and *Time, Inc. v. Hill,* the Warren Court extended the Sixth Amendment right to counsel to the states,[1] required that a person accused of crime be informed of his rights, including the right to counsel and the right to remain silent,[2] and required that state courts exclude evidence seized in warrantless searches by law enforcement officers (the exclusionary rule).[3]

The strengthening of the guarantees of both free press and fair trial was bound to bring them into collision. In several early cases, the Court came down on the side of the defendant's rights, chastening judges as much as the press. The justices started slowly, with a brief, per curiam opinion setting aside the federal conviction of one Howard R. Marshall of Colorado for unlawfully dispensing amphetamine tablets without a physician's prescription. The trial judge had refused to allow the government to present evidence that Marshall had previously practiced medicine without a license, on the ground that it could be prejudicial to the defendant, but some jurors read in local newspapers about this and a previous conviction for forgery. The Supreme Court sent the case back for a new trial, declaring, "The prejudice to the defendant is almost certain to be as great when that evidence reaches the jury through news accounts as when it is part of the prosecution's evidence."[4]

In 1965 the Court reversed the swindling conviction of a flamboyant Texan named Billie Sol Estes on the ground that obtrusive television crews operating in the courtroom had prejudiced his trial. The ruling was based on a violation of the defendant's right to due process of law under the Fourteenth Amendment rather than on the Sixth Amendment.[5] In a second trial Estes was found not guilty.

The Warren Court rose up in indignation in two cases involving heavily publicized murders. A rash of six murders near Evansville, Indiana, and in nearby Kentucky was extensively covered by the press and aroused great public indignation. When a man named Leslie Irvin was arrested, the newspapers, television, and radio told of crimes he had committed as a juvenile, convictions for arson twenty years ago, for burglary, and, by a court-martial, on AWOL charges during World War II. Then the media announced that Irvin had confessed to all six murders. Public outrage was so great that, even after 430 persons were called as prospective jurors in the Indiana trial, eight of the twelve who were finally seated admitted that before hearing any evidence they believed Irvin guilty. And so he was, of one count of murder, for which he was sentenced to death.

Irvin sought a writ of habeas corpus from the U.S. district court, in effect asking it to throw out his conviction on federal constitutional grounds. Although the district court and the court of appeals declined to do so, the Supreme Court did, ordering a new trial.[6] It was the first time the Supreme Court threw out a state conviction of murder because of prejudicial publicity. For a unanimous Court, Justice Tom Clark held up trial by jury as the "most priceless" safeguard of individual liberty and dignity received from England, stating, "Where one's life is at stake—and accounting for the frailties of human nature—we can only say that in the light of the circumstances here the finding of impartiality does not meet constitutional standards."[7] Tried again, Irvin was again convicted.

In an even more sensational murder case, the Supreme Court came to the same conclusion.[8] Sam Sheppard, a socially prominent osteopath, was accused of the second-degree murder of his pregnant wife in their home in a Cleveland suburb. The case was intensively covered nationwide. Sheppard blamed the murder on an intruder who, he said, beat him unconscious. He submitted to several hours of questioning without an attorney, but the press reported that he had refused to take a lie detector test. Other stories told of Sheppard's extramarital affairs, purportedly a motive for the crime, and of a detective's conclusion that the killer washed off a trail of blood from the bedroom; this was never presented to the jury. Front-page editorials pressed for action against Sheppard. A coroner's inquest was held in a school gymnasium and broadcast live. Sheppard's indictment, arrest, and arraignment got big headlines and inflammatory coverage. In a radio debate, news-

paper reporters complained that Sheppard's counsel was obstruct-
ing the prosecution and said Sheppard conceded his guilt by hiring a criminal lawyer. Sheppard's trial started two weeks before
an election in which the prosecutor and the trial judge were both
on the ballot. Names and addresses of all the prospective jurors
were published in the papers.

The media were allocated most of the seats in the courtroom
and occupied all the rooms on the courtroom floor, with private
phone lines installed. A TV station set up broadcasting facilities
next door to the jury room. Witnesses and jurors were photo-
graphed and televised as they came and went to the courtroom,
and Sheppard himself was presented for photographs in the courtroom prior to the start of each session. Reporters clustered inside
the bar of the courtroom, so close to Sheppard that he and his
lawyers often had to leave the room to talk privately. The reporters
made so much noise coming and going during the trial that witnesses could hardly be heard. Jurors were free to follow the inten-
sive press coverage and were pictured frequently in the newspapers
themselves. The trial lasted nine weeks, after which the jurors were
sequestered, but allowed to make phone calls home. All the "viru-
lent publicity" and innumerable departures from accepted trial
process were set forth in the Supreme Court's opinion reversing
the conviction as unconstitutional under the Sixth Amendment
and granting Sheppard's motion for a writ of habeas corpus.

Justice Clark again wrote for the Court. "The fact is," he stated,
"that bedlam reigned at the courthouse during the trial and news-
men took over practically the entire courtroom, hounding most
of the participants in the trial, especially Sheppard." He went on:
"Participants in the trial, including the jury, were forced to run
a gauntlet of reporters and photographers each time they entered or left the courtroom." Clark faulted the trial judge for not

controlling the access and behavior of the press, for not insulating the witnesses, and for not controlling statements to the press by counsel, witnesses, and "especially the Coroner and police officers." He noted that much of the derogatory "evidence" leaked to the press before the trial was never presented in court. To ensure a fair trial the judge could have delayed it until the publicity abated, or moved it to another county, or sequestered the jury, Clark suggested. "Since the state trial judge did not fulfill his duty to protect Sheppard from the inherently prejudicial publicity which saturated the community and to control disruptive influences in the courtroom, we must reverse the denial of the habeas petition," he declared.[9] Sheppard was retried and acquitted.

MEDIA GAINS, AND LOSSES

Under Chief Justice Warren Burger (1969–86) the Supreme Court began to accommodate the press, though not without a hiccup along the way. We mentioned in chapter 2 the Court's historic ruling against media "gag rules," a form of prior restraint, in *Nebraska Press Association v. Stuart,* involving a sensational murder of an entire family.[10]

However, the justices' unanimity in *Nebraska Press* dissolved three years later. In *Gannett v. DePasquale,* the Court affirmed a New York trial judge's closure of a pretrial hearing on suppression of evidence in the prosecution of two young men accused of murdering their fishing companion, Wayne Clapp, forty-two years old, of Henrietta, New York, a suburb of Rochester.[11] The story was relentlessly pursued by the Rochester newspapers. However, both the prosecution and the defense felt that press coverage of the hearing, in which the defense would seek to exclude the alleged murder weapon, Clapp's own pistol, might jeopardize the right to a fair trial. Judge Daniel A. DePasquale agreed. The Supreme Court affirmed the closure, but by a 5-4 vote, and there were five opinions, yielding no clear rule as to when a pretrial hearing could be closed without infringing on the First Amendment. Dissenters argued that trials in England and the United States presumptively had been open, in order to assure that the proceedings were conducted fairly. Nevertheless, trial judges around the country promptly seized on the ruling to grant motions to close a variety of criminal proceedings.

The Supreme Court was constrained to backtrack. Just a year later, in *Richmond Newspapers v. Virginia,* it struck down a Hanover County judge's order excluding the press and the public from a murder trial.[12] Chief Justice Burger, writing for the majority in a 7-1 decision, ruled that the First and Fourteenth Amendments guarantee the right of the public to attend criminal trials. He went on:

> There was no suggestion that any problems with witnesses could not have been dealt with by their exclusion from the courtroom or their sequestration during the trial. . . . Nor is there anything to indicate that sequestration of the jurors would not have guarded against their being subjected to any improper information. . . . Absent an overriding interest articulated in findings, the trial of a criminal case must be open to the public.[13]

The rash of trial closures abated.

In a series of rulings in the 1980s the Supreme Court further extended press and public access to criminal proceedings, but made the First Amendment workable by spelling out the limited circumstances that would justify reasonable exceptions.

The Court struck down a Massachusetts statute requiring the exclusion of the press and public during the testimony of a minor victim in a sex-offense trial.[14] The state's interests in protecting minors from further trauma and embarrassment, and in encouraging them to testify, could just as well be served, the Court held, by requiring the trial court to make a determination on a case-by-case basis of whether closure is appropriate. "Such an approach," Justice William Brennan wrote for the majority, "ensures that the constitutional right of the press and public to gain access to criminal trials will not be restricted except where necessary to protect the State's interest."[15] This time Chief Justice Burger dissented, noting that Brennan, in a *Richmond Newspapers* concurrence, had championed "the weight of historical practice." Burger continued: "Today, Justice Brennan ignores the weight of historical practice. There is clearly a long history of exclusion of the public from trials involving sexual assaults, particularly those against minors."[16]

PRELIMINARY HEARINGS

The publisher of the *Press-Enterprise,* in Riverside, California, asked that its reporters be allowed to cover the voir dire, the questioning and selection of jurors, in the Riverside County trial of Albert Greenwood Brown, Jr., for the rape and murder of a teenage girl. The trial judge assented partially, but closed that portion of the process dealing with the death penalty and other "special areas," which turned out to be all but three days of an extraordinary six-week voir dire. Media requests for a transcript were also denied. Brown was convicted and sentenced to death.

The California appellate court approved the closure, but the U.S. Supreme Court reversed, unanimously, based on the First

Amendment.[17] Chief Justice Burger, again writing for the Court, noted that the voir dire was historically open but stated that closure could be justified to protect the privacy of individual prospective jurors, in this manner: "those individuals believing public questioning will prove damaging because of embarrassment, may properly request an opportunity to present the problem to the judge *in camera* but with counsel present and on the record."[18]

Partly based on wiretap evidence, Georgia defendants faced gambling charges in connection with a lottery based on the prices of stocks and bonds on the New York Stock Exchange. They moved to suppress the wiretap evidence and to open to press and public a hearing on their motion to suppress. In most suppression hearings it is the defendant who wants the hearing closed, but in this case the prosecution requested closure because, under Georgia law, any disclosures involving persons not indicted could not be used in any future prosecution of those individuals. The judge closed the suppression hearing, which went on for seven days, the defendants were subsequently convicted, and the Georgia Supreme Court affirmed the convictions. But the U.S. Supreme Court reversed, ruling that the trial judge failed to give proper weight to the Sixth Amendment.[19]

Writing for a unanimous Court, Justice Lewis Powell cited *Globe Newspaper, Richmond Newspapers,* and *Press-Enterprise,* acknowledging that those decisions were based on the First Amendment. But he described the amendments as two sides of the same coin, not in conflict. He stated, "there can be little doubt that the explicit Sixth Amendment right of the accused is no less protective of a public trial than the implicit First Amendment right of the press and public." A suppression hearing should be open to public scrutiny, Powell went on, because a "challenge to the seizure of evidence frequently attacks the conduct of police and prosecutor. . . . The tapes lasted only 2 1/2 hours of the 7-day hearing, and few of them mentioned or involved parties not then before the court." Powell suggested that "closing only those parts of the hearing" might have been justified.[20]

A preliminary hearing for a California nurse, Robert Diaz, accused of murdering twelve patients by administering massive doses of a heart drug, evoked widespread press interest, another closure order by the Superior Court for Riverside County, and another challenge by the newspaper publisher Press-Enterprise Co. The hearing continued for forty-one days. The California Supreme Court ruled the closure justified. But the U.S. Supreme Court, in a majority opinion by Chief Justice Burger, held that the First Amendment right of access to criminal trials includes preliminary hearings as they are conducted in California, because "California preliminary hearings are sufficiently like a trial to justify the same conclusion."[21] He explained:

> In California, to bring a felon to trial, the prosecutor has a choice of securing a grand jury indictment or a finding of probable cause following a preliminary hearing. Even when the accused has been indicted by a grand jury, however, he has an absolute right to an elaborate preliminary hearing before a neutral magistrate. . . . The accused has the right to personally appear at the hearing, to be represented by counsel, to cross-examine hostile witnesses, to present exculpatory evidence, and to exclude illegally obtained evidence. . . . If the magistrate determines that probable cause exists, the accused is bound over for trial; such a finding leads to a guilty plea in the majority of cases. [citations omitted]

In this case, the Court held, the trial court failed to demonstrate a substantial probability that Diaz's right to a fair trial "will be prejudiced by publicity that the closure would prevent." Furthermore, the trial court "failed to consider whether alternatives short of complete closure would have protected the interests of the accused."[22]

Under Chief Justice Rehnquist (1986–2005), the Supreme Court applied *Press-Enterprise II* to a dispute arising in Puerto Rico when a journalist sought to attend a preliminary hearing and was turned down. Under Puerto Rico law, an accused felon is entitled to a preliminary hearing before a neutral magistrate who will decide whether there is probable cause warranting a trial. At the hearing, which at the time was normally closed, the accused is afforded counsel and has the rights to present testimony, to cross-examine, and in some instances, to challenge evidence as illegally seized. The Supreme Court, in a brief per curiam opinion, likened the Puerto Rico hearing to the California hearing and said it, too, violated the First Amendment. "The established and widespread tradition of open preliminary hearings among the States was canvassed in *Press-Enterprise* and is controlling here," the Court stated. As before, it added that if there is a "substantial probability" that the defendant's right to a fair trial would be jeopardized by an open hearing, a closure could be justified by specific findings demonstrating that threat.[23]

From the humiliating feeding frenzies of *Estes, Irvin,* and *Sheppard* to the near-total victories capped by *Press-Enterprise II,* it was an extraordinary run for the American news media. They celebrated their victories in *Nebraska Press Association* and *Richmond Newspapers* with prominent stories on the evening news and on newspaper front pages. The *Los Angeles Times* editorialized that *Nebraska Press Association* was "primarily a victory for the people's right to be informed by an unintimidated and unshackled press."[24] The *Chicago Tribune* put its editorial on page one, proclaiming that the decision "was an affirmation of the principle that the processes of justice must be open—that all citizens have the right to know how their rights are being protected in the courts."[25] The *New York Times,* applauding *Richmond Newspapers* as a celebration of "the public's right to know," took a disdainful swipe at the lone dissenter: "Only Justice Rehnquist was unable to find this principle spelled out in the Constitution and thus voted to approve closed trials."[26]

However, by the time *Press-Enterprise II* was delivered to them, the media seemed jaded by their own continuing success. The broadcast networks, including the Public Broadcasting System (PBS), ignored the decision on their evening newscasts, and most papers dropped it to inside pages. Editorial hosannas were hard to find, although the *Los Angeles Times* responded to that specifically California decision by calling it "an important and long-overdue ruling."[27]

A COMPARISON: CANADA

Journalists in other countries do not generally enjoy equivalent freedom to attend and report on criminal proceedings. Our neighbor to the north has a legal system based, like ours, on English common law, and the Canadian Charter of Rights and Freedoms adopted in 1982 contains a promise of "freedom of the press."[28] But it is not a guarantee. Like other rights of the charter, it is subject to balancing against other rights and freedoms. The Canadian Supreme Court in recent years has attached greater weight to the freedom of the press.[29] Nevertheless, as in the past, a Canadian trial judge still has the authority to close a proceeding, or simply to ban the press, if he deems the publicity a threat to the defendant's right to a fair trial, or to the "proper administration of justice."[30] A judge presiding at a preliminary hearing is required to ban the publication of evidence presented if the defendant requests it, and has discretionary power to issue such a ban if requested by the prosecutor.[31] In addition, journalists who write about a legal case before or during trial must guard against impairing the reputation of the court itself or prejudicing jurors, for instance, by describing a criminal suspect as "the prime suspect," even in a quotation from a law enforcement source. Transgressors are subject to being held in contempt of court, punishable by a fine or even jail.[32]

If there is a risk to justice in the more press-friendly American balance of press freedom against the defendant's right to a fair trial, a trial judge has several tools to minimize that risk. As Justice Clark wrote in *Sheppard,* a judge can order those involved in a trial not to talk to the press, he can delay the trial, he can sequester the jury, or he can initiate a transfer (a change of venue) to another location where publicity is less. Or, as Chief Justice Burger pointed out in *Nebraska Press Association,* careful examination of prospective jurors can eliminate those who have already formed opinions about the guilt or innocence of the defendant. Burger pointed to the 1807 treason trial of former Vice President Aaron Burr, at which Chief Justice John Marshall, sitting as a circuit court judge, presided. Burger elaborated:

> Few people in the area of Virginia from which jurors were drawn had not formed some opinions concerning Mr. Burr or the case, from newspaper accounts and heightened discussion both private and public. The Chief Justice conducted a searching voir dire of the two panels eventually called, and rendered a substantial opinion

on the purposes of voir dire and the standards to be applied. . . .
Burr was acquitted, so there was no occasion for appellate review
to examine the problem of prejudicial pre-trial publicity. Mr. Chief
Justice Marshall's careful voir dire inquiry into the matter of possible bias makes clear that the problem is not a new one.[33]

So, in an unlikely way, freedom of the press, like so much of
American law, is beholden to the first great chief justice.

FIVE

STATUTORY LIMITATIONS OF THE
MEDIA: A FIRM HOLD

In addition to its constitutional overview of the rights of the news media, the Supreme Court is the final authority on statutory limitations on the media enacted by Congress and administered by federal agencies. The most important statutes are the Freedom of Information Act (FOIA) of 1966[1] and the laws regulating electronic communication, in particular the Communications Act of 1934,[2] which created the Federal Communications Commission (FCC) and gave it sweeping authority to license and regulate radio and television. While the Supreme Court in recent decades has wrought a breathtaking reinterpretation of the First Amendment, it has been decidedly less activist in its review of these statutory limitations and the government's applications of them. We shall examine each area.

The Freedom of Information Act, though much younger than the Communications Act, has the greater reach and the broader impact on the work of the news media generally. It is intended to facilitate press and public access to government documents, upon request. Like nearly all statutes, the FOIA starts with certain definitions, and they are relevant here because they immediately outline and thus limit the scope of the law. One is "agency records," which means they are covered, and open to the press and public. An "agency" is any executive or military department or any regulatory agency, virtually the entire government, but significantly omitting Congress and the courts. The other crucial definitions are nine exceptions, categories of documents that may be kept secret, and they are extensive:

1. Documents required by an executive order of the president to be kept secret in the interest of the national defense or foreign policy
2. Documents regarding internal personnel practices
3. Documents specifically exempted by some other law (for instance, in one Supreme Court decision, the statute authorizing the Central Intelligence Agency to keep its sources secret)
4. Trade secrets and other proprietary business information gathered by government agencies
5. Internal or interagency documents used in the decision-making process, such as working papers or first drafts
6. Personnel, medical, or similar files whose disclosure would constitute a clearly unwarranted invasion of personal privacy
7. Law enforcement files, when disclosure would interfere with law enforcement or fair trial, invade personal privacy, disclose a confidential informant, or endanger someone's life or safety
8. Documents of agencies regulating banks and other financial institutions
9. Oil and gas exploration maps and data

When a government agency turns down a document request, the reporter or other person seeking the documents may ask for a review within the agency, and, if still unsuccessful, may appeal the rejection to the courts. The Supreme Court has considered a number of such cases, and several times has reversed decisions of the federal appellate courts.

In its first major review of an FOIA decision, the Court in 1973 overturned a ruling of the Court of Appeals for the District of Columbia Circuit, which had called for in camera examination by the U.S. district court of requested documents to determine whether they fell under either Exemption 1, national security, or Exemption 5, agency memoranda involved in internal decision-making. It was a high-profile case. U.S. Representative Patsy Mink of Hawaii and thirty-two other House members wanted to see reports by an interdepartmental committee on nuclear testing which reportedly had given President Nixon conflicting recommendations on the advisability of underground testing. The Supreme Court held that Exemption 1 did not countenance examination of the individual documents by a court, for these had been classified secret or top secret and that clearly met Exemption 1's description of matters "specifically required by Executive order to be kept secret in the interest of the national defense or foreign policy." Regarding Exemption 5, the Court noted that it protected only documents that would not be available to a party litigating against the agency, and so sent the case back to give the government an opportunity to address this point. Writing for a majority of five, Justice Byron White stated:

> The burden is, of course, on the agency resisting disclosure [citation omitted], and if it fails to meet its burden without *in camera*

inspection, the District Court may order such inspection. But the agency may demonstrate, by surrounding circumstances, that particular documents are purely advisory and contain no separable, factual information.[3]

Several times over a period of twenty-five years, the Supreme Court overruled the agency and granted access to the documents requested. In a highly visible controversy that followed a cheating scandal at the U.S. Air Force Academy, the Court ruled for New York University law-student researchers who sought the summaries of academy hearings on the violations, with the names of the cadets deleted, subject to in camera review of the records by the trial judge to ensure that any personal identification was stricken.[4] Later the Court required the Justice Department to provide copies of opinions of the federal courts in tax cases,[5] and it held that the Federal Bureau of Investigation (FBI) could not invoke the law-enforcement exception to reject automatically any request for a document that might identify a confidential source; a case-by-case consideration must be undertaken.[6] The Court also rejected a Bureau of Indian Affairs effort to keep its correspondence with Indian tribes confidential as "interagency" communications.[7]

More often, however, the Court has sustained the government's refusal to deliver requested documents. One prominent dispute involved President Nixon's national security advisor and later secretary of state, Henry Kissinger. His secretaries generally recorded his phone conversations and prepared summaries or transcriptions of them. Shortly before leaving office, without notifying either the State Department's document center or the National Archives, which is responsible for retention of government records, Kissinger quietly transferred his telephone records to the New York estate of former Governor Nelson Rockefeller, a longtime friend and colleague. However, months earlier *New York Times* columnist (and former Nixon staff member) William Safire had requested copies of certain phone records dating from Kissinger's earlier position at the White House. The request was turned down by the State Department.

The Supreme Court upheld the department's refusal, ruling that the phone records from the White House were not "agency records" because the president's personal assistants are exempt from the FOIA and the State Department did not generate or control the papers at any time. "We simply decline to hold," Justice William Rehnquist wrote for a majority of five, "that the physical location of the notes of telephone conversations renders them 'agency records.' "[8]

Later the Court ruled twice that "agency records" did not include documents of private organizations doing research for the government. In one such case the justices held that the Central Intelligence Agency could keep its sources secret even if no national security interest is involved. The Public Citizen Health Research Group, a Ralph Nader organization, had requested documents that contained the names of researchers and institutions that, from 1953 to 1966, had administered mind-altering drugs to unknowing subjects in research secretly financed by the CIA, research that was intended to counter perceived Chinese and Soviet advances in brainwashing and interrogation techniques. Some of the drugs, such as LSD, were dangerous and later banned; two of the test subjects died and others were believed to have been injured. Nevertheless, the Supreme Court noted that the National Security Act of 1947, which created the CIA, empowered its director to protect intelligence sources and methods from unauthorized disclosure, and held this statute to satisfy FOIA's Exemption 2, secrecy authorized by another law.[9]

Despite the FBI confidential-source decision mentioned above, the FBI generally has fared well in FOIA decisions, primarily under Exemption 7 for law enforcement files. For instance, the Court ruled, 5-4, that information held by the Nixon White House in a file of administration critics was not subject to disclosure because it had originally been gathered by the FBI in criminal investigations and thus was protected by the law-enforcement exception.[10]

PERSONAL PRIVACY UNDER THE FOIA

Several of the Court's pro-government rulings on FOIA requests have been based on the protection of personal privacy, mentioned explicitly in two of the act's nine exemptions and at least suggested in a third.

The Court held unanimously in a 1989 decision that FBI criminal identification records or "rap sheets" (24,000,000 of them, compiled from federal, state, and local law enforcement records) were beyond reach under Exemption 7(C), the law-enforcement exemption for "unwarranted invasion of personal privacy." A CBS reporter and the Reporters Committee for Freedom of the Press had asked the FBI for rap sheets of four members of the Medico family, whose company had been described by the Pennsylvania Crime Commission as dominated by organized crime figures, and which allegedly had obtained defense contracts through an improper arrangement with a corrupt member of Congress. The FBI released the rap sheets of three Medicos who were deceased, but withheld that of Charles Medico. Justice Stevens wrote for a unanimous Court:

[W]e hold as a categorical matter that a third party's request for law enforcement records or information about a private citizen can reasonably be expected to invade that citizen's privacy, and that when the request seeks no "official information" about a Government agency, but merely records that the Government happens to be storing, the invasion of privacy is "unwarranted."[11]

Privacy again trumped disclosure in 1997 when the Court held that an agency's mailing list need not be disclosed, on the grounds that it would shed no light on the agency's performance.[12] A few years later the Court bolstered the privacy exemption further by ruling that a deceased person's relatives may claim it. The Court sustained a decision to withhold photographs of the body of Vincent Foster, Jr., a high official in the Clinton administration and a longtime close associate of the president, who had stunned Washington by inexplicably committing suicide in a very public place, Rock Creek Park.[13]

In sum, the Supreme Court has only occasionally taken issue with agency decisions to withhold documents, and the constitutional freedom of the press does not figure in these interpretations of the Freedom of Information Act. However, the Court, in a number of its decisions, has at least noted the benefit of informing the public about the workings of its government.

COMMUNICATIONS STATUTES UPHELD

The picture is much the same as we consider the Supreme Court's interpretations of the statutes regulating electronic communication, especially the Communications Act of 1934, which created the Federal Communications Commission, and the FCC's numerous decisions and rules promulgated pursuant to these statutes. On several occasions aspects of these statutes have been challenged as unconstitutional, and the Supreme Court almost invariably has upheld them. Similarly, the rules and decisions of the FCC, which wields a pervasive control over television and radio that is unknown in the print industries, usually have prevailed at the Supreme Court.

Before looking at the cases, though, it must be noted that this supportive stance by the Court is no different from the pattern of its rulings on the decisions of other regulatory agencies, such as the Securities and Exchange Commission, the Nuclear Regulatory Commission, and the Federal Trade Commission. The Court gives them all deference because they are endowed with special statutory authority and they have expert knowledge of their fields. Federal law states that courts reviewing regulatory decisions must set them aside if they are unconstitutional or "arbitrary, capricious, an abuse of discretion, or otherwise not in accordance with law."[14] This is a difficult hurdle for any challenger to overcome, so the agencies have considerable latitude to exercise their specialized judgment and discretion. The courts, including the Supreme Court, readily acknowledge their deference. To do otherwise would clearly undercut the extensive regulatory role of the federal government, not to mention the uncertainty that would erupt in the industries regulated by these specialized agencies.

First, the statutes. Most importantly, in 1943 the Supreme Court upheld the constitutionality of the Communications Act of 1934, the foundation of all government regulation of broadcasting. The regulatory scheme was based on the scientific fact that the frequencies in the broadcast spectrum are limited and only a finite number of stations can broadcast over them. Therefore, Congress decided, the government should decide which broadcasters may operate, and regulate them.[15] The guiding principles for the regulator, the Federal Communications Commission, are the "public interest, convenience, or necessity." In the 1943 case, the National Broadcasting Co. (NBC) challenged the FCC's constitutional authority to regulate a chain or network of radio stations. The company then operated two networks embracing a total of 135 stations, out of 660 in the country. Among other concerns voiced by the FCC, NBC's affiliation contract with a local broadcaster gave the station the right to reject a network program, but in practice the network provided so little advance information on which to base such a decision that the right was meaningless. Therefore, the FCC concluded, local programming was in fact being determined by the network and advertising agencies, ergo, the local station was not fulfilling its obligation to broadcast in the public interest. This and other FCC views, embodied in a set of regulations, violated the First Amendment, NBC contended.

But Justice Felix Frankfurter, writing for a majority of six, declared: "The right of free speech does not include, however, the right to use the facilities of radio without a license. The licensing system established by Congress in the Communications Act of 1934 was a proper exercise of its power over commerce."[16] The Court also explicitly affirmed the FCC's use of its authority to promulgate the network broadcasting regulations. Years later the Court again cited the Communications Act in upholding FCC regulation of the earliest form of cable television, called community antenna television. The 1934 act gave the agency broad authority over wire and other communications, the Court ruled.[17]

In the 1990s, when new legislation empowered the Federal Communications Commission to regulate certain aspects of the cable television business, the Supreme Court firmly rejected constitutional challenges to those laws. The Court unanimously ruled against an appeal by a satellite master antenna TV operator alleging that a statutory requirement to obtain a municipal franchise violated the promise of equal protection implied in the Constitution's due process clause.[18] A 1992 cable TV law imposing broad restrictions on the industry[19] precipitated a number of First Amendment–based challenges that were turned back by the Court. It upheld a requirement that cable television operators must carry the local broadcast stations.[20] It declined to review two circuit court rulings, one affirming the constitutionality of a provision giving the FCC the power to set cable television rates,[21] the other upholding the FCC's limiting the number of subscribers a cable operator may reach.[22] The Court's denial of a writ of certiorari, as in these cases, did not constitute an affirmation of the lower court's ruling, but it left that decision standing.

On the other hand, in reviewing the 1992 cable statute's restrictions on programming that depicted sexual or excretory activities or organs, the Court issued a bifurcated decision. It upheld the constitutionality of a provision permitting local cable operators to decide whether or not to broadcast such programming on leased access channels, but declared unconstitutional a provision that required leased channel operators to segregate and block that programming, as well as a provision that applied to public educational and governmental channels, both on the grounds that they were not sufficiently tailored to achieve the stated interest of protecting children.[23]

In this long line of affirmations of communications statutes, the exceptions that prove the rule are of relatively modest import. The Supreme Court, reversing the Fifth Circuit Court of Appeals, ruled in 1999 that a statutory restriction of gambling advertising was unconstitutional as applied to broadcasters in Louisiana, where gambling was legal.[24] A year later the Court voided a provision of the massive Telecommunications Act of 1996[25] that required cable companies to scramble sexually oriented programming during daytime, finding this an unconstitutional content-based restriction on speech that could have been avoided by simply authorizing and promoting household-by-household signal blocking.[26]

AFFIRMING THE FEDERAL COMMUNICATIONS COMMISSION

Just as the Supreme Court has upheld the constitutionality of the broadcasting and cable regulatory scheme created by Congress, it has also by and large upheld the Federal Communications Commission's interpretations and applications of the statutes entrusted to it. Cases challenging FCC decisions generally come to the Supreme Court from the U.S. courts of appeals, which is where appeals of federal regulatory agency rulings must be presented first. Far more often than not, the Court lets FCC rulings—often a dozen or more are challenged in a single annual session of the Court—remain in place by simply denying the requested writ of certiorari. The Court turns down most of the thousands of petitions presented to it each year, and although this denial of "cert" occasionally leaves a legal question up in the air, when the Court declines a regulatory agency case it ineluctably indicates that the Court has no quarrel with the appellate court's ruling on the agency's decision, even though on occasion those rulings reverse the FCC. Therefore, along with a look at some FCC cases the Court accepted, we shall touch on several that the Court declined to review, because they presented significant questions.

FCC rulings appealed to the Supreme Court fall broadly into

two categories: decisions on the granting of broadcast licenses and other largely technical matters, and decisions more directly influencing what viewers will actually see. We qualify this distinction by noting that on occasion the granting or renewal of a license is contested and thus the FCC's award does determine, at least indirectly, what that station's programming will be.

The FCC's record of success before the Supreme Court is especially strong in the licensing and technical areas. Applicants for a license must be U.S. citizens and must meet the FCC's standards of character, financial and technical capability, and programming intentions. They must comply with nondiscrimination laws in employment practices, and with the FCC's limits on ownership of other media companies in the same market. Licenses are granted for eight years, contrasting sharply with the original three-year period set in the Communications Act of 1934. FCC licensing decisions have rarely been reversed by the Supreme Court.

Indeed, even before its *NBC* decision affirming the constitutionality of the Communications Act of 1934, the Court in 1940 quashed challenges to two FCC permits to construct a new radio station, one in Pottsville, Pennsylvania, the other in Dubuque, Iowa. In the Pottsville case, Justice Felix Frankfurter noted the act's mandate that the FCC be guided by the "public convenience, interest, or necessity" and stated: "While this criterion is as concrete as the complicated factors for judgment in such a field of delegated authority permit, it serves as a supple instrument for the exercise of discretion by the expert body which Congress has charged to carry out its legislative policy."[27] In Dubuque, an existing station had protested that it would be harmed by the new competition, and the District of Columbia Circuit Court of Appeals agreed. But the Supreme Court upheld the FCC's process and decision. Justice Owen Roberts wrote:

Plainly it is not the purpose of the [Communications] Act to protect a licensee against competition but to protect the public. . . .
We conclude that economic injury to an existing station is not a
separate and independent element to be taken into consideration
by the Commission in determining whether it shall grant or withhold a license.[28]

Years later, affirming a disputed FCC policy statement encouraging radio programming diversity, Justice Byron White wrote for
the Court:

Our decisions have repeatedly emphasized that the Commission's
judgment regarding how the public interest is best served is entitled to substantial judicial deference. . . . As we see it, the Commission's Policy Statement is in harmony with cases recognizing that
the [Communications] Act seeks to preserve journalistic discretion
while promoting the interests of the listening public.[29]

LICENSING AWARDS STAND

Many challenges to FCC licensing decisions have met with a
curt denial of certiorari by the Supreme Court. This includes
the longest-running, highest-stakes licensing dispute ever, which
slogged along for more than twenty years in the 1960s, '70s, and
'80s. The Court's refusal to hear this case actually cut both ways,
for and against the FCC, for that was the nature of the appellate
court's ruling.

The FCC denied license renewal applications by RKO General,
Inc., for its Los Angeles television station, KHJ-TV, now KCAL-
TV, and its stations in New York (WOR-TV, now WWOR-TV)

and Boston (WNAC-TV). The unusual reason was that RKO's parent, General Tire & Rubber Company (now GenCorp Inc.), had been accused by the Securities and Exchange Commission of questionable domestic and foreign payments and of falsifying corporate records to conceal them, in violation of federal securities laws. RKO resisted full disclosure of these matters to the FCC.

Loss of the three licenses would cost RKO General hundreds of millions of dollars. It appealed to the District of Columbia Circuit Court of Appeals, which upheld the Boston decision but sent the other two back for further consideration "because the FCC has not yet provided a principled explanation for RKO's disqualification as a licensee of those stations," in the words of Judge Abner Mikva.[30] RKO then turned to the Supreme Court, which responded simply, "Certiorari denied."[31]

TECHNICAL STANDARDS ACCEPTED

In its setting of technical standards, the FCC again has a high batting average at the Supreme Court. The commission in 1950 chose the color television transmission standards proposed by CBS over those proposed by the Radio Corporation of America (RCA), owner of NBC, and a third company. RCA protested that the decision was contrary to law and the public interest. Justice Hugo Black, writing for eight members of the Court, sustained the FCC and its deliberate process:

> The Commission's special familiarity with the problems involved in adopting standards for color television is amply attested by the record. It has determined after hearing evidence on all sides that the CBS system will provide the public with color of good qual-

ity and that television viewers should be given an opportunity to receive it if they so desire. This determination certainly cannot be held capricious.[32]

Justice Felix Frankfurter, in a puckish, separate opinion labeled *dubitante* rather than *dissenting,* protested eloquently that, given the immense creativity of the human mind, the commission and the Court should have been willing to wait before deciding, in the hope that another color system would be developed in a reasonable time, a system compatible with the existing black-and-white system, thus obviating new sets. The parties had agreed that compatibility was desirable, and RCA had held out hope for achieving it some day. Frankfurter, while describing himself as "no friend of judicial intrusion into the administrative process," asked rhetorically:

> What evil would be encouraged, what good retarded by delay? By haste, would morality be enhanced, insight deepened, and judgment enlightened? Is it even economically advantageous to give governmental sanction to color television at the first practicable moment, or will it not in fact serve as an added drain on raw materials for which the national security has more exigent needs?[33]

In later years the Supreme Court affirmed an FCC order prohibiting a television station from expanding its service,[34] as well as the agency's adoption of cable TV technical standards and its prohibition against more stringent standards by state and local governments.[35] The Court also upheld the FCC's designation of broadband cable modem service as an "information service" rather than a "telecommunications service."[36] Along the way the Court declined to consider appeals from an FCC ruling establishing procedures and a timetable for the introduction of digital technology

to existing TV stations,[37] the FCC's assessment of an $11,000 for-
feiture against the operator of a low-power FM station that violated an FCC ban on such stations,[38] and the FCC's decision not to
investigate alleged adverse health effects from nonthermal radiation
from cellphones and from radio, TV, and cellphone communications facilities (as opposed to effects from *thermal* radiation, which
the FCC already had addressed in regulatory guidelines).[39]

On the other hand, the Supreme Court denied certiorari to
an important but highly technical case in which the District of
Columbia Court of Appeals had struck down certain cable television rules that the FCC had promulgated in response to a congressional directive in the 1992 cable law. Congress was seeking
to ensure competition and diversity in the cable industry, both
in ownership of cable operators and in programming. Among
other rules triggered by the statute, the FCC imposed a 30 percent
"horizontal" limit on the number of nationwide cable subscribers
a multiple-system operator like Comcast or Time Warner could
serve, and a "vertical" limit of 40 percent of its channel capacity
(up to seventy channels) that an operator could fill with its own or
affiliated programming, reserving 60 percent for nonaffiliated program providers. The D.C. Circuit Court of Appeals ruled that the
FCC had not presented sufficient evidence to support its determination of the horizontal limit, and had restricted speech more
than necessary in setting the vertical limit, thus violating the First
Amendment.[40] The Supreme Court let the ruling stand.[41]

CONTENT REGULATION IS DICEY

Beyond the technical side of FCC regulation of broadcasting and
cable, the agency must wrestle with questions of who gets before

the microphone or camera, and sometimes, what they can say or do. This is regulation of content, as distinct from licensing.

While it is merely history now, a prominent example of content regulation was the FCC's long-standing requirement that public issues be presented on the air, and that the coverage be fair. This "fairness doctrine" evolved over time through a series of rulings, commencing with one by the Federal Radio Commission in 1929,[42] all grounded on the "public interest, convenience or necessity" mandate of the Communications Act of 1934. The doctrine was set forth in FCC regulations issued in 1967. One aspect of it was embraced by Congress as a Communications Act amendment, still in force, requiring that candidates for public office be afforded "equal opportunities."[43]

Despite the Court's support of the fairness doctrine,[44] it was abandoned by the FCC in 1987 for three reasons: it gave the government the right to second-guess the judgment of journalists; broadcasters were shying away from coverage of controversial issues for fear of invoking the doctrine; and new sources of information, notably cable TV, undercut the spectrum-scarcity justification for the doctrine. It was, therefore, deemed contrary to the First Amendment and to the public interest.[45]

The Supreme Court similarly was supportive of an FCC rule requiring cable operators to make time and studio facilities available for public access;[46] a decision permitting CBS to refuse all advertisements on public issues;[47] a ruling that the three broadcast networks, in denying President Jimmy Carter's request for thirty minutes of time to announce his reelection candidacy in December 1979, had violated a requirement of the Communications Act that candidates for federal office be granted "reasonable access" to the airwaves;[48] and an FCC interpretation of federal law that cable television systems in Oklahoma were required to transmit the signals of broadcast stations within thirty-five miles, including those across the state line, despite an Oklahoma ban on retransmitting alcoholic-beverage commercials from out of state.[49] In a case that caught the public eye and still is invoked in questions of broadcast indecency, the Court affirmed an FCC ruling against a twelve-minute radio monologue entitled "Filthy Words" by comedian George Carlin, in which he repeatedly used four-letter words and others avoided in polite speech. The FCC called the monologue a violation of a federal statute prohibiting the broadcast of "obscene, indecent, or profane language,"[50] in part because the monologue was broadcast during daytime when children might have been listening. Writing for the Court, Justice John Paul Stevens stated, "We hold that when the Commission finds that a pig has entered the parlor, the exercise of its regulatory power does not depend on proof that the pig is obscene."[51]

STRUGGLING OVER COMMON OWNERSHIP

In one highly controversial and high-stakes aspect of broadcasting control, the Supreme Court has not spoken the last word, at least not yet. This concerns the FCC's rule limiting the common ownership of broadcast stations and newspapers, an entirely new regulatory scheme promulgated in 1975 to promote diversity of news sources. The biggest sticking point, in the eyes of media companies, was a prohibition on common ownership of a television station and a daily newspaper in the same market. The FCC "grandfathered" most situations where common ownership already existed, as in the Tribune Company's ownership of both the *Chicago Tribune* and WGN-TV, which it had founded decades before. But mergers and acquisitions were severely limited, so the FCC, responding to business pleas, relaxed the rules in 2003, permitting cross-ownership and television station common-ownership "trio-polies" (up from "duopolies") in the country's largest markets. Most other rules restricting the ownership of radio and television stations were left unchanged, for instance, a statutory 39 percent limitation on the national audience share reached by TV stations owned by one company, and a limit of eight radio stations owned by a single company in the largest markets, those with forty-five or more stations.

However, before the new rules could take effect they were challenged by a host of broadcasting companies and public-interest advocacy groups, including a small low-power broadcaster in Pennsylvania called Prometheus Radio Project. The Third Circuit Court of Appeals, by a 2-1 vote, affirmed much of the FCC's order but nevertheless held, in the opinion by Judge Thomas L. Ambro, that

> the Commission falls short of its obligation to justify its decisions to retain, repeal, or modify its media ownership regulations with reasoned analysis. The Commission's derivation of new Cross-Media Limits, and its modifications of the numerical limits on both television and radio station ownership in local markets, all have the same essential flaw: an unjustified assumption that media outlets of the same type make an equal contribution to diversity and competition in local markets.

The circuit court sent the case back to the commission "to develop numerical limits that are supported by a rational analysis."[52] The Supreme Court denied a petition for a writ of certiorari.[53]

After much deliberation the commission in 2007 revised its proposed cross-ownership rule, calling for case-by-case adjudication of proposed newspaper-TV combinations. In the top twenty markets, the FCC stated, it would presume that a cross-ownership deal *is* in the public interest if the TV station is not among the top four in the market and at least eight independently owned voices, major newspapers and/or TV stations, would remain in the market following the merger. In smaller markets the FCC would presume that cross-ownership is *not* in the public interest, unless the newspaper or broadcasting station is failing, or if the proposed combination would produce a significant increase in local news coverage. All combinations would be evaluated for increasing local news coverage and for maintaining independent news judgment by each partner. These new cross-ownership rules were immediately challenged, and undoubtedly will require final adjudication by the Supreme Court, for the stakes remain high.

In its decisions upholding actions of the Federal Communications Commission, the Supreme Court remains faithful to the Founders' passion for open discussion of public affairs, as expressed in the Court's press clause rulings since the 1930s. Some of these decisions, in both FCC cases and First Amendment cases, have favored open discussion over other constitutional considerations, notably objections based on the due process clause of the Fifth Amendment. On the other hand, in its decisions supporting restrictive agency interpretations of the Freedom of Information Act, the Supreme Court has minimized the open-government purpose of the act. In some cases the Court has emphasized the privacy considerations stated in the act, but more often it has been content to endorse government claims that the act outranks open discussion of public affairs.

SIX

THE PRICE OF CONFIDENTIAL SOURCING

If the press is to be free, surely it follows that journalists must be free to talk to people, their everyday sources of information. Yet, in the eyes of journalists, that freedom is real only if a reporter can reliably promise a source that he or she may speak confidentially, without fear of embarrassing exposure or harmful retaliation. If an inside source has revealing, perhaps incriminating, information that she wants to disclose, she's highly unlikely to call a reporter if she fears she'll eventually be identified as the leaker. The states, which led the way in proclaiming the right to publish, began more than a century ago to protect journalists' confidential sources, enacting what are called reporter's shield laws.[1] They are of a piece with the common-law testimonial privileges: husband-wife, physician-patient, lawyer-client, and clergy-penitent. In other words, a person may not be compelled to testify against his spouse or patient or client or parishioner.

Today nearly all the states, through legislation or court interpretations of state constitutions or judge-made common law, recognize such a testimonial privilege for journalists. Although there are considerable variations among the states, the privilege essentially protects a reporter from legally coerced disclosure of names of confidential sources or other information obtained in confidence. The reporter may not be held in contempt of court and jailed for refusing to testify. It is difficult to imagine that the most probing journalism, much of it falling under the rubric of investigative journalism, can thrive without such a protection for journalists.

However, no such law or privilege exists at the federal level. Instead, the Supreme Court has ruled, and reiterated, that reporters subpoenaed by a grand jury must appear and testify, including even the disclosure of confidential sources regardless of whether the reporter had promised anonymity to them. The Court so held, though only by 5-4, in *Branzburg v. Hayes,* a 1972 case that tested the reach of the press clause, and still vexes the press today.[2]

Writing for the Court, Justice Byron White stated firmly:

> Misprision of a felony—that is, the concealment of a felony "which a man knows, but never assented to . . . [so as to become] either principal or accessory," 4 W. Blackstone, Commentaries, was often said to be a common-law crime. The first Congress passed a statute, 1 Stat. 113, § 6, as amended, 35 Stat. 1114, § 146, 62 Stat. 684, which is still in effect, defining a federal crime of misprision:
>
> > "Whoever, having knowledge of the actual commission of a felony cognizable by a court of the United States, conceals and does not as soon as possible make known the same to some judge or other person in civil or military authority under the United States, shall be [guilty of misprision]." 18 U.S.C. § 4.
>
> It is apparent from this statute, as well as from our history and that of England, that concealment of crime and agreements to do so are not looked upon with favor. Such conduct deserves no encomium,

and we decline now to afford it First Amendment protection by denigrating the duty of a citizen, whether reporter or informer, to respond to grand jury subpoena and answer relevant questions put to him. [footnotes omitted][3]

However, there was wiggle room in the Court's holding. Justice Lewis Powell, who was in the majority of five, also wrote separately that when a journalist moves to quash a subpoena because he believes the information sought has "only a remote and tenuous relationship" to the case or that the government is seeking confidential sources "without a legitimate need of law enforcement," each case "should be judged on its facts by the striking of a proper balance between freedom of the press and the obligation of all citizens to give relevant testimony with respect to criminal conduct."[4]

Justice Potter Stewart went further, writing one of the most influential Supreme Court dissents of modern times. Joined by Justices William Brennan and Thurgood Marshall, Stewart asserted that before calling a journalist to a grand jury, the government should be required to meet a three-point test:

1. show that there is probable cause to believe that the newsman has information that is clearly relevant to a specific probable violation of law;
2. demonstrate that the information cannot be obtained by alternative means; and
3. demonstrate a compelling overriding interest in the information.[5]

We have noted that the press has given abundant coverage to the Court's press clause rulings in recent decades, most of them favorable to the media, but not so with *Branzburg.* It was pushed off most front pages, and whittled down, by huge competition. It was announced on the last day of the Court's 1971–72 term; the dominant story that day was the Court's decision that the death penalty as then applied violated the Eighth Amendment's ban on cruel and unusual punishment.[6] Elsewhere, in the close race for the Democratic nomination for president, California decided to split its delegates proportionally according to the primary election vote, shifting important convention strength from Senator George McGovern of South Dakota (who nevertheless eventually secured the nomination) to Senator Hubert Humphrey of Minnesota. These two stories easily trumped *Branzburg,* reducing it to a brief reader on the evening newscasts. As for the wire services and the newspapers, how was a reporter covering *Branzburg* to assess, along with Justice White's formidable majority opinion, the relative importance of Justice Powell's concurrence (after all, he was part of the majority, too) and Justice Stewart's elaborate, cogent dissent?

A tip of the hat to the *New York Times.* Not only did the *Times* find room on page one (and a substantial jump inside) for *Branzburg,* but its story (unbylined) included quotations and paraphrases from Powell and Stewart that presciently captured the critical essence of their distinctive thinking. Those interpretations would live on. According to the *Times,* Justice Powell "declared that judges may still use the 'balancing' technique of weighing the First Amendment considerations in each case against the citizens' obligation to give information to grand juries."[7] In the following years this argument and Justice Stewart's dissent would be incorporated repeatedly into federal appellate and state court rulings and into state laws protecting journalists and their confidential sources.

Stewart's three-point test became part of the journalist's shield statutes now in effect in at least thirty-two states and the District of Columbia, most of them establishing a qualified testimonial privilege, that is, the right not to testify unless the three-point test is met by the government. (Among the state statutes, an *absolute* privilege for journalists, not dependent on any test, is provided in Alabama,[8] Montana,[9] Nebraska,[10] Nevada,[11] and Washington.[12])

So it is the federal government that is out of step here. However, while efforts to enact a federal shield law were opposed by the George W. Bush administration and remain unsuccessful, nine federal appellate courts, expressing a commitment to a free press, have interpreted *Branzburg v. Hayes* as providing a variously defined reporter's qualified privilege.[13]

Still, *Branzburg* remains the law of the land, and it is no idle law. Federal prosecutors repeatedly have relied on it, backed up by the courts, to pressure journalists to divulge confidential information. Notable manifestations include:

- Vanessa Leggett, a freelance writer, served 168 days in jail for refusing to hand over notes of an interview with a murder suspect who committed suicide in jail.[14]
- Three *Chicago Sun-Times* reporters were threatened with jail for refusing to turn over tapes of an interview with a key witness in a terrorism trial.[15]
- Jim Taricani, a Providence television reporter in ill health, was sentenced to home confinement for not naming the person who gave him a videotape of a city official apparently accepting a bribe.[16]
- Judith Miller of the *New York Times* served eighty-five days in jail for refusing to tell a federal grand jury the name of

her source for information (which the paper never published) disclosing the identity of an undercover CIA agent,
Valerie Plame.[17]

- Reporters were threatened with jail for refusing to name
  their sources for stories about former government scientist
  Wen Ho Lee, who was suspected by the government (and
  later cleared) of mishandling nuclear weapons information.[18]

- A freelance blogger, Joshua Wolf, was jailed for 226 days
  until he agreed to turn over a videotape he took of a
  public demonstration during a Group of Eight meeting in
  San Francisco.[19]

- The *San Francisco Chronicle* reporters who broke the
  BALCO baseball steroids scandal were found in contempt
  and sentenced to jail for not naming their source of confidential documents. (The source later came forward, and
  the ruling was dropped.)[20]

- Phone records of two *New York Times* reporters were ruled
  open to federal investigators pursuing the leak of a pending
  enforcement action in Chicago.[21]

- Judge Reggie Walton of the U.S. District Court in Washington, D.C., held former *USA Today* reporter Toni Locy
  in contempt of court and fined her $500 per day, escalating
  to $5,000 per day, for refusing to disclose her government
  sources for a story identifying former U.S. Army scientist
  Steven Hatfill as a possible suspect in the 2001 anthrax attacks that killed five people.[22] (After the government cleared
  Hatfill and settled with him for $5,800,000, the D.C. Cir-
  cuit Court of Appeals threw out the contempt ruling.[23])

Without the kind of aggressive reporting at issue in all the above
cases, investigative journalism, the stories that expose wrongdo-

ing in high places and bring public officials to account, would be thwarted. Most of these cases involved major stories that brought to light information important to a well-informed public.

Nevertheless, the Supreme Court refused even to hear Judith Miller's contempt-of-court case, and the voting records of the current justices, both as appellate judges and in their present roles, offer scant hope they will ever interpret the First Amendment to embody a reporter's testimonial privilege.

Does this end the matter? Not necessarily. Another possible response to the lack of a reporter's privilege may be found in the Federal Rules of Evidence, which are enacted by Congress. Rule 501 gives federal courts considerable discretion to apply the common law in order to determine testimonial privilege. Rule 501 states:

> Except as otherwise required by the Constitution of the United States or provided by Act of Congress or in rules prescribed by the Supreme Court pursuant to statutory authority, the privilege of a witness, person, government, State, or political subdivision thereof shall be governed by the principles of common law as they may be interpreted by the courts of the United States in the light of reason and experience. However, in civil actions and proceedings, with respect to an element of a claim or defense as to which State law supplies the rule of decision, the privilege of a witness, person, government, State, or political subdivision thereof shall be determined in accordance with state law.[24]

In adopting this general language, Congress considered but rejected a proposed listing of these specific, traditional, but non-constitutional testimonial privileges to be recognized in federal courts: required reports, lawyer-client, psychotherapist-patient, husband-wife, communications to clergymen, political vote, trade secrets, secrets of state and other official information, and identity of informer.

Instead, as explicated in House Report No. 93-650 by the House Judiciary Committee, Rule 501 left the law of privilege in its current state but expressly provided that privileges shall continue to be developed by the courts of the United States under a uniform standard applicable in both civil and criminal cases. That standard, derived from Rule 26 of the Federal Rules of Criminal Procedure, mandates the application of the principles of the common law as interpreted by the courts of the United States in the light of reason and experience.[25]

"What is the common law?" the U.S. Supreme Court asked itself more than a century ago, and then gave this answer:

> According to Kent: "The common law includes those principles, usages, and rules of action applicable to the government and security of person and property, which do not rest for their authority upon any express and positive declaration of the will of the legislature." 1 Kent. Com 471.
>
> . . .
>
> In Black's Law Dictionary it is thus defined: "As distinguished from law created by the enactment of legislatures, the common law comprises the body of those principles and rules of action, relating to the government and security of persons and property, which derive their authority solely from usages and customs of immemorial antiquity, or from the judgments and decrees of the courts recognizing, affirming, and enforcing such usages and customs; and in this sense, particularly the ancient unwritten law of England."[26]

A COMMON-LAW JOURNALIST'S PRIVILEGE

As early as 1979, the U.S. Third Circuit Court of Appeals relied on Rule 501 to fashion a reporter's privilege subject to a three-part test resembling Justice Stewart's: (1) an effort has been made to obtain the information from other sources, (2) only the journalist or his sources has the information, and (3) the information is crucial to the claim. The court granted a reporter's privilege to Geraldine Oliver of the *Delaware County Daily Times* because she was not an eyewitness, there was no allegation that she possessed evidence relevant to the criminal investigation, and the information sought had only a marginal relevance to the plaintiff's case.[27] The court considered it relevant that Pennsylvania law recognized a reporter's privilege.[28]

A year later the Third Circuit applied the common-law privilege in a criminal case,[29] but subject, as the court stated in a subsequent, similar case, to a balancing test "when constitutional precepts collide."[30] With a nod toward *Branzburg v. Hayes,* the court explained:

> This Court has taken a more reasonable view of the balance between the privilege and a criminal defendant's rights. We have previously adopted the formulation and the concurring opinion of Justice Powell in Branzburg:
>
>> [T]he asserted claim to privilege should be judged on its facts by striking a proper balance between freedom of the press and the obligation of all citizens to give relevant testimony with respect to criminal conduct. The balance of these vital constitutional and societal interests on a case-by-case basis accords

with the tried and traditional way of adjudicating such questions.[31]

The court, while stressing that the reporter's privilege has societal value in furthering the flow of public information, nevertheless affirmed the trial court's holding of a journalist in contempt of court for refusing to confirm or deny that she talked with a federal prosecutor who already had testified that such a conversation had occurred.

Subsequently reaffirming the reporter's privilege, a unanimous Third Circuit three-judge panel that included Judge Samuel Alito stated: "It is an interest of 'sufficient legal importance to justify some incidental sacrifice of sources of facts needed in the administration of justice.' Herbert v. Lando, 441 U.S. 153, 183, Brennan, J., dissenting."[32]

A Rule 501 journalist's privilege analysis was set forth in the Judith Miller contempt case by Judge David S. Tatel of the District of Columbia Court of Appeals. While concurring in the judgment against Miller, Tatel wrote an extensive, separate opinion advocating the creation of a limited federal privilege under Rule 501 rather than adopting the First Amendment theory propounded by Miller's counsel.[33]

Judge Tatel explained:

> Because I agree that the balance in this case, which involves the alleged exposure of a covert agent, favors compelling the reporters' testimony, I join the judgment of the court. I write separately, however, because I find *Branzburg v. Hayes* [citations omitted] more ambiguous than do my colleagues and because I believe that the consensus of forty-nine states plus the District of Columbia—

and even the Department of Justice [referring to a long-standing department policy discouraging the subpoenaing of journalists in civil and criminal investigations[34]]—would require us to protect reporters' sources as a matter of federal common law were the leak at issue either less harmful or more newsworthy.[35]

Looking beyond the case at hand to support the news-gathering function of the media and the chilling effects on it that forced disclosure of sources would inevitably create, Judge Tatel declared:

> If litigants and investigators could easily discover journalists' sources, the press's truth-seeking function would be severely impaired. Reporters could reprint government statements, but not ferret out underlying disagreements among officials; they could cover public governmental actions, but would have great difficulty getting potential whistleblowers to talk about government misdeeds; they could report arrest statistics, but not garner first-hand information about the criminal underworld.[36]

Judge Tatel advocated federal recognition of a common-law journalist's privilege in all but exceptional cases. Referring to the extensive state and federal recognition of a reporter's privilege, he wrote:

> To disregard this modern consensus in favor of decades-old views, as the special counsel urges, would not only imperil vital news-gathering, but also shirk the common law function assigned by Rule 501 and "freeze the law of privilege" contrary to Congress's wishes, *see Trammel,* 445 U.S. at 47.[37]

TESTIMONIAL PRIVILEGE CHANGES BY THE SUPREME COURT

Judge Tatel referred to *Trammel v. United States,* one of three cases in which the Supreme Court has in fact applied Rule 501 to modify traditional common-law testimonial privileges. In these cases the Court limited one privilege, broadened another, and created a new privilege.

The Court in *Trammel* affirmed a decision by the Tenth Circuit Court of Appeals to curtail the privilege that precludes forced testimony by one spouse against another.[38] One Otis Trammel, indicted for importing heroin from Thailand, objected to testimony by his wife, who had agreed to testify against him in return for leniency, for she, too, had been arrested trying to carry concealed heroin from Thailand into the United States. She was not charged. The trial court allowed the adverse testimony on the grounds that it did not concern a confidential communication between spouses but rather was her own firsthand knowledge of their joint smuggling operation, and the Tenth Circuit affirmed.[39]

The appeal to the Supreme Court was bottomed on its holding in *Hawkins v. United States,* twenty-two years earlier, that the testimony of one spouse against the other is barred unless both consent.[40] But in *Trammel* the Court determined that "the existing rule should be modified so that the witness-spouse alone has a privilege to refuse to testify adversely."[41] The Court based its conclusion on two factors: Federal Rule of Evidence 501, and what it deemed a progressive narrowing of the spousal privilege in state law.

Just a year later the Supreme Court addressed another ancient privilege, that protecting the confidentiality of private communications between a lawyer and his client, and broadened it to include communications between a company's general counsel and its employees.[42] In an opinion by Justice William Rehnquist, the Court cited both Rule 501 and a line in its *Trammel* decision: "The lawyer-client privilege rests on the need for the advocate and counselor to know all that relates to the client's reasons for seeking representation if the professional mission is to be carried out."[43]

The Internal Revenue Service (IRS) was investigating whether an Upjohn Co. foreign subsidiary had made payments to foreign government officials. The IRS subpoenaed internal questionnaires about the matter answered by foreign managers at the request of the corporation's general counsel, and notes of the general counsel's interviews of corporate employees. Justice Rehnquist noted that the IRS was free to interview the same employees, and in fact had interviewed about twenty-five of them:

> While it would probably be more convenient for the Government to secure the results of petitioner's internal investigation by simply subpoenaing the questionnaires and notes taken by petitioner's attorneys, such considerations of convenience do not overcome the policies served by the attorney-client privilege.[44]

In 1996, with Rehnquist as chief justice, the Supreme Court created a new testimonial privilege under Rule 501. Citing *Trammel* once more, the Court recognized a psychotherapist-client privilege and extended it to protect confidential communications with a licensed social worker in the course of psychotherapy.[45]

The Court affirmed a ruling of the Seventh Circuit Court of Appeals in a lawsuit brought by the administrator of the estate of an Illinois man shot and killed by a police officer responding to a call of a fight in progress.[46] The police officer, shaken by her experience, sought counseling from a licensed clinical social worker and participated in about fifty sessions with her. The lawsuit sought the social worker's notes. But the appellate court said no, invoking Rule 501, noted that all fifty states had adopted some form of psychotherapist-patient privilege, and that the Illinois law specifically covered social workers.[47]

Affirming, the Supreme Court placed especial weight on the pervasive action by the states:

> Because state legislatures are fully aware of the need to protect the integrity of the factfinding functions of their courts, the existence of a consensus among the States indicates that "reason and experience" support recognition of the privilege. . . . Denial of the federal privilege therefore would frustrate the purposes of the state legislation that was enacted to foster these confidential communications.[48]

ARGUING FOR A RULE 501 REPORTER'S PRIVILEGE

These Rule 501 rulings could serve as influential precedents for the Supreme Court's consideration of a common-law journalist's shield along the lines of those existing in nearly all the states, either by statute or court rule based on common law or state or federal constitutions. In fact, the arguments of "reason and experience" in favor of such a federal common law vastly exceed the arguments presented in favor of a corporate attorney-client privilege and a psychotherapist-patient privilege, because the "experience" of a free press in America is nearly three centuries old and because a free press so clearly satisfies the courts' expectation that any impairment of legal fact-finding under Rule 501 will be outweighed by a greater societal good.[49]

Might the conservative justices who control the Court buy into such an argument? It's quite clear that at least one will not. Justice Scalia dissented forcefully in *Jaffee v. Redmond,* the psychotherapist-patient case. In an opinion joined by Chief Justice Rehnquist, he called the Court's holding "inexplicable" and "a judgment in favor of suppressing the truth."[50] But the conservatives broke ranks on this one: Justices Clarence Thomas, Anthony Kennedy, and Sandra Day O'Connor joined the Court's opinion by Justice John Paul Stevens along with Justices David Souter, Ruth Bader Ginsburg, and Stephen Breyer. In other words, with Rehnquist, O'Connor, Stevens, and Souter no longer present, four of the seven majority votes in *Jaffee* are still on the Court, and one of the newcomers, Justice Alito, when ruling in *In re Madden*[51] at the Third Circuit Court of Appeals, affirmed that court's precedents recognizing and granting a journalist's privilege under Rule 501. (Justice Sonia Sotomayor did not participate in a Rule 501 case while on the Second Circuit Court of Appeals, and Justice Elena Kagan has not taken a public position.) An appropriate case will give the media a fighting chance at the Supreme Court bar.

PART THREE
PRESS COVERAGE OF THE SUPREME COURT

SEVEN

EXPANDING BUT LIMITING
GOVERNMENT POWER

The Supreme Court was not originally a plum appointment. The justices and the Court itself had little power or prestige. The anomalous, part-time job was burdened by the necessity to "ride circuit," meaning to sit on the U.S. courts of appeals scattered around the country. Other positions were much more important. While serving as the first chief justice, John Jay went abroad on a major diplomatic mission, to negotiate trade and financial disputes with Great Britain, which culminated in the Jay Treaty of 1795. Then he resigned to advance to the governorship of New York. The Court's most important early decision, an assertion of its authority to try a state in a private lawsuit, was soon reversed by the Eleventh Amendment.[1] Alexander Hamilton, Patrick Henry, and Justice William Cushing declined President Washington's entreaties to take the chief justiceship. Senator Oliver Ellsworth of Connecticut stepped up, but then he absented himself to undertake, at the president's behest, a diplomatic assignment that led to an important international agreement. He resigned from the Court after only four years. Washington asked Jay to return, but he declined on the ground that the Court had not gained sufficient respect.

So it was almost providential that President John Adams, defeated for reelection in 1800 by Thomas Jefferson, asked Secretary of State John Marshall, as they both were about to exit in early 1801, to become chief justice of the United States. Marshall was then forty-five years old, a distinguished Virginia lawyer and briefly a member of Congress, where he often spoke in support of the Adams administration. But Marshall was best known for his 1797–98 diplomatic mission, with Charles Pinckney of South Carolina and Elbridge Gerry of Massachusetts, to deal with French attacks on American shipping. The mission to Paris, which paved the way for a subsequent agreement, is remembered as the XYZ Affair, for the three representatives of France's revolutionary government with whom the Americans dealt. XYZ demanded bribes for an agreement. The Americans turned them down, quite publicly, and were welcomed home as heroes.

The Supreme Court in 1801 still had little stature, reflected in the fact that it was to be housed humbly, almost as an afterthought, in an unfinished, ground-floor committee room in the new Capitol building, sharing space with the federal courts for the District of Columbia. Nevertheless, Marshall accepted the president's appointment. The Federalist-dominated Senate, soon to come under Republican control, confirmed him, and Marshall took the oath of office in the makeshift courtroom. "As befitted the Court's low profile, the event was little noted and sparsely attended," according to Marshall biographer Jean Edward Smith. He adds in a footnote: "The leading Washington newspaper, the *National Intelligencer*, stated only that the justices had 'made a court.' "[2]

Nevertheless, the chief justiceship of John Marshall, which lasted thirty-five years until his death, was to be celebrated in American history. In fact, in many respects it *defined* American history. For the Marshall Court set the United States on its course to greatness in two ways: it defined federal law in a fashion that strengthened the power of the Court, the federal government generally, and at times the states as well, while also limiting the federal and state governments so as to protect individual liberties; and it avoided, as had the Constitution, challenging slavery, thus averting or at least postponing a cataclysmic national rupture over this irreconcilable issue.

Although it was already prominent in early 1801, in fact the *National Intelligencer and Washington Advertiser,* a triweekly costing five dollars a year, had commenced publication only the previous October, just before the presidential election. Its founder and sole employee was Samuel Harrison Smith, only twenty-eight years old, a Jefferson admirer who had moved from Philadelphia in hopes of capturing government printing business should the Virginian be elected. In that Smith was successful, but not before he had been banned from the House of Representatives, which he regularly covered, allegedly for inaccurately reporting the detention of a spectator who had disrupted House proceedings. Soon after, Smith published a sharp, anonymous criticism, signed "A Friend to Impartial Justice," of judicial appointments made by the departing President Adams, contending that they imperiled the authority of the legislative and executive branches of the government. As a result, the article averred, President Jefferson viewed the courts with disdain: "There, where reason and truth, unagitated, and unimpaired even by suspicion, ought to preserve perpetual reign, he contemplated the dominance of political and personal prejudice, habitually employed in preparing or executing partial vengeance."[3]

Himself one of those late appointments, John Marshall took

such offense that, sitting on the Circuit Court for the District of Columbia, he joined in ordering the district attorney to commence a criminal libel prosecution against Smith. Covering the dispute in his own paper, Smith asserted his First Amendment rights of free speech and press, while quoting Marshall's self-characterization as a supporter of freedom of the press who was nevertheless opposed to its excesses which "agitated the public mind" with "most un-warranted liberties, and descended to the most shameful scurrility and abuse."[4] However, the grand jury declined to indict Smith, and Marshall did not pursue the matter.

Despite his close call, Smith was unrelenting. He strongly op-posed the Federal Judiciary Act of 1801, passed by the Federalists just before ceding power, which created new circuit courts whose sixteen judges President Adams then appointed, greatly expanded federal jurisdiction at the expense of the states, and ended the onerous circuit-riding responsibilities of the Supreme Court jus-tices. Congress took up a repeal bill late in 1801, and the *National Intelligencer* gave extensive coverage to the debate. The newspaper's historian records that "Smith editorialized on the brilliance of speeches he heard relative to the repeal of the judiciary bill" and celebrated passage of the repeal, which meant abolition of the new circuit court judgeships and thus a continuation of circuit-riding by the Supreme Court justices.[5]

The tiff with Samuel Harrison Smith would not be Marshall's last run-in with the press, but it bred a strange and historic twist. Adams's judicial appointments fiercely criticized in the *National Intelligencer* became the center of the first major constitutional holding by the Marshall Court, *Marbury v. Madison,* decided less than two years later.[6]

The issue was joined by William Marbury, who along with several others had been appointed justices of the peace by the departing president but had never received their commissions. (Ironically, the responsibility for delivering them, apparently overlooked, was Secretary of State Marshall's.) Marbury sought a writ of mandamus ordering the new secretary of state, James Madison, to deliver his commission, which Madison refused to do. In one of the most masterful opinions in American judicial history, Marshall, for a unanimous court of five, held on February 24, 1803, that Marbury was entitled to his commission, but the Court lacked the power to require Madison to deliver it. Marshall reasoned that the Judiciary Act of 1789, empowering the Court to issue such writs, went beyond the scope of Article III of the Constitution, which created the Court and granted it original jurisdiction to hear certain kinds of cases, and was therefore unconstitutional. He declared that "the particular phraseology of the Constitution of the United States confirms and strengthens the principle supposed to be essential to all written constitutions, that a law repugnant to the constitution is void; and that *courts,* as well as other departments, are bound by the instrument."[7] Thus Marshall claimed for the Court the authority to hold statutes unconstitutional, a cornerstone of the Court's power ever since. The Constitution itself did not explicitly grant this authority, but Marshall's inoffensive assertion of it stood.

Nevertheless, despite the overarching significance of the ruling, which Marshall understood and history later would, the Court on that decision day exemplified an indifference to the role of the press that continues to the present day. There was no printed opinion available, not even the original that reporters could read and quote from. The justices simply failed to recognize that only the press could inform the public of the important work of the Court. It had no way of distributing its opinions. That was left to the newspapers, which clearly could have communicated the important decision much more effectively if they had had access to the printed opinion. Apparently it was not yet written.

In obvious frustration, one paper, the *Washington Federalist,* resorted to paraphrasing the holding in a few short paragraphs, without detail or quotations. It explained:

> Time does not permit at present a more full account of the opinion of the court—which considered each point at great length, and with great ability. Besides, it would be too much to hazard a report of the opinion from notes. As soon however, as a copy can be obtained from the Reporter, this interesting and highly important opinion shall be given at length.[8]

The *National Intelligencer* chose to wait, not even mentioning the decision until the 11,000-word opinion became available weeks later, but then printed it in its entirety. Other papers did so as well. In three separate installments engulfing its densely black front pages on March 18, 21, and 25, 1803, the *National Intelligencer* ran first a long, straightforward, and highly detailed preamble of the facts and the legal arguments, still not stating the result but setting the stage for the entire text.

With three weeks to reflect, did the *Intelligencer* grasp the monumental importance of the ruling? No, but two months later it reprinted a long, angry, anonymous diatribe from the *Virginia Argus* that sensed the overriding meaning. Addressed "To the Chief Justice of the United States," it fulminated: "The acts of the Executive government are then subject to the scrutiny and controul of this pipowder [dusty-footed] court. The idea is too ridiculous to excite alarm, disgust or even merriment." It was signed LITTLETON.[9]

Marbury v. Madison was the only case of Marshall's long tenure in which the Court held an act of Congress unconstitutional, but it invoked similar authority over state actions, commencing in 1809 with *United States v. Peters.*[10] Pennsylvania, by an act of its legislature, had defied a federal court decision holding the state liable for payment of a judgment in a dispute stemming from the Revolutionary War seizure of a British vessel. Marshall, though expressing regret that such a holding was necessary, nevertheless declared firmly: "the state of Pennsylvania can possess no constitutional right to resist the legal process which may be directed in this cause."[11] The press almost totally ignored the case, until the governor of Pennsylvania two weeks later published a notice to the legislature announcing that he was calling out the militia to resist the Court's ruling. During the next several days a number of newspapers up and down the eastern seaboard reproduced the notice without describing the dispute that prompted it. They missed an important story. (The state later backed down.)

THE CONTRACTS CLAUSE RISES, QUIETLY

Also underreported by the press, at least initially, were several important decisions of the Marshall Court that applied the contracts clause of the Constitution to undergird ordinary business and real estate agreements, which were normally in state jurisdiction. The Constitution declares, in Section 10 of Article I, "no State shall . . . pass any Law impairing the Obligation of Contracts."

In the first of these cases, *Fletcher v. Peck,*[12] the Supreme Court voided an act of the Georgia legislature that rescinded a previous grant of 35,000,000 acres, the "Yazoo grant," because the rescission was demonstrably brought about by widespread bribery of legislators and others. The legislature's action set aside subsequent sales of parcels of the land, too, penalizing innocent, bona fide purchasers along with speculators. Marshall held this a violation of the contracts clause, declaring that "when absolute rights have vested under that contract, a repeal of the law cannot divest those rights."[13]

Although both the plaintiff and defendant were New Englanders, and a party in interest was called the New-England Land Company, the good news was slow to appear in New England newspapers. The *New-England Palladium,* of Boston, reported mysteriously a week after the decision: "The Supreme Court of the U. States yesterday confirmed the decision of the court below in all its points, in favor of the New-England Land Company. (Yazoo) Baltimore paper, Mar. 17."[14] Over the next ten days several other New England journals followed suit, equally briefly. They conveyed no sense of the significant novelty, much less the historical import, of these decisions. As biographer Smith puts it, "In landmark cases like *Marbury v. Madison* and *Fletcher v. Peck,* it [the Court] was not only announcing the law authoritatively but was shaping the nature of the Union for future generations."[15]

Once the Supreme Court had breathed life into the contracts clause, would the press be more alert to contracts cases? *Dartmouth College v. Woodward* brought to the Court Daniel Webster, a Dartmouth graduate, a former congressman from New Hampshire and a formidable advocate, to plead his alma mater's cause. Striving to bring privately operated Dartmouth under the dominion of the state, New Hampshire's legislature had amended the college's royal charter of 1769 to create a state-chartered Dartmouth University controlled by gubernatorial appointees. Webster characterized the royal charter as a contract to which the state of New Hampshire had succeeded, and argued that it was protected from legislative interference by the contracts clause. Although the argument extended over three days, the newspapers failed to cover it. Afterward many papers, most of them in New England, noted that it had taken place or that the case was pending. However, the *Salem Gazette,* of Salem, Massachusetts, and later other papers, published this fascinating report from an unidentified person who admitted he was not there, either, but had heard about the argument from others:

> Mr. Webster opened the cause in that clear, perspicuous, forcible and impressive manner, for which he is so much distinguished, and for two or three hours enchained the court and the audience with an argument, which, for weight of authority, force of reasoning, and power of eloquence, has seldom been equalled in this or any court.[16]

When Marshall later announced a 4-1 decision for Dartmouth College, dozens of newspapers gave it notice, most of them in a single paragraph, but an anonymous correspondent of the *Columbian Centinel,* of Boston, was carried away. He reported that the chief justice had

> delivered the most able, and elaborate opinion, which, perhaps, has ever been pronounced in a Court of Judicature, on the far-famed question relative to *Dartmouth College. . . .* The opinion of the Court goes the whole length with the plaintiffs—overthrows every ground of defence relied on by the defendants, and shows most conclusively that *both* acts of the Legislature of *New-Hampshire,* interfering with the vested rights of the College, were *violations of the Constitution,* and, therefore, were void.

The writer said it was a unanimous decision, causing the newspaper to add that other reports stated there was one dissenter, which was correct.[17]

Marshall, once again, wrote carefully but broadly. He declared that the donors to the young college had entered into a contract backed by "valuable consideration"—their gifts—that the contracts clause prohibited the state from altering. He went out of his way to elaborate on the virtues of corporate charters:

> They enable a corporation to manage its own affairs, and to hold property without the perplexing intricacies, the hazardous and endless necessity, of perpetual conveyances for the purpose of transmitting it from hand to hand. It is chiefly for the purpose of clothing bodies of men, in succession, with these qualities and capacities, that corporations were invented, and are in use.[18]

However, the newspapers carried no quotations from Justice Marshall's expansive opinion, and there was little recognition in the many stories and commentaries of its broad constitutional, social, and civic significance, to wit, its encouragement of all manner of human endeavor in corporate form. But the press can hardly be faulted, for Marshall again, despite the lapse of nine months between the oral argument and the decision, delivered his opinion orally. He provided no written opinion until several weeks later. This allowed a rumor to be repeated in several papers that the decision of the Court was not final and would be reconsidered— a tall tale that could not have arisen had Marshall's emphatically unequivocal written opinion been immediately available.

The decision in a later important test of the contracts clause, *Ogden v. Saunders,*[19] was leaked to the press. On February 20, 1827, the *Republican Star and General Advertiser,* of Easton, Maryland, carried this item:

IMPORTANT INTELLIGENCE

We have been informed that letters have been received from Washington, containing the important intelligence, that a majority of the Judges of the Supreme Court of the U. States, will decide that the State Insolvent Laws are constitutional, so far as they relate to contracts entered into between citizens of the same State, subsequently to the passage of the State Insolvent Laws.[20]

The tip was correct. Other papers picked it up in the next few days. In fact, the Court had already decided the case, just the day before the rumor was first printed, but the decision was not yet known.

Ogden v. Saunders found Marshall, for the only time, dissenting from the Court's ruling on a constitutional question, an anomaly that should have attracted press attention but did not. A 4-3 majority ruled that contract rights in fact were not absolute, that a New York insolvency statute granting relief to debtors under certain circumstances did not violate the contracts clause, at least insofar as the statute applied to a contract whose parties were both in New York. But the law could not be applied against an out-of-state party. In his opinion Marshall contended, as before, that "an act of the legislature does not enter into the contract, and become one of the conditions stipulated by the parties; . . . that contracts derive their obligation from the act of the parties, not from the grant of government."[21] It was a complex decision, with Marshall actually in a majority of four on the out-of-stater aspect of it, but in a minority of three on the main question, and the justices wrote a number of individual opinions. Although Marshall's dissent was noted in the newspapers, as with previous Court coverage there were no quotations, no exploration of the legal reasoning despite the notable clash, no recognition that it was his first dissent, after twenty-six years, on a constitutional question.

It appears that, again, the justices' opinions were not immediately available to the press. Witness the confusion admitted by the *National Intelligencer* in this report picked up by the *Connecticut Courant,* a report which in fact accurately described the Court's dual holding:

> Of course, we cannot recapitulate the heads of argument and grounds of decision, embraced in these very elaborate opinions; and, perhaps we may not be entirely accurate in stating their results.... We are not entirely certain, we repeat, that we have accurately described the general result of the whole case, or that we entirely comprehend it. If, however, our conception of the result be right, the Court has so left the question, that State discharges, where the contract was posterior to the law, are good against creditors living in the State, but not good as against other creditors.— *National Intelligencer.*[22]

This examination of press coverage of some historic decisions is not to suggest that other, more mundane cases were not covered. In 1827, the year of *Ogden v. Saunders,* several newspapers reported a Supreme Court decision requiring the city of Washington, D.C., to pay $100,000—truly a king's ransom in those days—to a lottery winner named Christian Clark, who had been left holding an empty bag when the lottery agent hired by the city defaulted.[23]

THE NECESSARY AND PROPER CLAUSE
GROWS TEETH

Like the contracts clause, the vague "necessary and proper" clause of the Constitution was endowed with lasting potency by the Marshall Court.[24] In the leading case, *McCulloch v. Maryland*,[25] the press took early notice, mentioning the three days of oral argument, though apparently no newspaper actually covered that one either. The topic was politically flammable: it was the Second Bank of the United States. Chartered by Congress in 1816, the bank was mismanaged, too easy with credit and then too stingy, bringing down many state-chartered banks, especially in the South and West. It was highly unpopular. Moreover, when the case came to the Supreme Court the economy was ailing, done in by postwar extravagance and a flood of cheap imports that hurt manufacturing. According to legal historian Charles Warren, when banks in the West, Kentucky, and the Carolinas "stopped payment, the general public placed the responsibility on that 'monster,' the Bank of the United States."[26]

With all eyes on the Supreme Court, the case posed two important questions: did the U.S. government, lacking any explicit constitutional authorization, nevertheless have the authority to charter a national bank, and did a state, here Maryland, have the power to tax a branch of the bank? For a unanimous Court, Marshall noted that Section 8 of Article I authorizes Congress to lay and collect taxes, to borrow money, to regulate commerce, to raise an army and navy and declare war, and to enact laws "necessary and proper" to carry out these enumerated powers. So, Marshall ruled, just three days after the oral argument, that a national bank was an appropriate means of carrying out such powers. He wrote in sweeping, even majestic language:

We admit, as all must admit, that the powers of the government are limited, and that its limits are not to be transcended. But we think the sound construction of the constitution must allow to the national legislature that discretion, with respect to the means by which the powers it confers are to be carried into execution, which will enable that body to perform the high duties assigned to it, in the manner most beneficial to the people. Let the end be legitimate, let it be within the scope of the constitution, and all means which are appropriate, which are plainly adapted to that end, which are not prohibited, but consist with the letter and spirit of the constitution, are constitutional.[27]

Thus Marshall gave life to the doctrine of "implied powers." He also held that Maryland could not tax an entity over which it had no authority. "The power to tax involves the power to destroy," he wrote famously.[28]

Not surprisingly, a prominent Baltimore newspaper, *Niles' Weekly Register,* while calling the decision important, took issue with the concept of implied powers and criticized the ruling for apparently meaning "that congress may grant *monopolies,* almost at discretion, to any set of men, and for almost any purpose, if the price is paid for them, or without any pecuniary consideration at all."[29]

"Marshall's opinion in *McCulloch* immediately drew national attention," reports Marshall biographer Jean Edward Smith. He continues:

In the North and East, where the bank was still popular and the recession less severe, the decision drew substantial support. . . . Re-action in the South and West was mixed. . . . [A] Mississippi news-paper said, "The last vestige of the sovereignty and independence of the individual States composing the National Confederacy is obliterated at one fell swoop." . . . Opposition was fiercest in Virginia.[30]

A Tennessee paper raged, "This Court, above the law and beyond the control of public opinion, has lately made a decision that prostrates the State sovereignty entirely." One Kentucky newspaper echoed that the decision "must raise an alarm throughout our widely-extended empire."[31]

A week after *McCulloch* was handed down, the *National Intelligencer* praised the decision as important and proudly announced: "We have therefore taken some pains to procure a copy of this interesting and elaborate opinion for publication, and have the pleasure to-day of presenting it to our readers."[32] It occupied the entire front page, all five columns, and then some. Other papers picked it up from the *Intelligencer* and also published it in full; the *City of Washington Gazette* needed two days to accommodate it all. Though the first stories reporting the historic decision contained no details or quotations from the opinion, the Court made the text available comparatively promptly, so the totality of the coverage by the national press was by far the fullest to date of any decision of the Supreme Court.

THE COMMERCE CLAUSE GIRDED FOR STARDOM

Another fulcrum of the Marshall Court's nation-building was the commerce clause in Section 8 of Article I, Congress's power "to regulate Commerce with foreign Nations, and among the several States, and with the Indian Tribes." The Court first applied the clause to state regulations affecting interstate commerce. Later, commencing with the enactment of the Interstate Commerce Act of 1887 and the Sherman Antitrust Act of 1890, the clause would become the principal constitutional source of federal power, reaching well beyond purely commercial matters to underpin such actions as civil rights legislation.

Gibbons v. Ogden set the stage, in 1824.[33] New York had granted steamboat pioneer Robert Fulton the exclusive right to operate his vessel in the state, but the monopoly was challenged by Thomas Gibbons, who operated boats between New Jersey and New York under a federal coasting license. The Supreme Court, unanimous as it often was under Marshall, ruled that Gibbons's federal license, and the federal statute under which it was granted, nullified New York's monopoly:

> This act demonstrates the opinion of Congress, that steam boats may be enrolled and licensed, in common with vessels using sails. They are, of course, entitled to the same privileges, and can no more be restrained from navigating waters, and entering ports which are free to such vessels, than if they were wafted on their voyage by the winds, instead of being propelled by the agency of fire.[34]

Despite the importance of the case, well recognized even before the decision, the Supreme Court and the press were still not in sync, more than three decades after the Court commenced operations. The *Baltimore Patriot and Mercantile Advertiser* reported lamely two days after the decision:

> The high importance, as well as reputed ability and conclusiveness of the Opinion of the Supreme Court, yesterday declared, in the case of the celebrated Steam Boat controversy, have induced us to solicit of the Chief Justice a copy for publication, which has been

politely afforded. We shall be able to present it to our readers, either to-morrow, or on the day following. It is of considerable length, and is decisive against the right of the state of New York to constitute the Steam Boat monopoly.[35]

Although the newspapers were slow to report, "with virtually no exceptions, the nation's press rejoiced at the destruction of the obnoxious steamboat monopoly," records Jean Edward Smith. "Many New York papers published the opinion in full. . . . Newspapers in Kentucky, Georgia and Missouri joined the chorus. Even in South Carolina the holding was greeted with approval. . . . Negative reaction centered in Virginia, and even there it was moderate."[36]

CHIEF JUSTICE TANEY CARRIES ON

John Marshall died in 1835. He was succeeded by Roger Brooke Taney, of Maryland, who would preside for twenty-eight years and become infamous as the author of the 1857 Dred Scott decision that deemed a slave property rather than a person.[37] Taney, a prominent Maryland lawyer and a dedicated supporter of President Andrew Jackson, had served as his attorney general and briefly as secretary of the Treasury before being appointed at age fifty-nine to succeed Marshall. Having previously been rejected by the Senate for a seat on the Court, Taney was a controversial appointee, but ultimately was confirmed by a vote of 29-15. However, except for a blind eye to slavery, Taney proved to be a pragmatist who effectively led the Court, at least until the Dred Scott case. His Court sometimes elevated the role of the states in economic matters, but only so long as their regulations did not conflict with federal law. The decisions extended Marshall's construction of the legal framework of a national economy, notably in cases involving the contracts clause and the commerce clause.

First up was *Charles River Bridge v. Warren Bridge,* a Massachusetts case which at least purported to be a test of the contracts clause.[38] The proprietors of the Charles River Bridge, who had been authorized by the legislature decades earlier to build the bridge and collect tolls, sought to prevent the construction of a competing bridge also approved by the legislature. The new Warren Bridge company was represented by Daniel Webster, then a U.S. senator from Massachusetts. In a rare, indeed enchanting, look inside the courtroom, an unnamed correspondent of the *Mississippian* later reported:

> Sir—I have been listening to-day to an argument by Mr. Webster, delivered in the Supreme Court . . .
>
> He starts out in his argument, by the most lucid and forcible statement of his proposition. There is no possibility of mistaking what he intends to establish. Having made his points, he continues their demonstration by a logical method and chain of reasoning, unsurpassed, if not unrivalled . . .
>
> Woe to his opponent, if his propositions are loosely stated, or defended by inappropriate terms. Mr. W. at once grasps them with his wonderful power of analysis, strips them of all disguise, holds them up to the naked eye, with a sarcasm of comments, which makes their author's cheeks mantle with blushes . . .
>
> He always makes his superiority *felt.* He sometimes, too, drops a sneer, which is as icy and chilling as a spirit from the frozen ocean.[39]

Unlike most decisions of the Marshall Court, here the justices were sharply divided, ruling just 4-3 for competition. While the minority saw an implied contract protecting the Charles River Bridge, Taney, writing for the majority, saw no such contract. He pointed out that the legislature's authorization of the second bridge also extended the Charles River Bridge's authorization to collect tolls. The legislature contemplated no exclusivity, he ruled, nor would that comport with the experience of turnpike proprietors who were used to seeing competitive roads built subsequently. If the Court ruled for the Charles River Bridge, Taney wisely wrote,

> [t]he millions of property which have been invested in rail roads and canals, upon lines of travel which had been before occupied by turnpike corporations, will be put in jeopardy. We shall be thrown back to the improvements of the last century, and obliged to stand still, until the claims of the old turnpike corporations shall be satisfied; and they shall consent to permit these states to avail themselves of the lights of modern science, and to partake of the benefit of those improvements which are now adding to the wealth and prosperity, and the convenience and comfort, of every other part of the civilized world.[40]

The newspapers, even in New England, were slow and perfunctory in their reporting of the decision, perhaps because the opinion was not published promptly. But the *New Hampshire Patriot and State Gazette,* of Concord, later rejoiced that "vested rights as they are called, are not sacred and intangible nor to predominate over the public good."[41]

In the midst of its historic march, the Supreme Court paused at one point to respond publicly to an unusual invitation from a group of congressmen. The *Vermont Chronicle,* of Bellows Falls, reported that the justices were invited "to attend the funeral of the

Hon. Jonathan Cilley, late a member of the House of Representatives, and it being well known that the deceased was killed in
a duel lately fought by him." Dueling was illegal, so the Court
voted formally, "Resolved, . . . the Justices of the Supreme Court
cannot, consistently with the duties they owe to the public, attend,
in there [sic] official characters, the funeral of one who has fallen
in a duel."[42]

Over the next several years the Supreme Court ruled on a number of commercial cases now seen as fundamental in economic
nationalization, though they did not all favor federal authority
over state. Unfortunately the newspapers, still covering the Court
only occasionally and often relying on other papers, primarily the
renamed *Daily National Intelligencer* in Washington, gave them only
modest coverage. It should be noted that in the 1840s the *Intelligencer* played a unique role in Supreme Court coverage, publishing
not only news stories and occasionally full texts of opinions, but
detailed listings of attorneys admitted to practice before the Court,
cases argued, the attorneys involved, decisions announced and the
winners, and sometimes statements by the attorney general of con-
dolences for attorneys recently deceased.

BALANCING STATE AND FEDERAL AUTHORITY

Just as the contracts clause did not stand in the way of the Warren
Bridge decision, neither did the commerce clause prevent New
York from checking ship passenger manifests to block entry by
indigents and aliens. In *New York v. Miln* the interstate transit of
slaves lurked in the background, so the Court, in an opinion by
Justice Philip Barbour of Virginia, veered from the pro-federal
holding of *Gibbons v. Ogden*. Barbour made a distinction between

goods and persons and thus upheld the New York statute as a permissible use of a state's police powers, the right to protect the health and welfare of its citizens.[43] But the Court once again set aside state action in *Bank of Augusta v. Earle,* upholding the validity of debts owed to out-of-staters.[44] *Swift v. Tyson* set an important precedent in the nationalization of the economy, directing federal judges to apply general principles of commercial law, or common law, even if contrary to state court decisions.[45] Decisions in other tussles between state and federal authority produced confusion because the justices, always eyeing the potential impact on slavery questions, wrote multiple opinions.[46]

The Taney Court's most coherent holding on the commerce clause, *Cooley v. Board of Wardens of the Port of Philadelphia,* upheld local levies on ships despite an earlier, contrary ruling by the Court. Philadelphia required that a vessel not employing a local pilot pay one-half the usual pilotage fee into a fund for infirm pilots and pilots' widows. Deeming pilotage laws local, the Court, by a vote of 6-2, found no burden on interstate commerce.[47] In historical hindsight it was an important decision, but it was ignored by the newspapers, including the recently founded *New-York Daily Times,* which was on newsstands for a penny.

Any examination of news coverage in the United States in the nineteenth century needs to emphasize the development of the electrical telegraph by Samuel F. B. Morse, which he tested successfully in 1837. It drastically improved newspapers' and the public's awareness of current events. In fact, after a special line financed by the government was completed in 1844, Morse's first public demonstration of his telegraph took place in the Supreme Court chamber, where he sent his famous "What hath God wrought" to the Baltimore & Ohio Railroad depot in Baltimore. But the device needed wires, and years were required to develop an eastern network, which was then connected to the West in 1861. After the Civil War ended in 1865 the breadth of news coverage, notably from Washington, increased greatly.

THE CHASE COURT GETS PRESS

Roger Taney died in 1864, and once again the secretary of the Treasury was named chief justice. President Abraham Lincoln selected Salmon P. Chase, fifty-six years old, a former Ohio governor and U.S. senator who had been one of Lincoln's rivals for the presidency in 1860.

Though preoccupied by race and Reconstruction questions that produced split decisions, the Chase Court affirmed federal supremacy in two cases with economic impact. It ruled in *Texas v. White* that Congress had the constitutional authority to reestablish state governments after the war, that Congress had recognized the new, provisional government of Texas, that therefore Texas could sue in federal court, and finally that the state was entitled to recover certain securities sold by its Confederate government.[48]

Press coverage of the Texas case was extensive, enhanced by the fact that the Court made its printed opinion available immediately. The decision was well reported the following day by the *Daily National Intelligencer,* which proceeded to print the entire opinion a day later, along with an editorial endorsing it. The *New York Times,* the *Milwaukee Daily Sentinel,* and other papers also published the complete text. The *Chicago Daily Tribune* provided extensive coverage, and in an editorial predicted public acceptance: "The time for frantic appeals by parties to the courts for partisan judgement will be forgotten, and the people, North and South, will once more address themselves to the improvement of their material interests, every day realizing more strongly the blessings of peace and of an indissoluble Union."[49] But the *Weekly Georgia Telegraph* reported acidly: "In the Texas bond case the court decides that Texas, notwithstanding secession, continued to be a State of the Union, and yet also decides that Congress had the right to adopt measures of reconstruction. It needs all the Chief Justice's ingenuity to harmonize these two points."[50]

Somewhat to its embarrassment, the Supreme Court first invalidated, then only a year later affirmed, the constitutionality of the Legal Tender Act of 1862, which declared that the paper money called greenbacks issued by the federal government during the Civil War (ironically, by Chase as Treasury secretary) was legal tender for debts and taxes.[51] The Court compounded its clumsiness by mishandling the release of the second decision. First there was a leak, perhaps a deliberate effort to smooth out the reversal, for the *Atlanta Constitution* reported confidently three days before the decision that the justices "met in council" and five "voted to sustain the constitutionality of the act" while four "voted in the negative."[52] Then, confounding public anticipation of the decision, the Court undermined its own announcement by stating it only partially, as reported by the *New York Times:* "Mr. Justice Clifford read a brief paper" stating the result and concluding, "The opinion of the Court, and the reasons for dissent will be read before the close of the adjourned term."[53] Other papers ignored the peculiar announcement. The *Constitution*'s beat was correct: the vote was indeed 5-4.

In economic regulation the Chase Court took a step now widely regarded as backward with the *Slaughterhouse Cases.*[54] By another vote of 5-4, with the chief justice among the dissenters, the Court rejected a challenge to a monopoly granted by a Louisiana statute to a newly formed New Orleans slaughtering company, driving other local butchers out, a measure justified as enhancing health regulation of the business. The majority rejected a cogent argument that the statute ran afoul of the postwar Fourteenth Amendment, which among other admonitions to the states forbade enforcement of "any law which shall abridge the privileges or immunities of citizens of the United States." This language, the Court ruled, was intended to protect the rights of the newly freed slaves, not the freedom to work, thus making a fussy but potent distinction between the rights of state and national citizenship.

Reports of the decision, most of them stating correctly the Fourteenth Amendment argument and noting the four dissents, appeared in newspapers the following day. Crediting a "special dispatch" to the paper, the *Boston Daily Advertiser* summarized the decision and then a day later reported that the justices spent the day reading their opinions: "The decision of yesterday in the so-called slaughter-house case was given to an almost empty court room, and has as yet attracted little attention here outside of legal circles, although the judges of the court regard the case as the most important which has been before them since the Dred Scott decision."[55] The *Daily Arkansas Gazette* regretted that "the court was so equally divided—the ablest judges dissenting from the majority."[56] On the other hand, the *Chicago Daily Tribune* once again approved: "The Court in its decision very clearly condemns the theory that it was the intention of the framers of the Fourteenth Amendment to bring the entire domain of civil rights, heretofore belonging to the States, within the power of Congress."[57] The *New York Times* agreed, hoping that the ruling dealt "a severe and, one might almost hope, a fatal blow to that school of constitutional lawyers who have been engaged, ever since the adoption of the Fourteenth Amendment, in inventing impossible consequences for that addition to the Constitution."[58]

By this time some papers were providing copious coverage of Washington, including sometimes humdrum news of Congress and federal agencies as well as of the Supreme Court. The *Milwaukee Daily Sentinel* reported in 1873: "The Supreme Court rendered a large number of decisions to-day, many of them having no general interest." But it described several of them anyway.[59]

THE FULLER COURT: SLOWDOWN

Through most of the 1870s and 1880s the Supreme Court busied itself with civil rights cases testing the reach of the post–Civil War amendments—Thirteen (freeing the slaves), Fourteen (guaranteeing them equal protection of the laws), and Fifteen (granting them the vote). But with President Grover Cleveland's appointment in 1888 of a Chicago business lawyer, Melville Fuller, fifty-five years old, as chief justice, the Court focused increasingly on property, business, and labor matters, often limiting government authority, state as well as federal.

The justices waded into a hornets' nest when they agreed to consider the constitutionality of an income tax enacted in 1894.[60] As it turned out, the case had no enduring significance, for it was overridden in 1913 by the Sixteenth Amendment specifically authorizing an income tax, but public agitation about the issue and daily newspaper coverage of it were intense and unprecedented. Partly because the Supreme Court had approved a temporary income tax levied during the Civil War,[61] there was a general expectation that the new tax, to be levied only on incomes exceeding an above-average $4,000 a year, would be upheld. The *Washington Post* reprinted this story from the *New York Herald:*

> Bridgeport, Conn., March 3—In order to get money to pay the income tax is the reason given by Dr. Warner, the head of the big corset factory of the Warner Brothers Company, for the reduction of the wages in the factory, where hundreds of girls are employed. The reduction will take effect in a few days.[62]

Public anticipation of the oral argument before the Court ran so high that merchandisers strove to capitalize on it. A display advertisement in the *New York Times* listed prominent people sick with a common malady called grip, warning that "grip may prevent Senator Edmunds from appearing in the Income Tax Cases" and touting a remedy called simply "77."[63]

George Edmunds, actually then a prominent former senator from Vermont (he had twice sought the Republican presidential nomination), miraculously managed to appear for the historic argument after all. For more than a week members of Congress, lawyers, and other spectators jammed the courtroom, now situated in more spacious and dignified Capitol quarters originally occupied by the Senate. Edmunds was one of several prominent attorneys opposing the tax, primarily on the grounds that it was unconstitutional as a violation of a provision of Article I, Section 9: "No Capitation, or other direct, Tax shall be laid, unless in Proportion to the Census or Enumeration hereinbefore directed to be taken." The *Washington Post,* paraphrasing a perhaps tongue-in-cheek statement by Edmunds, reported that he, "to adorn his discourse," questioned "how many of the gentlemen who voted to enact that law intended to or who would pay the alleged tax they imposed upon others." (He had resigned from the Senate before the tax was proposed.) Edmunds argued, according to the *Post,* that it was commonly believed that 90 percent of the tax would be paid by fewer than 2 percent of the "male voters" and declaimed: "And they call this equality; this they call liberty."[64]

Similar hyperbole was employed in defense of the tax. Attorney General Richard Olney characterized the attack as a blatant end run around the legislative process:

> It is nothing but a call upon the judicial department of the government to supplant the political in the exercise of taxing power; to substitute its discretion for that of Congress in respect to the subject of taxation, the plan of taxation and all the distinctions and discriminations by which taxation is sought to be equitably adjusted to the resources and capacities of those who have it to bear.[65]

The national drama went on and on. The Court upheld the lower court ruling in favor of the tax, but by an unsatisfactory 4–4 vote because Justice Howell Jackson, seriously ill, was at home in Tennessee. Exhorted by Chief Justice Fuller, Jackson rose from his sickbed and returned to Washington to hear reargument of the case, then voted with three others to uphold the tax. But one justice switched sides to form a five-vote majority that invalidated the tax on the ground that it was indeed a direct tax not apportioned among the states according to population. (Worn out, Jackson died three months later.)

Newspapers resounded with the decision. The *New York Times* gave it top billing on page one, quoting Chief Justice Fuller's opinion while also describing in these strong terms Justice John Marshall Harlan's dissent:

> The most rampant Populist could not have used more vehement expressions or shown greater contempt for the views of the majority than Justice Harlan did in the long harangue to which he treated the court and the spectators. It was little less than a stump speech crowded with inflammatory statements and thinly disguised sneers.[66]

But the *Times* editorialized with satisfaction, "Never was the 'wisdom of the fathers' more conclusively demonstrated nor more happily invoked."[67]

The *Boston Daily Globe* agreed: "Now that the Supreme Court has spoken it is unlikely that there will be a serious attempt to renew income tax agitation, so far as action by the general government is concerned, for many a year to come."[68] But the *Atlanta Constitution* noted the "extravagance" of the federal government and predicted presciently that new revenues could and would be found:

> The country is beginning to be embarrassed by overgrown fortunes which are year after year becoming more potent in controlling legislation and in the dictation of public opinion. We believe that the conditions are rapidly crystallizing to bring about such a state of affairs as will, in the near future, call for heroic treatment and which will force overgrown and indolent fortunes to bear their just part of the public burden.[69]

The income tax case opened a new era in press coverage of the Supreme Court. The Court made important, exciting news. Its decisions mattered, at least some of them. The public was engaged, and so were editors and reporters. Washington news bureaus were growing, and they would give more attention than ever before to major cases—the oral arguments, the decisions, and their ramifications. Editorial writers back in the papers' home offices would weigh in more frequently, too.

In the face of Chief Justice Fuller's reluctance to expand federal authority, other justices assembled majorities to extend the federal reach in two significant cases. A 5-4 majority took an important regulatory leap by upholding under the commerce clause a statute prohibiting the interstate transportation of lottery tickets.[70] Justice Harlan wrote for the Court that lottery tickets had value and that the transport of them was commerce. The holding would prove significant as the first of several that interpreted the commerce clause to support a federal police power like that of the states, which had the power to protect public health, safety, and morals. Justice Harlan declared that the Constitution would not support a claim of a right to conduct interstate commerce in items "that will be confessedly injurious to the public morals."[71]

The *Chicago Daily Tribune,* noting that the case had been tried in Chicago, correctly saw the broader implications of the holding:

> WASHINGTON, D.C., Feb. 23—[Special.]—Justice Harlan today handed down a decision of the United States Supreme court in a lottery case which reaffirms the power of congress to prohibit interstate commerce within certain limits. . . . The decision ended with a denial that it is intended to lay down a rule on the validity of all acts under the commerce law, but said it meant simply to define a lottery ticket as an article of commerce, and as such subject to the regulations of congress.[72]

A year later, in 1904, the Court voted 6-3, Chief Justice Fuller again in dissent, to uphold Congress's use of the taxing power to regulate the production of oleomargarine. The Court held that the ten-cents-per-pound tax, on oleo colored to resemble butter, did not violate any express constitutional limitation on the taxing power, and so established it as another basis for federal police power.[73] However, as the Supreme Court closed out its term with a flood of decisions, the oleo case was not well covered. The *Chicago Daily Tribune* took notice, but was more concerned about the decision's economic impact than its constitutional significance: "In Chicago last night, as well as in Washington, men familiar with the trade, expressed the belief that the butterine industry had received its death blow. As they understood the ruling and its effect, the immense industry, built up in recent years, was doomed."[74]

THE WHITE COURT: UNCERTAINTY ON FEDERAL POWER

Chief Justice Edward Douglass White (1910–21) was not a consistent supporter of federal authority. Yes, he had voted in the minority to uphold the federal income tax in 1895, and he had written the Court's opinion in the 1904 oleomargarine case that expanded the taxing power.[75] But when the power to tax came up during his chief justiceship, he recanted, dissenting from a 5-4 ruling on the grounds that a tax on heroin sales was merely an attempt by Congress to exert a power not delegated by the Constitution, the police power, which White deemed reserved to the states.[76] Major newspapers took no notice.

The White Court vacillated over the reach of the commerce clause. It cited the clause in sustaining the Mann Act of 1910, the so-called White Slave Act that prohibited the interstate transport of women for prostitution.[77] On the other hand, by a 5-4 vote the Court ruled unconstitutional a 1916 federal statute prohibiting the interstate shipment of products made by children under age fourteen, on the ground that manufacturing was local and thus beyond the reach of the commerce clause.[78] Newspapers noted a strong dissent by Justice Holmes in the child labor case, but it caused no stir. The *New York Times* was supportive of the ruling: "When there are forty-eight varieties, more or less, of temperance laws and child labor laws there is proved to be such a wide variance of opinion that it would not be right for intolerant opinion on those subjects to impose its will upon others equally entitled to their opinions."[79]

THE TAFT COURT: THE COMMERCE CLAUSE WORKS

Chief Justice White died in 1921 and was succeeded by the man who had appointed him, William Howard Taft. Warren G. Harding, whom Taft had supported for president in 1920, made the appointment on June 30, 1921, and the Senate confirmed the nomination the same day without even referring it to a committee. However, there were four no votes, three by his fellow Republicans. One objected that Taft was more politician than lawyer, but the *Boston Daily Globe* commented that "our strongest Chief Justices have all been politicians. Marshall, Taney, Chase and White came to the office from the field of politics, where they had been intensely active."[80] The *Los Angeles Times* praised Taft for his World War I support of President Woodrow Wilson, who had defeated him in 1912, and declared: "No one mentally honest will be inclined to accuse the new Chief Justice of being influenced by political considerations."[81]

In the commerce clause Chief Justice Taft saw a congressional strength. Once, when the Court invalidated a commodity-futures regulation statute that was based on the taxing power, he explicitly advised Congress how to get it right. In his opinion the chief justice asked, quite gratuitously because the commerce clause was not at issue, "We come to the question then, Can these regulations of boards of trade by Congress be sustained under the commerce clause of the Constitution?" He answered his own question, in the affirmative.[82] So Congress wrote the same scheme of federal regulation into a new statute citing the commerce clause as its authority, and the Court bought it.[83]

Without mentioning the unusual role of the chief justice, newspapers noted appropriately that the new legislation was based on the commerce clause rather than the taxing power. The *Wall Street Journal* wrote that the act brought trading under the regulation of the secretary of agriculture, who would have authority to discipline traders manipulating the market. But, the *Journal* went on, quoting no one and citing no sources, "There is nothing else in the law that prevents the trade from operating as it now does. . . . This is an annoyance but is not destructive. . . . There is nothing else in the law to raise or depress prices, help or hurt the trade."[84] In the home city of the Chicago Board of Trade, the center of the controversy, the *Tribune* found similar equanimity. It reported that the decision "was viewed favorably here last night by prominent Board of Trade men. They assert that the chief importance of the decision rested in the fact that the grain exchanges now have the sanction of the government."[85]

THE HUGHES COURT AND THE NEW DEAL

In ill health, Taft resigned from the Court in 1930, just a month before his death, and was succeeded by Charles Evans Hughes

(1930–41). The Hughes Court is remembered as an obstacle to President Franklin Roosevelt's ambitious New Deal programs designed to cope with the catastrophic Great Depression that had begun in 1929. Such New Deal legislative pillars as the National Industrial Recovery Act of 1933, the Agricultural Adjustment Act of 1933, the Tennessee Valley Authority Act of 1933, the National Labor Relations Act of 1935, and the Social Security Act of 1935 asserted a radical expansion of federal authority and sometimes injected the government into the market economy. States also invoked extraordinary new authority to deal with the crisis, which idled one-fourth of the American workforce. Despite its reputation today, the Hughes Court, though sharply divided, in fact sustained a number of the early federal and state economic measures.

Also responding to the national emergency, the press rose to new heights in covering government efforts to cope with the Depression, including the critical role of the Supreme Court. Newspapers provided extensive coverage of important decisions, often including the constitutional or statutory reasoning and quotations, sometimes lengthy, from majority and minority opinions. Interpretive bylined articles, both straight news reports and commentary, reflected a more comprehensive and confident grasp of the sometimes subtle facts and forces influencing the justices' thinking.

Early in 1934 the Supreme Court, in identical 5-4 rulings, gave its sanction to two state measures challenged as violative of the U.S. Constitution. The Court ruled that a Minnesota statute empowering the courts to block mortgage foreclosures did not violate the constitutional admonition against impairment of contracts, *Fletcher v. Peck, Dartmouth College,* and *Charles River Bridge* notwithstanding, because a state had the authority to safeguard the welfare of its citizens.[86] With similar reasoning, the Court upheld a New York statute that authorized fixing the retail price of milk (set at nine cents per quart), although four dissenters deemed it a violation of the due process clause of the Fourteenth Amendment.[87]

Reporting the milk decision, the *Chicago Daily Tribune* went straight to the heart of the matter:

> WASHINGTON, D.C., March 6—[Special.]—The United States Supreme Court today, for the second time since the New Deal came into being, decided 5 to 4 in favor of a major principle of the Roosevelt program.
>
> A five dollar fine imposed upon an insignificant Rochester, N.Y., storekeeper became, through the majority opinion of the court, a vital factor in the future determination of the constitutionality of such national policies as those of the agricultural adjustment administration and the NRA.[88]

The *New York Times,* also looking for deeper meaning, editorialized judiciously: "There will probably be several cases of that general sort, and yesterday's decision by the Supreme Court does not indicate directly what view it would take of them."[89] *Times* columnist Arthur Krock, witnessing the justices' delivery of their clashing opinions, gave an emotional, human twist to the historic drama:

> WASHINGTON, March 5—In some respects the most exciting place in the New Deal capital is not the White House, the NRA or AAA headquarters or either Congressional chamber. It is the small, stuffy room where sits the Supreme Court of the United States. . . . The decision in the Rochester milk-price case today, and some of the language in the majority and minority opinions, make it

clear that a grave and deep chasm of political and social philosophy separates the distinguished jurists. There must be heavy hearts that beat these days behind the black gowns. The expressions on the faces of the Justices today were of patriots who have divided at an ominous fork in a road and are concerned because they cannot march on together.[90]

Again divided 5-4, the Court went on to uphold a congressional abrogation of any requirement in public or private contracts that payment be made in gold, an effort to conserve the government's bullion reserves. Holders of corporate and Treasury bonds claimed violations of the contracts clause and the due process clause, but Chief Justice Hughes held that Congress had a constitutional right to regulate the nation's monetary system.[91]

Nevertheless, these decisions sustaining state and federal efforts to cope with the Depression quickly faded into distant memory when the Court in 1935 and 1936 invalidated a number of Roosevelt initiatives: a bankruptcy act amendment giving relief to farmers who had defaulted on their mortgages,[92] the president's removal of a recalcitrant regulator,[93] the National Industrial Recovery Act,[94] the Agricultural Adjustment Act,[95] the Bituminous Coal Conservation Act of 1935,[96] and, for good measure, a New York minimum-wage law for women and children.[97] Most of the decisions found violations of the necessary and proper clause, the commerce clause, the due process clause of the Fourteenth Amendment, or the Tenth Amendment's reservation of undelegated powers to the states or to the people.

Newspapers erupted with intense coverage. On May 28, 1935, the day after the Supreme Court handed down three unanimous opinions adverse to the New Deal, the *New York Times* carried no fewer than thirty-one stories about the decisions and their ramifications. The *Chicago Daily Tribune* ran sixteen stories, the *Los Angeles Times* twelve, and the *Atlanta Constitution* and the *Wall Street Journal* nine each. One *Tribune* story comprised excerpts from editorial opinion of nineteen papers around the country, most of them chiding the president and celebrating the Constitution and the Court. The *Journal* declared that some economic restrictions might have been warranted by the Depression,

> [b]ut to say that in the name of emergency it was necessary to jail a pants presser for undercutting his competitors by a nickel or that it was necessary to build up a Washington bureaucracy for the purpose of determining whether a good lady clerking in a small town store should or should not have an extra half hour for lunch is to enter into a realm of unreality of which Lewis Carroll himself never dreamed.[98]

Supreme Court decisions voiding New Deal measures continued to rain down in early 1936. President Roosevelt was reelected in a landslide that fall, and soon afterward threw down the gauntlet to the Court. He proposed legislation, quickly dubbed his "court-packing plan," to enlarge the Court by one seat for each sitting justice over age seventy, up to a maximum of six. There were then, not coincidentally, exactly six justices over seventy, four of whom had consistently voted against New Deal actions. The papers were as cool to this as they had been kindly toward the Court's decisions. The *Washington Post* editorialized:

> So dangerous, and so really indefensible, is the President's plan to pack the Supreme Court that many will wonder if the underlying long-range idea is perhaps to bring this institution into public con-

tempt. Certainly if an American President should ever harbor dictatorial ambitions, that would be an effective course to pursue.[99]

However, in March 1937, four months after the election and just one month after the president unveiled his proposal, the Supreme Court changed course. It has long been said that "the Supreme Court reads the election returns," and this was the prime example of that. Chief Justice Hughes and Justice Owen Roberts, who previously had been among the naysayers, switched sides to provide the deciding votes in the Court's upholding of two anti-Depression statutes, one federal and one state. By a vote of 5-4 the Court articulated a new, broader interpretation of the commerce clause to affirm the National Labor Relations Act of 1935, known as the Wagner Act, which encouraged the formation of unions and created the National Labor Relations Board.[100] And in another 5-4 decision, the Court turned back a challenge to a Washington State minimum-wage law for women.[101] The Washington holding overturned a decision of the Taft Court which was based on a pro-employer, judge-made concept called the freedom of contract. "What is this freedom?" Hughes snorted indignantly for the majority of five. "The Constitution does not speak of freedom of contract. It speaks of liberty and prohibits the deprivation of liberty without due process of law. . . . There is no absolute freedom to do as one wills or to contract as one chooses."[102]

Shortly afterward the Court, by a vote of 7-2, sustained the old-age benefits of the Social Security Act of 1935.[103] After that, Roosevelt, still facing ferocious congressional opposition to his court-packing plan, quietly dropped it. But his objective, a Supreme Court more amenable to his expansive reading of the federal government's constitutional powers, had been achieved. With the Wagner Act decision, the press generally accepted the changed Court. In another survey of newspaper editorials, the *Chicago Daily Tribune* included this from the *Hartford Courant:* "It [the Court] has given an interpretation to the commerce clause that must delight even the President himself. Neither packing the Supreme court nor the adoption of a far-reaching amendment to the constitution could possibly give Mr. Roosevelt more."[104] But Arthur Krock of the *New York Times,* who opposed the court-packing plan, blustered: "It is a reportorial duty to record the fact that, so far as Washington is concerned, the Supreme Court conclusions today in the Wagner act cases were assayed exclusively on the scales of politics and not on the scales of law. Elsewhere in the United States it may be that the analyses were legal. Not here."[105]

Krock went beyond his usual role of commentator in 1938 when, prompted privately by Justice Harlan Fiske Stone, he reported that his colleagues of the press had missed a very important decision of the Court. And indeed they had. It was called *Erie Railroad v. Tompkins,* a case studied by all first-year law students ever since.[106] It threw out a century-old Supreme Court doctrine under which the federal courts had ignored state common law— the accepted interpretations of commercial, corporate, real estate, torts, and other laws as declared by the state supreme court—to decide cases by what was termed "general federal common law," in other words, case law determined by federal judges. Interpreting the federal Judiciary Act of 1789, the Hughes Court surprisingly ruled, 6-2, that there was no general federal common law, and that unless the Constitution or a federal statute was at issue, the law to be applied by federal courts in any diversity case (parties located in different states) was state law. It was a shocker. And yet, not a single reporter noticed the decision. So Krock puckishly began his column this way:

If the Supreme Court, like so many other arms of the government, had a publicity agent, eight days would not have passed before the importance of its decision in the Tompkins case became known. Though Justice Brandeis delivered this transcendently significant opinion a week ago yesterday, it has generally eluded public notice.[107]

THE STONE COURT LEANS FEDERAL

Charles Evans Hughes resigned as chief justice in 1941 and was replaced by Associate Justice Harlan Fiske Stone, who was then sixty-eight years old. Stone had been the dean of Columbia Law School as well as a prominent practitioner in New York City. Although deemed a Republican, for he had been appointed to the court by President Coolidge in 1925, Stone had dissented from several of the Hughes Court's 1935–36 rulings against New Deal legislation. That gave President Roosevelt good reason to promote him to chief justice.

On one very busy day in February 1942 the Stone Court handed down three decisions sustaining extensions of federal authority, two of them upholding federal agricultural regulations as a proper exercise of the commerce clause, the third deferring to a presidential international agreement as a function of the supremacy clause of the Constitution.[108] Only one decision was unanimous, and the new chief justice, despite his known predilection for federal authority, dissented in the other two. But even this showing of internal dissonance was not enough to persuade the press that the federal-state rivalry was still front-page news. The *New York Times* covered the decisions on page 21, the *Los Angeles Times* on page 22. The *Chicago Daily Tribune* accorded them a bit more prominence, page 11, apparently because one decision, involving a Chicago dairy, authorized federal price regulation of milk produced and sold entirely within the state of Illinois.

A similar agriculture ruling late in 1942 received more attention. In *Wickard v. Filburn* the Court upheld the Second Agricultural Adjustment Act of 1938 and its enforcement against Roscoe C. Filburn, a small Ohio farmer who used his entire crop of wheat for food, feed, or seed, selling none of it. But he sowed 12 acres more than authorized by the government, yielding 239 bushels, upon which the government imposed a penalty of 49 cents per bushel.[109] A unanimous Court reasoned that Filburn and thousands of other small farmers who consumed their own grain were depressing market demand and thus the price of wheat, so the commerce clause could be invoked. The *Wall Street Journal* lamented:

> What a long way we have travelled since Gibbons vs. Ogden! . . . The average citizen . . . may well wonder whether in the simple routine of his day he may not find himself engaged in "interstate commerce" at any moment that Congress decides to say so. Is this what Assistant Attorney General Thurman Arnold had in mind when a few years ago he characterized the Constitution as a collection of "myths and folklore"?[110]

The *New York Times* agreed, if more soberly:

> If the farmer who grows feed for consumption on his own farm competes with commerce, would not the housewife who makes herself a dress do so equally? . . . The net of the ruling, in short, seems to be that Congress can regulate every form of economic activity if it so decides, a decision that may be of considerable

importance in view of our increasing trend toward a regulated economy.[111]

In a different sphere, the Stone Court upheld the federal regulation of broadcast companies. Chain broadcasting regulations issued by the Federal Communications Commission under the Communications Act of 1934 were challenged by the National Broadcasting Co. and the Columbia Broadcasting System, Inc. But the Court ruled, 5-2, that the rules were issued under a valid congressional delegation of legislative authority, and that the commission's regulatory and broadcast-station licensing powers, governed by the "public interest, convenience, or necessity," were not unconstitutionally vague and indefinite.[112]

The story was well covered, notably by the Associated Press:

> Of the six commission regulations the one most strongly attacked by NBC and CBS in a long and thus far losing fight was that restricting the system by which the radio chains obtained exclusive options from hundreds of American stations to clear [broadcast] their big national programs on arranged schedules.

The story went on to explain that the two companies wanted to sell commercial time to advertisers with a promise of uniform, nationwide exposure, and so objected to the FCC rule that allowed individual stations to sell that option time to other sponsors. The AP also reported testy reactions from NBC and CBS. They suggested that congressional amendment of the Communications Act might be in order. But a third radio network, the Mutual Broadcasting System, expressed satisfaction.[113]

Following the story well, the *Wall Street Journal* wrote a day later:

The broadcasting industry was ready to take initial steps yesterday to conform to the Supreme Court's Monday decision, one of the most important in radio's history. . . . One important factor to N.B.C. and C.B.S. was that the Commission has indicated that it will allow ample time, probably up to a year, for adjustment of contracts between the networks and their affiliates.[114]

The *Chicago Daily Tribune* applauded the Court's decision, calling NBC and CBS "arrogant and domineering."[115] However, in what today would be considered a breach of journalistic ethics, the paper failed to note in its editorial that it stood to benefit from the ruling as the owner of an independent radio station, WGN.

THE VINSON COURT CONFRONTS THE PRESIDENT

Chief Justice Stone died in 1946, after only five years on the job. To replace him President Harry S. Truman selected Fred Vinson, fifty-six years old, a former New Deal congressman and federal appellate judge who had held a variety of positions in the wartime Roosevelt administration, followed by a stint as postwar secretary of the Treasury under Truman. In the most significant test of federal power during his seven-year term, Vinson dissented from the Court's 1952 ruling against the president's seizure of the steel industry during the Korean War.[116] The issue gripped the nation. To avert a strike scheduled by the United Steelworkers of America, Truman directed his secretary of commerce to take control of the mills and keep them operating. The steelmakers cooperated but filed suit, and the dispute moved quickly to the Supreme Court.

When the Court ruled the seizure unconstitutional, denying the "inherent power" claimed by the president, newspapers blared banner headlines and covered every angle of the epic struggle: the justices' majority and minority opinions, gratification expressed by steel executives, reactions of members of Congress and other citizens, implications for the economy and the conduct of the war. The *Wall Street Journal* captured the momentous courtroom scene during the justices' reading of their several opinions:

> But the bulkiest of the lot was the dissenting opinion, a 44-page affair offered by Chief Justice Vinson. He read it with considerable force—shaking a pencil frequently and appearing red-faced and angry. . . .
>
> The justices spent more than two hours reading their opinions to a courtroom packed with industry, union and Government lawyers and other spectators. Almost 200 more would-be spectators waited outside the courtroom in the hope of being admitted to hear the historic decision.[117]

Editorials published immediately were so thoughtful that they might have been drafted in anticipation of the ruling. Some took an appropriate long view and are still worth quoting a half-century later.

The *Los Angeles Times:*

> The Supreme Court's holding, 6 to 3, that President Truman acted illegally when he seized the steel industry will go down among the great historic decisions of that court.
>
> It is a rebuff to the Truman administration, and to President Truman personally, such as has not been given since a unanimous Supreme Court decided the National Industrial Recovery Act was unconstitutional back in the early days of the Roosevelt administration. . . .

This is believed to have been the first decision ever made by the Supreme Court on the inherent powers of the Presidency. The reason for this may be that no President, prior to Harry S. Truman, ever asserted that he had such inherent powers.[118]

The *New York Times:*

> Under this opinion the trend toward an indefinite expansion of the Chief Executive's authority is deliberately checked. There can be no legitimate answer to that decision except a new decision or an amendment to the Constitution. For a decision of the Supreme Court is, under our system of government, the Constitution.[119]

The *Washington Post:*

> It is noteworthy that the majority includes two former Attorneys General—Justices Jackson and Clark. Neither could stomach the "inherent power" arguments of Administration spokesmen.... [Vinson's dissent] is unimpressive.... This is dangerous doctrine. It is a rationale for the President to do what he thinks necessary irrespective of what the Constitution or Congress say. Stripped of its gilding, it is a formula for executive dictatorship.[120]

THE WARREN COURT CHECKS CONGRESS

Under Chief Justice Earl Warren (1953–69), the Supreme Court became known for its exaltation of constitutional rights, but at least one decision of the Warren Court restricted an important aspect of federal power: the congressional power to investigate. In *Watkins v. United States* the Court invoked the Fifth Amendment's guarantee of due process of law[121] to set aside a contempt-of-Congress conviction.[122] It held that Congress does not have the authority to expose individuals' private affairs unless clearly justified by a legitimate congressional function, and that it may not engage in law enforcement or trial-like processes to determine guilt. On the same day, the Court reversed the federal convictions of fourteen California Communists on charges of advocating the overthrow of the government,[123] and it set aside the State Department's dismissal of a foreign service officer for alleged disloyalty.[124] The decisions prompted the *New York Times*'s James B. Reston to write:

> WASHINGTON, June 17—The Supreme Court today warned all branches of the Government that they must be more faithful to the constitutional guarantees of individual freedom. . . . [T]he court . . . is asserting that the Legislative and Executive Branches of the Government and the lower courts must be more sensitive to procedures that may affect a citizen's liberties or good name.[125]

By the early 1960s the reach of federal power in its broadest constitutional sense—under the contracts clause, the commerce clause, the taxing power, and the necessary and proper clause—was generally well settled. By contrast, future Supreme Court cases invoking or challenging federal authority would involve primarily the Bill of Rights, the due process and equal protection guarantees of the Fourteenth Amendment, and regulatory powers granted by statute. Press coverage of these cases will be considered in the next four chapters.

Newspaper coverage of the Supreme Court, too, was well settled by the early 1960s. Though most newspapers did not closely monitor the Court's docket and decisions, the *New York*

Times and the *Washington Post* did. The *Wall Street Journal* and the Washington *Evening Star,* a fine afternoon paper that later folded, provided steady coverage as well. Reliably good stories by the experienced, full-time reporters of the Associated Press and United Press International (UPI) enabled any paper to provide its readers with good coverage of the Court, depending on individual editors' judgment.

THE BURGER COURT CHECKS THE PRESIDENT

Under Chief Justice Warren Burger (1969–86) the Court, rather than grappling with questions about the extent of federal power,[126] settled some intramural clashes of authority within the government. Of these, none was more important than the question of whether the president could withhold recordings of his office conversations under an extravagant claim of almost unlimited power termed "executive privilege." This was *United States v. Nixon,* the 1974 case that led directly to Nixon's resignation in disgrace for his cover-up of the Watergate burglary.[127] In its opinion the Court recognized a presumption of executive immunity and privilege, but ruled unanimously that Nixon was not above the law in this dispute and ordered him to turn over the audiotapes to a special prosecutor appointed to investigate the matter. The tapes revealed Nixon's personal involvement in the cover-up, and he stepped down.

Major newspapers ran several stories each on the momentous decision and its ramifications, including the text of the opinion or portions of it, and approving editorials that explored both the law and the politics of the messy situation. The *Los Angeles Times:*

The strength of the position taken by the Supreme Court goes to the fundamental problem of maintaining what the court itself called "the constitutional balance of 'a workable government.'" This balance would be impaired, and with it the rule of the courts, according to the justices, if they had sustained Mr. Nixon's claim for "an absolute, unqualified presidential privilege of immunity from judicial process under all circumstances." Nothing in the whole Watergate affair has been more disturbing than the evidence of abuses of power, abuses which have tended to disrupt the balance of authority in government. This decision will help restore that balance.[128]

THE REHNQUIST COURT AND FEDERALISM

Questions of federal authority arose under Chief Justice William Rehnquist (1986–2005), not in regard to extensions of national power but in the context of federalism, the relationship between the federal government and the states. Rehnquist favored the states. Thus the Rehnquist Court, especially after the appointments of conservative Justices Antonin Scalia (by President Ronald Reagan) in 1986 and Clarence Thomas (by President George H. W. Bush) in 1991, applied a view of federalism that trimmed federal authority in various respects.

In 2001 the Court rejected a contention by the U.S. Army Corps of Engineers that its jurisdiction over navigable waters extended to ponds in an abandoned sand and gravel pit not connected to other waters but used occasionally by migratory waterfowl.[129] The Corps contended the birds were protected under its own Migratory Bird Rule, issued under the Clean Water Act.

A consortium of twenty-three Chicago suburbs wanted to fill a small portion of the huge pit and use it for the disposal of solid waste packaged in protective bales. Although the state of Illinois had approved the meticulously engineered plan, the Corps of Engineers denied a permit. However, the Supreme Court ruled that the agency's interpretation of "navigable waters," long justified under the commerce clause, was unreasonably broad. Chief Justice Rehnquist wrote for a five-member majority that permitting "federal jurisdiction over ponds and mudflats falling within the 'Migratory Bird Rule' would result in a significant impingement of the States' traditional and primary power over land and water use."[130] Four justices dissented.

The press attributed considerable importance to the decision. The *Christian Science Monitor* reported: "Business groups and local governments applaud the court ruling, which effectively returned oversight to the states. But environmental groups worry that many hard-fought federal protections are being swept away as the court continues to erode federal power."[131] Comments were as divided as the Court itself. The *Atlanta Journal and Constitution* called the decision "a sensible ruling made on the legal merits of the case, protecting local governments' reasonable land-use options and resisting the emotional extremism of those who not only would welcome a fed at every whiskey-barrel water garden, but are convinced the federal Clean Water Act should govern your bath water, too."[132] But the *Capital Times* of Madison, Wisconsin, fretted that the ruling "could wipe out protection for more than 4 million acres of Wisconsin wetlands, a state official says."[133]

In a peculiar test of executive authority, a closely watched 2005 case involving Vice President Dick Cheney was effectively decided in his favor.[134] The Court, by 7-2, declined to require Cheney, as head of an energy policy task force making recommendations to the president, to disclose its records in accordance with the Federal Advisory Committee Act. The Court remanded the case for determination of a separation-of-powers defense raised by Cheney.

The case had gained special notoriety because there was widespread suspicion that representatives of oil refiners and other companies not members of the task force had participated in its meetings, and also because while the case was pending before the Court Justice Scalia had gone hunting with the vice president. Asked to recuse himself, Scalia declined, and voted with the majority.

Despite the years-long controversy, coverage of the decision was spotty. Network evening news treatment varied from three minutes and forty seconds on Fox to nothing on NBC. ABC and Fox referred vaguely to "special considerations" in the case, but CBS described the essence of the dispute.[135] Gina Holland of the Associated Press crafted a fine lead for her story, which unfortunately was not widely picked up by newspapers, and not featured when it was:

> WASHINGTON, June 24 (AP)—The Supreme Court protected the Bush administration Thursday from having to reveal potentially embarrassing details about Vice President Dick Cheney's energy task force until after the election, sending the case back to a lower court and noting a "paramount necessity of protecting the executive branch from vexatious litigation."[136]

Even the *New York Times* relegated the high-profile dispute to page A19, while editorializing that the holding was "unfortunate" and "likely to frustrate" the Federal Advisory Committee Act's purpose of public monitoring of "the influences exerted on government policy makers."[137]

It must be noted here that the Rehnquist Court uncharacteristically opted for federal supremacy in its most momentous decision, *Bush v. Gore*,[138] which we will consider in chapter 10 on voting rights.

THE ROBERTS COURT SEES THINGS FEDERALLY

John G. Roberts, Jr., highly experienced in Supreme Court advocacy as a government lawyer and private practitioner, and a former federal appellate judge and onetime law clerk to Chief Justice Rehnquist, was appointed by President George W. Bush to succeed Rehnquist when he died in 2005. Only fifty years old, Roberts became the youngest chief justice in more than 200 years. The Roberts Court soon gained a reputation for strengthening the authority of the federal government and especially of its executive branch.

In 2008 the Court, confronting a novel test of federal authority in *Winter v. Natural Resources Defense Council,* sided with the U.S. Navy when an environmental group obtained an injunction limiting ships' use of sonar in training exercises off southern California in waters containing at least thirty-seven species of marine mammals, including dolphins, whales, and sea lions.[139] The Court held, 6–3, that the navy's failure to prepare an environmental impact statement, sought by environmental groups, did not constitute a violation of the National Environmental Policy Act of 1969. The majority opinion by Chief Justice Roberts stated that "there is no basis for enjoining such training in a manner credibly alleged to pose a serious threat to national security." He quoted President Theodore Roosevelt as saying that "the only way in which a navy can ever be made efficient is by practice at sea."[140] But Justice Ruth Bader Ginsburg, in dissent, quoted the navy's own environmental assessment as predicting "substantial and irreparable harm to marine animals."[141]

Although the confrontation of dolphins and the United States Navy had gained substantial prior media coverage and considerable public interest, when the Court's decision came down it did not get priority news attention. In the evening news broadcasts NBC and CBS gave it twenty seconds each, and ABC a minute and forty seconds well down in the broadcast. On the Public Broadcasting System the *NewsHour with Jim Lehrer* devoted far more attention to a Supreme Court oral argument that day in a religious monument controversy,[142] but regular PBS visitor Marcia Coyle of the *National Law Journal* concisely summarized Chief Justice Roberts's opinion in *Winter:* "Yes, there may be harm to marine mammals, but top senior officials of the Navy said that, under these restrictions, the Navy cannot prepare, cannot train for war, cannot protect national security. He said it was not a close question which interest should prevail."[143]

Even a leading California newspaper, the *San Francisco Chronicle,* put *Winter* in the Metro section.[144] Editorial comment was muted. "The court struck a reasonable balance," said the *Washington Post.*[145]

The multitude of Supreme Court rulings that determined the scope of federal power, and thus the nature of our country, is the longest trail we follow in this book, for it began first and still continues today, if in less critical manifestations. What the Court has wrought, especially under John Marshall, is history well appreciated. But this look at news coverage, often slow and limited in the nineteenth century, sporadically good and weak in the twentieth, opens a new door on our understanding of the waxing of our nation. What did the public know? From the start the Court underestimated, indeed misunderstood, the need for good press coverage to communicate and explain its decisions. It habitually dropped clusters of significant decisions in great globs on the press at the end of each term. Not until the 1920s did the Court begin to regularly provide timely printed copies of its opinions. In the mid-twentieth century the Court began to record its oral arguments but kept the practice secret, only recently releasing occasionally an audiotape after an especially newsworthy case is heard. Today the Court, lagging far behind the state supreme courts, still shuns the public enlightenment of television cameras. More on this later.

The press, too, fell short, especially in the nineteenth century as the Supreme Court was slowly constructing the legal framework of a powerful national government, while at the same time, as we shall see, consistently denigrating human rights. Early Court coverage sometimes consisted of publishing the text of an important opinion, but it usually wanted summarization and explanation to call it journalism. That is still what is required of good Supreme Court journalism, and the 24-hour news cycle puts greater pressure than ever on reporters to get it right and get it out—fast. We will explore this further as we proceed.

EIGHT

STRUGGLING OVER SLAVERY AND INDIVIDUAL RIGHTS

From the beginning the Supreme Court tolerated slavery. Although no case challenging the institution of slavery came before the Marshall Court, Marshall himself was known to be hostile to slavery,[1] and his Court did hand down one decision at variance with the "property, not persons" rule later enunciated by Roger Taney in the Dred Scott case. In a civil lawsuit seeking damages for four slaves lost in a Kentucky boating accident, Marshall held that slaves were intelligent beings and thus more akin to passengers than cargo, meaning the ship operator could be held liable only if gross neglect were found, which it was not.[2] The decision was briefly noted in the press, but without explication or comment. More significantly, though the case was unrelated to slavery, the Marshall Court handed down a major constitutional ruling that the guarantees of the Bill of Rights applied only against the federal government.[3] Observing this precedent, the Taney Court (1835–64) usually deferred to state law on slavery issues—except when that law favored the slaves.

After the Civil War, Supreme Court decisions shamelessly eviscerated the three postwar amendments for more than a half-century. Alongside these discriminatory rulings, commencing in the 1880s, came others against Chinese immigrants, then against other peoples of color drawn under U.S. rule during the nation's imperial period, and later, World War II rulings against Japanese Americans.

In the clarity of historical hindsight, it's not a pretty picture. A ripe target for high-minded journalists? We shall see. This chapter also looks at the coverage of later Court decisions applying constitutional freedoms in such diverse realms as national security, the rights of the criminally accused, and the rights of post-9/11 detainees.

The Taney Court decided several slavery cases, always supporting domestic slavery and the internal slave trade with various legal reasoning. When a Mississippi constitutional amendment forbidding the importation of slaves into the state for sale was not implemented by a statute, the Court held the amendment was not self-enforcing, and thus validated a slave importer's note given for imported slaves.[4] When the federal Fugitive Slave Act of 1793, requiring the return of escaped slaves, conflicted with the law of Pennsylvania, a free state, the Court opted for the federal statute, despite the justices' usual preference for state law.[5] Federal priority was reaffirmed in a civil suit against an Underground Railroad conductor accused of sheltering a fugitive slave.[6] In another case, two Kentucky slaves who had spent time in Ohio, a free state, relied on that fact to claim permanent freedom, but the Taney Court held that Kentucky law governed over the law of Ohio.[7]

Neither the Northern nor the Southern press took much notice of these decisions. The first case, *Groves v. Slaughter,* was overshadowed by the Court's decision in that of the *Amistad,* which set free fifty-three African slaves who had taken over their Spanish ship and found themselves in New London, Connecticut. Former President John Quincy Adams passionately pleaded their cause in the Supreme Court, drawing attention to the case. The Court ruled that the Africans were not cargo and thus not required to be returned under a 1795 treaty with Spain.[8] The Kentucky case, *Strader v. Graham,* elicited a comment from a Mississippi paper that the pro-slavery result "will probably give general satisfaction to the bar and the country."[9] But the *Liberator,* of Boston, concurred in a comment attributed to Daniel Webster that *Strader* was "not a respectable decision."[10]

The world was watching when, in 1857, as the nation seethed over the slavery question, the Taney Court came down hard on Dred Scott.[11] He was a slave in Missouri who had lived temporarily (with his master, an army surgeon) in Illinois, a free state, and in western territory where slavery was forbidden by the Missouri Compromise of 1820. He returned to Missouri voluntarily, then sued for his freedom under a Missouri principle of "once free, always free," which the Missouri Supreme Court abandoned to rule Scott still a slave. The Taney Court affirmed. By a vote of seven (five were Southerners) to two, it held that the slavery prohibition of the Missouri Compromise was unconstitutional (the first overturn of a federal statute since *Marbury v. Madison* in 1803), that Scott was property protected by the Constitution, that he was not a citizen of the United States entitled to sue in its courts, and that therefore his status was governed by the courts of Missouri.

The decision is seen in historic terms as having exacerbated the sectional struggle over slavery and contributed to the start of the Civil War three years later. But at the time, most newspapers expressed no sense of imminent cataclysm. In the South, the stories were straightforward and factual, mentioning and even publishing the two dissenting opinions (whose reading Taney delayed by a day), and editorial comment was restrained but certain. The *Charleston Mercury* was especially gratified by the Court's voiding of the Missouri Compromise's prohibition of slavery in the territories, declaring confidently that "henceforth slavery in the Territories is an issue which must be decided by the laws of climate, products, races, and the natural laws of our population and migration; for Congress henceforth can have nothing to do with the subject."[12]

But there was a sense of triumph, too. Playing on the South's longtime contention that states could nullify obnoxious federal statutes, the *Fayetteville Observer* took pleasure in reporting: "The decision has produced a sensation at the North. The Republicans in the N.Y. Legislature have already a resolution to 'consider the decision.' We suppose they will resolve that it is not law, and should be nullified."[13]

In the North, some newspapers seemed relieved. The *Pittsfield Sun* editorialized: "If the sectional question be not now settled then we may despair of the Republic. We believe it is settled, and that henceforth sectionalism will cease to be a dangerous element in our political contests."[14] But most Northern papers were at least indignant. The *New-York Daily Times* praised the dissenting opinions as "among the proudest monuments of the Court," contending that they "completely annihilated the positions of the majority."[15] The *Milwaukee Daily Sentinel* dubbed the decision "this enormous heresy" and declared that the Court "dishonored itself and the age and our free institutions."[16]

There were a few ominous comments, too. The *New York Herald* exclaimed: "No sooner does the fire threaten to go out for want of fuel than this Supreme Court appears, and loads the embers with dry combustible material."[17] The *Whig and Courier,* of Bangor, Maine, warned: "That the decision will reopen the slavery question, in a form, too, more bitter and dangerous than we have yet seen it brought forward, there can be little doubt."[18]

The *Lowell Daily Citizen and News* managed to find humor in disappointment: "All the great men of former times, Jefferson, Madison, Marshall, Adams, Clay, Jackson, Webster, who believed the Missouri Compromise constitutional, were fools! John C. Calhoun was the only wise man in history!"[19]

CHIEF JUSTICE CHASE: A DIFFERENT VIEW

The political opposite of Taney, his successor Salmon P. Chase (1864–73), advocated equal rights for the former slaves, but his court was divided on both civil rights and postwar Reconstruction issues. Chase dissented when the Court upheld a prewar slave purchase contract and later upheld the Illinois Supreme Court's rejection of a qualified white woman's application to practice law.[20] The latter was one of the Court's first interpretations of the Fourteenth Amendment, adopted in 1868; its "privileges and immunities" clause did not confer a right to practice law, the Court ruled.[21] The case was little reported, but the *Boston Daily Advertiser* noted with approbation:

> Mr. Justice Bradley, in an eloquent opinion, cited the common and civil law, the law of nature, and divine law, to prove that it was never intended that women should practise law, but that women's sphere was her home and she violated all law in endeavoring to force her way into professional and public life.[22]

WAITE COURT DENIES THE POSTWAR AMENDMENTS

Chase's successor as chief justice, Morrison R. Waite of Ohio (1874–88), represented another turnaround of Supreme Court leadership on issues of civil rights. Fifty-seven years old when plucked from relative obscurity by President Ulysses S. Grant, Waite favored state authority over federal, and he took a narrow view of the rights granted by the post–Civil War amendments. In fact, his court ran roughshod over them.

In April 1873, following a hotly contested gubernatorial election, sixty-two or more former slaves assembled at a courthouse in Colfax, Louisiana, were killed and mutilated by a well-organized white mob. It became known as the Colfax Massacre. Ninety-eight men were indicted for violations of the Negroes' constitutional rights and the Enforcement Act of 1870, which prescribed criminal penalties for denials of those rights.[23] A mere three men were convicted but asked the Supreme Court to dismiss their indictment. The Court did, unanimously, finding that the indictment failed to allege properly the denial of federal rights. The opinion by Chief Justice Waite made no mention of the massacre.[24]

Southern newspapers looked kindly on the decision. "At last the United States Supreme Court ... has pronounced the Enforcement act, commonly known as the Kuklux act, to be unconstitutional," wrote the *Galveston Daily News,* of Houston, in only a slight overstatement.[25] In fact, in another decision that same day, the Court did rule a key section of the Enforcement Act unconstitutional.[26] Looking at both cases, the *Constitution,* of Atlanta, affirmed: "It is not claimed that these tardy decisions go as far as they should, but they are at least an important advance in the right direction."[27]

Even some Northern papers, concerned that the federal government had indeed sought to encroach on legitimate state law-enforcement authority, expressed satisfaction. "The decisions of the Supreme Court on the Enforcement Act come very opportunely to settle certain controverted points on the subject of State rights," the *Boston Daily Globe* declared, predicting that as such questions came before the Court in the future, "there is no reason for doubting that its decisions will be cheerfully accepted and acquiesced in by the people of the whole country."[28]

The *New York Times* gushed:

> The decisions deal with constitutional questions of the highest order, and deal with them in a way to render still more firm the confidence of the people in the impartiality and wisdom of the court, and to enhance the value of that department of the Government as a means of securing the rights of citizens.[29]

The Waite Court went on to rule that a Louisiana statute requiring nondiscrimination in public transportation was unconstitutional because it interfered with Congress's authority to regulate interstate commerce,[30] that the consistent absence of colored people from a county's juries trying cases against colored defendants did not constitute a violation of the Fourteenth Amendment's guarantee of equal protection under the law,[31] and that the federal Civil Rights Act of 1875, barring discrimination in public accommodations, transportation, and amusements, was an unconstitutional encroachment on individual conduct because the Fourteenth Amendment limited only state action.[32]

In this last case the sole dissenter was Justice John Marshall Harlan, who frequently found himself in the minority in his thirty-four years on the Court (1877–1911), but whose positions (e.g., his dissent in *Plessy*) were later adopted by Court majorities in a number of important decisions. He had not yet written his opinion when the decision was announced, merely stating his dissent. But a month later the *Los Angeles Times,* recognizing the strength of his argument, ran on page one a long excerpt from his dissent, in which he argued that Congress had authority to "protect colored people against deprivation on account of their race of any civil rights enjoyed by other freemen in a State." Furthermore, Harlan declared, "railroad corporations, keepers of inns and managers of places of public amusement are agents of the State, because amenable to public regulation and a denial by these instrumentalities, to a citizen because of his race of that quality of civil rights secured him by law is a denial of his civil rights by the States."[33] This statement remarkably foretold a public accommodations provision of the Civil Rights Act of 1964, which of course passed constitutional muster.

Press reaction to this case was mostly ho-hum. The *Milwaukee Daily Journal* commented placidly, "The decision is at once important and interesting and will give rise to many discussions and theories before it is settled. At best, the negro takes a long stride backwards to-day."[34] A *New York Times* correspondent reported laconically from Washington that the "general opinion" of "public men here" was that "the view of the Supreme Court would not entail any hardship on the colored people or deprive them of any privileges which they have enjoyed since the war."[35] The *North American,* of Philadelphia, declared indifferently, "The decisions of the Supreme Court yesterday that the provisions of the Civil Rights bill by which Congress gave to colored people privileges in excess of those possessed by white citizens are unconstitutional will perhaps surprise some people, but it will hardly offend anybody."[36] On the other hand, the *Atlanta Constitution* celebrated the decision with "deep and perfect satisfaction."[37]

THE FULLER COURT DEFERS TO THE STATES

The Morrison Waite view of civil rights, deferring to the states, was perpetuated under Chief Justice Melville Fuller (1888–1910). In the words of Fuller biographer James W. Ely, Jr.,

> Although the Fuller Court was willing to give heightened protection to the rights of property owners and the operation of the national market, the justices were generally unconcerned with guarding other asserted rights from government regulation. Hence the Supreme Court during Fuller's tenure displayed little sympathy for the claims of racial minorities, women, criminal defendants, dissidents, or individuals who breached accepted codes of moral behavior.[38]

The Fuller Court upheld a series of statutes restricting the immigration and reentry of Chinese after many had flooded into the West for mining and railroad construction jobs since mid-century. In San Francisco particularly, where an estimated 50,000 Chinese immigrants lived, hostility toward them had arisen. Although a restrictive 1888 statute conflicted with U.S.-Chinese treaty obligations, the Court declared unanimously that the treaties did not deprive Congress of the authority to exclude Chinese laborers.[39] Four years later the Court, by 6–3 (the chief justice dissented in this one), upheld a new statute that required Chinese laborers to obtain a certificate of residence, on penalty of summary deportation.[40]

Newspapers engaged this last case energetically with full reports of the majority and minority opinions, reactions to the decision, and a variety of thoughtful editorial opinions. From San Francisco the Associated Press reported that the ruling "created great excitement among the Celestials, who gathered in groups about their bulletin boards and jabbered in the most excited manner. . . . The Chinese vice consul . . . said . . . 'It will be a great blow to business in Chinatown.' "[41] In Boston, "Chinatown was deeply moved last night," reported the *Boston Daily Globe,* referring to that city's own Chinese community. The paper quoted one "Chinaman," a member of a Baptist church choir, as saying, "We are tired of this constant haggling about us. We don't want to stay here if we are not wanted." And a Methodist minister recently returned from Asia declared: "It is a shame for this government to abuse the Chinese. I would be an ingrate if I did not lift up my voice and demand that they receive as least as fair treatment as the scum of the other nations that comes to our shores."[42]

Some papers questioned whether the ruling could be enforced, saying that the deportation of 100,000 unregistered Chinese would cost $16,000,000, far beyond the funds available. Although its headline blared, "Now They Leave," the *Galveston Daily News,* of Houston, speculated that "it is hardly probable that the next congress will appropriate the enormous sums required." The *News* also noted concerns about possible retaliation against American missionaries and others in China, but said, "the News correspondent is informed at the state department that the Chinese government has so far shown the broadest generosity in the matter and has given this government to understand that whatever may be its course the government has no idea of retaliatory measures."[43] The *Chicago Daily Tribune* opined that there would be no enforcement problem because "most of them . . . will hunt up their witnesses and prove that they are entitled to certificates."[44] The *Milwaukee Journal* faulted both the Court majority and Congress, commenting that "the minority opinion of the supreme court on the Chinese registration act is very popular. There has been a great revulsion of feeling on the subject and now most people believe that the new law was not warranted."[45]

There was no such journalistic indignation, however, when the Fuller Court took a similar hard line against the former slaves, ruling that a Mississippi separate-but-equal railroad accommodations statute constituted no burden on interstate commerce, a holding directly counter to an earlier decision of the Waite Court on a Louisiana statute.[46] Six years later the Court handed down *Plessy v. Ferguson,* which would stand for more than half a century.[47] Writing for a majority of seven, Justice Henry Billings Brown said the Louisiana statute in question did not suggest one race was inferior, it was just that one race chose to see it that way. Justice Harlan dissented in immortal terms, declaring "our Constitution is color-blind."[48]

In newspapers the *Plessy* ruling, remarkably, was lost in the Supreme Court's end-of-term tide of decisions. North and South it received mostly routine, brief, straightforward coverage, and little editorial comment. But the *Atchison Daily Globe,* in Kansas, declared: "The whites and blacks will not mix, whatever the law may say they must do. The fourteenth amendment was adopted when there was a good deal of patriotism on the surface; the late decision comes nearer representing the actual necessities of the case."[49] The *Atlanta Constitution* editorialized:

> Such a thing as mixing the whites and blacks together in the same coaches cannot be required in reason. The people of the northern states but rarely come in contact with the negro, and for that reason but little objection is raised in that section.... [T]he negro himself ... is thoroughly satisfied with the custom which is universally observed by southern railroads.[50]

However, the *Boston Daily Globe* reported that in a meeting of the Colored National League there was considerable criticism. One Rev. W. H. Scott exclaimed, "It is useless for a colored man to aspire to be anything in this country. I am now training my boys to speak Spanish, so they can go to South America or some other country, where ability and not color is a test for advancement."[51]

Between 1901 and 1904 the Fuller Court handed down more than a dozen rulings, known as the Insular Cases, holding that the Constitution and therefore the Bill of Rights did not apply in U.S. territories, notably the islands acquired in the Spanish–American War of 1898. In one of these rulings the Court, by 5-4 with the chief justice in dissent, sustained a manslaughter conviction in Hawaii while recognizing that the prosecution, which involved an indictment not handed up by a grand jury, and a conviction by only nine of twelve jurors, did not meet the standards of the Fifth Amendment (due process of law) and the Sixth Amendment (fair trial). Justice Henry Billings Brown wrote improbably: "[T]he two rights alleged to be violated in this case are not fundamental in their nature, but concern merely a method of procedure which sixty years of practice had shown to be suited to the conditions of the islands, and well calculated to conserve the rights of their citizens to their lives, their property and their well-being."[52] If any newspaper challenged the notion that due process and fair trial are "not fundamental," it could not be discovered.

Similarly, the Court a year later declined to require a jury trial in the case of two Manila newspaper editors convicted of criminal libel. Justice William R. Day justified an exception to the Sixth Amendment jury-trial guarantee on the ground that "the uncivilized parts of the archipelago were wholly unfitted to exercise the right of trial by jury."[53] Justice Harlan dissented vigorously in both the Hawaii and Philippines cases, calling the denial of the jury-trial right "utterly revolting" and asserting: "No power exists in the judiciary to suspend the operation of the Constitution in any territory governed, as to its affairs and people, by authority of the United States."[54]

Newspapers reported the Philippines jury-trial case and prominently noted Harlan's forceful dissent. "No Trial by Jury in the Philippines," headlined the *New York Times*.[55] The *Atlanta Constitution* railed: "Surely we have fallen upon evil times so far as our boasted constitutional liberties are concerned." Identifying the two convicted editors as "natives of the United States" and "fellow-citizens of ours," the paper exclaimed, "Here are the bitter fruits of imperialism with a vengeance!" and quoted Harlan at length.[56] It was a high-water mark of press scrutiny of the Fuller Court's decisions on individual rights.

THE WHITE COURT: WHAT FIRST AMENDMENT?

Individual rights fared no better under Chief Justice Edward Douglass White (1910–21). The Court ignored a due-process claim from a Georgia business owner convicted in a circus atmosphere of murdering a thirteen-year-old female employee,[57] upheld another state separate-but-equal railroad law (on the ground that the plaintiffs had not actually tested it),[58] and sustained another newspaper contempt-of-court conviction for editorial criticism of a court, over a claim of freedom of the press.[59] Again, newspapers reported but acquiesced.

The most important civil rights decisions by the White Court were its four post–World War I decisions overriding First Amendment claims of free speech and free press to sustain convictions under the 1917 Espionage Act, which forbade obstruction of military recruiting,[60] or under the 1918 Sedition Act, which banned publications intended to hinder the war effort.[61] The decisions were prominently covered, but rather briefly. Some papers quoted portions of Justice Oliver Wendell Holmes's eloquent *Abrams* dissent, which gained historical stature: "the ultimate good desired is better reached by free trade in ideas—that the best test of truth is the power of the thought to get itself accepted in the competition of the market."[62] But, sadly, the convictions were quickly subsumed in anxious press coverage of several conflicting trial-court rulings on whether the recently passed Volstead prohibition-enforcement act was constitutional, a question of great national concern that Chief Justice White agreed to consider promptly.[63]

TAFT COURT EXTENDS THE FIRST AMENDMENT

Under Chief Justice William Howard Taft (1921–30) the Supreme Court weighed constitutional rights against convictions under state sedition laws. One case was particularly important. *Gitlow v. New York* affirmed the conviction of Benjamin Gitlow, a former member of the New York legislature, for violation of New York's Criminal Anarchy Law, which prohibited advocating the violent overthrow of the government.[64] Gitlow had published in a Socialist newspaper a "manifesto" calling for mass revolutionary action to overthrow the government. Nevertheless, in its opinion the Court for the first time held that Bill of Rights protections apply against the states, by virtue of the due process clause of the Fourteenth Amendment. Here the Court referred only to the First Amendment freedoms of free speech and free press, but this process of "incorporation," as it came to be called, continues to the present day, with major ramifications for state trials and other actions.[65]

The decision was significant as well for another memorable dissent by Justice Holmes, who, joined by Justice Louis Brandeis, argued that the law should distinguish between inflammatory words and criminal actions, which were not alleged against Gitlow. His article, Holmes declared in one of many quotable phrases, "had no chance of starting a present conflagration."[66] This minority view, too, had legs; it would be adopted by the Supreme Court in the 1960s.

In a story that was widely used, the Associated Press reported *Gitlow* with extensive quotations and views of both sides. Justice Edward Sanford for the majority of seven: "the freedom of speech and of the press . . . does not confer an absolute right to speak or publish, without responsibility." Justice Holmes: "there was no present danger of an attempt to overthrow the government by force on the part of the admittedly small minority who shared the defendant's views."[67] The *New York Times,* in its own extensive story on page one, highlighted the Holmes dissent, but commented editorially, "Revolutionists retain their old privilege of perishing gloriously in arms, but they can't incite others to perish and hope to get off themselves scot free."[68] The *Carroll* (Iowa) *Times* rebutted the dissent, arguing that even if Gitlow's "utterances" posed no immediate danger, "there is such a thing as a moral peril in addition to one merely physical. . . . [T]he revolutionists must be prepared to undergo the penalty of failure."[69]

It is noteworthy that the majority opinion's application of the First Amendment against the states, though a pronounced transformation of well-established Supreme Court doctrine, went unnoticed by the press. Two years later, when the Court upheld a California criminal syndicalism law directed against the Industrial Workers of the World, again overriding a due process–First Amendment dissent by Holmes and Brandeis, the newspapers yawned.[70]

STONEWALLING JAPANESE AMERICANS

During the brief tenure of Chief Justice Harlan Fiske Stone (1941–46), the Supreme Court dealt with challenges to the World War II forcible relocation and internment of more than 100,000 Japanese nationals and Japanese Americans on the West Coast. These actions were first ordered by President Franklin Roosevelt in February 1942. Half a century later, an apologetic United States paid $1,600,000,000 in reparations to 82,000 surviving internees or their heirs. The Stone Court first upheld curfews imposed on the Japanese Americans.[71] Then a year later the Court sustained their detention in *Korematsu v. United States,* though in a separate case it revoked the detention of one young native-born American, Mitsuye Endo, who worked in the California Department of Motor Vehicles, and whose brother was in the U.S. Army.[72] These decisions were announced in December 1944, one day after the Roosevelt administration announced it would end the internment, and they may have been delayed in deference to the president's decision.[73]

The opinions, resembling those in the post–World War I sedition cases, are devoid of considerations of personal freedom and constitutional rights, focusing instead on war powers and military judgments, upholding both. However, three justices dissented forcefully in *Korematsu.* Frank Murphy called the prosecution of Fred Korematsu, also a native-born U.S. citizen, and who had tried unsuccessfully to enlist in the navy, "a clear violation of constitutional rights."

Korematsu, the most important decision, was given second billing or worse by some major papers. The *Los Angeles Times*'s front-page headline focused instead on *Endo:* "Supreme Court Rules Loyal Nips Held Illegally."[74] "Supreme Court Defines Rights of

Race Groups" said a fuzzy headline on page 11 of the *Chicago Daily Tribune.* The story led with a Court decision on a railroad union's discrimination against its black members,[75] then *Endo,* and last, *Korematsu.* The *Tribune* noted, as did others that day, that the government was in retreat on this matter: "The war department only yesterday revoked its order excluding Japanese from the west coast with unfavorable reaction from some congressional circles."[76]

THE VINSON COURT: RELIGION, SCHOOLS, AND HOUSING

During the chief justiceship of Fred Vinson (1946–53), questions of constitutional rights began to affect more Americans, including school children and home owners. Press coverage responded accordingly.

In 1947 a divided Court ruled that the religion clauses of the First Amendment, protecting free exercise of religion while prohibiting the establishment of a state religion, are applicable to the states through the Fourteenth Amendment (an example of "incorporation"), but it found no violation of church-state separation in a New Jersey statute's authorization for public school boards to reimburse the bus transportation costs of children attending parochial schools.[77] On the other hand, a year later, in *McCollum v. Board of Education District 71, Champaign County,* a case brought by an Illinois atheist, the Court blocked voluntary religious education in public schools as contrary to the establishment clause.[78] In a controversy closely watched as civil rights began to take hold in the public mind after World War II, the Court declared in *Shelley v. Kraemer,* actually two cases from Missouri and Michigan, that racially discriminatory restrictive covenants in real estate deeds were unenforceable, under the equal protection clause of the Fourteenth Amendment, thus opening better housing opportunities to minority buyers.[79]

The press saw nuances in the several opinions the justices wrote in *McCollum,* reflecting its sweeping implications. "Justice Frankfurter," the Associated Press reported, "in a separate opinion which in effect was a concurrence with the majority contended that each program of school–religious group co-operation stands on its own feet. He said many may be constitutionally proper. Justices Jackson, Rutledge and Burton joined in Frankfurter's argument."

The local implications were immediately explored. The *Washington Post:* "Two religious education classes in nearby Maryland will be abolished and a program of interdenominational religious education in Virginia may have to be abandoned because of the Supreme Court ruling Monday outlawing religious classes in public schools."[80] The *Chicago Daily Tribune* reported a pushback: "Dr. Roy G. Ross, general secretary of the International Council of Religious Education, yesterday proposed a three-fold program to the council's 4 denominations to meet the religious education situation created by Monday's Supreme court decision, which forbids such education in public schools."[81]

Shelley, and a related case barring restrictive-covenant enforcement in Washington, D.C.,[82] struck an even more sensitive chord with the press. The *New York Times* blanketed the story. Its page-one report pointed out prominently:

> Even though the two opinions were unanimous, they were decided by a bare legal quorum. Justices Stanley F. Reed, Robert H. Jackson and Wiley Rutledge did not participate. The assumption around the court was that one or more of them might have owned,

or were interested in, property restricted by covenants. They disqualified themselves when the cases were argued in January."[83]

As if for emphasis, Arthur Krock of the *Times* summarized the decisions in his column, portraying the result as a compliment to Chief Justice Vinson: "The clearest insight which the Chief Justice of the United States has publicly given of his legal equipment and his political philosophy is to be found in two opinions he wrote for a unanimous Supreme Court today."[84] In a separate story, the *Times* reported: "Negro and Jewish organizations and church and labor groups hailed last night the ruling of the Supreme Court forbidding use of the courts to enforce racially restrictive real estate covenants."[85]

A black-owned weekly, the *New York Amsterdam News,* thanked the Justice Department and the private civil-rights organization that provided the legal muscle behind *Shelley* and other discrimination challenges throughout the nation:

> It marks another notable achievement for the National Association for the Advancement of Colored People and its representatives on the front lines of defense of the civil rights of American citizens. To Walter White, executive secretary, Thurgood Marshall, special legal counsel, and Charles H. Houston, of Washington, are due the appreciation and gratitude of all believers in human rights.[86]

The *Washington Post* looked at an integrated neighborhood, and reported:

> White families in the 100 block of Bryant st. nw. reacted with deep disappointment and some disillusionment yesterday to the

Supreme Court ruling that stripped the armor from their racial covenants. Negro families—who now occupy all but a half dozen or more of the covenanted houses—greeted the high court decision with unbridled relief and glee. . . . At no. 136, an elderly white couple, Mr. and Mrs. Frederic Hodge, said they would keep their house as a matter of principle. The Hodges spearheaded the little group of Bryant st. owners who fought to save the covenants. "It's all over now. There's nothing to say. But we're staying right here," said Mrs. Hodge.[87]

The *Chicago Daily Tribune* reported shortly after the decision: "The first Chicago court ruling on restrictive covenants since the United States Supreme Court on Monday outlawed private agreements forbidding ownership of real estate by persons of designated race or color was made yesterday by Judge Frank M. Padden in Superior court."[88] Two days later the arch-conservative *Tribune* commented idealistically: "We do not believe that untoward incidents will arise as a consequence of the decision. If they do, the fault will lie with the churches, schools, and other agencies which have failed to perform their duty of enlightenment."[89]

THE WARREN COURT: *BROWN,* AND MORE

During the tenure of Chief Justice Earl Warren (1953–69), a deluge of Supreme Court rights-expanding decisions so angered conservatives that an outcry to remove the chief justice drew a broad audience and reverberated for years. Yet, as Warren biographer Jim Newton notes, "the decisions that launched the movement to impeach Earl Warren—the desegregation of schools, the insistence on free and fair elections at all levels of government, the curbs on prosecutions of Communists, the end to government-sponsored prayer in public schools—are such settled facts of American society that they barely stir dispute."[90]

It all started very quickly. When Warren was appointed, the justices already were wrestling with *Brown v. Board of Education,*[91] which actually denoted several cases challenging "separate-but-equal" schools. Warren, the veteran politician, worked the room patiently for months to gain unanimity on this most sensitive issue. He succeeded. On May 17, 1954, the justices unanimously overruled the Fuller Court's *Plessy v. Ferguson,*[92] declaring that separate schooling was inherently unequal and therefore violated the equal protection clause of the Fourteenth Amendment. In a remarkably brief opinion by the chief justice focusing on education rather than constitutional argument, the Court declared simply: "In these days, it is doubtful that any child may reasonably be expected to succeed in life if he is denied the opportunity of an education. Such an opportunity, where the state has undertaken to provide it, is a right which must be made available to all on equal terms."[93]

The press reflected the enormity of the decision. Newspapers and wire services played the story big, straight, and for the most part with a positive dignity. The United Press nailed it:

> Washington (UP)—The Supreme Court ruled today in an historic decision that racial segregation in public schools is unconstitutional.
>
> Speaking for a unanimous court, Chief Justice Earl Warren said education must be available to all on an equal basis.
>
> The decision, a sweeping victory for Negroes, is probably the most important in U.S. race relations since the famous Dred Scott

decision of 1857, which held that a Negro was not a citizen. The Civil War reversed that decision.[94]

Alongside its front-page story, the *Charleston* (West Virginia) *Daily Mail* editorialized:

> There is no doubt that this will cause difficulties, ill-feeling and some heartbreak. Segregation is embedded in the Constitution of West Virginia and in the minds of many people who are far from lacking in charity and breadth of outlook.... The course of those who disagree and doubt is clearly indicated: We shall continue to live, as we always have, under the law and the Constitution.[95]

The *San Antonio Express* wrote, "Few problems were envisioned for San Antonio when Alamo City schools move to comply with the edict against segregation handed down Monday by the U.S. Supreme Court."[96]

To be sure, some politicians groused, as the Associated Press reported from Atlanta: "White political leaders of the Deep South reacted all the way from bitter criticism and near-defiance through milder anger and on to quiet caution."[97]

From Savannah the *New York Times* reported on a luncheon meeting of a Rotary Club where the decision was announced: "The announcement was greeted with some applause. Few of the members seemed much concerned.... [One said] 'It's a good thing.... We can now practice the true Christian principles of brotherhood.'"[98]

The *Times* excerpted a variety of newspaper opinion in both segregated and nonsegregated states, under these headlines from the former: "Wise and Fair Ruling" (*Washington Evening Star*); "Painful Implications" (*Baltimore Sun*); "No Time for Hasty Action" (*Atlanta Constitution*); "Decision Is Regretted" (*Birmingham News*); "Will Meet Situtation Calmly" (*Chattanooga Times*); "More Time Is Needed" (*Richmond Times-Dispatch*); "A Mortal Blow" (*Louisville Courier-Journal*).[99]

Newspaper errors about Supreme Court decisions sometimes are created by headline writers. Another prominent Warren Court civil-rights decision struck down state laws prohibiting racially mixed marriages.[100] The *Albuquerque Journal* put the story on page one, but this headline blew it: "Supreme Court Upholds Racially Mixed Marriages." The story, by United Press International, was quite correct, stating that the Court held such antimiscegenation laws a violation of the equal protection clause.[101]

THE WARREN COURT ON PERSONS ACCUSED

Over several years the Warren Court handed down a number of decisions broadening the constitutional rights of persons suspected or accused of crime. A Fourth Amendment search-and-seizure ruling, *Mapp v. Ohio,*[102] extended the federal exclusionary rule, barring the use of evidence illegally obtained, to the states through the due process clause of the Fourteenth Amendment, another step toward the "incorporation" of Bill of Rights protections initiated decades earlier in *Gitlow v. New York.*[103] *Gideon v. Wainwright* extended to the states the Sixth Amendment's right to counsel, again through the due process clause.[104] The accused, Clarence Earl Gideon, had unsuccessfully defended himself in a Florida court on a breaking-and-entering charge, but after his Supreme Court victory he was acquitted when represented by a lawyer provided by the trial court. The *St. Petersburg Times* celebrated his success: "Most persons, we are sure, will be thankful that the Supreme Court clings to the ancient democratic tradition of protecting the individual against the tyranny of any governmental agency."[105]

In *Escobedo v. Illinois* the Court threw out a murder confession because the suspect, in police custody, had not been allowed to see his lawyer and had not been advised of his right to remain silent, in violation of the Sixth Amendment right to counsel.[106] Two years later the justices, divided 5–4, specified in *Miranda v. Arizona* that the Fifth Amendment privilege against self-incrimination requires that a person held for questioning must be advised that he has a right to remain silent, that anything he says may be used against him, that he has a right to counsel, and that if he cannot afford a lawyer, one will be provided.[107]

Much of the press was alarmed by *Miranda,* not over the Court's constitutional reasoning, but because the police were. United Press International quoted a Philadelphia detective captain as saying the ruling "puts the police department out of business."[108] The head of Washington, D.C.'s robbery squad told the *Washington Post* that the decision "puts another handcuff on the police."[109] The *Fresno Bee,* in a story based on UPI and AP dispatches, quoted Garland, Texas, Police Chief Henry C. Ashley: "It's the damnest thing I ever heard of."[110] The *Chicago Tribune* commented: "Taken in conjunction with a long series of holdings by the court, the decision throws up another roadblock in the path of the police and prosecutors."[111] Arthur Krock of the *New York Times* wrote that law enforcement officials attributed rising crime in part to "previous court decisions which have steadily increased the weight given to constitutional protections of offenders over those of their victims."[112] Ronald J. Ostrow, Supreme Court reporter of the *Los Angeles Times,* declared in an opinion piece that "the court's emphasis on the rights of suspects, even poor suspects, probably is running ahead of public opinion."[113] But the *Washington Post* respected the Court's legal reasoning: "What's all the bleating about, anyway? American cops are not about to throw in the sponge in their long conflict with the robbers. The country needs . . . painstaking, patient, expensive attention to the causes and sources of crime. But it really doesn't need to junk its Constitution and its freedom."[114]

In Chief Justice Warren's final six months, as the Vietnam War dragged on, the Court handed down two notable protections of free speech under the First Amendment. It sanctioned a high school student's wearing of a black antiwar armband to class,[115] and it limited punishment of speech advocating illegal action to situations where the "advocacy is directed to inciting or producing imminent lawless action and is likely to incite or produce such action."[116] This latter decision tightened the Court's long-standing "clear and present danger" doctrine and overturned its 1927 ruling in *Whitney v. California,*[117] where the state statute at issue was identical to the Ohio statute now before the Court.

The armband decision did not receive the wide coverage that might have been expected during a time of strident Vietnam War protests, and the stories emphasized the practicalities of school enforcement rather than the First Amendment issue at stake. They also played up a strong dissent. In its second paragraph, United Press International reported that the decision "brought a wrathful outburst from Justice Hugo L. Black who asserted the ruling subjects every public school student 'to the whims and caprices of their loudest-mouthed . . . students' and will encourage the current wave of student defiance."[118] The *Chicago Tribune* reported, "Several suburban school superintendents expressed cautious agreement" but quoted one as saying, "If free expression encourages anarchy in a school, then this decision is not a sound one."[119] The *Tribune* also complained editorially, "Maintaining discipline and order in the nation's schools will be more difficult as a result of a decision by the United States Supreme court, which is always ready to meddle in local affairs."[120] But the *Washington Post* contended, "There is nothing in the case to suggest that the Court is giving license to violence on the campus or the disruption of educational programs. There was no disorder in connection with the wearing of the armbands."[121]

The Court's second major free-speech decision that year, *Brandenburg v. Ohio,* came down in June, and so, like many important cases over the years, was nearly lost in the end-of-term crunch.[122] Many newspapers gave greater attention to a Senate speech by Strom Thurmond of South Carolina demanding Justice Douglas's resignation from the Court because of his involvement with a foundation Thurmond termed "socialist." It was not Thurmond's first such attack on Douglas, but it drew coverage because he was challenged on the Senate floor by a young Senator Edward Kennedy of Massachusetts. At one point Thurmond mispronounced a Latino name and was corrected by Kennedy. The Associated Press reported this from Thurmond: "Are you an expert because you went to Harvard? What was your record at Harvard?"[123] It was an obvious allusion to Kennedy's well-publicized expulsion from Harvard for cheating. (After two years in the army, he returned and graduated.) Further upstaging the Court that day, the Senate confirmed President Richard Nixon's appointment of Warren Burger to succeed Earl Warren as chief justice.[124]

Even the *New York Times* relegated to page 24 the historic *Brandenburg* ruling, in which the Court reversed itself to strike down as a violation of the First and Fourteenth Amendments an Ohio statute prohibiting the advocacy of violence to achieve political change. On page one, instead, the *Times* reported the Thurmond-Kennedy altercation[125] as well as two other Court decisions, one requiring a hearing before garnishment of a debtor's wages[126] and another upholding the Federal Communications Commission's fairness doctrine requiring that broadcasters give a right of reply to personal attacks and political editorials.[127]

A LOOK AT TV LOOKING AT THE COURT

During the tenures of Earl Warren (1953–69) and Warren Burger (1969–86), encouraged by the growing public impact of Supreme Court decisions and controversy surrounding them, television emerged as a significant new dimension of journalism at the Court. By the early 1970s all three broadcast networks had reporters with law degrees covering the Court, an educational standard not matched by the print media. A study by Ethan Katsh of TV coverage from 1976 to 1981 published in *Judicature* magazine found that "[o]ne in ten Supreme Court decisions were reported or analyzed by the network's legal affairs correspondent" as opposed to a brief mention by the anchorman. These stories were "one to three minutes in length" and "individual rights cases are almost twice as likely to be reported than cases involving an economic issue."[128] All abortion decisions (*Roe v. Wade*[129] was decided in 1973), according to the study, were covered by at least one network, and more than half of free-speech, free-press, and freedom-of-religion cases received network coverage. Cases involving antitrust, taxation, patents, copyrights, and trademarks were less well covered, and even "[c]riminal cases also seem somewhat neglected."[130]

In a rejoinder published in the same issue of *Judicature,* Tim O'Brien, ABC's Supreme Court reporter and a lawyer, pointed out that Katsh's study was limited to the networks' regular evening newscasts, but that on ABC considerable additional Court coverage was provided on mornings, weekends, *Nightline,* and special broadcasts. "Last term, for example," O'Brien wrote, "of 141 signed decisions, the network had 'correspondent coverage' of 29 cases, or 20.6 percent—nearly twice Katsh's average." He went on: "Are there surveys comparing the networks' selection of cases with that of middle America's leading newspapers? I am aware of none, but I suspect any difference in cases reported between the newspapers and television would be negligible."[131] This despite television's time constraints and the lack of pictures. But Katsh's findings also led O'Brien to acknowledge that "many legal issues confronting the Supreme Court fail to get the attention they deserve from television news."[132] The same could fairly be said of newspapers.

THE BURGER COURT: AFFIRMING FEDERAL REMEDIES

The Burger Court (1969–86) rendered important decisions affirming federal authority to remedy past racial injustice. The Court was unanimous in sustaining a federal district court order to bus students to achieve a racial mix in each school that would resemble the racial composition of the entire school district.[133] Later, though divided 6-3, the Court upheld Congress's authority to require a 10 percent set-aside for minority business enterprises in federal public works, a ruling that stimulated other minority set-asides by federal, state, and local governments.[134]

Both decisions were front-page news, if not universally celebrated. "The United States Supreme Court's new school desegregation rulings," United Press International reported, "were denounced yesterday as 'tragic' and 'discriminatory' by some southerners, but civil rights leaders hailed them as a sign that America is headed toward an integrated society. 'I am not surprised at anything the court does,' said Gov. George C. Wallace of Alabama."[135] On the minority set-aside, the *Wall Street Journal* perceptively scrutinized the Court's opinion:

> The endorsement of an explicit quota based on race strays a long way, in our view, from the equal protection principle. And, in this particular case, unlike some school desegregation cases, even the evidence of past discrimination in the award of contracts falls somewhat short of persuasive. Some day, we suspect, the courts will have to back away from what they have entered here. The deeper they go, the harder it will be.[136]

THE REHNQUIST COURT: RATCHETING DOWN

The Rehnquist Court (1986–2005) took a more conservative stance in cases dealing with the rights of criminals and other individual rights, a cluster of them in 1989. That year the Court upheld the death penalty for minors who commit murder[137] and for mentally retarded murderers.[138] It also ruled unconstitutional a minority set-aside program[139] and limited the use of civil rights laws to challenge discrimination.[140] It permitted white firefighters in Birmingham to challenge a court-approved consent decree favoring black firefighters.[141] But it set aside a conviction under a Texas statute that prohibited burning the flag.[142]

Newspapers emphasized especially the minority set-aside ruling. Tony Mauro wrote in *USA Today:*

For more than 20 years, the Supreme Court breathed life—and power—into the Civil Rights Act with rulings that interpreted it expansively. Now, civil rights lawyers and scholars fear the court is marking the 25th anniversary of the act by sapping its strength. The result, they fear, is that the law's success in encouraging the hiring and promotion of minorities will end with doors being shut in their faces.[143]

Marshall Ingwerson, on page one of the *Christian Science Monitor:*

The United States Supreme Court has virtually assured a new political confrontation over affirmative action.... In practice, government agencies all over the country that either settled or avoided politically charged discrimination suits by creating court-sanctioned affirmative action plans now fear that white employees can challenge them, even years later.[144]

Some editorial writers critical of the Rehnquist Court's decisions blamed President Reagan, who had appointed Antonin Scalia, Sandra Day O'Connor, and Arthur Kennedy; they generally voted with Chief Justice Rehnquist in these cases. The *St. Louis Post-Dispatch:*

The second Reconstruction period has ended.... A new court majority, created by Ronald Reagan in his own image and—like him—out of touch with reality, ignored shocking examples of racial discrimination in an Alaska cannery (separate dining and housing facilities, for instance) but managed to muster ultimate sympathy for white firefighters in Birmingham, Ala.[145]

The *Arkansas Democrat-Gazette* was biting:

> Everyone figured that a primary assignment of the Court's present majority would be to halt and where possible turn back the legal impetus for the civil rights movement. The Court is just hitting its stride in these matters, but there is every indication it will live down to expectations.[146]

The following term, 1989–90, was marked by a number of profound disagreements within the Rehnquist Court, many of them on questions of individual rights under the First Amendment or the Fourth Amendment. It was noteworthy that network television responded, reporting certiorari petitions, oral arguments, and decisions on 32 (of 139) cases, as set forth in a fine study by Elliot E. Slotnick and Jennifer A. Segal.[147] They found that all three networks broadcast the decisions in a dozen cases raising issues ranging from free expression (political hiring and promotion disapproved,[148] new federal flag-burning prohibition struck down[149]) and the First Amendment's establishment clause (after-school Bible club permitted,[150] Oregon law banning peyote use upheld[151]) to abortion (judicial bypass of parental notification upheld[152]), the right to die (removal of life support permitted only if the patient so indicated in advance[153]), and search-and-seizure (Michigan sobriety checkpoints on roads upheld,[154] limited protective search of premises by police upheld[155]).

DENIAL OF CERTIORARI: WHAT DID THE COURT DECIDE?

However, Slotnick and Segal also reported network errors in 22 stories (out of 29 reported) on Court denials of certiorari, finding them ambiguous, misleading, or "clearly wrong."[156] Although such a denial simply means the justices declined to hear the case, rendering no decision on it, "[t]he most frequently used word to characterize the Court's action in such stories was *upheld*." The researchers cite several specific misstatements by Tom Brokaw of NBC, Bob Schieffer and Dan Rather of CBS, and Ted Koppel and Peter Jennings of ABC:

> On April 30, Brokaw stated in a story about one of the cases of random drug testing that "the Court *upheld* random drug testing of thousands of air traffic controllers and other Transportation Department employees in safety-related jobs." The clear implication of these and other stories was that the Court had made a decision on the merits of the cases rather than denying them certiorari.
>
> Other reports included the equally misleading and erroneous words *ruled* or *ruling,* stating clearly that a decision had been made. Bob Schieffer of CBS News, when reporting on a case regarding special education programs in public schools for handicapped children, stated that "in effect, today's *ruling* means that these schools must keep trying to find programs that will help these children." (November 27, 1989)[157]

"The data clearly underscore," Slotnick and Segal conclude, "that coverage of the Court's docketing decisions by the network newscasts is cursory at best."[158]

In fact, this mistreatment of denials of certiorari is one of the most common errors by newspapers, too. Justice Ruth Bader Ginsburg comments that "too often, in my view, the press overstates the significance of an order denying review." She continues:

> Headlines, particularly, may be as misleading as they are eye-catching. For example, when we declined to review a decision

of the Illinois Supreme Court in what has come to be known as the "Baby Richard" case [*In re Petition of John Doe and Jane Doe to Adopt a Baby Boy,* 627 N.E.2d 648 (Ill. 1993)], one headline read: "Controversial Illinois Adoption Rule Upheld: Without Comment, Supreme Court Affirms Biological Father's Right to 'Baby Richard.'" [*Wash. Post,* Nov. 8, 1994, at A6.] And when we declined to hear a constitutional challenge to a curfew for minors in Dallas, Texas, a headline reported: "High Court Appears to Uphold Curfews." [*Balt. Sun,* June 1, 1994, at 1A.][159]

Linda Greenhouse of the *New York Times* recalls ruefully the Supreme Court's denial of a petition to review "a state court judgment of liability for the death of a child who was treated by prayer instead of medicine." Her story, which reported the denial correctly, ran on page one under this headline: "Christian Scientists Rebuffed in Ruling by Supreme Court." In fact, the Court had not ruled at all.[160]

THE REHNQUIST COURT: CRIME SCENES

A 1990 decision upheld Oregon's classification of the hallucinogen peyote as an illegal controlled substance over a "free exercise of religion" claim by two Native Americans.[161] Writing for the majority, Justice Antonin Scalia said the decision was consistent with the Court's prior rulings, including one that exempted Amish children from attending school until age sixteen as required by Wisconsin law.[162] Conservative columnist George Will, usually of one mind with Scalia, challenged that statement, not to dispute the peyote ruling, which he pronounced "constitutionally correct," but to chastise the justice for not overruling the Amish case. "Scalia should have forthrightly said that the 1972 Old Order Amish decision was mistaken," he asserted.[163]

Despite its toughness on crime, the Rehnquist Court ruled unconstitutional two anticrime statutes, one federal and one local. The federal law, banning possession of guns within 1,000 feet of a school, was overturned on the ground that it was unrelated to Congress's authority under the commerce clause.[164] A Chicago ordinance prohibiting street gang members from loitering in any public place was deemed too vague to satisfy the due process clause of the Fourteenth Amendment.[165] The voiding of the federal statute was widely covered, many of the stories appearing on page one, with emphasis duly given to this new limitation on the commerce clause. The Associated Press reported in its second paragraph: "The 5-4 decision throwing out the 1990 Gun-Free School Zones Act stood in sharp contrast to a long-standing court trend of deference to congressional power to regulate interstate commerce."[166] Joan Biskupic of the *Chicago Sun-Times* pointed to the decades-long progressive expansion of the commerce power, adding,

> This week, the court put the brakes on, in an opinion experts called breathtaking and historic. . . . Lawmakers immediately expressed concerns that the decision opened the door to future rejections of their efforts to control crime. "What comes next, drugs?" asked Sen. Arlen Specter (R-Pa.). "I think that crime is a national problem. . . . Guns and drugs are the principal instrumentalities of crime."[167]

The Court's rejection of the Chicago ordinance received less coverage but some editorial support. However, there was dismay in Chicago, where public officials said the law was effective in policing the streets. Jan Crawford Greenburg of the *Chicago Tribune* perceived that divisions among the justices effectively narrowed the holding:

> The court sidestepped sweeping civil liberties concerns in its majority decision, which fell far short of declaring all anti-gang loitering laws illegal. Some justices even suggested ways Chicago could rework the ordinance to make it constitutional, prompting city officials to vow they would quickly respond with such an effort.
>
> "We will go back and correct it, and then move forward," Mayor Richard M. Daley said of the law, which he strongly supports. "You have to look at the quality of life. People are saying, 'Mr. Mayor, how do I get by? There are 25 people (on the corner).' These are known gangbangers and dope dealers. What do I do, throw a picnic for them?"[168]

The Gun-Free School Zones Act case was one of nine in the 1994–95 term that, according to the Slotnick and Segal study, attracted coverage by all three television network evening news broadcasts on decision day and, in some cases, earlier, when the Court granted certiorari or when it heard oral argument. The study also found that total network coverage in that term had declined to just 15 (out of 86) cases; compared with the 1989–90 term, when 32 cases were covered, there was "a relative paucity of coverage" underscoring "the diminishing interest in the Supreme Court by the network news."[169]

As in the earlier term, according to the Slotnick-Segal study, most of the cases covered by television concerned the scope of constitutional rights. Some examples: the First Amendment establishment clause (not a barrier to a university student activities fund's payment of the printing costs of a student Christian publication along with other student publications,[170] and not a barrier to Christmastime placement of a cross by the Ku Klux Klan on a public plaza surrounding the Ohio statehouse[171]); First Amendment free expression (organizers of Boston's St. Patrick's Day parade could not ban a gay and lesbian group[172]); the Fourth Amendment (school athlete drug tests upheld[173]); and the Fourteenth Amendment (race-based congressional redistricting disallowed[174]).

Among several rulings on the rights of persons accused or convicted of crimes, rulings generally favorable to law enforcement, the Rehnquist Court in 2005 reversed itself to hold that the death penalty for juveniles violates the Eighth Amendment's proscription of cruel and unusual punishment. The vote was 5-4. In dissent, Justice Scalia, joined by the chief justice, protested that the majority based the ruling in part on practices in other countries, which they deemed irrelevant.[175]

In reporting the decision, both television and newspaper stories focused on the victims of crimes committed by offenders under eighteen. The *Richmond Times Dispatch* told the story this way:

> Robert Kinney Jr. is 14 now, and he will never have more than the faintest memory of his mother.
>
> She was raped and murdered when he was just 3.
>
> Her killer, Shermaine Ali Johnson, was found guilty and sentenced to death. But yesterday's U.S. Supreme Court decision changes everything for Kinney and his family—and for Johnson....
>
> He was just 16 in 1994 when he stabbed to death Kinney's mother, Hope Hall, a 22-year-old part-time producer for WWBT-Channel 12.
>
> "I think it's a horrible, horrible decision," said Kinney's father, Robert Kinney Sr.[176]

The *Galveston County Daily News* wrote: "For almost 12 years, Melissa Pena has waited for the execution of five gang members who raped and killed her teenage daughter and a friend and left their bodies to rot in a Houston field. On Tuesday, she learned that day would never come."[177] The *Houston Chronicle* reported that several victims' families held a news conference to protest the ruling: "The Supreme Court decision outraged Adolph and Melissa Pena. The couple's daughter Elizabeth Pena, 16, and her friend Jennifer Ertman, 14, took a shortcut home June 24, 1993, and unwittingly walked into a drunken gang initiation in northwest Houston. The Waltrip High School sophomores' badly mauled bodies were found four days later."[178]

However, another Texas paper, the *Austin American-Statesman,* called the decision "welcome" and pointed to the "racial disparities and legal inconsistencies of Texas' death penalty system for juvenile offenders."[179] In fact, despite the emphasis on victims in many news stories, most editorials were favorable. The *Milwaukee Journal Sentinel* called the ruling "enlightened" and declared, "We've simply moved beyond such barbarism as executing minors."[180] The *Las Vegas Review-Journal* endorsed the decision but objected, like Justice Scalia, to its reliance on foreign disdain for executing juveniles: "The majority justices could have reached a similar conclusion without subordinating U.S. jurisprudence to European public opinion."[181]

THE SUPREME COURT AND THE WAR ON TERROR

In two major decisions on the same day in 2004 dealing with the rights of prisoners captured by the United States in its war on terror, the Court countermanded White House assertions of presidential authority. It held, 6–3, in *Hamdi v. Rumsfeld,* a petition for habeas corpus, that an American citizen seized in Afghanistan and held in the United States since 2002 without due process of law was entitled to a meaningful opportunity to rebut before a neutral decision maker the government's reasons for holding him.[182] In *Rasul v. Bush* other habeas corpus petitions, filed by aliens held without charges or hearings at the U.S. naval base in Guantanamo Bay, Cuba, also were validated by the Court, again 6–3, which directed a federal trial court to consider them.[183]

Coverage of these prominent cases was universal. The stories emphasized *Hamdi,* pointing out that it applied to 600 prisoners and looking ahead to its future ramifications. Frank Davies of the *Miami Herald* called it a "historic decision" and "a rare, sharp reversal of a president's assertions of wartime powers," adding: "The ruling may also open the door to U.S. courts for terrorism suspects held elsewhere. Defense Department officials did not immediately respond to the decision."[184] *USA Today* saw uncertainty ahead: "Some former military lawyers said federal courts could be inundated with cases and forced into complicated judgments."[185]

Newspaper editorials evaluated wartime policy and national ideology as well as legality, and were decidedly mixed. The *Christian Science Monitor* said the justices' "scattered views reflect a similar mix of uncertain opinions among Americans on how much liberty and convenience to sacrifice in order to prevent more terror attacks."[186] The *Columbus Dispatch* believed the Court acted "in Americans' best interest" because "America can't be that 'shining city on a hill' that former President Reagan spoke of unless it holds fast to the protection of due process."[187] But the *Omaha World-Herald* thought the Court was meddling: "[T]he ruling constitutes second-guessing by the courts of a commander-in-chief's wartime decisions. It's extraordinarily forgiving—even the Geneva Conventions don't require the release of prisoners of war prior to the end of hostilities."[188]

Two years later, with John Roberts in the center chair, the Court invalidated President Bush's military commissions to try detainees, evoking similar intense coverage and comment.[189] The vote was 5-3, with the chief justice not participating, and Justices Thomas, Scalia, and Alito in dissent. Editorials were generally supportive. The *Boston Herald* declared that "the rule of law under which we are privileged to live extends to those on what is technically U.S. soil (even if it is on a Cuban shore). And what the court said in a 5-3 decision was that there are no shortcuts in applying the law. . . . [I]t never should have come to this."[190] But the New York *Daily News* contended that "the court went wrong" and quoted with approval Justice Scalia's dissent that President Bush had the authority to create the commissions. The editorial went on: "It is not clear where the Court derives the authority—or the audacity—to contradict this determination."[191]

In still another hotly disputed Guantanamo ruling, the Supreme Court in 2008 declared unconstitutional a new statute denying alien detainees the right of habeas corpus, and said they were entitled to a meaningful opportunity to contest their "enemy combatant" status before a federal court. The Court again split, 5-4 this time. Chief Justice Roberts and Justice Scalia wrote angry dissents. "The Nation will live to regret what the Court has done today," Scalia declared. "It will almost certainly cause more Americans to be killed."[192]

While giving prominence to Scalia's bitter words, newspapers stressed that the decision was still another rebuke from the Court to President Bush for his detention policies. The *Washington Post* accompanied its report on page one with a second story about the

Bush administration's dilemma: "The ruling throws into disarray the administration's detention strategy, almost certainly leaving to Bush's successor and the next Congress the dilemma of what to do with the Guantanamo Bay detainees."[193]

Editorial writers could hardly have been more enthusiastic about the decision. "Rule of Law Wins" was the headline on the editorial page of the *Seattle Post-Intelligencer*.[194] The *Salt Lake Tribune* celebrated the ruling as "a ringing affirmation that the United States means what it says about individual freedoms and the due process of law."[195] Even in the military town of Norfolk, Virginia, the *Virginian-Pilot* pointed with alarm to the dissenters, saying that they "have revealed themselves as activists in the sense most pernicious to this nation's values."[196]

THE ROBERTS COURT DIVIDED

Contrasting with its rulings favoring detainees, the Roberts Court in 2007, 2008, and 2009 rejected other claims of individual-rights violations. All the decisions were by divided votes. The justices, 5-4, threw out the pay-discrimination claim of Lily Ledbetter, retired from Goodyear Tire & Rubber Company's plant in Gadsden, Alabama, on the ground that the limited time for filing such a claim, 180 days, commenced with the decision regarding her pay, rejecting her claim that each paycheck represented a discriminatory act.[197] By a vote of 6-3 the Court turned down the free-speech claim of Joseph Frederick, a Juneau, Alaska, high school student who had been suspended because he defied his principal's direction at a school outing to view the passing of the Olympic torch to take down a banner reading "Bong Hits 4 Jesus," which the principal took to be promoting illegal drug use.[198] Interpreting the Eighth Amendment's ban on cruel and unusual punishment, the Court voted 7-2 to reject the claim of Ralph Baze, a condemned inmate in Kentucky, that a lethal injection not properly administered could result in such significant pain as to render that method of execution unconstitutional.[199] In another 5-4 decision, the justices ruled that William Osborne, an Alaska inmate serving twenty-one years for raping, beating, and shooting a prostitute, did not have a due-process right to DNA testing at his own expense of sperm found in a condom at the scene.[200]

These split decisions received prominent coverage, with quotations from both majority and dissenting opinions, and considerable editorial comment. Approving of the pay-discrimination decision, the *Contra Costa* (California) *Times* declared that "it is not the court's responsibility to rewrite the law, only to interpret it and to make sure there are no constitutional violations."[201] However, most papers were critical of the decisions, and the *New York Times* was especially outspoken, addressing the justices' legal reasoning as well as the policy implications. "This oblique reference to drugs," it complained about the Alaska student's case, "hardly justifies such mangling of sound precedent and the First Amendment."[202] The *Times* termed the lethal injection decision "regrettable."[203] But the *Times* unleashed its biggest salvo at the DNA ruling, calling it "appalling." The editorial observed that in his majority opinion Chief Justice Roberts noted the "unparalleled ability" of improved DNA testing, not available at the time of the crime, to determine guilt or innocence. Yet, the *Times* argued, "he treated that breakthrough more as an irritant than an opportunity. . . . Thursday's ruling will inevitably allow some innocent people to languish in prison without having the chance to definitively prove their innocence and with the state never being completely certain of their guilt."[204]

In a long-awaited decision on the Second Amendment, the

right to bear arms, the Roberts Court held invalid a District of Columbia prohibition on handguns. A majority of five stated that the amendment, though referring to the need for a "well regulated militia," protects an individual's right to possess a firearm unconnected with service in a militia and the right to use that firearm for traditionally lawful purposes such as self-defense within the home. However, in his majority opinion Justice Scalia also declared that the decision should not be taken to invalidate such existing prohibitions as gun possession by felons and the mentally ill, and weapons bans in such places as schools and public buildings.[205]

It was the top story in newspapers and on the network news, all reporters pointing out prominently that the ruling did not wipe out all gun regulations. CBS ran the story for an extraordinary six-and-a-half minutes, and ABC for five minutes and forty seconds. NBC's Pete Williams called it "a landmark ruling," no overstatement, while noting that it "doesn't say much about what other kinds of limitations on gun ownership might be constitutional."[206]

Linda Greenhouse of the *New York Times* focused on the constitutional argument, stating the Second Amendment in full: "A well regulated militia being necessary to the security of a free State, the right of the people to bear Arms, shall not be infringed." She continued:

> According to Justice Scalia, the "militia" reference in the first part of the amendment simply "announces the purpose for which the right was codified: to prevent elimination of the militia." The Constitution's framers were afraid that the new federal government would disarm the populace, as the British had tried to do, Justice Scalia said.

But he added that this "prefatory statement of purpose" should not be interpreted to limit the meaning of what is called the operative clause—"the right of the people to keep and bear arms, shall not be infringed." Instead, Justice Scalia said, the operative clause "codified a pre-existing right" of individual gun ownership for private use.[207]

Editorials tended to support the ruling or at least acknowledge it as correct. "Thank you, Supreme Court," gushed the *Arkansas Democrat-Gazette*.[208] "The right to bear arms is a real right," said the *Capital Times* of Madison, Wisconsin.[209] The (Portland) *Oregonian* stated: "The court was correct to define gun ownership as an individual right, rather than merely as a collective right to form militias."[210] But the *Berkshire Eagle*, in Pittsfield, Massachusetts, called the ruling "disturbing"[211] and the *Chicago Sun-Times* worried that "more guns will flood into Chicago."[212] The *Boston Globe*, echoing the sentiments of a number of papers, said: "The important work now is to determine what constitutes 'reasonable' regulation of murderous weapons.... Some Americans may feel safer owning a gun for self-defense. But guns will kill 80 people today in homicides, suicides, or accidents. This ruling won't change that."[213]

Looking back now on two centuries of Supreme Court decisions on slavery and individual rights, it is clear that the Court was slow to apply the nation's high ideals as expressed in the Constitution. This observation is not new, but we observe, too, that the press generally was indifferent, both professionally and idealistically. Coverage of decisions, even after the advent of the telegraph, was often spotty, itself an indication that the press, like the Court, failed to recognize and declare that the Constitution, the Bill of Rights, and the post–Civil War amendments set forth higher human-rights standards than the Court's decisions reflected.

Only when the Court began to give more recognition to those standards in the mid-twentieth century did the press recognize and celebrate them. As the Court's high-impact decisions waxed, the media provided better staffing, more newspaper space, and for a time anyway, more broadcast minutes. These basic ingredients of better journalism enabled more extensive coverage of the Court's work, and for the most part the press was supportive, though racial issues posed a never-ending challenge to southern media whose values and audience were grounded in a culture distinct from that of the nation at large.

NINE

REFEREEING BUSINESS AND LABOR

Unlike its clear statements of individual rights, the Constitution sets forth almost no ground rules by which the courts are to determine the rights and responsibilities of businesses and working people. In the early days few such decisions were rendered by the Supreme Court. However, as noted in chapter 7 on nation-building, in its interpretations of the constitutional powers of government the Court did lay down some important, fundamental precepts governing business.

The Marshall Court (1801–35) ruled that the contracts clause barred a state from enacting legislation that impaired contracts or land titles,[1] and that the contracts clause prohibited a state from altering the terms of a corporate charter[2] and from legislating the discharge of preexisting debt,[3] but that the contracts clause was not violated by a New York insolvency statute that operated only prospectively, that is, not impairing the obligations of contracts signed before the enactment of the statute.[4] The Marshall Court also held that the commerce clause gave primacy to a federal steamboat license over a state's monopoly grant.[5]

Under Chief Justice Taney (1835–64) the Court ruled that a

state charter did not constitute a state monopoly;[6] that an Ohio River bridge constituted an impediment to interstate commerce and must be raised to permit the passage of large steamboats;[7] that the commerce clause did not prohibit state regulation of alcoholic beverages imported from other states[8] nor did it prohibit local pilotage laws;[9] and, in one of several 1850s patent decisions, that Samuel F. B. Morse was indeed the inventor of the electromagnetic telegraph and that his patent had been infringed by certain other telegraph operators.[10]

The Chase Court (1864–73) ruled that the Fourteenth Amendment did not bar a Louisiana statute, bottomed on the state's police power, that created a slaughterhouse monopoly in New Orleans.[11] Similarly, the Waite Court (1874–88) found no Fourteenth Amendment barrier to an Illinois law regulating grain elevator rates in Chicago,[12] but it did find a violation of the Fourteenth Amendment in a San Francisco licensing ordinance that discriminated against Chinese-owned laundries.[13]

THE FULLER COURT VERSUS LABOR

A rising tide of business and labor cases came to the Court starting in the 1890s and continues to the present day. Under Chief Justice Fuller (1888–1910) the Court imposed a due process requirement on business regulation and thus voided a state statute that did not permit judicial review of the rates set.[14] The Fuller Court also ruled unconstitutional a federal income tax.[15] A number of other cases dealt with the rights of workers and unions. Their rights eventually were prescribed in the first national labor legislation, enacted in 1935, but the earlier cases, like most of those in chapters 7 and 8, raised questions of constitutional law or other broad legal principles, and the Fuller Court decided many, all against workers.

For instance, the Court upheld the contempt-of-court sentences of Eugene Debs and other union leaders who had defied a government-requested injunction ordering them to cease interference with railroad operations by strikes and boycotts directed against the Pullman Palace Car Company, in Chicago. Pullman had sought to cope with the depression of the early 1890s by drastically cutting its workers' wages.[16] Over a sharp dissent by Justice Harlan, the Fuller Court upheld a federal statute that authorized U.S. marshals to enforce seamen's contracts by physically delivering them to their ships.[17] The Court reversed the conviction of a creditor in Georgia for violating a federal statute against forcibly returning a person to peonage, or forced labor to work off his debt, on the ground that there was no proof that the debtor had been in peonage previously.[18] The Court set aside federal convictions of three Arkansas white men for frightening and coercing eight African Americans to abandon their job contracts, reasoning that the Thirteenth Amendment abolishing slavery did not give the federal government jurisdiction to criminalize such an act.[19]

Most prominently, in *Lochner v. New York* the Fuller Court invalidated a New York statute limiting the hours of bakery workers to ten a day and sixty a week, on the ground that it violated a concept called freedom of contract.[20] Not to be confused with the contracts clause, the freedom of contract was derived by judges from the Fifth and Fourteenth Amendments, which both prohibit the deprivation of liberty or property without due process of law. As applied to employment, freedom of contract meant that states could not deprive a person of the freedom to agree to his own work terms, which in practice severely disadvantaged workers and strengthened the hand of employers.

A majority of five, this time including the chief justice, deemed the New York work-hours statute a violation of the freedom of contract, and thus beyond the state's police power and infringing on the Fourteenth Amendment's due process clause. Justices John Marshall Harlan and Oliver Wendell Holmes, the two most eloquent dissenters of that era, wrote powerful dissents arguing that the Court was deciding social policy and should have deferred to the judgment of the legislature.

Newspaper coverage was widespread but routine. Freedom of contract, despite its lack of constitutional provenance, largely escaped scrutiny. However, the *Boston Daily Globe* saw a greater significance. Under a two-column photograph of Justice Harlan, the paper stated in the second paragraph of its story: "Justices Harlan, White, Day and Holmes dissented, and Justice Harlan declared than [*sic*] no more important decision had been rendered in the last century." The *Globe* went on to quote Harlan at length, including this:

> Our duty, I submit, is to sustain the statute as not being in conflict with the Federal Constitution, for the reason—and such is an all-sufficient reason—it is not shown to be plainly and palpably inconsistent with that instrument. Let the State alone in the management of its purely domestic affairs, so long as it does not appear beyond all question that it has violated the Federal Constitution.[21]

Seeing the potential local impact of the ruling, the *Globe* reported that "Massachusetts has several statutes fixing the hours for the employment of labor by municipal and private corporations which may be analogous, in principle to the New York law."[22]

The *Globe* did not overstate the importance of *Lochner.* For the next three decades the case would be cited by the Court as the basis for holding unconstitutional other state statutes regulating business and labor.

Another labor case before the Fuller Court dealt with an Alabama statute characterized by the U.S. attorney general as an attempt to legalize and maintain a system of peonage in violation of the Constitution and federal law. Nevertheless, the Court affirmed the conviction of an Alabama man for accepting fifteen dollars for work with intent to defraud, that is, to not work.[23]

When Congress declared that railroads were liable for employees' work accidents, the Fuller Court held the statute unconstitutional as beyond the authority granted by the commerce clause.[24] A similar finding voided a federal statute that made it a crime to discriminate against a railroad employee because he was a union member.[25] Chief Justice Fuller himself wrote for a unanimous court in the famous Danbury Hatters case, which surprisingly applied the Sherman Antitrust Act of 1890 to a labor union's organizing efforts, including a strike and a boycott, deeming them an illegal restraint of trade.[26]

Most of these anti-labor decisions by the Fuller Court were not widely reported, although the *Rocky Mountain News* labeled its story on the seaman's contract case "Involuntary Servitude" and devoted most of it to Justice Harlan's dissent. The paper followed up with a cogent editorial criticism, contending that "an ordinary laborer . . . may enter into a contract to work and failing to do so, he cannot be arrested and compelled to work. But under this decision if a seaman changes his mind he can be arrested, held like a felon, and toted off to sea to be flogged to death if he does not work."[27]

One possible reason for the light coverage of the Fuller Court's decisions that today seem ideologically skewed may have been the persistence of the Court's century-old bad habit of announcing a decision from the bench but not releasing the printed opinion until days later, when it was no longer news. This hampered reporters and sometimes produced errors. The *Atlanta Constitution* reported *Hodges v. United States,* the case of coercion against African American workers, this way:

> WASHINGTON, May 28—The case of Reuben Hodges and others v. the United States was decided by the supreme court of the United States today, which refused to take jurisdiction in the matter. The decision was announced by Justice Brewer, but owing to the fact that the dissenting opinion in the case was not ready for filing, the controlling opinion also was withheld.[28]

The story contained no quotations, no legal reasoning, and a serious error. The Court did not decline jurisdiction; in fact it overturned the convictions of the Arkansas men. The Court granted their motions to dismiss their indictment on the ground that the federal courts had no jurisdiction to consider such charges because Congress, in turn, had no authority under the Thirteenth Amendment to enact such a statute. This strained reasoning was surely hard to follow without the printed text. Other newspapers made the same mistake.

On the other hand, the *Lochner* decision voiding the New York bakers' hours law was well covered, and when the Court handed down Danbury Hatters, its third consecutive anti-labor ruling in early 1908, the press made a point of it. The *New York Times* said the decision was "of more far-reaching effect than either of the two which preceded it," continuing: "It is the most damaging blow organized labor has received, and, carried to its full import, means that hereafter any union which undertakes a boycott renders every one of its members personally liable for threefold damages to the firm or individual boycotted." At the end of its lengthy story the *Times* stated: "The decisions must have an effect on the political situation. It is one which would seem to call for another message from the President."[29] Along with its story the *Los Angeles Times* ran a photo of the chief justice, artistically embellished by a border of penciled hearts, under the headline "Nation's First Jurist Restrains Unionists," and with this caption below: "Chief Justice Fuller, of the United States Supreme Court, which yesterday rendered decision which is knockout blow to labor unions."[30] Strangely, the *Wall Street Journal,* despite its obvious interest in such matters, printed only this single nonsentence: "The Supreme Court decision of to-day, against labor unions, together with others that have preceded it during the past few weeks, but has caused consternation in labor union circles."[31]

The press soon reported significant Washington reaction to these labor cases. Bills were introduced to give unions greater protection and power. The *Los Angeles Times* wrote: "It is understood the President will advocate the passage of the Townsend Compulsory Arbitration Bill, which provides for settlement of labor disputes."[32]

Incredibly, as the controversy simmered, the justices contributed some reaction of their own, leaking this story to a few papers, including the *Chicago Daily Tribune:*

> WASHINGTON, D.C., Feb. 9—Some of the justices of the United States Supreme court have taken counsel together regarding the present day political tendencies in both parties, so far as these seem to the justices to menace the constitution. They have determined that upon them rests the burden of standing between the constitution and the popular passion.

They intend at every point to meet these subversive tendencies and defeat them. . . .

The justices are not confident that congress can be relied upon to stand permanently between the constitution and what one of the justices calls "the mob," and they are determined to fulfill their ancient function of bulwark.[33]

However, the brouhaha did not stand in the way of a contemporaneous dinner speech by President Theodore Roosevelt lauding the Supreme Court and a retiring justice, nor of favorable press comment about the Court, which had just completed another term. Despite occasional opposition stirred up by the Court's rulings, the *Chicago Daily Tribune* stated, "the president is right in his statement that the criticism which the court has sustained is a small and trivial thing compared with the deep reverence felt by the people for it."[34]

FEDERAL STATUTES, FEDERAL AGENCIES

Note that these Fuller Court decisions were governed by constitutional or other broad legal principles rather than by specialized business or labor regulatory statutes. But these were beginning to flow from Congress at the same time, starting in 1887 with the Interstate Commerce Act regulating railroads. These statutes, and the detailed rules they spawn, typically are complex and defy ready interpretation by a layperson. This makes the cases brought under these statutes and rules more challenging for reporters and therefore less subject to critical journalistic scrutiny. These cases fall into four main categories: antitrust, labor (after the National Labor Relations [Wagner] Act of 1935), intellectual property (patents, trademarks, and copyrights), and rulings of regulatory agencies such as the Federal Trade Commission, Federal Communications Commission, Securities and Exchange Commission, and Food and Drug Administration. Each such agency was created by a separate act of Congress to limit the operation of the free market for reasons deemed to be in the public interest, such as ensuring that prescription drugs are safe and efficacious. Each statute specifies the powers and responsibilities of the agency, giving it considerable discretion to interpret and apply the broad mandate of the statute. The agencies issue licenses or permits to operate and they lay down enforceable rules of conduct in the marketplace. They adjudicate disputes arising under those rules, and are empowered to levy fines and issue cease-and-desist orders akin to court injunctions, ordering a transgressing firm to alter its behavior. Some of these agency decisions are appealed to the federal appellate courts, and ultimately a few are reviewed by the Supreme Court. In weighing such disputes, however, the courts accord considerable deference to the agencies' interpretations of their own statutes.

In 1890, amid public concern about the advent of anticompetitive business combinations such as cartels, mergers, holding companies, and trusts deemed capable of controlling markets and prices, Congress passed the Sherman Antitrust Act. Its stated objectives were to prevent monopoly, attempts to monopolize, and other restraints of trade or commerce. It left the definition and policing of these practices up to the U.S. Justice Department and the courts. That process started badly. In 1895 the Fuller Court, with Justice Harlan again in dissent, threw out the government's prosecution of the Sugar Trust, created by one company's acquisition of all the stock of its leading competitors, on the questionable rationale that manufacturing is distinct from commerce and therefore the lawsuit was trying to reach intrastate activity beyond the authority of the commerce clause and the Sherman Act.[35] Subsequently, however, the Court supported applications of the act, though by fractured votes that produced clashing opinions about its scope. The Court, by 5-4 and then 5-3, upheld government challenges of a rate-setting agreement among a group of 18 railroads[36] and another among 31 railroads.[37]

This was important news, well covered, though generally from the viewpoint of the railroads, with comments from "railroad men" but none from shippers or passengers. The *Chicago Daily Tribune* reported: "Railroad officials here and especially those connected with traffic associations were almost prostrated" by the decision, which meant that "[c]ompetition will keep the rates on freight and passengers down to the lowest notch unless the railroads succeed in prevailing upon Congress to pass a law permitting the formation of pools."[38] The Associated Press wrote that "some railroad men are inclined to think that the companies will get along fairly well by instituting again the system of 'gentlemen's agreements,' as a substitute for the association."[39] The *New York Times* quoted one railroad president: "I do not fear any rate cutting or demoralization of railroad rates. Of course, I do not know what will be done, but I guess that the railroads will get along."[40] The Portland *Oregonian* was unusual in recognizing a consumer side to the story, if only to dismiss it:

> It will, we imagine, generally be considered that the decision is a triumph of the public interest over the interests of monopoly; but there is room here for serious doubt. . . . The business of the country generally, we believe, would prefer to see some arrangement assuring stability in transportation rates, and, on the whole would probably not object to leaving the matter in the hands of

the railroad men, subject to their sense of what is expedient and just.[41]

In another major antitrust case, President Theodore Roosevelt, a determined opponent of business combinations inimical to competition, directed Attorney General Philander C. Knox to bring the Sherman Antitrust Act to bear on Northern Securities Company, which had acquired the stock of two major, competing western railroads. Reversing the lower courts, the Supreme Court, again sharply divided, ordered Northern Securities dissolved, thus extending the Sherman Act's reach to the ownership of shares and questioning, if not answering, whether any horizontal mergers or other such combinations of competitors could pass muster under the act.[42] Major newspapers made a sharp turn. They abandoned their earlier pro-railroad stance and devoted whole columns to the decision. A four-column, two-line, all-caps headline on page one of the *Boston Daily Globe* proclaimed:

NORTHERN SECURITIES
COMPANY AN OUTLAW.
Court Stood
5 to 4.
Justice Holmes in Minority.
Knox Reassures All Timid People.
Government Not to Run Amuck, He Says.

The *Globe*'s story, with photographs of all nine justices and how they voted, termed the close decision "one of the most important ever rendered by that court" and "a narrow squeak for the government," but devoted much of the top of the story to this novel-like, thoroughly engaging description of the courtroom scene:

As the solemn procession of black-gowned justices filed into their place, led by the little chief justice with his flowing white hair and mustache, they saw before them a room crowded to its full capacity. . . .

Atty. Gen. Knox and several of his assistants . . .

Many senators were scattered about the bar . . .

Judge Taft, who according to common expectation, is himself some day to sit upon the great bench, was the only cabinet member present besides the attorney general.

Two score of newspaper men, paper and pencil in hand, and dozens of Wall-st. men and their agents waiting to rush to the telegraph and telephone wires, rounded out the picture of nervous expectancy.

It required but little effort of the imagination to see in the vast background millions of American citizens awaiting the outcome of this judicial battle of the government against daring financiers and millionaires in their offices waiting for the decree from which there is no appeal.[43]

The *Chicago Daily Tribune* called the decision "a great legal victory" for the government, but cautioned that the two railroads, the Great Northern and the Northern Pacific, "are controlled by men who do not believe in free and unrestrained competition. The communities served by the two roads will see no change in the situation so far as they are concerned after the decision."[44] In a front-page editorial the *Wall Street Journal* applauded even more enthusiastically, finding the decision "in the best interests of the whole country" because "[i]f that monopoly had been upheld, there would have been nothing to prevent its extension to include all the railroads of the United States, and that would have been the first step toward government ownership, and perhaps industrial socialism."[45]

It is doubtful that any current antitrust decision by the Supreme Court could command the extensive news coverage and fervent commentary the newspapers accorded to *Northern Securities Co. v. United States.* President Roosevelt's personal commitment, making the antitrust cause a public concern, undoubtedly was a factor. Surely another was the spirited opposition of four justices including Oliver Wendell Holmes and the influential Edward White, forging a distinguished record that would one day make him chief justice.

THE WHITE COURT ON ANTITRUST

Under Chief Justice White (1910–21) the Court further interpreted the Sherman Antitrust Act. In the spring of 1911 it handed down three major decisions that still are regarded as historic. By a 7-1 vote with Justice Holmes dissenting, the Court struck down a resale-price maintenance agreement between Dr. Miles Medical Co., a maker of proprietary medicines, and its wholesalers on the ground that it destroyed retail price competition and injured the public interest.[46] In *Standard Oil v. United States,* White's opinion established a new, pro-business "rule of reason" meaning that only "unreasonable" restraints of trade were forbidden by the Sherman Act, but even that easier rule was breached by the oil company's acquisitions of competitors and resultant market dominance.[47] Applying the rule of reason in *United States v. American Tobacco Company,* the Court, also by White, found both restraint of trade and monopolization because the company had acquired not only other tobacco companies, deemed horizontal competitors, but the dominant makers of tinfoil and licorice paste needed for plug tobacco. Justice Harlan dissented from the rule of reason (as he had in *Standard Oil*), arguing that it "in effect amends an act of Congress."[48] In both *Standard Oil* and *American Tobacco* the Court ordered divestiture or dissolution to bring the companies' operations into compliance with law.

The Sherman Act clearly had teeth, but they were uneven. Although the rulings of these cases were clear as to the companies involved, they were unclear on exactly what business behavior was proscribed, and the sharp dissents by Holmes and Harlan further clouded the picture. The newspapers coped well with that uncertainty, giving prominence to Justice Harlan's *American Tobacco* dissent as part of lavish coverage of the Court's decision.

The *New York Times* employed several sidebars to tell the story, including lists of *American Tobacco*'s multiple defendants: 29 individuals and 65 American and 2 English companies, stating American Tobacco's stock ownership in each. Like other papers, the *Times* immediately looked ahead to the breakup of the combines, noting in the third paragraph of its *American Tobacco* lead story that the reorganization "will be taken as the model set up by the courts of the form in which big business may proceed without fear of being in violation of the law."[49] In a separate story on Harlan's dissent, which was termed "exceedingly caustic," the *Times* noted that he "delivered his opinion orally" because, he stated, "the opinion of the court was not delivered to me until late Saturday evening, and it has been impossible for me since then to put in writing the views which I deem necessary to express." Nevertheless, the *Times* then quoted several paragraphs verbatim, undoubtedly reflecting the fact that most reporters of that era knew shorthand.[50]

Editorials were supportive, if cautious. "It leaves the legitimate business man feeling that his interests will be protected," said the *Boston Daily Globe,* "and warns monopoly builders that their combinations will not be tolerated."[51] The *Wall Street Journal* took issue with Harlan's dissent, saying his literal interpretation of the act "would amount to nothing less than simple anarchy" and calling the law as applied by the Court majority "a protection and not a menace."[52] The *Chicago Daily Tribune,* suggesting that the coming reorganizations might be ineffective, talked tough: "It may turn out that nothing short of criminal proceedings will bring those men to terms."[53]

The papers were not amiss in giving heed to Harlan's dissent. The Roosevelt administration did, too. It promptly dispatched a cabinet member to plant this counterstrike, as reported by the Associated Press:

> Administration officials, after consideration and study of the tobacco decision and a thorough comparison with the Standard Oil decision, today were agreed that "the rule of reason" is no new feature of the Supreme court's interpretation of law, and one member of the cabinet, whose views have always been regarded as reflecting those of the administration, made a comprehensive statement to that effect. The statement was attributed to "an official close to the administration."

The story consisted primarily of a long verbatim quotation from the unnamed official describing an earlier decision of the Supreme Court, joined by Harlan, in which, according to the official, "the light of reason" was invoked to void the prosecution of a New York church for contracting with an English clergyman to fill its pulpit, in a literal violation of immigration law.[54]

In all of this immense coverage, none of it included any reaction from the presumed beneficiaries, American consumers, nor any estimate of those presumed benefits.

THE TAFT COURT DEMURS

Slowing the advance of antitrust enforcement, the Taft Court (1921–30) handed down several decisions against the government in 1926 and 1927. It dismissed a Justice Department allegation that United States Steel Corporation had grown so large that it inhibited competition.[55] It found no Sherman Act violation in General Electric Company's licensing the manufacture of its incandescent bulbs to competitor Westinghouse Electric and Manufacturing Company and fixing the resale price.[56] It dismissed a government allegation that International Harvester Company was not abiding by a prior consent degree to limit its sales agencies and divest some of its farm machinery lines in order to enhance competition.[57] It held the Colorado antitrust law unconstitutionally vague under the due process clause of the Fourteenth Amendment because it necessitated the determination of a "reasonable profit."[58]

However, the Taft Court affirmed the Sherman Act conviction of 20 individuals and 20 corporations for fixing the prices of sanitary pottery,[59] and it judged a stonecutters union's refusal to work on limestone quarried by workers who were not members of its union an illegal restraint of trade under the Sherman Act. In the limestone case the Court also invoked another antitrust law, the Clayton Act of 1914, to order an injunction against the union. Justice Louis Brandeis dissented, joined by Justice Holmes.[60]

In sharp contrast to the newspapers' immense attention to the earlier antitrust decisions, the coverage of these cases was spotty. The limestone case fared better than most. The *Washington Post* and the *Chicago Daily Tribune* put it on page one, and the *New York Times* wrote a fine story, noting the invocation of both the Sherman and Clayton acts, and quoting both the majority opinion and the dissent of Justice Brandeis, who said the Court's decision "reminds of involuntary servitude."[61]

When it came to labor matters, the Taft Court's view was simple: the Constitution did not support pro-labor legislation. The Court struck down an Arizona law banning injunctions against picketing as a violation of the due process clause and the equal protection clause of the Fourteenth Amendment;[62] held that Congress's taxing power could not sustain a renewed effort to limit child labor;[63] and ruled 5-3 that a District of Columbia minimum wage law for women violated the liberty of contract guaranteed by the due process clause.[64]

Newspapers jumped on the District of Columbia minimum-wage story, and went beyond it. The *Boston Daily Globe,* an afternoon paper, reported the decision that same day, then on the following day, along with other papers, printed a scathing criticism by Samuel Gompers, president of the American Federation of Labor, of the ruling: "It demeans humanity. Women and girl wage-earners are to be bought over the counter."[65] The *Globe* also quoted a state labor official as saying that enforcement of the Massachusetts minimum wage law would not be affected by the decision.[66] But the *Los Angeles Times* quoted a state commission member as expecting the Court decision to presage invalidation of California's minimum wage for women of sixteen dollars per week.[67]

Even though the decision was the Taft Court's third in a row against labor regulation, editorial comment was muted. In fact the *Washington Post* supported the ruling, declaring that although the District of Columbia law benefited some persons, "it opened the way to the curtailment of the rights of other groups, and in the long run would have been detrimental to the public interest."[68]

THE HUGHES COURT AND ANTITRUST

The Hughes Court (1930–41) went both for and against the government in antitrust cases. In its first three years it found no Sherman Act violation in an agreement among oil companies to license patents for "cracking" gasoline,[69] nor in a "price-stabilization" marketing agreement among Appalachian coal companies struggling to cope with the Depression.[70] But the Court declined to modify a 1920 consent decree in which the major meatpackers agreed to halt their expansion into the grocery business.[71] This was front-page news in Chicago, home of the packing companies, although the Supreme Court provided an even bigger page-one story for the *Chicago Daily Tribune* that day by declining to hear Al Capone's petition for review of his income tax evasion conviction. "PRISON TONIGHT FOR CAPONE" screamed the banner headline.

The *Tribune*'s lead on the meatpacking story was tart: "Past days of monopolistic power were raked up by the United States Supreme court today and thrown into the faces of the meat packers as the court refused to consent to the modification of the packers' consent decree of 1920." A day later the *Tribune* offered a cogent editorial observation that the packers' rights under the law "were more than a little vague thanks in part to the Supreme court itself. To this day business men do not know and their lawyers cannot tell them with much assurance what the courts will probably decide the Sherman and Clayton acts permit and what these laws forbid."[72]

A STONE TURNED

The most important business case decided by the Court during the tenure of Chief Justice Stone (1941–46) was a challenge to Congress's empowerment of the Federal Communications Commission to grant station licenses and promulgate broadcasting rules, as set forth in the Communications Act of 1934. The case was *National Broadcasting Co. v. United States.*[73] The Court, recognizing that the broadcast spectrum is limited, held that the grant of regulatory authority to the FCC was constitutional and that the Chain Broadcasting Regulations specifically at issue in the case were a proper exercise of that authority. The Associated Press reported crisply:

> Regulations prohibiting exclusive broadcast contracts between a network and a radio station and otherwise restricting their relationships were upheld today by the Supreme Court as a valid exercise of the Federal Communications Commission's licensing power in the "public interest, convenience or necessity."[74]

As unexceptionable as the decision may seem in today's regulated world, it seriously ruffled some broadcast and newspaper feathers at the time. Both NBC and CBS were so incensed, according to another AP story, that they "spoke of the possible desirability of changes in fundamental radio law."[75] Columnist David Lawrence whined, "The first step toward abridging the freedom of the press in America has been taken by five members of the Supreme Court of the United Sates in a decision, which, while it puts radio broadcasting into a government strait-jacket, opens the way for strangulation of the newspapers of America."[76] The *Wall*

Street Journal was appalled, calling such a regulatory scheme "a grotesque absurdity" and raging facetiously:

> If the logic of the Supreme Court's majority—and for that matter of the minority—is sound the Constitution of the United States and particularly the Bill of Rights and some other amendments, is little more than empty verbiage, and might be replaced by the "welfare clause" with a single commission to give it effect.[77]

As with the antitrust coverage, no one thought to ask the putative beneficiaries of the decision, in this case independent radio stations and radio listeners, what they thought, or told how the decision might actually impact them.

THE WARREN COURT: AGGRESSIVE ON ANTITRUST, TOO

Although it is best known for its decisions on free expression, racial discrimination, criminal procedure, and voting rights, the Warren Court (1953–69) decided a number of antitrust cases, most of them establishing much tighter interpretations of antitrust law, often reversing lower courts and generally favorable to the government's trustbusters. In June 1957 the Court ruled that the Du Pont Company's acquisition of 23 percent of General Motors stock nearly forty years earlier violated section 7 of the Clayton Act, which prohibited stock acquisitions or mergers that tend to create a monopoly. The Court said the stock ownership enabled Du Pont to become the dominant supplier of fabrics and finishes to the number one carmaker. The decision was novel for two reasons: the acts judged illegal had taken place long ago, when auto manufacturing was a fragmented industry, in sharp contrast to GM's 50 percent market share when the Justice Department filed suit; and the Court for the first time applied section 7 of the Clayton Act to an acquisition of stock in another industry, not just the horizontal acquisition of a competitor's stock that the act clearly targeted or the supplier–customer vertical acquisitions that probably were in mind, too.

The basis for the decision was wobbly, with a majority comprising only four justices, while three abstained for various reasons. Justice Harold Burton filed a stinging dissent, joined by Justice Felix Frankfurter, protesting that "[e]very corporation which has acquired a stock interest in another corporation after the enactment of the Clayton Act in 1914, and which has had business dealings with that corporation is exposed, retroactively, to the bite of the newly discovered teeth of § 7."[78]

Despite its lack of relevance for consumers, the story was widely reported, commonly on page one. Unfortunately, the Associated Press account run by many newspapers, a story that may have been slighted under another end-of-term avalanche of important decisions, failed to emphasize the sweeping legal novelties of the decision and the sharp disagreement within the Court. But some major papers did so very well, with ample detail and useful quotations from the dissent. In Chicago, where a federal judge had dismissed the government's suit after a months-long trial, the *Tribune* noted appropriately that, in the view of the two dissenters, "the government had not proved there was a 'reasonable probability' in 1917 of restraint of trade or monopoly."[79] The *New York Times* ran several clear, informative stories on the decision, with ample interpretation. *Times* columnist Arthur Krock commented that it "disregards both the language and the purpose of the Clayton Act and all precedents 'save one district court decision.'"[80] The

Wall Street Journal agreed that the decision was "so sweeping that it throws suspicion on any company that does business with any other company any of whose stock it may own."[81]

Among the other significant decisions handed down by the Supreme Court that same June day, the papers gave good coverage to a ruling that grievance-arbitration clauses in labor union contracts may be enforced in the federal courts.[82]

The Supreme Court again surprised much of the business world when it ruled against the merger of Brown Shoe Company, Inc., and G. R. Kinney Company, Inc., both manufacturers and retailers of men's, women's, and children's shoes.[83] Brown's share of the manufacturing market was 4 percent, Kinney's less than one-half of one percent. Of the total national sales by 70,000 stores selling shoes, Kinney had a market share of one and two-tenths percent; none was given for Brown, yet the decision was based on a prospective retail market position of the merged company that the Court deemed anticompetitive under the Clayton Act.

The Court noted a trend toward consolidation in the industry, enabling manufacturers to better retail their products through their own stores, and judged that Brown's resulting control of two and three-tenths percent of the nation's shoe outlets might substantially lessen competition in shoe retailing. Chief Justice Warren's opinion, fifty-one pages long, was more speculation than fact: "In an industry as fragmented as shoe retailing, the control of substantial shares of the trade in a city may have important effects on competition," he wrote for a six-judge majority. "If a merger achieving 5% control were now approved, we might be required to approve future merger efforts by Brown's competitors seeking similar market shares. The oligopoly Congress sought to avoid would then be furthered and it would be difficult to dissolve the combinations previously approved."[84]

Although the *Wall Street Journal* and the *Washington Post* recognized the case as especially significant,[85] it was just one small part of a tidal wave of Supreme Court decisions and orders—245 of them, including a number of other important rulings on such issues as school segregation, narcotics addiction, lunchroom sit-ins, contempt of Congress, taxes, and even several other antitrust cases—on that final day of the 1961–62 term. One was a stunning decision banning a state-prescribed prayer in public schools.[86] This story, not surprisingly, dominated the front pages throughout the country. The papers simply could not keep up. Even the *New York Times* relegated a number of important cases to a page-18 summary of Court actions, with just this for *Brown Shoe:* "Held unanimously that acquisition by the country's fourth largest shoe manufacturer, making about 4 per cent of the nation's shoes, of the largest national family shoe store chain violated section 7 of the Clayton Act as amended in 1950."[87] Some papers used the Associated Press story, which like the *Times* misleadingly mentioned manufacturing-market share, but neither the AP nor the more extensive articles in the *Journal* and the *Post* made it clear that the basis for the Court's ruling was the prospective impact on shoe retailing. Nor did they state the tiny shares of that market held by Brown and Kinney. An opportunity for incisive journalism lost.

In quick succession in the spring of 1967, the Warren Court four times reversed lower courts to lay down additional tighter antitrust rules. In April the Court held that household products giant Procter & Gamble Co.'s acquisition of Clorox Chemical Co. violated the Clayton Act because P&G's advertising power might discourage competition in the market for household liquid bleach.[88] Then the Court ruled that falling prices of frozen pies in Utah could rationally be attributed to illegal price discrimination, blamed on national companies trying to take market share from the dominant, local company, an effort that might, in the end, lessen competition.[89] It was crystal ball–gazing piled on supposition piled on speculation. Louis M. Kohlmeier of the *Wall Street Journal* wrote, "One yea, one nay for price competition," adding: "If, as the Supreme Court repeatedly has said, price competition is the greatest boon the free enterprise system can bestow on consumers, the consumers have been cheated."[90]

In June the Court ruled that exclusive sales territories delineated by mattress maker Sealy, Inc., and bicycle manufacturer Arnold, Schwinn & Co. were unlawful under the Sherman Antitrust Act because they limited competition as part of price-fixing schemes.[91] These decisions were important antitrust markers and had clear implications for consumers. On the same day the Court upheld two significant rulings of the National Labor Relations Board under the National Labor Relations Act of 1935. The Court ruled that a union at tractor maker Allis-Chalmers Manufacturing Co. could fine recalcitrant members who continued to work during a strike,[92] and that an employer was required to pay accrued annual vacation benefits even after its union contract expired and the workers had gone out on strike.[93]

These four important decisions clearly warranted public dissemination, but, once again, they were but grains of sand in a windstorm, for the Court, wrapping up its term that day, inundated reporters with 184 decisions and other rulings. Though Arnold, Schwinn was a prominent Chicago company, the *Chicago Tribune* made do with a short Associated Press story, and it ignored the labor rulings.[94] The *Washington Post* reported one labor decision but omitted the other. The *Los Angeles Times* covered neither the labor nor the antitrust cases.

But the decisions were not entirely ignored. The *Washington*

Post wrote a short story on the antitrust cases with a punchy lead: "The Supreme Court yesterday ruled that two important methods of licensed or franchised product distribution violate U.S. antitrust laws."[95] The *New York Times* put one labor case, the fines for nonstriking union members at Allis-Chalmers, on page one, with extensive quotations from both the majority and minority opinions, appropriate for a 5-4 decision. At the end of his story *Times* reporter David R. Jones mentioned an unusual local angle: "Allis-Chalmers had been joined in its fight against the fines, which ranged from $20 to $100, by 23 New York Times advertising salesmen who were fined up to $1,500 each by the American Newspaper Guild for crossing picket lines in a 1965 strike."[96] Back on page 84, the *Times* wrapped the two antitrust cases together.[97]

THE REHNQUIST COURT AND INTELLECTUAL PROPERTY

Though the Supreme Court of Chief Justice Rehnquist (1986–2005) was known more for conservative restraint, especially in regard to civil liberties, affirmative action, and criminal law, and for a federalism that favored the states, that Court did not hesitate to hand down novel and expansive interpretations of intellectual property law, often reversing lower courts.

The Court made two such rulings, both unanimous, in March 1994. It held that a prevailing defendant in a copyright case was equally entitled to recover his attorney fees as a prevailing plaintiff.[98] Then it declared that a parody of a copyrighted song may be exempt from copyright infringement as a "fair use," which is usually available only to limited copying for school classes, research, comment, and such. The holding overturned an appellate court ruling that the popular song "Pretty Woman" by rap group 2 Live Crew infringed a copyright by Roy Orbison of his rock ballad "Oh, Pretty Woman." The Supreme Court sent the case back to the trial court, instructing it that the determination of fair use required that other factors, including the substantiality of the portion used and the effect on the market for the copyrighted work, must be considered along with the commercial nature of the new work.[99]

The attorney-fee ruling was too esoteric to excite the newspapers, but they swarmed around the 2 Live Crew case. In a page-one story the *Philadelphia Inquirer* quoted a 2 Live Crew lawyer as saying, "This is a very important victory for Saturday Night Live, the Capitol Steps, Mark Russell, Mad magazine, the Harvard Lampoon and many others who make their living through the commercial use of parody."[100] The *New York Times* also put the story on the front page, declaring that the Court was "carving out a safety zone for parody,"[101] and the next day expressed editorial delight. Was it a question of "commercial ripoff" or "legitimate artistic commentary"? asked the *Times*. "The Supreme Court . . . deftly split the difference. . . . Parodists no less than their targets— original creators of literature, music and other arts—have their place in a free, competitive society. Now when they clash they will have reasonable guidance and ground rules from the Supreme Court."[102] The *Washington Post* just loved it:

> It's a rare Supreme Court opinion that's actually fun to read. But the copyright infringement case . . . meets the test. . . .
>
> [I]n setting out the reasoning of the unanimous court, Justice David Souter revealed his expertise not only on the Crew's lyrics

("Big hairy woman ... Bald-headed woman") but in details like bass riffs and the fact that the group plays "a regional, hip-hop style of rap from the Liberty City area of Miami." ...

The essence of the ruling is a rousing reaffirmation of the right of an artist, writer or performer to parody someone else's work without infringing copyright.[103]

However, another big-name copyright dispute drew little attention, perhaps because it concerned older art. The owners of the Alfred Hitchcock classic movie *Rear Window,* including James Stewart, one of its stars, were found to have violated the copyright on the original short story when they rereleased the film in the 1980s. The *New York Times* and the *Washington Post* put the story on the front of the business section. The *Times* featured a three-column image of a film scene with Stewart and Grace Kelly, and Linda Greenhouse provided useful numbers: "As a result, the movie's owners, including the actor James Stewart, who was one of its stars, will have to pay damages and a portion of the movie's profits to a literary agent who in 1972 acquired the copyright to the short story for $650. 'Rear Window' generated more than $12 million in gross revenue in commercial distribution during the 1980's."[104] The *Wall Street Journal* emphasized the burden placed on the movie industry:

> "This has put a whole number of works in limbo," said Louis P. Petrich, who represented MCA and the other defendants. "All the works created from 1962 to 1977 [a new Copyright Act took effect in 1978] that are subject to renewal are going to become like lepers, because if you use them in creating a new work, there's always the potential that they're going to be like a little time bomb."[105]

The Rehnquist Court took up matters of interest to advertisers and consumer-goods manufacturers, such as whether a color could be trademarked (yes)[106] and whether Wal-Mart Stores, Inc.'s deliberate knockoffs of a manufacturer's children's clothing could constitute a violation of the manufacturer's trademark. The answer to this question was that the aggrieved party must show that its product's design was distinctive because it had acquired "secondary meaning." In a unanimous opinion reversing an appellate court, Justice Scalia noted that the Lanham Trademark Act provides for the registration of any trademark "by which the goods of the applicant may be distinguished from the goods of others," including "a mark used by the applicant which has become distinctive of the applicant's goods in commerce," or, in Scalia's words, a mark "which is not inherently distinctive but has become so only through secondary meaning."[107] The Court sent the case back to the trial court to make the determination.

Though Justice Scalia's opinion was phrased mostly in negatives—a unique design like an orange Tide bottle is not sufficient—several papers made his meaning clear. Lorrie Grant wrote in *USA Today* that "in the apparel industry, long rife with imitations, the test for inherent distinction has been cloudy. A company had to prove either that its products were inherently distinctive or that consumers had to recognize that the product came from a certain source. Now it must do both."[108] The *Washington Post* helpfully quoted an authority:

> "This is an age-old issue," said retail expert Christiana Shi of McKinsey & Co., a management consulting firm. "There are always broad trends that everyone follows. But the court's decision does up the ante for name brands to find additional ways to really put unique source content into their product design."

Unfortunately the *Post* topped its good story with a misleading headline proclaiming "Knockoffs Legal"—not at all what the Court decided.[109]

A must case for the press was *New York Times Co. v. Tasini,* a 2001 ruling that publishers' placement of freelance writers' work in electronic databases violated the authors' copyrights. The Court, by 7-2, affirmed an appellate court decision, but suggested that authors and publishers "may enter into an agreement allowing continued electronic reproduction of the Authors' works."[110] It was but one of 235 decisions and other actions announced by the Court on that final day of its term, and a 5-4 campaign-finance limit decision warranted the big play,[111] but the copyright ruling got a share of the next day's ink. Warren Richey wrote in the *Christian Science Monitor:* "The US Supreme Court has just wrenched a key part of US copyright law out of the age of the printing press and into the age of digital cyberspace."[112]

The *New York Times* announced its own loss on page one, with an inside story adding, "Newspaper and magazine publishers ... began preparing yesterday to cull thousands of articles from Lexis-Nexis and other online databases while positioning themselves for the next round in the battle with writers' groups."[113]

As the federal copyright law was about to expire in 1998, intense lobbying pitted Walt Disney Co. and other holders of valuable old copyrights against Internet practitioners and other advocates of free public access to such older works. Acting under the authority of the copyright clause of the Constitution, which authorizes Congress to "promote the Progress of Science and useful Arts, by securing for limited Times to Authors and Inventors the exclusive Right to their respective Writings and Discoveries," Congress extended the term of existing and future copyrights by 20 years, to a term of 70 years after an author's death, and for "works made for hire," essentially for corporations, 95 years from publication. A New Hampshire Web publisher of classic books, Eric Eldred, sued Attorney General John Ashcroft to overturn the statute, contending that the extension exceeded the "limited times" authorized by the copyright clause and that it also violated the First Amendment's guarantee of free speech. However, the Supreme Court found no constitutional violation and sustained the statute.[114] Justices John Paul Stevens and Stephen Breyer dissented forcefully.

It was a Hollywood story. Pamela McClintock of *Daily Variety* reported from Washington:

> Handing the entertainment biz an enormous win Wednesday, the U.S. Supreme Court upheld a 1998 law giving Hollywood nearly a century before having to release copyrighted pics into the public domain and lose exclusive rights to sell coveted classics.
>
> In a 7-2 ruling worth billions to showbiz, the Robes said Capitol Hill was perfectly within its rights when it extended the life of copyrighted works by two decades, from 75 to 95 years.
>
> Industryites say the ruling provides an important investment incentive, both for future projects and for hundreds of existing works.[115]

Bill Hillburg of the Los Angeles *Daily News* said the ruling kept Mickey Mouse "in Disney's cast until 2024." He noted that Justice Ruth Bader Ginsburg in her majority opinion sustaining Congress's right to make such policy judgments added, "however debatable or arguably unwise they may be."[116] Lyle Denniston of the *Boston Globe* noted the frustration of the minority: "Dissenting from the ruling along with Justice Breyer was Justice John Paul Stevens, who accused the majority of operating on 'the mistaken premise that this court has virtually no role in reviewing congressional grants of monopoly privileges to authors, inventors, and their successors.' "[117]

Critics of the ruling pulled no punches. Dan Gillmore, the technology columnist of the *San Jose Mercury News,* called the statute "a brazen heist. . . . Who got robbed? You did. I did. Who won? Endlessly greedy media barons will now collect billions from works that should have long since entered the public domain."[118] The *New York Times* was somber:

> In effect, the Supreme Court's decision makes it likely that we are seeing the beginning of the end of public domain and the birth of copyright perpetuity. Public domain has been a grand experiment, one that should not be allowed to die. The ability to draw freely on the entire creative output of humanity is one of the reasons we live in a time of such fruitful creative ferment.[119]

The federal government exercises immense influence over the private economy through independent regulatory agencies like the Federal Communications Commission and the Securities and Exchange Commission. More often than not the Court affirms agency decisions, so the news is not surprising. Therefore it is instructive to consider a case that did not go the agency's way, and, unlike many regulatory actions, was a case of immediate, broad public significance.

The case was *Whitman v. American Trucking Associations, Inc.,* decided in 2001.[120] Christine Todd Whitman was the administrator of the Environmental Protection Agency (EPA), whose national ambient air-quality standards for particulate matter and ozone were challenged by business organizations as unconstitutional and improper under the Clean Air Act.

In a multifaceted decision sending the standards back for revision, the Supreme Court ruled, reversing a prominent decision of the District of Columbia Court of Appeals, that Congress had not unconstitutionally delegated legislative power to the EPA to decide such matters.[121] Justice Scalia wrote for the Court that what Congress delegated in the Clean Air Act was merely an acceptable "certain degree of discretion." But he faulted the agency's application of its authority, saying it could not consider implementation costs in setting air quality standards, and therefore held that the EPA's interpretation of the Clean Air Act in implementation of the ozone standards was unlawful.[122] There were no dissenters, but Scalia's opinion was not entirely satisfactory to all the justices. Three wrote concurrences explaining their own reasoning. In an unusual pas de deux, Justice Thomas and Justice Stevens, ideological extremes, questioned in separate opinions the majority's conclusion that the statute was not an unconstitutional delegation of legislative power.

Press coverage was not universal, but the newspapers that ran the story saw it as both important and constructive. Editorial comment was uniformly favorable. A "wise ruling," said the Syracuse *Post-Standard*.[123] The *Palm Beach Post* declared, in bland approval, "national sentiment clearly is on the side of regulation that benefits the public good."[124] The *New York Times* reported the decision on page one, calling it "one of the court's most important environmental rulings in years." Dealing prominently with the issue of delegating legislative power, Linda Greenhouse wrote that the District of Columbia appellate court, ruling on the case two years earlier, had "startled much of official Washington and the legal world by reviving the so-called nondelegation doctrine, which the Supreme Court had used to strike down two New Deal programs in 1935 but that had fallen into great disfavor since then."

She continued: "On the current court, Justice Scalia and Chief Justice William H. Rehnquist had, in past opinions, indicated the most interest in reviving the nondelegation doctrine. It was therefore particularly interesting that the chief justice, exercising his power to assign opinions, asked Justice Scalia to write the court's opinion."[125] The *Times* noted in an approving editorial, "Justice Antonin Scalia briskly disposed of this [constitutional] argument by asserting that the delegation of authority had been no greater than delegations to other administrative agencies that the court had upheld over the years."[126]

With or without constitutional interpretations, there are inevitably winners and losers in Supreme Court rulings on business and labor. In the early nineteenth-century cases, they were usually just the parties to the case—the bridge builders, the specific workers, and so on. But from the 1890s on, most Court rulings in the economic realm have had implications reaching well beyond the parties, to many other companies or unions or workers similarly situated. Although, with some exceptions that we have noted, the press has not universally covered these sometimes difficult opinions, even the good stories typically have gone little beyond the text and reactions from the parties. Missing are other businesses and industries affected, and how. Consumers, in particular, the alleged beneficiaries of antitrust and regulatory statutes, are absent, too. Do they notice? Do they care? Would further reporting and additional stories tell us?

Editorials on Court opinions, as on all issues of public policy, are helpful in focusing citizen attention on important questions. But editorials on business and labor decisions (few on the latter) comment primarily on the results in a political sense, as public affairs, shying away from challenging or even analyzing the legal reasoning that is the essence of every Supreme Court opinion. Is it too much to hope that editorial writers will have the necessary knowledge and sophistication? Sometimes little more than common sense and ordinary journalistic skepticism are needed, as in assessing the Warren Court's arbitrary and speculative rulings such as *Brown Shoe* on what sort of business conditions foster competition and consumer benefit. Although *Brown Shoe* held that the merger of two companies would impair competition at the retail level, the Court never stated what that combined market share would amount to nor what the legal limit might be, nor why growth by merger should be any different to the consumer from a company's organic growth. Nor did the papers seize on this ideal opportunity for commentary.

The Court's omission of quantitative reasoning, of economic data, particularly in its antitrust opinions, is striking when viewed today. The *Wall Street Journal* reported in the mid-1960s that economists were beginning to play a larger role in the government's antitrust decisions,[127] but the numbers, if any, used to support subsequent Supreme Court antitrust decisions were little more than market shares. Credible assessments of prevailing market conditions, judging competition by prices rather than by the number of competitors, could be instructive. Could journalists have originated such observations, or obtained them from economists or other experts? If we judge such insights to be above a reporter's or editorial writer's pay grade, we admit a serious shortcoming.

TEN

VOTING RIGHTS AND CIRCUMSCRIBED ELECTIONS

We might think of voting rights and elections as being legal issues born in the second half of the twentieth century, posited by both the Supreme Court and Congress. In one sense that is true, for a new generation of such issues originated then. But voting issues arose occasionally even before the Civil War. Then after it a host of voting questions, mostly involving former slaves' right to vote, swirled about. Here again, as with cases involving other individual rights, we have a visible, clear standard to measure results against, at least since 1870: the guarantee of the Fifteenth Amendment: "The right of citizens of the United States to vote shall not be denied or abridged by the United States or by any State on account of race, color, or previous condition of servitude." The amendment also provides that "[t]he Congress shall have power to enforce this article by appropriate legislation." Note that this guarantee, unlike some others in the Constitution, applies equally to the state and federal governments. A stout benchmark, indeed.

We define "voting rights" here to encompass the conduct of elections, including the drawing of legislative districts and the rules governing campaign finances. All these matters were traditionally in the province of the states, governed by state statutes and administered by local governments. Even voting for federal offices—members of Congress, president, and vice president—was state-controlled.

A harbinger of later intense clashes on voting rights, one early complaint actually led to rebellion. Urban voters in Rhode Island were deeply distressed at being disenfranchised and malapportioned under the still-operative 1663 royal charter. So in 1842 they seized on the guarantee of a "Republican Form of Government" in Article IV of the Constitution[1] to call a rump constitutional convention for the state. They drafted a new constitution, conducted a vote ratifying it, and elected Thomas Wilson Dorr as governor of Rhode Island. It was Dorr's Rebellion. The actual governor declared martial law, and state judges convicted Dorr of treason. But when a case challenging a home break-in and an arrest by a Rhode Island militiaman came before the Supreme Court, Chief Justice Roger Taney ducked the constitutional issue by enunciating a doctrine of "political questions"—matters that the executive and legislative branches should decide.[2] Reports of the decision appeared in several New England newspapers, though not always prominently. Buried as the tenth item in a long column of news briefs, this was the entire story in one New Hampshire paper:

> The U.S. Supreme Court (Judge Woodbury excepted) has decided that the Rhode Island Dorr insurrection was decidedly out of order.[3]

The dissent by Justice Levi Woodbury of New Hampshire brought him some grief. A correspondent for the New York *Ex-*

press identified only as E. B., in a report of the decision picked up by at least two New England newspapers, averred:

> Much of the respect which has hitherto been attached to the unity and opinions of the Court is fast fading away, in consequence of a want of unity of opinion among the Judges.
>
> Even where there is a concurrence of opinion, there is often a dissent from the reasons of that opinion, the effect of which is often a loss of confidence, in law, law courts, judicial decisions, and the high tribunals of justice.
>
> Mr. Woodbury is the chief of sinners in these innovations, and he takes thereby much more from the dignity and stability of the Bench, of which he is a member, than he adds to his own reputation from any opinion of his, however able.
>
> Mr. Woodbury's Report this morning was long beyond the patience of most listeners, and nearly two hours were occupied in the delivery.[4]

Because of E. B.'s dependence on the oral delivery, and because there were no quotations from the opinion in his substantial story, we may infer that the Court provided no printed opinion on decision day.

The Supreme Court under Chief Justice Waite (1874–88) was, as we have seen, not receptive to the new rights created by the three post–Civil War amendments. But in 1875 the Court derogated several provisions of the original Constitution and the Bill of Rights as well as the Fourteenth Amendment in ruling that a state could deny women the right to vote. No such right was conferred, the Court ruled unanimously, by the amendment's citizenship clause or its "privileges or immunities" clause,[5] or by the "republican form of government" clause of Article IV, or by the due process clause of the Fifth Amendment, or by the Article I prohibition of bills of attainder, laws that inflict punishment without trial or verdict. "The Constitution, when it conferred citizenship," the chief justice wrote, "did not necessarily confer the right of suffrage."[6]

A year later the Waite Court also brushed aside the Fifteenth Amendment and its implementing statute, the Enforcement Act of 1870. In a Kentucky case involving the refusal to register a former slave, the Court ruled 8-1 that the amendment prohibited only exclusion on racial grounds, and that the Enforcement Act's operative section was invalid because it did not repeat the Fifteenth Amendment's words "race, color, or previous condition of servitude."[7]

Egregious though they were by modern standards, these decisions received scant notice from the press at the time. The Kentucky case suffered by its release on the same day as *United States v. Cruikshank,* the notorious Grant Parish or Colfax Massacre whitewash described in chapter 8.[8] The few papers that covered the voting case did so by merely publishing most of the opinion, fussy legal reasoning, and providing no summary, explanation, or interpretation. As the *Boston Daily Advertiser* reported,

> In the Kentucky election case the court says the fifteenth amendment does not confer the right of suffrage upon any one. It prevents the States or the United States, however, from giving preference in this particular to one citizen of the United States over another on account of race, color or previous condition of servitude.[9]

This was a gross misstatement of the Fifteenth Amendment. It prohibits denying or abridging the right to vote. It says nothing about "giving preference." The press let it pass.

It was not only former slaves whose attempts to vote got short shrift from the Waite Court. It rejected an attempt by John Elk, a Native American, to register to vote, although he was native-born and had severed his tribal relationship to reside in Omaha. The justices grounded their refusal in the fact that Elk had not been naturalized and thus was not "born or naturalized in the United States, and subject to the jurisdiction thereof," the description of citizenship in the Fourteenth Amendment. Two justices dissented, Harlan declaring testily that the Court's ruling meant that

> there is still in this country a despised and rejected class of persons, with no nationality whatever; who, born in our territory, owing no allegiance to any foreign power, and subject, as residents of the States, to all the burdens of government, are yet not members of any political community nor entitled to any of the rights, privileges, or immunities of citizens of the United States.[10]

A news story, perhaps by the Associated Press although not attributed, appeared in several papers, written in the chronological style of the day. The *Atchison* (Kansas) *Daily Globe:* "A decision was rendered yesterday afternoon on a long series of cases which have arisen out of the adoption of the fourteenth and fifteenth amendments to the constitution." Although the story went on succinctly to state the Court's holding—that Elk "is not a citizen of the United States within the meaning of the first section of the fourteenth amendment" and therefore "has been deprived of no right secured by the fifteenth amendment"—the pointed dissent unfortunately was reduced to this one sentence: "Justice Harlan read a long dissenting opinion in behalf of Justice Woods and himself."[11]

THE FULLER COURT IN DENIAL

Like the Waite Court, that of Chief Justice Melville Fuller (1888–1910) handed down voting decisions that mirrored its cramped view of civil rights generally. The Court dismissed three cases from Alabama brought by Negroes who had been denied registration to vote. In the first decision, a complicated and circular exercise in legal reasoning announced orally without a written opinion available, Justice Holmes wailed that if the state constitution registration scheme, which included literacy and property requirements, were fraudulent, "how can we make the court a party to the unlawful scheme by accepting it and adding another voter to its fraudulent lists?" He brushed aside the Fourteenth and Fifteenth Amendments and advised the would-be voters to look to the political process, ironic in view of the fact that they had been refused participation in that process. Furthermore, noting that the colored man's plea "imports that the great mass of the white population intends to keep the blacks from voting," Holmes said that "to meet such an intent something more than ordering the plaintiff's name to be inscribed ... will be needed." Justice Harlan, one of three dissenters, stated simply, without offering a constitutional argument, that "the plaintiff is entitled to relief in respect of his right to be registered as a voter."[12]

A year later the Fuller Court dismissed two similar registration-denial cases on the ground that it lacked jurisdiction because the Alabama courts' decisions were based on state law only. "We do not perceive how this decision involved the adjudication of a right claimed under the Federal Constitution," the Court declared.[13] Justice Harlan again dissented, though without writing an opinion.

The first Alabama decision was widely reported, most papers using some version of the same story, apparently from a wire service. But the papers conveyed quite different results to the reader, depending on whether they ran the story long or cut it short, because the Court's ruling was not stated at the top of the story, simply that a decision was announced. In the *Waterloo* (Iowa) *Daily Reporter* and other papers, the story ran only two paragraphs, ending with this: "The relief sought was denied on the ground that the case was political. Justice Holmes, who delivered the opinion, said that for the court to interfere would be unheard of relief in cases presenting only political questions."[14] But in other papers the same story continued on for several more paragraphs, noting that the justices hesitated to consider the case because the appellate court had ruled that it lacked jurisdiction, but then decided it after all. "He then announced that it would be impossible to grant the relief asked," the *Atlanta Constitution* reported.[15] But why? None of the half-dozen papers that used that story got around to explaining how the Court managed to sidestep the obvious mandate of the Fifteenth Amendment and dismiss the case. Whoever the reporter was, a printed opinion surely would have helped him.

IN SEARCH OF THE FIFTEENTH AMENDMENT

More than six decades after its adoption the Fifteenth Amendment still did not resonate at the Supreme Court.[16] In 1935, under Chief Justice Hughes (1930–41), the Court held unanimously that the Texas all-white Democratic primary election did not violate the Fifteenth Amendment or the Fourteenth.[17] The story was smothered, however, by the Supreme Court's decision that same day to reverse for the second time the notorious Alabama rape convictions and death sentences of the Negro "Scottsboro boys."[18]

The *Chicago Daily Tribune* wrote the two cases together, on page one, leading with Scottsboro, and then noting that "the court rebuffed the colored race in another opinion. This was a decision that the Democratic party in Texas is a voluntary association, not subject to control by the state legislature, and as such may exclude colored persons from voting in its primaries." But the *Tribune* gave the decision some perspective: "Previously the court had ruled invalid a state law barring colored persons. A state cannot deny colored persons the right of franchise, but a party can.... This sweeping decision as to what a political party can do led to immediate speculation about the ideas it might inspire in some dictator like Huey Long of Louisiana."[19] The *New York Times* put the Scottsboro story on page one, voter registration on page 15, but quoted the voting opinion at length and enhanced the story with this amplification: "The Texas case has attracted more than ordinary interest because of the ruses and devices whereby Negroes are prevented from voting in various Southern States, where the 'grandfather clause,' tests of high intelligence, poll taxes and even a requirement to expound a passage of the Bible are employed as tests."[20] The story played differently in Texas, where the Associated Press reported from Austin:

> Texas Democrats, comprising a vast majority of the white residents of the State, have at last found a legal way to prevent negroes from voting in their primaries.... The general opinion here was that Democrats of other Southern States could follow Texas' lead and exclude negroes by convention action unless State laws prohibited such a procedure.[21]

Nine years later the Supreme Court, with seven new members and a new chief, Harlan Fiske Stone, abruptly reversed ground to hold, seventy-four years after the adoption of the Fifteenth

Amendment, that the Texas Democratic primary's exclusion of Negroes did indeed violate that promise. A lone dissenter was Justice Owen Roberts, author of the earlier opinion.[22] This decision was much more widely reported, but Texas was not amused. The *Amarillo Daily News* topped a half-dozen World War II stories with an eight-column banner headline:

PRIMARY VOTE FOR NEGRO DENOUNCED

> WASHINGTON, April 3 (AP)—Supreme court action today, upsetting a decision of nine years' standing in ruling that negroes have the right to vote in Texas Democratic primary elections, brought bitter denunciations from southern members of Congress. The ruling, which prompted Justice Roberts to protest the tribunal's opinions are getting to be like a railroad ticket, good only for one day in one train, was branded an assault on states' rights....
> The decision has far-reaching implications for the South, where success in a primary usually is tantamount to election, but whether it will lead to any great increase in the number of negro voters is considered doubtful.

A second front-page story in the Amarillo paper, also by the Associated Press, reported that Texas Democrats "unofficially indicated party machinery might be reorganized to preserve exclusive white participation."[23]

Arthur Krock of the *New York Times,* while describing the Court's reasoning, had his own take on "the real reason for the overturn. It is that the common sacrifices of wartime have turned public opinion and the court against previously sustained devices to exclude minorities from any privilege of citizenship the majority enjoys."[24] The *Washington Post* praised the decision as "a bold stroke for democracy"[25] and the *Los Angeles Times* commented, "At last the nation knows where it stands."[26]

Despite the copious coverage of the Texas primary case, just two years later, in 1946, the press missed what would become a momentous voting issue. The Court considered a novel question: whether the Constitution could be invoked to remedy disparities in the size of congressional districts. The answer, by just 4-3, was no, but the decision received little coverage and no attention to the constitutional issues, which were clearly stated in Justice Black's dissent if not in Justice Frankfurter's opinion for the Court. Frankfurter declared that districting was a political matter to be decided by the legislature and "courts ought not to enter this political thicket," a term that would resound for many years to come.[27] (Recall that Chief Justice Taney in *Luther v. Borden,* concerning Dorr's Rebellion in Rhode Island, similarly ducked a "political question," although Justice Frankfurter did not cite that ruling as precedent here.) The Court rejected an allegation by three voters in Illinois, where congressional districts varied between 914,000 residents and 112,000, that the unequal weight of their votes violated the Fourteenth Amendment's equal protection clause and the provision of Article I, Section 2 that representatives "shall be . . . chosen . . . by the People of the several States."

Once again, a major decision came down on the Court's busy last day of its term, but all the decisions announced that day were overridden by yet another Court event, an unprecedented public attack by one justice on another. It mesmerized Washington and got top billing everywhere. FEUD RIPS SUPREME COURT! screamed the eight-column banner headline in the *Chicago Daily Tribune,*[28] while an adjacent story spelled out the accusation by Justice Jackson that Justice Black had persuaded the Court to favor a former law partner in a recent case. "Obviously seething," the *Tribune* reported, "because President Truman had selected Treasury Secretary Vinson for the post of chief justice, left open by the death of Chief Justice Stone, Jackson indicated his belief that he did not get the position because of reports spread by Black and others."[29] The Illinois districting decision also made page one, but it was written by a political reporter in Chicago who made no mention of the constitutional issues.[30] The *New York Times,* although it, too, put the story on the front page, also neglected the constitutional questions.[31] The pity was that, as in so many other divided Supreme Court rulings, the dissenters' reasoning, of which the public learned almost nothing, was so powerful that it would one day be adopted by the Court, in this instance completely altering the constitutional nature of U.S. election law.

THE WARREN COURT REWRITES ELECTION LAW

Under Chief Justice Warren (1953–69), the Supreme Court unleashed a flood of election law rulings, boldly rewriting this area of the law, but not without sharp disagreement among the justices. First the Court plunged into legislative districting, a close relative of the congressional districting that the Court had shied away from in 1946. Legislative-district maps traditionally were drawn by state legislators to suit their own interests, usually slighting urban areas by giving them districts more populous than rural districts. So the Court stunned the nation—especially state legislators—by ruling in *Baker v. Carr,* a case brought by voters in Memphis, Nashville, and Knoxville, that their claim of discrimination was indeed justiciable in federal courts under the equal protection clause of the Fourteenth Amendment. Revising the Court's Illinois holding, the vote was 6-2, with five opinions running 163 pages. One was a concurrence by Justice Tom Clark, who despaired of any prospective remedial action by Tennessee and would have preferred an immediate adjudication by the Supreme Court.[32]

As the newspapers said, it was truly monumental. The banner headline at the top of page one of the *New York Times:*

SUPREME COURT GIVES U.S. JUDGES
VOICE IN STATES' REAPPORTIONING;
URBAN-RURAL STRUGGLE AT ISSUE[33]

James E. Clayton, on the front page of the *Washington Post,* wrote, "The decision will almost surely rank in importance with such judicial landmarks as the pre–Civil War Dred Scott case and the 1954 ruling outlawing segregation in public schools."[34]

However, the papers devoted far more attention to interpreting and commenting on the likely impact of the decision than to describing the Court's reasoning and the vigorous dissents by Justices John Marshall Harlan and Felix Frankfurter, who contended that this political struggle had no place in federal court. William Beecher of the *Wall Street Journal* delved so deeply into possible political results in several states that his description of the Court's opinion did not commence until paragraph 24.[35]

The Associated Press filed a number of stories emphasizing the implications of the decision, and many papers favored these interpretive articles over the Court's opinion. The case "is likely to set off court suits and special legislative sessions in many states," one AP story declared. "One suit was filed within two hours after the decision was handed down Monday. A taxpayer in Atlanta asked that Georgia's county unit system be thrown out." Another AP story quoted politicians wondering, presciently, "if the U.S. courts can decide such matters it might not be long until they were asked to consider congressional districting."[36] The AP also produced a number of stories about the impact in individual states. Among four page-one AP stories on the case in the *Newport* (Rhode Island) *Daily News,* one quoted state officials on the prospect of prompt legislation to reapportion the state house of representatives. According to the article, a Republican legislator said "yesterday's U.S. Supreme Court decision will be an incentive to prod the Democrats into reapportioning the House, but, at least until yesterday, the chances for reapportiontment were exceedingly slim."[37] Still another AP story reported that a Mississippi lawyer, "representing a group of six Gulfport businessmen, said he would seek an immediate hearing on a suit to force reapportionment."[38]

Editorial writers and columnists could not resist the case. Most supported the decision, although William S. White maligned it as "rewriting the Constitution and meddling in politics to suit the wishes of some—but only some—of nine unelected men."[39] On the other hand, Roscoe Drummond predicted that the "ultimate consequence of the supreme court action will be to increase the capacity of the states to discharge their responsibilities to their citizens and thus to protect states' rights by exercising them rather than neglecting them."[40] Even conservative David Lawrence backed the decision: "One feels like giving a cheer for the Supreme Court of the United States for its temerity in cracking, even slightly, a precedent of nearly 100 years on which it has hitherto based a refusal to decide case after case involving so-called 'political questions.' "[41] The *New York Times,* like William S. White, read the decision as "a reinterpretation of the Constitution,"[42] but supported it so strongly that a day later it commented again, saying the case "imposes a clear duty on the New York Legislature to reexamine the basis on which its members are elected. . . .

The apportionment formula in use since 1894 results in a grossly unfair weighting of both houses in favor of the lesser-populated rural areas."[43] The *Charleston* (West Virginia) *Gazette* called the decision the Court's most important "since the verdict outlawing racial discrimination in the public schools." It asserted that the states, now "forewarned, . . . must act. If they don't, as Justice Clark indicated, the federal judiciary will."[44] Clearly, the press rose to the historic occasion.

A year later the Supreme Court declared the principle of "one man, one vote." It came in a case challenging Georgia's primary-election system of voting by county units, which also diluted urban votes.[45] Another year found the Court invalidating—as unconstitutionally disadvantaging urban voters—Georgia's congressional districts[46] and the legislative districts in fifteen states, declaring that both houses must be based substantially on population.[47] In the leading state case, *Reynolds v. Sims*, from Alabama, Chief Justice Warren wrote this memorable line: "Legislators represent people, not trees or acres."[48] Holding to his prior views, Justice Harlan was a lone but vehement dissenter in *Reynolds*. (He was joined by Justices Stewart and Clark in dissenting in cases from Colorado and New York.[49])

Anthony Lewis of the *New York Times* called *Reynolds* "a decision of historic importance" under a five-column, three-line headline on page one. "Not since the school segregation cases 10 years ago had the Court interpreted the Constitution to require so fundamental a change in this country's institutions," Lewis went on. "The big gainers from redistricting will be the cities and especially now the fast-growing suburbs."[50] It was one of eighteen *Times* stories that day about the case. The *Wall Street Journal* noted prominently in its story that "The High Court's decision—loaded with repetitive phrasing put there seemingly to avoid any misunderstanding—clearly rejected arguments that a state may apportion at least one house of its legislature along geographical or similar lines." Further, the *Journal* stated, "[t]he High Court's decision is its first effort to provide specific guidelines to states since its 1962 landmark decision that Federal courts have authority over legislative apportionment."[51]

The Associated Press again provided comprehensive coverage, including stories about many individual states and the likely impact there. "Practically every state in the Union," the AP reported, "faces an explosive change in its lawmaking and politics which eventually should give city voters a more equal voice in their state governments."[52] Among its numerous stories AP took the unusual step of writing separately and at length about Justice Harlan's dissent:

> Harlan said today's decision gives support to a "current mistaken view of the Constitution and the constitutional function of this court."
>
> He continued: "This view, in a nutshell, is that every major social ill in this country can find its cure in some constitutional principle, and that this court should take the lead in promoting reform when other branches of government fail to act."[53]

Smaller papers, too, featured the election cases. "The court got biting criticism for all three decisions, and high praise," wrote James Marlow of the Associated Press in a story that was widely published. "The country quickly adjusted to the first two and will to the third." The cases' perceived local impact was news everywhere, and politicians were not reluctant to be quoted. "Clark County legislators," the AP reported from Las Vegas, "were exultant Monday over a U.S. Supreme Court decision which meant to them Southern Nevada would have a bigger voice in the future destiny of the state."[54] Some papers gave greater attention to critics, most of them legislators who found themselves directly in the line of fire. "That Court's going crazy again," a South Carolina state senate leader told United Press International.[55] Some papers, reflecting uncertainty if not disdain, buried the story. The *Corpus Christi Times* led with a story on a Japanese earthquake and put *Reynolds* on page 7, publishing only a reaction story and none on the decision itself.[56]

Editorial comment on *Reynolds* by the national newspapers was less favorable than on the more philosophical *Baker v. Carr.* In support, the *Washington Post* declared, "Equal representation can mean the beginning of a constructive approach to urban problems."[57] The Court "is clearly right," said the *New York Times,* noting that the state's apportionment formula since 1894 "gives one vote for Assemblyman in Schuyler County the same weight as fourteen in Suffolk."[58] But the *Wall Street Journal* hooted at the Court's constitutional reasoning: "Well, if the legislature itself is an illegal body, can it perform legal acts? . . . How can anything an unconstitutional legislature does be anything but null and void?"[59]

The *Chicago Tribune,* defending the Illinois Senate's apportionment based on geography, worried that the Chicago Democratic Party boss, Mayor Richard J. Daley, would take over the state: "there are sound practical reasons for a legislative apportionment which protects the remainder of the state from domination by the large city. Large cities almost invariably are under the thumb of a political machine which is likely to be a one-man dictatorship."[60] (At the same time a *Tribune* news story reported that "Daley said it is merely 'propaganda' to say Chicago or Cook county would control the legislature."[61]) The *New Mexican* of Santa Fe also criticized the Court for its inclusion of senate seats, allocated one per county in that state: "we can't agree to its thoughts on the Senate. Without using the federal system, we have no need for two houses in our State Legislature."[62] Columnist David Lawrence fulminated, "No such usurpation of power by the judicial branch of the government has been recorded before in the whole history of the republic."[63]

However, for some papers *Reynolds v. Sims* represented not a national constitutional catastrophe but a local political opportunity. The *Delta Democrat-Times* in Greenville, Mississippi, noted that its congressional district, the largest in the state, "has almost 200,000 more people than the second largest," and asserted, "[w]e deserve a fairer congressional district shake than we have now, and the Supreme Court has indicated we can get it."[64]

BUT LOCAL ELECTIONS ARE DIFFERENT

The Supreme Court's first one-man, one-vote rulings were nearly unanimous, with only one dissenter in most cases, but when the Court in 1968 extended the rule to local government, Justices Abe Fortas and Potter Stewart joined Justice Harlan in vigorous opposition.[65] Local government, they contended, is different. Harlan declared that "the greater and more varied range of functions performed by local governmental units implies that flexibility in the form of their structure is even more important than at the state level." In this case, *Avery v. Midland County,* concerning the Midland County (Texas) Commissioners Court, Harlan contended it "performs more functions in the area of the county outside Midland City than it does within the city limits. Therefore, each rural resident has a greater interest in its activities than each city dweller. Yet under the majority's formula the urban residents are to have a dominant voice in the county government."[66] The Court held that the four county commissioner districts must be apportioned on a population basis, though 95 percent of the people lived in the city of Midland, which occupied just one of the four districts.

Wire services and newspapers noted the three dissents, but largely ignored their telling arguments. The *Chicago Tribune* simply reported "vigorous dissent."[67] The *Washington Post* consigned the dissenters' arguments to the last paragraph: "As a practical matter, the Midland commissioners exercised limited powers and their reapportionment will deprive rural residents of any voice in government, Fortas said."[68] The Associated Press alluded to the same remark.[69]

The *Los Angeles Times* gave more attention to the dissenters: "Under the redistricting scheme required by the high court, Fortas said, 'only the city population will be represented, and the rural areas will be eliminated from a voice in the county government to which they must look for essential services.' "[70]

The *New York Times* put the Court story on page one and excerpted substantial portions of the majority and minority opinions. Fred P. Graham reported that Justice Harlan "foresaw the possibility of 'an avalanche of reapportionment cases,' in which the equal-district principle might not work as well as it has with Congressional and state legislative districts." And he quoted Justice Stewart's statement that "the apportionment of a county government is far too subtle and complicated a business to be resolved as a matter of constitutional law in terms of sixth grade arithmetic."[71] But nowhere did the newspapers or the wire services mention the important fact that the Texas Supreme Court, whose ruling the U.S. Supreme Court vacated, had already found the Midland County districts in violation of the equal protection clause of the Fourteenth Amendment, the only difference being that the Texas court would have permitted factors other than population, such as area, miles of county roads, and taxable values, to be considered in the redistricting.

Newspapers promptly addressed the implications of the Supreme Court's ruling for local governments. Harley Dadswell reported succinctly at the top of page one of the *Middlesboro* (Kentucky) *Daily News:*

> Bell County Fiscal Court is apparently the most glaring example of districts with population inequality in this area. Middlesboro has over one-third of the county's population but has only one of the eight Fiscal Court seats. Others who must check to see that their voting districts have population equality are Bell County School Board, Pineville City Council, Middlesboro City Council, Clairborne County Court, and Lee County Board of Supervisors.[72]

Editorial commentary was limited and expectant. The *Abilene Reporter-News* said "the Texas Legislature ... can and surely at its next regular session in 1969 will, enact legislation requiring such redistricting.... It would be wiser for all concerned—commissioners, courts and citizens—to wait on the legislature and see what guidelines, if any, are set out in the law."[73] The *Daily Herald* in suburban Chicago said the *Avery* decision "makes it evident basic organization of county-level government will change in the next few years, either through voluntary action by local and state leaders or by court decree."[74]

THE VOTING RIGHTS ACT OF 1965

In 1965 Congress passed the Voting Rights Act, requiring "preclearance" by the U.S. Justice Department of all changes in election methods in jurisdictions with a history of disenfranchising minority citizens. So subsequent Supreme Court voting-rights decisions dealt as much with the new statute as with the equal protection clause. Together they were the basis for several cases raising new questions regarding the voting rights of ethnic groups as opposed to individuals. Here the Court fragmented and vacillated.

Under Chief Justice Warren Burger (1969–86) the Court handed down three important voting decisions on one day, June 18, 1973, the penultimate decision day of its term. More than some Supreme Court opinions, these required careful reading to report their combined holdings accurately and to include the strong, important views of dissenters. To make matters even more challenging for reporters and editors, the Court competed with itself for coverage by announcing on the same day a major decision affirming the authority of the Food and Drug Administration (FDA) to withdraw from the market drugs that it found ineffective.[75]

On its front page the *Washington Post* nicely wrapped up the voting decisions:

> Vowing to cut back drastically on judicial review of state reapportionment plans, the Supreme Court declared yesterday that deviations as high as 10 per cent from the "one person, one vote" ideal are too minor for court attention.
>
> At the same time the justices held firmly to the rule that when it comes to congressional districting, even relatively small departures from the principal [sic] of equal populations among districts must be justified in court.
>
> And for the first time in a decade of reapportionment cases, the court held unconstitutional multimember districts in the Texas legislature on grounds that they submerged the voting power of blacks in Dallas and Mexican-Americans in San Antonio.

Providing good perspective, the *Post* story went on to note that the Court earlier had permitted a wider variation in a legislative apportionment case, up to 16 percent from the average, because "the state's desire to follow county lines justified the deviations." And the *Post* noted: "Dissenting were three survivors of the former Warren Court majority which had set exacting reapportionment standards—Justices William J. Brennan, Jr., William O. Douglas and Thurgood Marshall. Brennan called the action 'a substantial and very unfortunate retreat from the principles established in our earlier cases.' "[76]

The *New York Times,* giving priority to the FDA case, buried the voting story on page 64 and failed to mention that the Texas multimember districts had been found unconstitutional.[77] The Texas decision was especially significant because just two years earlier the Supreme Court had ruled quite differently that multi-member districts in another urban area, around Indianapolis, were constitutional because, the Court held, they were not drawn purposefully to discriminate against minority voters.[78]

In addition to its national stories on the cases, the Associated Press provided regional stories that focused more on impact than on the opinions. In Texas, the state most affected, for instance: "The U.S. Supreme Court, in two separate decisions, has ordered a reshaping of Texas legislative and congressional districts that may change the future of regional politics in the state."[79] In states not involved in the cases, local stories also stressed impact. Richard Rodda of McClatchey Newspapers reported in California: "The US Supreme Court's relaxation of reapportionment guidelines may help end a 2 1/2-year-old battle in the legislature over congressional and legislative district lines."[80]

Turning to the Voting Rights Act, the Supreme Court, again divided, ruled in 1975 that a 1970 annexation of a predominantly white suburban area by Richmond, Virginia, whose city council was elected at large, would violate the statute if the sole reason was racially discriminatory. The annexation reduced the proportion of blacks in Richmond from 52 percent to 42 percent. But, the Court said, even if racial discrimination had been the original purpose, if the city now could present sound administrative and economic reasons for the annexation, its plan to establish wards, one-half of them with black majorities, would be in compliance with the act. The Court sent the case back to the district court to make that judgment. Justices Brennan, Douglas, and Marshall again dissented, contending that the annexation was intended "to avert a transfer of political control to what was fast becoming a black-population majority."[81]

The nuances in the decision proved a challenge for the press, producing different emphasis, different lead paragraphs, and misleading headlines. Even papers that ran a good UPI story wrote quite different headlines. "The Supreme Court," wrote UPI's veteran Supreme Court reporter Charlotte Moulton, "in a 5-3 ruling yesterday, gave southern cities subject to the 1965 Voting Rights Act some hope they can annex predominantly white suburbs without running afoul of the law." Correct. But the *Syracuse Post-Standard*'s headline declared, "Annexations Approved by Top Court."[82] Incorrect. In the *Pocono* (Pennsylvania) *Record* the UPI story bore this headline: "Supreme Court Eases Up on Annexation of Suburbs."[83] The *Argus,* of Fremont, California, wrongly credited the case to the suburbs: "Southern White Suburbs Win Partial Victory."[84] Even the black-owned *Chicago Defender* headlined the UPI story incorrectly: "OK City-Suburb Merger."[85]

Under the headline "Court Backs Richmond Annexation," the *Kingsport* (Tennessee) *Times* ran a southern-oriented story that began: "The Supreme Court has ruled that black majority voting control of city governments may be blocked by city annexation of predominantly white suburban areas—as long as the annexation is done for 'verifiable, legitimate reasons' and not to discriminate against black voters."[86] Even the *New York Times,* despite a fine story, went overboard in its headline: "High Court Backs Richmond's Annexation of White Suburb That Altered Racial Balance," ignoring the important qualification that the Court sent the case back to the trial court for final determination.[87] But the *Washington Post*'s headline captured nicely the subtlety of the Court's decision: "Annexation in Richmond Given Boost."[88]

The subject of voting rights necessarily encompasses election and campaign finance rules enacted by Congress in the aftermath of the Watergate scandal of 1972 in an effort to limit the influence of money on voters. In a major 1976 case, *Buckley v. Valeo,* considering the constitutionality of the Federal Election Campaign Act, enacted in 1971 and fortified in 1974, the Supreme Court took the unusual step of announcing its decision in a special session on a Friday, because its ruling would bear immediately on the presidential campaign already well under way. The Court upheld the validity of the act's purpose, to limit actual or perceived corruption resulting from large financial contributions, and of the Federal Election Commission (FEC), created by the statute to enforce it. It also upheld the act's limits on contributions to presidential and congressional candidates by individuals ($1,000 per candidate per election) and by political committees ($5,000 per candidate per election), financial disclosure and gift reporting requirements, and public financing of presidential campaigns, this last deemed authorized by the general welfare clause of Article I of the Constitution.[89]

However, the Court rejected the act's other limits on spending: on a candidate's own spending, on an individual's or a committee's spending independent of a campaign, and on overall campaign spending (except presidential candidates who accept public financing), all seen as restrictions on the First Amendment's freedom of expression. The Court also rejected a provision that a majority of the members of the commission be appointed by Senate and House leaders, considered a violation of the appointments clause of Article II of the Constitution, which empowers the president to appoint ambassadors, ministers, judges "and all other Officers of the United States." This had the effect of disabling the FEC and invalidating its actions; the Court gave Congress thirty days to fix the law.

The multipronged opinion was a strange construct: per curiam (by the court) on behalf of the eight justices participating, but only three justices signed on to the entire opinion, while Chief Justice Burger and four others wrote separate opinions concurring in part and dissenting in part, so there were different majorities for different parts of the Court's opinion. The interweaving complexity ran 295 pages, including appendices of the statutory language.[90]

With at least a dozen candidates then actively campaigning for president, many newspapers emphasized the political implications and several candidates' reactions rather than the decision itself. The page-one story in the *Oakland Tribune,* for instance, was an Associated Press report stating that President Gerald Ford, a candidate himself, "will call in congressional leaders to discuss the need for legislation to reconstitute the Federal Election Commission" and that "he is asking his campaign committee to limit its expenditures to the level established under the 1974 election campaign law."[91] The *Des Moines Register*'s front page carried an Associated Press "news analysis" stating: "Presidential candidates are in no hurry to change their campaign game plans as a result of the Supreme Court's overhaul Friday of election finance rules—

but some of them may be getting unexpected, backdoor bonuses from the big money crowd."[92]

Linda Mathews of the *Los Angeles Times,* on page one, came to grips with the Court's unwieldy opinion by reporting candidly:

> The justices held, with very little explanation, that any presidential candidate who had received federal subsidies for his campaign still must observe the act's spending limits of $10 million for the primaries and $20 million for the general election. . . . Both supporters and opponents of the federal election law hailed the decision as a victory, apparently because the 137-page majority opinion was so confusing, in places even inconsistent, that it seemed to provide a little something for everyone.[93]

Most editorials accepted the reality of the decision, but the *El Paso Herald-Post*'s did not: "One of the more promising reforms in American political history has been severely crippled by a Supreme Court decision which opens the way, once again, to the corrupting influence of big money in presidential and congressional election campaigns."[94] On the other hand, the *Wall Street Journal* drubbed the Court for not extending its First Amendment reasoning even further: "It seems to us the court was absolutely right in overthrowing the keystone of the law, a blatantly unconstitutional limit on campaign expenditures. . . . [T]he campaign law serves no one's good. We hope, without much hope, that Congress will strike a blow for the public interest by permanently putting it to rest."[95]

The *Washington Post* and the *New York Times* could not get enough of the story, addressing it from several angles. But the *Times,* too, buried the Court decision (and extensive abstracts from the opinions) in favor of reaction stories up front. Warren Weaver, Jr., wrote that the decision "will probably not have a great deal of effect on the 1976 Presidential election,"[96] while Linda Greenhouse reported, "Campaign finance law in New York, New Jersey, Connecticut and 32 other states will require drastic revision."[97]

The *Washington Post* did put the Court story on the front page, along with a reaction story that proved akin to the "greatly exaggerated" report of Mark Twain's death. The *Post* reported that the Federal Election Commission, just eight months old, "probably will not live to see its ninth monthly anniversary."[98] The FEC lives on. The *Post*'s editorial was an unusual salute to the constitutional argument set forth by the Court, stating that its

> well-reasoned opinion has afflicted us with some sober second thoughts about our advocacy of spending controls. While we persist in our belief that we had our eye on the right problem—the inequitable advantage which easy access to money gives to some well-situated candidates—we may well not have had the right solution. We are persuaded by the constitutional questions raised by the Court.[99]

The Burger Court continued to struggle with voting rights issues. In 1980 it held that an at-large election for Mobile, Alabama, city commissioners did not violate the Fourteenth Amendment or the Voting Rights Act because there was no intent to discriminate against black voters. The vote was 6-3. Justice Thurgood Marshall wrote an angry dissent.[100] Congress responded by deleting from the act the "intent" requirement and substituting a "totality of circumstances" measure to guide the courts. Shortly after President Reagan signed the amendment, but without regard to it, the Court abandoned its Mobile ruling to decide, again by 6-3, that a Georgia county's at-large election of commissioners was unconstitutional. Even though there was no showing of discriminatory intent, the Court ruled, the *effect* of the at-large system was to exclude blacks from the political process. Even the liberal Justice John Paul Stevens dissented from that tortured logic.[101]

THE REHNQUIST COURT CASTS ITS VOTE

Under Chief Justice Rehnquist (1986–2005), the Supreme Court ruled unconstitutional, by a vote of 7-2, California's "blanket primary," a strange animal that gave all voters regardless of party affiliation a single ballot enabling them to vote for candidates of any party. The law violated a political party's First Amendment right of association, the Court held.[102] Though the ruling, according to Linda Greenhouse of the *New York Times,* "cast serious doubt on the more common open primary, in use in more than half the states,"[103] the decision was swept off page one or more commonly out of the paper and the evening newscasts altogether by other Court rulings that busy June day. The justices held that their *Miranda* warning for criminal suspects may not be overruled by Congress,[104] and that only a jury can decide whether a crime is motivated by hate, a case in which four dissenters warned of potential widespread disruption in criminal sentencing.[105] But still another case, just a request for Supreme Court review, grabbed top billing that day. It was a last-ditch plea by Miami relatives of a suddenly famous six-year-old Cuban refugee named Elian Gonzalez, that the Supreme Court block his court-ordered return to Cuba with his father.[106] (The Supreme Court declined to consider the case, and Elian returned home.)

Will history record that the most important decision by the Rehnquist Court was *Bush v. Gore?*[107] Probably, but what interests us here is the unprecedented media coverage. The uncertain outcome of the presidential election of 2000, and especially its denouement in Florida, gripped the nation for more than a month after election day, November 7. A nearly tied vote in Florida, whose electoral votes would decide the presidency, led to a laborious recount and the televised spectacle of "hanging chads" that baffled election officials and the nation. On Saturday, December 9, the U.S. Supreme Court suspended the Florida recount by temporarily staying an order of the Florida Supreme Court to continue the recount past December 12, the date set by both federal and state law to submit the results to the Electoral College, which was to meet on December 18. On Monday, December 11, the Court heard oral argument and the next day, December 12, at 10 P.M., it announced that by 5-4 vote it reversed the judgment of the Florida court and remanded the case "for further proceedings not inconsistent with this opinion."[108] That effectively ended the recount with George W. Bush ahead by 537 votes in Florida.

The Court majority declared in an unsigned, per curiam opinion that the extended recount and what it deemed the lack of a uniform statewide recount standard violated Florida voters' right to equal protection guaranteed by the Fourteenth Amendment, and that there was no time to rectify it all by December 12, the Electoral College deadline, and also, of course, the date of the decision. Chief Justice Rehnquist and Justices Kennedy, O'Connor, Scalia, and Thomas constituted the majority. Justices Breyer, Ginsburg, Souter, and Stevens wrote harsh dissents. Florida's 25 electoral votes and the presidency went to Bush with a total of 271 against 266 for Vice President Al Gore. After more than 105,000,000 votes were cast, a half-million more for Gore than for Bush, the winner was decided by one.

Massive media coverage chronicled the weeks-long legal process in minute detail as the nation—and the world—watched and waited. When the Court released its decision late on Tuesday evening, broadcasters in particular struggled with it. Their reporters on the steps of the Supreme Court went live as they received and hurriedly scanned the opinion, their anchors and commentators standing by in the studios. Peter Marks of the *New York Times* aptly described their dilemma:

> Viewers across the channels were given the opportunity to watch as anchors and reporters struggled mightily to digest and summarize a complex, voluminous decision. It was a task so confusing and rife with tension that at times, analysts sitting next to each other at the network anchor desks could not agree on even the most basic implications of the historic ruling.
>
> Some were quick to declare it the definitive victory for Gov. George W. Bush; others thought it still held out some sliver of hope for Mr. Gore. But talking heads on every channel seemed to agree that the job of parsing it on the air was monumental.
>
> "It may take an army of lawyers to translate this thing," Dan Rather said on CBS at 10:18 P.M., Eastern Standard Time, about 20 minutes after the opinion was released. To which his colleague Bob Schieffer, searching for the appropriate adjective, added, "'Complicated' is the understatement of the year." . . .
>
> When Ms. [Jackie] Judd [of ABC] apologized for the attenuated effort at getting the gist of the opinion, Mr. [Peter] Jennings stopped her. "Nobody," he said, "should be embarrassed about working through a Supreme Court decision" before a national audience.[109]

In Wednesday's papers the decision's immediate and historic political implications overrode the justices' constitutional reasoning.[110] But the Court opinion stories stated that reasoning well, including dissenters' criticisms, notably, as the *Philadelphia Daily News* put it, "a withering dissent by Justice John Paul Stevens that laid bare the deep divisions inside the court on whether it should decide the presidency."[111] A number of papers quoted this from Justice Stevens: "Although we may never know with complete certainty the identity of the winner of this year's Presidential election, the identity of the loser is perfectly clear. It is the Nation's confidence in the judge as an impartial guardian of the rule of law."[112] Joan Biskupic of *USA Today* wrote:

> Souter emphasized that if the high court had allowed the state to carry out the recounts, there might not have been any reason for the justices to get involved and any "political tension" could have been worked out in Congress under federal rules for the appointment of presidential electors. . . .
>
> Ginsburg stressed that the high court has rarely issued such an outright rejection of a state court's interpretation of its own law.[113]

A fine insight was provided by Linda Greenhouse of the *New York Times,* who noted that two of the dissenters agreed with the majority that the recount lacked uniform standards, but obviously disagreed with the Court's decision to terminate it: "What the court's day and a half of deliberations yielded tonight," she wrote, "was a messy product that bore the earmarks of a failed attempt at a compromise solution that would have permitted the vote counting to continue."[114] Most stories appropriately focused on the December 12 reporting date deemed imperative by the Court though not actually required by federal law.[115] The *Chronicle Tele-gram* of Elyria, Ohio, cleverly placed this quotation from the Court opinion in boldface type just under the paper's masthead, above the story's headline and photos of the justices:

> Because it is evident that any recount seeking to meet the December 12 date will be unconstitutional for the reasons we have discussed, we reverse the judgment of the Supreme Court of Florida ordering a recount to proceed.[116]

Editorial writers and commentators tapped on into the night. The *Lancaster* (Pennsylvania) *New Era* declared confidently:

> The court has made the correct decision—a decision it did not welcome but which was forced upon it by a Florida Supreme Court determined to rewrite election rules after the election at the prompting of an aggressive challenge to certified results by Al Gore.
>
> Never in his wildest dreams could Bush have imagined that events would magnify his challenge to this extent. If he rises to this occasion, his long ordeal by dimpled ballot and divided court may become merely a brief prelude to a distinguished presidency.[117]

The *Denver Post,* which had supported Bush, took issue with the December 12 "deadline" and railed: "The fractured percuriam decision will exacerbate, rather than ease, our national division.... For Bush to pull a successful presidency out of the court's cynical ruling will take a miracle.... The passionate dissent filed by Justice Paul Stevens, in our view, appropriately describes the damage the court has inflicted on itself."[118] The *San Jose Mercury News* called it "a messy and ugly ending to a messy, ugly, and not at all satisfying election."[119] The *St. Louis Post-Dispatch* declared, "It would have been far better if the court had allowed every vote to be counted in Florida. But the court has spoken and the nation should respect that decision."[120]

David M. Shribman of the *Boston Globe,* while acknowledging that "the campaign could have been conducted with more depth, the coverage of the election could have been conducted with more precision," commented that "the high court's action raised questions about the independence of one of the few national institutions that retains the public's respect."[121] The *New York Times* was crestfallen but stoic: "It is incumbent on citizens and elected officials alike to respect the authority of the ruling and the legitimacy of the new presidency whether or not they agree with the court's legal reasoning."[122]

Apparently at least two of the majority justices were sensitive to criticisms that their decision was more political than legal, for the next day they took the extraordinary step of denying it. Laurie Asseo of the Associated Press reported that Justice Thomas spoke "in a televised question-and-answer session with high school students. . . . 'We have no axes to grind, we just protect this,' Thomas told the students, holding up a copy of the Constitution." As Thomas was speaking, the story went on, Chief Justice Rehnquist happened to drop in at the Court's Public Information office, which is adjacent to the pressroom. "Told by reporters that Thomas had just said politics did not enter into the court's overall decision-making, the chief justice responded, 'Absolutely, absolutely.'"[123]

However, the Rehnquist Court was not finished with dicey election questions. Its 2003 decision in another important case, *McConnell v. Federal Election Commission,* raised more hackles. By various majorities subscribing to three different opinions regarding the five titles of the Bipartisan Campaign Reform (McCain-

Feingold) Act of 2002, a fragmented Court upheld the statute's ban on "soft" money contributions, the large, unregulated donations by corporations, unions, and wealthy individuals to political parties for such purposes as advertising and get-out-the-vote drives. Also sustained was the law's prohibition of pre-election communications by a union or corporation (except the media) naming a candidate.[124]

The majority opinions were by Stevens and O'Connor jointly, Rehnquist, and Breyer, while partial dissents of varying scope were filed by Scalia, Thomas, Kennedy, Rehnquist, and Stevens. The opinions totaled 193 pages. Justice Thomas, referring to the Court's 1976 decision upholding the Federal Election Campaign Act and its $1,000 contribution limit, stated, "I have long maintained that *Buckley* was incorrectly decided and should be overturned." He pilloried the majority opinion as "the most significant abridgement of the freedoms of speech and association since the Civil War. . . . The chilling endpoint of the Court's reasoning is not difficult to foresee: outright regulation of the press."[125]

Gina Holland of the Associated Press wrote crisply that

> unless there is a showing of harm, the divided court said Wednesday, the nation is better off with limits on the financial influence of deep-pocket donors even if money can never be divorced from politics. . . . The court ruled 5-4 that rooting out corruption, or even the appearance of it, justifies limitations on the free speech and free spending of contributors, candidates and political parties.[126]

As a result, reported Julia Malone of Cox Newspapers in the *Atlanta Journal-Constitution,* "Democrats and Republicans said they will be turning more to independent groups that are free from many of the new fund-raising restrictions . . . the burgeoning independent groups that are planning voter mobilization programs and ad campaigns."[127]

Although the decision admittedly curtailed the First Amendment, most newspapers did not object. The *Austin American-Statesman,* supporting the ruling, said soft money "had been perverted into political advocacy ... diverted into individual political campaigns, and both parties accepted the reality with a wink and a nod."[128] Explicitly addressing Justice Thomas's dissent, the *Boston Herald* responded, "Somehow we think the First Amendment and editorial pages will survive."[129] The *Milwaukee Journal Sentinel* quoted Justice Scalia's dissenting remark, "This is a sad day for freedom of speech,"[130] and retorted: "It is nothing of the sort."[131] The *St. Louis Post-Dispatch* said the First Amendment restrictions were acceptable in light of the majority's view that "protecting the integrity of elections has a free-speech benefit: improving 'public participation in political debate.' "[132]

But the *Charleston* (West Virginia) *Daily Mail* quoted Thomas and called the decision a "ridiculous abridgement of free speech.... No faux sanitizing of the political process justifies that."[133] And the *Las Vegas Review-Journal* howled that the Court had "eviscerated the First Amendment."[134] The *New York Post* quoted the First Amendment, "Congress ... shall make no law ... ," and protested that "Congress made just such a law.... If a majority on the Supreme Court can assert the right to curtail political speech here, it will assert the same right in other areas as well."[135]

All network evening news broadcasts reported the ruling, though ABC confined it to a fifty-second reader. The *NBC Nightly News* devoted a full five minutes to the decision and the role of money in the 2004 presidential race, which was then in the preprimary stage. The McCain-Feingold law was named (it was not by CBS or CNN), as was Justice Scalia's "sad day" dissent. Reporter David

Gregory commented, "there's a lot of money going into politics. In the end, this law may simply shift it around."[136] Nina Totenberg of National Public Radio provided good historical perspective:

> The court's majority opinion was in stark contrast to the Supreme Court's last major campaign reform opinion in 1976, when the justices upheld some key provisions of the post-Watergate reform law, but struck down others, in essence cherry-picking the law and making enforcement over the next quarter-century often very difficult. This time, the court accepted the complex law as a whole, invalidating only a couple of minor provisions.[137]

THE ROBERTS COURT ON REDISTRICTING AND CAMPAIGN FINANCE

Voting and election controversies have materialized several times at the Supreme Court under Chief Justice Roberts (2005–). In 2006 the Court rejected, 7-2, an allegation that a Republican redrawing of congressional districts in Texas was an unconstitutional gerrymander. Yet, in the same case, a majority of only five justices (Roberts not among them) ruled that changes to a Latino-majority district to shore up a Republican incumbent with waning Latino support amounted to a dilution of the voting strength of Latinos that violated the Voting Rights Act. The district was just one of thirty-two in an audacious, mid-decade redrawing engineered by the U.S. House majority leader, Representative Tom Delay, Republican of Texas. It was designed to pick up six seats in Texas and cement Republican control of the U.S. House of Representatives. Six justices wrote opinions totaling 122 pages. Justice Kennedy said the Court saw no "reliable standard for identifying unconstitutional political gerrymanders." However, he went on, "[t]he State chose to break apart a Latino opportunity district to protect the incumbent congressman from the growing dissatisfaction of the cohesive and politically active Latino community in the district." Dissenting from this aspect of the ruling, the chief justice argued that the concomitant creation of a new Latino-majority district elsewhere helped create a statewide districting plan that did satisfy the Voting Rights Act.[138]

Press coverage emphasized the political aspect of the decision rather than the legal. "In a partial victory for Texas Republicans," wrote Warren Richey of the *Christian Science Monitor,* "the US Supreme Court on Wednesday upheld most of a 2003 redistricting that helped the state GOP win a near 2-to-1 advantage in congressional seats while igniting all-out partisan warfare with the state's Democrats."[139] In all stories this priority subordinated the Court's finding that the Voting Rights Act was violated, which unfortunately led to omission of the chief justice's cogent dissent that it was not.

Editorial writers fumed. "Unlike obscenity," remarked the *Austin American-Statesman,* "the Supreme Court apparently can't recognize partisan redistricting when it sees it."[140] The *Boston Globe* termed the decision a "weak-kneed refusal to call a halt when politics runs amok."[141] The *Milwaukee Journal Sentinel* called it "a threat to truly representative and effective government."[142] But the *Omaha World-Herald* was comfortable with the decision and with the statute, saying "the Voting Rights Act remains a fundamental part of American jurisprudence, still guiding redistricting decisions in crucial ways."[143]

The Bipartisan Campaign Reform (McCain-Feingold) Act again came before the Court in a closely watched case called *Fed-*

eral Election Commission v. Wisconsin Right to Life. Ironically, the statute's cosponsor, Senator Russ Feingold, himself was in the picture. WRTL, a not-for-profit advocacy group, wanted to run advertising before the 2004 primary election asking Wisconsin citizens to urge Senator Feingold, then an unopposed candidate for renomination, and Senator Herb Kohl, both Democrats, to oppose a Senate filibuster of President Bush's nominees for federal judgeships. The Federal Election Commission said the ad would violate McCain-Feingold's prohibition on pre-election candidate advertising by independent organizations. But by 5-4, with new Justice Samuel Alito providing a critical vote, the Court reversed. It ruled that the ad merely advocated a position, and though it mentioned a candidate, was not an electioneering communication prohibited by McCain-Feingold. Loosening the statute a bit, Chief Justice Roberts wrote that "a court should find that an ad is the functional equivalent of express advocacy only if the ad is susceptible of no reasonable interpretation other than as an appeal to vote for or against a specific candidate. Under this test, WRTL's three ads are plainly not the functional equivalent of express advocacy."[144]

Concurring only in the judgment, Justice Scalia quarreled anew with both *Buckley* and *McConnell,* contending that "the effect of BCRA has been to concentrate more political power in the hands of the country's wealthiest individuals and their so-called 527 organizations, unregulated" by the statute.[145] Justice Souter, dissenting for himself and three others, protested that the decision in effect overruled *McConnell*'s holding only four years earlier that the relevant section of the law was constitutional.

Robert Barnes of the *Washington Post* seized the essence of the decision, and its significance:

> The Supreme Court yesterday substantially weakened restrictions on the kinds of television ads that corporations and unions can finance in the days before an election, providing special interest groups with the opportunity for a far more expansive role in the 2008 elections.
>
> Chief Justice John G. Roberts Jr. wrote the 5 to 4 decision, saying the McCain-Feingold campaign finance act's prohibition against the use of a candidate's name in such ads in the days before an election was an unconstitutional infringement on the groups' rights to advocate on issues.[146]

This story required a reporter to touch several bases, and although the networks did cover it, the narrative style that broadcasters sometimes prefer, letting the story progressively unfold, did not work well here, at least not for the Fox network. Reporter Jim Angle got off on the wrong foot by saying the relevant provision of the McCain-Feingold Act banned "references" to candidates when in fact it banned use of their names. Then he left important elements of the story, such as citing the First Amendment, to be woven into and among several interviews, and in the process he incorrectly stated that the law targeted ads within sixty days of a general election (*any* election was covered, and the case actually involved a primary election). Angle let an interview with Senator John McCain, cosponsor of the law, make the essential point that the *Post* made in its lead, that the statute's target here was big corporate and union money. And Fox ignored the dissenting opinion by Justice Souter, even though he spoke for four justices.[147]

A challenge to the constitutionality of the Voting Rights Act, based largely on changes in southern politics since 1965, was expected by many observers to be the most important case of the 2008–09 term. But the Court sidestepped that ultimate question to rule narrowly that a tiny utility district in Texas was eligible to apply for exemption from the act and its preclearance requirement.[148]

Although the ruling was unexpectedly limited, the press covered it prominently. Most stories conveyed a precision that unfortunately was not emulated by some headline writers. Jess Bravin wrote accurately in the *Wall Street Journal:* "The Supreme Court dodged a constitutional showdown over the 1965 Voting Rights Act, leaving intact the federal government's power to review election procedures in certain states to ensure minorities are not disenfranchised." But the *Journal*'s headline was mistaken: "Court Upholds Voting Rights Act."[149] The headlines in the San *Francisco Chronicle* and the *Washington Post* made the same error.[150]

In Austin, Texas, the location of the utility district, there was confusion about the Court's ruling that the district could seek an exemption from the act. "The 8-1 decision gives a Northwest Austin neighborhood the right to conduct utility district elections without federal oversight," declared the *Austin American-Statesman* in an overstatement. A sub-headline also went too far when it stated, "Decision Lets More Governments Opt Out of Federal Election Oversight," for the act merely provided an opportunity to seek exemption, not a unilateral "opt-out."[151] The Web site of the *Dallas Morning News* was equally incorrect: "Supreme Court Exempts Texas District in Voting Rights Case," read the headline over an equally incorrect Associated Press story rushed out shortly after the decision was announced: "The Supreme Court has ruled narrowly in a challenge to the landmark Voting Rights Act, exempting a small Texas governing authority from a key provision of the civil rights law."[152] The error was caught and eliminated in later AP stories.[153]

The *Washington Post* editorialized, with relief and praise: "In refusing to disturb the carefully considered judgment of lawmakers, the justices rendered a decision far less dramatic than anticipated. In doing so, they also bolstered the legitimacy of their own institutional roles."[154] Also approving, the *New York Times* dismissed Chief Justice Roberts's suggestion that changed circumstances might no longer support the constitutionality of the act, saying Congress removed any such doubt when it extended the statute in 2006 by overwhelming votes in both houses. The *Times* called for a future reaffirmation of the law: "The next time it considers the question, the Supreme Court should make clear that Section 5 is still needed and still constitutional."[155] However, the next time was *Citizens United v. Federal Election Commission,* decided 5-4 in January 2010, in which the Supreme Court declared violative of the First Amendment the law's ban on independent campaign spending by corporations, including not-for-profit advocacy organizations, immediately preceding elections.[156] The decision prompted the *New York Times* to lament, "the Roberts court demonstrated its determination to act aggressively to undo aspects of law it found wanting, no matter the cost."[157] McClatchy Newspapers reported that "corporations and unions are now freer to run attack ads—or, for that matter, ads touting their positions—and to praise or criticize specific candidates, right up until Election Day."[158] The *Denver Post* embraced the ruling, editorializing that "Concerns about money-in-politics should not allow for censorship of political speech, and thanks to the high court's ruling, the system has gained significant new freedoms it ought to have had all along."[159]

As we have seen, press coverage of Supreme Court voting and election decisions increased and improved greatly over a century and a half, ramping up sharply, and necessarily, with the Warren Court's stunning decisions of the 1960s. However, throughout this long period there was a widespread lack of commitment, call it indifference, by newspapers to the fairness and the integrity of this vital aspect of American civic life. Inasmuch as most papers strive to stand up for the right and for the oppressed, should they not have taken early notice of how disparate were the promise of the Fifteenth Amendment and the Court's rulings that flouted it? Instead they usually just reported them, giving insufficient attention to the forceful reasoning of the first Justice John Marshall Harlan and other dissenters.

This shallowness was not limited to Fifteenth Amendment cases. The press missed the Court's first consideration, in the Illinois case of *Colegrove v. Green,* of whether voting and election questions might also come under the equal protection clause.[160] To be sure, journalists hardly could have anticipated that the Court one day would apply that constitutional protection so forcefully to election cases. Nevertheless, once that door was opened, the press could have given the public a better understanding of this novel constitutional reasoning, most readily by laying out the contrasts between each Court opinion and the dissenters' thinking.

The Voting Rights Act of 1965 and later the Bipartisan Campaign Reform Act of 2002 added still other dimensions to the voting questions coming before the Court, and such statutory interpretations are more difficult for journalists to cover because there is no bright and shining constitutional star to guide them. But the high degree of political controversy surrounding both statutes has stimulated the wide coverage to which the public is entitled. Yet, in the coverage there was a faint reminder of the press's indifference to the Court's constricted interpretation of the First Amendment in the post–World War I sedition cases. Few newspapers reflected in their stories or editorials on campaign-speech restrictions any concern, though it was voiced by political critics and eventually by Justices Scalia and Thomas in their *McConnell* dissents, that this curtailment of the First Amendment might eventually lead to others. Moreover, for reasons not apparent, Court decisions on voting and elections have proved especially vexing for headline writers and of insufficient interest to the editors who select and position the stories.

An exception to the shortcomings of the press in covering election cases is the *New York Times,* which, at least since *Baker v. Carr* in 1962, usually has accorded prominent coverage to decisions of the Court (though not without headline glitches) and has ardently championed editorially the fairness of voting and elections, as well as seeing the potential, broader issue of undermining the First Amendment.

ELEVEN

THE SOCIAL SCENE

It is a phenomenon of relatively recent times. Privacy, abortion, desecration of the American flag, classroom prayer and other school controversies, affirmative action, and so on. Hot political issues, all emotionally charged, many of them more likely to touch our everyday lives than most of the Supreme Court issues we have examined thus far. They are, at bottom, disputes about the extent of our constitutional rights, but they have a certain edge, a comparative simplicity and a high public awareness that call for special treatment here. For the news media they are especially challenging because the issues and often the specific cases are in the public eye, engendering a heightened demand for speed, precision, and interpretation by print as well as broadcast journalists. These cases have opened a whole new public window on the world of the Supreme Court of the United States.

School prayer, still a contentious subject nearly five decades later, is a good place to start. In a 1962 case called *Engel v. Vitale,* the Warren Court (1953–69) held that a teacher-led recitation of an optional, state-written, nondenominational prayer at the start of the day in New York public schools was "a practice wholly inconsistent with the Establishment Clause" of the First Amendment.[1] Justice Hugo Black's majority opinion went on to say, "It is neither sacrilegious nor antireligious to say that each separate government in this country should stay out of the business of writing or sanctioning official prayers and leave that purely religious function to the people themselves and to those the people choose to look to for religious guidance." A lone dissenter, Justice Potter Stewart, argued, "A religion is not established in the usual sense merely by letting those who choose to do so say the prayer that the public school teacher leads."[2]

Delivered at the end of the term after much press and public attention to the case, the decision took center stage. The *New York Times* ran on the front page three stories on the ruling and local reactions to it; another was inside, accompanied by the complete text of the Black and Stewart opinions and a concurrence by Justice William O. Douglas. Anthony Lewis of the *Times* summed up the ruling concisely:

> WASHINGTON, June 25—The Supreme Court held today that the reading of an official prayer in New York public schools violated the Constitution.
>
> The prayer was drafted by the New York Board of Regents and recommended in 1951 for recital aloud by teachers and children in each classroom at the start of every school day. It is nondenominational and just twenty-two words long. It reads:
>
> "Almighty God, we acknowledge our dependence upon Thee, and we beg Thy blessings upon us, our parents, our teachers and our country."[3]

The *Chicago Daily Tribune*'s banner headline read, "Supreme Court Bans School Prayers," and the paper ran the prayer text before starting its story, a clever way to focus the reader's attention. In the story reporter Joseph Hearst observed, "The decision will have far reaching effects in other states," though not in Illinois. Hearst pointed out: "Black brushed aside the argument that the prayer is non-denominational and that no child is required to say the prayer."[4] James E. Clayton of the *Washington Post* noted that "Justice Black began to read his opinion with a great deal of emotion in his voice."[5] The *Post*'s editorial page praised the decision as "an act of liberation" and said Black's "learned, illuminating and richly eloquent opinion" showed that "one of the principal purposes of the Amendment was to preserve religion in the United States from the inevitably corrupting influence of secular authority."[6]

Many smaller papers emphasized the widespread national and local opposition to the decision. The *Lake Charles* (Louisiana) *American Press* featured an Associated Press story on the decision that led with the negative reaction: "A Supreme Court ruling striking down the saying of official prayers in public schools has stirred a cauldron of criticism from churchmen and members of Congress."[7] The *Emporia* (Kansas) *Gazette* placed on page one this Associated Press report: "A constitutional amendment to get around the Supreme Court ruling against official prayers in public schools was introduced in the House today and others were in the planning stages in both houses of Congress."[8] Another prominently played AP follow-up began this way:

> The U.S. Supreme Court decision against the recitation of official prayers in public schools is viewed by some groups as a challenge to many types of religious observations in the schools.
>
> Those observances include Bible readings, the Lord's Prayer, Christmas carols and plays, Easter plays and other religious practices permitted in some states.[9]

Robert J. Donovan of the Herald-Tribune News Service wrote:

> Washington (HTNS)—The Supreme Court, it is now quite clear, has stuck its head into a mighty hornets' nest in the school prayer decision.
>
> Indeed real concern is being expressed privately among some leading constitutional lawyers here that the court's prestige among the rank-and-file of the people may be seriously impaired as a result. . . .
>
> Former Presidents Dwight D. Eisenhower and Herbert Hoover led a list of distinguished citizens who spoke critically of the decision yesterday. . . . [T]he denunciations in Congress yesterday were harsh, though not unanimous.[10]

In a page-one local story the *Southern Illinoisan,* of Carbondale, Illinois, wrote, "Most area ministers and parents interviewed today oppose yesterday's Supreme Court decision against the saying of prayers in public schools."[11]

Widely read conservative columnist Westbrook Pegler declaimed, "the Supreme Court was absolutely wrong and, I submit, immoral in this decision. . . . [T]he First Amendment was invoked and it was not violated or even involved in any way."[12] Another conservative columnist, David Lawrence, also objected: "Morality can be discussed and taught in the public schools without violating the Constitution of the United States."[13]

Is the reporting of reactions an appropriate extension of the press's coverage of the Supreme Court? Yes. Although at times reaction reporting seems to supplant legal reporting, the Court ultimately depends on the trust and good faith of the public to carry out its work. And on this matter, the criticism was not hyperbole, for the Court was subsequently called on to resolve other disputes over school prayers and the use of school facilities for religious meetings, and such issues continue to reverberate.[14]

A NEW RIGHT: PRIVACY

Although the subject of prayer may well have been on the minds of the authors of the Bill of Rights, would any of them have imagined that the use of a birth control device, even by married couples, would one day command the attention of the Supreme Court and give rise to a new constitutional right? It is the right to privacy, specified in many state constitutions but nowhere to be found in the U.S. Constitution. At least, not until Justice Douglas, writing for five members of the Warren Court (two others concurred in the result) in *Griswold v. Connecticut,* in 1965, fashioned one of the Court's most creative opinions ever, marshaling the First Amendment (stretched to guarantee a "right of association"), the Third (no quartering of soldiers in a house without permission of the owner), the Fourth (the home is secure against unreasonable search and seizure), the Fifth (government cannot compel self-incriminating testimony), and the Ninth (rights not enumerated here are retained by the people). These guarantees, Douglas declared memorably, "have penumbras, formed by emanations from those guarantees that help give them life and substance. . . . Various guarantees create zones of privacy." He concluded, "We deal with a right of privacy older than the Bill of Rights," and declared that therefore the Connecticut anticontraceptive statute of 1879 was unconstitutional. In dissent, Justice Black, while emphasizing that he found the statute as offensive as did the other justices, nevertheless objected to the creation of the new right: "I like my privacy as well as the next one, but I am nevertheless compelled to admit that government has a right to invade it unless prohibited by some specific constitutional provision." Justice Stewart also dissented, finding "no such general right of privacy in the Bill of Rights, in any other part of the Constitution, or in any case ever before decided by this Court."[15]

Despite its novelty, its constitutional importance, and its easily understood message, *Griswold* was scantily covered, if at all, by most newspapers. For it was the last day of the Court's term, and once again a torrent of significant rulings came tumbling down, amid a total of sixty-four decisions and orders. Most papers gave top billing to the Court's reversal, mentioned in chapter 4, of the swindling conviction of Billie Sol Estes on the ground that extensive and disruptive televising of his trial violated his due process right under the Fourteenth Amendment.[16] Other decisions that day dealt with unions (they won three)[17] and whether evidence-exclusion rulings by the Court were retroactive (no).[18] The Associated Press's wrap-up of the day's decisions subordinated *Griswold* to *Estes*. The *Chicago Tribune* played *Griswold* on page 12, the *Billings* (Montana) *Gazette* put it on page 35, the *Albuquerque Journal* on page 20, and the *Los Angeles Times* took a pass altogether.

On the other hand, the *New York Times* managed to find space on page one for Fred P. Graham's good report:

> WASHINGTON, June 7—The Supreme Court struck down the Connecticut birth-control law today in a sweeping decision that established a new constitutional "right of privacy." . . .
>
> The seven justices in the majority were divided on the proper constitutional provision to use in striking down the law, but they agreed that married couples had private rights that could not be abridged in such a manner.[19]

The *Washington Post* also placed *Griswold* on the front page, and editorialized in favor of it, saying that Justice Black's dissenting call for greater deference to state legislatures "ignored, we think, the Court's obligations as a sentinel of freedom to construe the provisions of the Bill of Rights not in their literal terms but in their larger design as the postulates of a free society."[20]

SCHOOL BUSING

How to desegregate the public schools, an extremely volatile issue in segregated northern cities like Chicago as well as in the South, was largely up to the federal district courts, and occasionally a controversy over a desegregation plan reached the Supreme Court. In 1971 the Burger Court (1969–86) approved the busing of school children for this purpose, and laid down guidelines for the district courts, in a North Carolina case called *Swann v. Charlotte-Mecklenburg Board of Education*.

The Charlotte-Mecklenburg school district was partly urban, partly rural, and large, covering 550 square miles. It operated more than 100 schools with 84,000 pupils, 29 percent of them Negro, concentrated in one part of Charlotte. The U.S. district court had adopted an ambitious plan, to supersede a more modest plan that already entailed busing, that would integrate all of the district's 76 elementary schools, achieving proportions of Negro students ranging from 9 to 38 percent, by transporting an additional 13,000 students in more than 100 new buses at an annual cost of more $500,000. The Supreme Court unanimously approved. Directed at "dual" or segregated school systems, Chief Justice Burger's opinion upheld the use of mathematical ratios and the use of busing to achieve them, while adding significantly, "The constitutional command to desegregate schools does not mean that every school in every community must always reflect the racial composition of the school system as a whole." The opinion explicitly held open the possibility of federal court desegregation orders in school districts that had not historically operated separate, segregated systems.[21]

It was the lead story, running more than three-and-a-half minutes on the *CBS Evening News* with Walter Cronkite, and on front pages everywhere, thanks to the wire services. United Press International wrote forcefully: "The Supreme Court has laid it on the line once more: State-imposed segregation in public schools must go."[22] The Associated Press was tough, too: "In a sweeping smash at segregated schools, the Supreme Court approved unanimously Tuesday massive busing and limited racial balancing as proper ways of assuring black children an integrated education."[23]

The AP cast a wide net for reactions, reaching well beyond the civil rights groups and race-dependent politicians whose comments were predictable. One elected official, Governor Linwood Holton of Virginia, whose children were attending desegregated schools in Richmond, was quoted as saying calmly: "Virginia will abide by the law of the land." The school superintendent of Clarke County, Georgia, whose desegregation plan also was governed by the Court's ruling, told the AP: "I am extremely happy that the Supreme Court has finally made a decision on this matter so that all of us in education will know what is expected of us." On the other hand, the AP said, two members of the Charlotte-Mecklenburg school board "predicted large numbers of white children being transferred to the 12 private schools that have opened in the area during the last year."[24]

Still another AP story reported that President Richard Nixon's stated preference for neighborhood schools was "trumped by the Supreme Court." So, the story went on, a White House spokesman merely "called on the American people to obey the ruling" even though, the AP pointed out, President Nixon's "legal views were largely turned back by the court whose unanimous opinions were written and delivered by Warren E. Burger, the man Nixon named chief justice." A number of papers played this political angle higher than the report of the Court's decision. The *Santa Fe New Mexican* gave it a seven-column banner headline across the top of the front page: "White House Bows to Rule on Busing."[25]

The *Fresno Bee Republican,* attaching "great significance" to the Court's unanimity, editorialized optimistically that the decision "should put an emphatic halt to all the evasions and subterfuges by which [school desegregation] has been thwarted, not only in the Deep South but in most parts of the country."[26] Surprisingly, the *Chicago Daily Defender*'s top story quoted two Chicago "prominent black educators" who criticized the decision as "a blow to efforts by blacks to gain decision-making power over their neighborhood schools" and a threat to the teaching jobs held by blacks.[27] The *Chicago Tribune* reported that an unnamed attorney for the Chicago Board of Education said the Court decision appeared to apply only to "willful segregation" of schools "rather than segregation caused by housing patterns, as is the case in Chicago."[28] That would turn out to be incorrect.[29] Indeed, the *Los Angeles Times* editorialized presciently that the Court's opinion left "open the possibility that even in non-Southern school districts, which never operated overtly separate school systems, discriminatory action by school authorities," as in selecting locations for new schools and drawing district lines, "would require remedial action by the courts."[30]

ROE V. WADE

For intense public interest, however, even the Charlotte-Mecklenburg decision—not to mention all others—was topped by *Roe v. Wade* in 1973. The case involved challenges to criminal abortion laws in Texas and Georgia. By a vote of 7-2 the Burger Court held, with surprising specificity, that a woman, in consultation with her physician, has a virtually unrestricted right to choose an abortion in the first trimester of pregnancy, but that states could regulate abortion in the second trimester and severely restrict it in the third. Justice Harry Blackmun, who at one time had been counsel to the Mayo Clinic, wrote in a long, scholarly opinion that "the Court has recognized that a right of personal privacy, or a guarantee of certain areas or zones of privacy, does exist under the Constitution." He cited *Griswold v. Connecticut* and other cases but concluded that the right of privacy is "founded in the Fourteenth Amendment's concept of personal liberty and restrictions upon state action." This was a new basis for constitutional privacy, but, curiously, Blackmun did not insist on it for his ruling. He embraced what he described as the approach of state-court abortion decisions that "the right of privacy, however based, is broad enough to cover the abortion decision."[31] Justices Byron White and William Rehnquist protested that the "judgment is an improvident and extravagant exercise of the power of judicial review that the Constitution extends to this Court. . . . This issue . . . should be left with the people and to the political processes."[32]

A Vietnam peace agreement in Paris seemed imminent that day, and former President Lyndon B. Johnson died unexpectedly of a heart attack, but the *CBS Evening News* reported *Roe v. Wade* at the top of the broadcast and ran it three minutes and forty seconds. The other networks gave it three minutes as well. NBC, though not stating the Court's constitutional reasoning, related the decision to a current New York controversy over repeal of its two-year-old law permitting abortions; the report included interviews with a Planned Parenthood official and a spokesman for the New York Roman Catholic archdiocese who called the Court's ruling a "shocking action" and "a horrifying decision."[33]

Many newspapers gave more page-one space to opinions and reactions than to the Court's ruling and the justices' opinions. The constitutional source of the majority opinion, the Fourteenth Amendment, was hard to find. The *Newport* (Rhode Island) *Daily News* focused on a state legislator who planned to introduce a bill conforming with the Supreme Court decision.[34] The *Morning Herald* of Hagerstown, Maryland, featured an Associated Press story that was all reaction: "The U.S. Supreme Court ruling on abortion Monday drew comments ranging from 'beautiful' to 'disgraceful.' There were indications that the decision could affect all but four of the 50 states."[35] The *Billings* (Montana) *Gazette* ran a United Press International story that briefly cited the Fourteenth Amendment, and alongside it a local story reporting that the impact in Billings was uncertain, but "[t]he only known result is that there will be no abortions performed in the city in the near future."[36] Next to excerpts from Justice Blackmun's opinion the *Des Moines Register* reported, "A bill revising Iowa's 115-year-old abortion law along lines of Monday's U.S. Supreme Court decision was introduced in the Iowa Senate Monday."[37] The *Los Angeles Times* editorialized, "It is a sensible decision, persuasive both by its historical and legal arguments," without explaining why, and said that "[t]he impact of the decision in California will be minimal."[38] The *New York Times* put the story on the front page, but even its long and detailed report mentioned the Fourteenth Amendment source only obliquely: "Justice Blackmun concluded 'the word "person," as used in the 14th Amendment, does not include the unborn,' although states may acquire, 'at some point in time' of pregnancy, an interest in the 'potential human life' that the fetus represents, to permit regulation."[39] By contrast, the *Chicago Tribune* focused editorially on what it considered the shortcomings of the Court's interpretation of the Fourteenth Amendment, saying "it has not answered the question basic to the entire controversy: When does life, in constitutional terms, actually begin? . . . When do the provisos of this amendment apply? Is it not until birth, or is it at some arbitrary point between the sixth and seventh month of pregnancy? The court has not clearly said."[40]

REVERSE DISCRIMINATION IN ADMISSIONS

Allan Bakke, a white man in his thirties, was a sympathetic figure, and his plea, reverse discrimination, resonated widely. Already established in an engineering career with the National Aeronautics and Space Administration in California, Bakke twice applied to and twice was rejected by the medical school of the University of California-Davis. The school had an affirmative action program that reserved 16 places in the class of 100 for minorities whose undergraduate grade-point average was exempt from the 2.5 minimum required of the other applicants. Bakke sued under the Civil Rights Act of 1964, which prohibits racial or ethnic preferences in programs receiving federal funds, and under the equal protection clause of the Fourteenth Amendment, pointing out that his grade-point average and admission-test scores were significantly higher than those of minority candidates who were admitted.

The case attracted national media attention when it was tried in the California courts. Bakke won at the California Supreme

Court, which ordered his admission,[41] and coverage was heavy when the university filed its petition for certiorari at the U.S. Supreme Court and when the Court granted it.[42] It was the Court's first major constitutional test of affirmative action.

Television in particular embraced Allan Bakke's story. The three broadcast networks ran a total of thirty-seven evening news stories about him and his quest even before the Supreme Court, in 1978, decided his case.[43] Political scientists Elliot E. Slotnick and Jennifer A. Segal not only counted the stories, they watched them all, for a microscopic and illuminating study of TV's coverage of the case.[44] "On decision day," they found, "six correspondents joined the anchors of ABC's and NBC's *Bakke* coverage, while four correspondents joined Walter Cronkite on CBS."[45] To report the decision and its aftermath, the networks produced another 23 stories, for a total of 60, almost evenly divided among the three. Fifty-five percent of the stories mentioned the legal issues involved, "although the cynic would take note that a full 45 percent of *Bakke* stories lacked specific content about the nature of Bakke's claim or the factual scenario underlying it." Furthermore, "attention to the facts of the case dissipated the longer the story was in the news."[46]

Despite the networks' immense attention to the case, Slotnick and Segal found, their reporting was hampered by a lack of television's great strength, pictures:

> [T]he most frequently utilized visual was a sterile picture or drawing of the Supreme Court's building, an image present in nearly four out of ten (38.3%) stories. Nondescript college campus scenes served as a backdrop in more than a quarter (26.7%) of the stories, suggesting that the case had something to do with education. Allan Bakke's visage appeared in fifteen (25%) stories, either through an

artist's drawing, a photograph, or an "action" scene of his efforts to avoid cameras. (*Bakke* coverage may have been even more difficult for television reporters than many other Supreme Court cases, since the main protagonist refused to be interviewed and remained a very private person throughout the litigation process.)[47]

In addition, Slotnick and Segal faulted the television coverage for often referring to the admitted minority students as not meeting the medical school's admission requirements: "to the extent that such reporting suggested that blacks admitted under the UC-Davis plan were 'unqualified' (and, on balance, the reports appeared to do just that), news coverage misreported and misrepresented an important fact in the case."[48]

To Slotnick and Segal, "[i]n a public setting fraught with ambiguity and ambivalence about affirmative action, the public's posture toward the issue could be uniquely affected by the media's message regarding the unfolding *Bakke* litigation."[49]

The media prepared extensively for the decision, which finally came down at the end of the term, in late June 1978. According to *Newsweek,* "NBC, for example, began on May 1 to station two camera crews equipped with microwave transmitters for instant transmission at every Court session."[50] When Justice Lewis Powell, Jr., who provided a swing vote in Bakke's favor, prepared to speak from the bench, he offered an unusual acknowledgment of the enormous media coverage. The *Los Angeles Times* reported:

> Powell, the first of the justices to read from his opinion, noted to the rapt courtroom audience at the outset that "perhaps no case in memory has received so much media attention and scholarly commentary . . . and advice." Acknowledging the lack of unanim-

ity on the court, he added: "Perhaps it's fair to say we needed this advice."[51]

So, what did the Court decide in this celebrated controversy? It was not easy to decipher, for the justices wrote six opinions, none commanding a majority. Justice John Paul Stevens, writing for a plurality of four, said the medical school's reservation of sixteen places in the entering class for minority applicants—places that Bakke could not compete for—violated the Civil Rights Act's prohibition of racial discrimination in any publicly funded program. Justice Powell adopted this view, producing a majority of five that ordered Bakke admitted. At the same time Powell agreed with an opinion by Justice William Brennan, for himself and the three other justices, that racial considerations in admissions were constitutionally permissible because the university had a legitimate interest in promoting racial diversity.

Reporters waded through 156 pages. Glen Elsasser and Jack Fuller wrote concisely in the *Chicago Tribune:*

> WASHINGTON—The Supreme Court ruled Wednesday that the University of California at Davis must admit Allan Bakke to its medical school because its admissions program illegally discriminated against whites.
>
> At the same time, a majority of the justices agreed that at least some university admissions programs that take race into account by giving preference to minority applicants would be valid under the Constitution.[52]

However, the *Tribune* story did not mention the Fourteenth Amendment or, specifically, the Civil Rights Act of 1964, just "a

1964 federal civil-rights law." The *New York Times* published four-teen *Bakke*-related stories that day, but its lead story, too, neglected to mention the Fourteenth Amendment.[53] The *Wall Street Journal,* which in those days rarely placed a breaking-news story in its outside columns on page one, did, citing both the statute and the amendment.[54] Editorials were immediate and supportive. Among its twenty-one *Bakke*-related articles, the *Los Angeles Times* commented: "The U.S. Supreme Court's ruling in the Allan Bakke case is a cautious and reasonable decision that does not require any drastic shifts in the direction of national policies to ensure civil rights."[55] The *Washington Post* declared, "Everybody won."[56]

Journalists sought out reaction from high and low, particularly among college administrators and professors who were themselves struggling to make sense of the multiple opinions. In Syracuse, New York, home of Syracuse University and near other colleges, the *Post-Standard*'s banner headline was not the decision but the local implications: "Bakke's Victory Unlikely to Affect SU." The story reported that college affirmative action officers found the decision "confusing" but were in agreement that it "does support affirmative action in higher education." However, a Syracuse University affirmative action officer was quoted as greeting the ruling "with displeasure," and a law school professor commented that it "doesn't make sense."[57] The *Waterloo* (Iowa) *Courier* reported that "[t]he president of the University of Northern Iowa said Thursday he is 'as much up in the air as anybody.... But it would appear that at least for this university, not much will change—although we will have to review what we're doing,' Dr. John Kamerick said."[58] The *New York Times* revealed that Bakke's lawsuit had been quietly urged by the medical school's own admissions officer, who "sympathized with Mr. Bakke and tacitly encouraged him to challenge the minority preference program in court."[59]

BUT, AFFIRMATIVE ACTION AFFIRMED

The Burger Court subsequently upheld two other affirmative action programs. By a vote of 5-2, it ruled that the Kaiser Aluminum Company's training program for unskilled production workers, intended to alleviate racial discrepancies in the workforce but in which half the slots were reserved for whites, was acceptable under the Civil Rights Act of 1964 on the ground that it did not condemn all private, voluntary, race-conscious affirmative action plans.[60]

Then, in a case called *Fullilove v. Klutznick,* the Court affirmed congressional authority to require a 10 percent set-aside for minority contractors in the Public Works Employment Act of 1977.[61] The vote was 6-3, with the majority justices putting forth different rationales. Three, citing Justice Brennan's opinion in *Bakke,* found no violation of the equal protection clause because the set-asides supported the achievement of a compelling governmental interest in remedying the effects of past discrimination, and because they did not grant superiority by race to any individual or group. Three other justices in the majority, relying on congressional authority under the spending and commerce clauses of Article I and the Fourteenth Amendment's enforcement clause, said Congress need not "act in a wholly 'color-blind' fashion."[62]

In a huge contrast to *Bakke,* the decision was not well covered by newspapers generally, although the *Los Angeles Times,* the *Washington Post,* and the *New York Times* put it on page one. Linda Greenhouse of the *Times* pointed out in her second paragraph, "The 6-to-3 ruling marked the first time the Supreme Court had explicitly endorsed the awarding of Federal benefits based on the race of the recipients."[63] Smaller papers that used a wire-service story buried it. The *Daily Intelligencer* of Doylestown, Pennsylvania, for instance, put it on page 51; the Associated Press story reported: "Once again deferring to the power of Congress, the Supreme Court has endorsed the use of racial quotas to guarantee minority owned businesses a fixed share of government grants."[64] Once more, it was the last day of the term with a number of important decisions handed down. Some news organizations were more interested in *Richmond Newspapers v. Virginia,* the case mentioned in chapter 5 in which the Court declared that trials must be open to the public and the press.[65] Another important ruling that day rejected more rigorous government standards for workers exposed to benzene.[66] Also, *Fullilove v. Klutznick* had no personal protagonist like Allan Bakke to humanize the issue.

Despite the lack of a personal focus, the television networks gave *Fullilove* more prominent coverage than most newspapers. The *NBC Nightly News* led with a Court package that ran nearly six minutes, with *Fullilove* first. The *CBS Evening News* accorded a similar priority to the Court that day, its package running nearly five minutes. ABC's *World News Tonight* chose to lead with *Richmond Newspapers* but followed immediately with *Fullilove* and gave it nearly two minutes. All the networks included several interviews with such experts as union leaders, lawyers, and the statute's congressional sponsor, as well as quotations from Chief Justice Burger's plurality opinion and Justice Stewart's dissent.

SCHOOL PRAYER

In a case testing the Warren Court's decisions on school prayer, the Burger Court in 1985 held unconstitutional an Alabama statute that authorized a moment of silence for prayer or meditation. The vote was 6-3, with the chief justice and the future chief,

William Rehnquist, in dissent. Justice Stevens's majority opinion said "the statute had *no* secular purpose" and was designed to promote religion, while Justice Rehnquist insisted the First Amendment does not impose a wall of separation between church and state.[67]

The television networks gave the decision top billing and interviewed several informed sources plus some predictable critics like the Reverend Jerry Falwell and the conservative South Carolina senator Strom Thurmond. ABC's *World News Tonight* devoted an extraordinary seven minutes to the story, including quotations from the majority and dissenting opinions, the background of previous Supreme Court decisions on prayer, and interviews with the Alabama protagonists as well as advocates of a constitutional amendment to overturn the ruling.[68]

Major dailies also featured the decision, sometimes with excerpts from the justices' opinions. Philip Hager pointed out in the *Los Angeles Times:* "The court indicated that those laws enacted for a neutral purpose, such as meditation or reflection, are permissible—but those that specifically endorse prayer or are intended to promote religion are not permissible."[69] In one of its several stories on the case, the *New York Times* described a surprising reaction from the winner, an Alabama agnostic named Ishmael Jaffree:

> Mr. Jaffree said he was glad he had challenged the Alabama statute, but he added: "I'm still sorry for my children. They have told me that they wish I'd never filed the suit. They said they have lost friends over it." Mr. Jaffree, a 41-year-old black lawyer who works for the Legal Services Corporation of Alabama, also said he was "sort of persona non grata in the black community now, but the black community doesn't understand: I was never opposed to religion."[70]

Smaller papers gave much less attention to the Court's decision, emphasizing instead national and local reaction and the perceived ramifications of it. The *Gettysburg Times,* without reporting the decision on page one or elsewhere, ran this Associated Press story on page 17:

> Some members of the religious right are so outraged over the newest Supreme Court ruling on prayer in the schools that they are calling it "an act of war against this nation's religious heritage." But to civil libertarians, Tuesday's decision is "a major victory to keep religious activity out of the nation's public schools."[71]

Another AP story about the case, played under a banner headline on page one of the *Santa Fe New Mexican,* reported the decision very briefly in the first paragraph: "Strongly reaffirming its 1962 ban on organized prayer in public schools, the Supreme Court on Tuesday outlawed daily moments of silence if students are told they may pray during that time." But then local and national reaction constituted nearly all the remainder of the story.[72] The front-page story in an Indiana paper, the *Pharos-Tribune,* was a compilation of United Press International and staff reporting that brushed quickly past the Court's ruling to localize the story: "A U.S. Supreme Court decision to prevent states from endorsing prayer in schools will not affect Indiana law or the practice of most schools in Indiana."[73] The *Daily Herald,* in suburban Chicago, without reporting the decision, ran this from Springfield, the state capital: "Afraid that Illinois' current law may now be unconstitutional, some local lawmakers said they will consider sponsoring a new state law requiring a moment of silence, but not necessarily prayer, in all public schools."[74] The *Syracuse Herald-Journal,* also

minimizing coverage of the decision itself, was quick to editorial-
ize against it:

> We were inclined to think our justices of the U.S. Supreme Court
> should have better things to do with their time than to split hairs
> over whether teachers can say, "prayer," in the schoolroom. . . . In
> our mind, we tend to agree with Chief Justice Warren E. Burger . . .
> Burger belittled the majority's decision, saying [it] "borders on, if
> does not trespass into, the ridiculous."[75]

THE REHNQUIST COURT GOES SOCIAL

During the chief justiceship of William Rehnquist (1986–2005)
the Supreme Court accepted a steady stream of cases dealing with
highly charged social issues. Many were decided by a divided vote.

In one of several disputes over affirmative action, the Court in
1989 threw out, by 6-3, a Richmond, Virginia, 30 percent set-aside
for minority contractors, saying it violated the equal protection
clause of the Fourteenth Amendment. Significantly, the Court
adopted a high standard of "strict scrutiny" in judging the constitutionality of affirmative action plans based on race, meaning they
must be based on a showing of past discrimination in the locale,
must be closely related to a "compelling" government interest,
and must be "narrowly tailored" to address that interest. Writing
for the majority, Justice Sandra Day O'Connor declared, "The
30% quota cannot in any realistic sense be tied to any injury suffered by anyone." She differentiated the case from *Fullilove v. Klutznick,*[76] which sustained a federal set-aside of 10 percent, on the
ground that the Fourteenth Amendment empowers the federal

government to enforce it, but the states have no such mandate. In an angry dissent, Justice Thurgood Marshall accused the majority of mistakenly regarding

> racial discrimination as largely a phenomenon of the past.... In constitutionalizing its wishful thinking, the majority today does a grave disservice not only to those victims of past and present racial discrimination in this Nation whom government has sought to assist, but also to this Court's long tradition of approaching issues of race with the utmost sensitivity.[77]

Turning out a model Supreme Court story, Linda Greenhouse clearly explained the ruling, both the legal reasoning and the likely impact on the law, on page one of the *New York Times:*

> WASHINGTON, Jan. 23—The Supreme Court today cast constitutional doubt on a wide variety of government hiring and contract programs to aid minorities. It did so by invalidating a law in Richmond that channeled 30 percent of public works funds to minority-owned construction companies.
>
> The Court ruled 6 to 3 that the Richmond ordinance, similar to minority set-aside programs in 36 states and nearly 200 local governments, violated the constitutional rights of white contractors to equal protection of the law. The decision upheld a ruling by the United States Court of Appeals for the Fourth Circuit, in Richmond.
>
> The opinion, written by Justice Sandra Day O'Connor, said such programs could be justified only if they served the "compelling state interest" of redressing "identified discrimination," either by the Government itself or by private parties.

Many affirmative action programs will fail to meet this test, known in constitutional doctrine as "strict scrutiny."

In a dissenting opinion, Justice Thurgood Marshall said the Court had set a "daunting standard" that "sounds a full-scale retreat from the Court's longstanding solicitude to race-conscious remedial efforts directed toward deliverance of the century-old promise of equality of economic opportunity."

Justice Marshall would uphold such efforts if they served "important governmental objectives," a less stringent constitutional test than the "strict scrutiny" that Justice O'Connor applied today.[78]

Other newspaper and television stories studiously avoided the term "strict scrutiny," critical to the Court's decision and requiring definition. Thus they failed to convey the same precision.

THE SYMBOLISM OF THE FLAG

In a less complex ruling, a divided Rehnquist Court held in 1989 that the First Amendment protects desecration of the American flag as a form of symbolic speech.[79] Gregory Johnson, ostentatiously defying a Texas statute, had burned a flag at the 1984 Republican National Convention in Dallas to protest Reagan administration policies. He was convicted, fined $2,000, and sentenced to a year in jail. Both the majority and dissenting opinions invoked history. Justice William Brennan, writing for a majority of five, said:

> Our decision is a reaffirmation of the principles of freedom and inclusiveness that the flag best reflects, and of the conviction that our toleration of criticism such as Johnson's is a sign and source of

our strength. Indeed, one of the proudest images of our flag, the one immortalized in our own national anthem, is of the bombardment it survived at Fort McHenry.[80]

Dissenting, Chief Justice Rehnquist cited, among other national treasures, Ralph Waldo Emerson's "Concord Hymn," Revolutionary War flags bearing slogans such as "Don't Tread On Me," and Francis Scott Key's 1812 poem that became the national anthem, which Rehnquist set forth in full. He also quoted the entirety of John Greenleaf Whittier's Civil War poem "Barbara Frietchie," in which she confronts advancing Confederate soldiers:

> "Shoot, if you must, this old gray head,
> But spare your country's flag," she said.[81]

Following suit, television, so adept at stoking emotions, milked the story. The *NBC Nightly News* interviewed an "unrepentant" Gregory Johnson, who said he had intended to be offensive: "I wanted to very much offend that whole America uber alles event," and now, with his favorable ruling, "we should turn up the heat on the flag and we should turn up the heat on the system of U.S. imperialism that that flag represents." An American Legion representative said that "our first reaction is one of anger, and our second reaction is one of sadness."[82] ABC's *World News Tonight,* in a five-minute lead story, reviewed the history of the flag in photos and movies, and showed reaction from Senator Robert Dole, who was disabled in World War II, and the Veterans of Foreign Wars. ABC and CBS also interviewed the inflammatory Johnson.

Newspapers would not be outdone. Tony Mauro of *USA Today* wrote:

The ruling roused strong emotions. Justice John Paul Stevens—a Bronze Star recipient in World War II—took the unusual step of reading his dissent from the bench. His voice cracking, Stevens recalled "the soldiers who scaled the bluff at Omaha Beach" and said, "The American flag is more than a proud symbol." Permitting burning will "tarnish its value."[83]

The *San Diego Union-Tribune* featured veterans' angry reactions:

> For 30 years, Leonard Howell has proudly displayed the U.S. flag in his front yard, saluting it in the morning when he leaves home and again when he returns in the evening.... So the idea that someone could desecrate the flag with impunity makes Howell see red, white and blue. "They ought to get five years in jail, at least."[84]

The United Press International reported from St. Louis:

> The Supreme Court's decision that the burning of the American flag is protected by the First Amendment brought hundreds of calls to a radio station Thursday and prompted the station to sponsor a "day of mourning" for the flag.[85]

The *Syracuse Herald-Journal* ran an Associated Press story date-lined Dallas that began with comments from Gregory Johnson and his lawyer, followed by a melancholy quotation from Fort Worth resident Dan Walker, a Korean War veteran, who had recovered the remains of Johnson's flag. Walker got the headline: "Veteran Who Retrieved Ashes of Burned Flag Grieves over Ruling."[86]

Editorials were few. The *New York Times* called the decision "a victory for ordered liberty that gives flag-waving a good name."[87] The *Washington Post* deemed it a "decision that defends free speech and the kind of symbolic acts that have to be counted as speech."[88] But the Syracuse *Post-Standard* said "the high court has sanctioned the fouling of our own nest."[89]

WILL *ROE* SURVIVE?

An important abortion case called *Webster v. Reproductive Health Services* generated considerable partisan interest long before the Supreme Court decided it,[90] because it raised the possibility that the Court might revise its historic ruling in *Roe v. Wade,* and perhaps even overturn it.[91] In fact, the ruling turned out to be comparatively modest, at least from a legal standpoint. By 5-4 the Court upheld various abortion restrictions enacted by Missouri, including prohibitions on the use of public facilities and on the participation of public health employees in abortions, and a requirement of medical tests to determine whether the fetus would be viable outside the womb when, in the doctor's judgment, it was twenty or more weeks from conception. In their study of television coverage of the Supreme Court, Elliot Slotnick and Jennifer Segal counted 60 network evening news stories about *Webster,* starting well before the decision, of which 48 "placed the case in a political context." As a result, "the *Webster* case provided unusual grist for the media's speculative mill, both with regard to prognostications from interview subjects as well as television journalists themselves."[92] They continue:

> In the absence of television-worthy litigants (like Bakke) around which *Webster* could be presented, the case became a vehicle

through which television portrayed the ongoing societal battle of two well-organized political forces, the "pro-life" and "freedom of choice" camps in the American polity.... On the eve of the decision, ABC's Tim O'Brien reported from the Court: "This is the eye of the storm.... Tranquil tonight but a ruling is expected tomorrow on abortion—a ruling many believe is more likely to elevate this highly charged debate than it is to solve it" (July 2, 1989).[93]

Slotnick and Segal counted the television news appearances of well-known advocates of the opposing sides in the political debate. One was Kate Michelman of the National Abortion Rights Action League, "who, while not a direct party in the litigation, was present in one out of three (20) *Webster* stories." Another was Susan Smith, a spokeswoman for the National Right to Life Committee, who was in nine stories.

Newspapers, while reflecting the political and social controversy surrounding abortion, did not let that distract them from the legal reasoning of the Court when it handed down the decision. But it was another difficult challenge for reporters. There was no majority opinion. Chief Justice Rehnquist's plurality opinion took issue with *Roe*'s trimester rules and inclined toward giving the states considerable leeway to restrict abortions. It was joined by only two other justices. But Justices O'Connor and Scalia wrote concurrences, Scalia wanting to overrule *Roe* and O'Connor resisting that, at least for the moment. Thus was the majority mustered to uphold Missouri's abortion restrictions. Justices Blackmun and Stevens issued strong dissenting opinions with different reasoning.

Under a sweeping banner headline, Linda Greenhouse of the *New York Times* looked beyond the immediate decision: "the majority made it clear that the Supreme Court is now prepared to uphold state restrictions on abortion that have been ruled unconstitutional for the past 16 years." She added human touches: "The tense silence in the crowded courtroom was in contrast to the frenzied activity of the crowd chanting and waving placards on the plaza outside the Court building. . . . Justice Harry A. Blackmun, the author of the Roe v. Wade opinion, read his dissent in a weary and sorrowful tone."[94]

Also with an eye on prospective abortion cases, Ethan Bronner of the *Boston Globe* wrote, "Yesterday's decision—dealing with the use of public facilities for abortions and testing fetal viability—will affect only a handful of the abortions performed in this country, but opened the way for curtailments of much greater impact."[95]

Many papers ran several articles on the decision and the reactions it provoked, though most of the stories concerned the entire abortion issue rather than the Court's ruling. Karen L. Koman wrote in the *St. Louis Post-Dispatch:* "Both sides of the abortion issue said Monday that they would take their fight to the streets, to the abortion clinics and to every state legislature in the country. . . . The two sides held a day of marches and press conferences after the decision, which freed states to impose further restrictions on abortion."[96]

Editorials and other commentary, like political and personal reactions, were strong. Columnist Ellen Goodman predicted that state "sexual politics" would now determine the issue, and rasped, "the national message is clear. Don't count on the Constitution to protect rights. Count votes."[97] But columnist George Will, calling *Roe v. Wade* "extreme and incoherent," said the Court did not go far enough: "Let us hope the court soon drives out of the intellectual cul-de-sac it took a wrong turn into in 1973. It should restore to the states that right to regulate abortions."[98]

Slotnick and Segal find the television coverage of the Court's decision inadequate:

> The nuances of the Court's division and the lack of a true majority opinion did not receive crisp or clear coverage on any newscast. . . . The least explicit attention to the actual case decision came in Carl Stern's coverage on NBC . . . outlining the explicit holdings in the Missouri law's provisions without any mention of Rehnquist's plurality authorship or identification of voting coalitions.

And the researchers detect errors, for instance, "Rita Braver's decision coverage on CBS News . . . characterizing Rehnquist's opinion as the 'majority opinion.'" Their assessment of the networks' overall *Webster* coverage is that a legal story was "transformed into a story more suitable for television coverage" while "a thorough vetting of the issues, both legal and policy-oriented, that could have been brought to public view, received lesser attention."[99]

GAYS' RIGHTS, AND OTHERS'

Another sensitive social controversy, the rights of homosexuals, was the issue in *Romer v. Evans,* decided in 1996. The case challenged a Colorado constitutional amendment approved by referendum that prohibited all state or local government actions designed to protect those rights. The Supreme Court, affirming a judgment of the Colorado Supreme Court, held by a 6–3 vote that the amendment violated the equal protection clause of the Fourteenth Amendment on the ground that it withdrew from homosexuals alone specific legal protection from injuries caused by discrimination.[100]

The ruling made page one of the *Boston Globe,* the *New York Times,* and some other papers, but it was relegated to an inside page of the *Washington Post* and others. The Associated Press story mentioned "equal protection" but not the Fourteenth Amendment.[101] Some editors gave higher priority to the reaction. The *Santa Fe New Mexican* reported at the top of page one: "Gay-rights advocates were celebrating Monday in the wake of the U.S. Supreme Court decision striking down Colorado's anti-gay initiative, saying that the opinion handed their movement both a crucial legal win and an enormous symbolic boost."[102] The decision was reported only as a reader on *CNN World View,* but it was the lead story on the broadcast networks. NBC, while neglecting to mention the Fourteenth Amendment, gave it three minutes, including a brief question-and-answer between anchorman Tom Brokaw and Court reporter Pete Williams about any possible impact on the legality of gay marriage and gays in the military (none).[103] The Colorado story competed for news attention that day with another Supreme Court decision, a curiosity case in which the justices threw out a $2,000,000 punitive damage award to an Alabama doctor who discovered that his new car had been damaged and repainted before delivery to him.[104]

A dispute that had only limited application nevertheless commanded top attention from the media. The Court held in 1996 that Washington State's ban on assisted suicide did not violate the due process clause because the law, which provided severe criminal penalties, was rationally related to a legitimate government interest, and because due process does not guarantee a right to assistance in committing suicide. The vote was unanimous, though the justices wrote six separate opinions, five of them concurring in the judgment but for differing reasons. The ruling explicitly left open the legal and moral issue of whether a state might authorize physician-assisted suicide.[105]

The denial of a constitutional right to assisted suicide was the lead of most stories. But not a few papers got the ruling wrong, misapprehending that Washington's ban applied only to medical assistance. "A unanimous U.S. Supreme Court ruled yesterday," reported William Goldschlag in New York's *Daily News,* "that terminally ill patients have no constitutional right to medically assisted suicide."[106] The *Chicago Sun-Times:* "States have the right to ban doctor-assisted suicide, the Supreme Court ruled Thursday."[107] And the *Houston Chronicle:* "The justices ... upheld laws ... that bar physician-assisted suicide."[108] The *New York Times:* "[T]he court rejected constitutional challenges to laws ... that made doctor-assisted suicide a crime."[109] The Associated Press: "The court upheld laws ... that make it a crime for doctors to give life-ending drugs."[110] The networks also gave prominence to the story, leading their evening news broadcasts with it, though CNN and NBC omitted mention of the constitutional basis for the ruling.[111]

GO MICHIGAN

Two affirmative action cases involving state university admissions, both from the University of Michigan, became nationwide news well before they were decided by the Rehnquist Court in 2003. The lawsuits were instituted by rejected white applicants. By a vote of 5-4, the Court found no violation of the equal protection clause in the law school's policy of considering race along with such factors as an applicant's essay, the enthusiasm of recommenders' letters, and the difficulty of the applicant's undergraduate course selections, all credited in an effort to enroll more members of underrepresented minority groups.[112] But the decision was different when it came to the university's undergraduate admissions, which gave minority applicants 20 points out of about 100 needed for acceptance.

The Court held, 6-3, that the policy made race decisive for virtually every minimally qualified minority applicant, and thus the policy violated the equal protection clause because it was not narrowly tailored to achieve the state's compelling interest in promoting diversity.[113] The Court cited its prior affirmative-action holdings in *Adarand Constructors v. Pena*[114] and *Richmond v. J. A. Croson Co.,*[115] which required "strict scrutiny" of racial preferences by government; *Fullilove v. Klutznick,*[116] specifying "narrow tailoring" of actions to further compelling governmental interests such as diversity; and Justice Powell's *Bakke* opinion calling for individual consideration of an applicant's "potential contribution to diversity."[117]

The Michigan decisions led the evening news shows of all four commercial television networks, each story running three minutes or longer, though some of that time was devoted to broadening the affirmative-action issue to other campuses, the military, and business. *CNN NewsNight* gave the story a big five minutes and forty seconds, with reporter Bob Franken mentioning the equal protection clause and *Bakke* as the legal basis for the decisions before shifting to reaction at the University of Michigan, including an interview with one student who admitted she would not have been there if not for affirmative action.[118] ABC's *Nightline* devoted its entire half-hour to the story.

Newspapers put it on page one, most of them nicely summarizing the two rulings. John Aloysius Farrell wrote in the *Denver Post:* "A divided Supreme Court kept alive the use of affirmative action in American society Monday, ruling that a university may consider an applicant's race as a guiding factor in the admissions process to secure the benefits of a diverse student body."[119] Warren Richey of the *Christian Science Monitor,* after stating that the rulings turned on "constitutional principles of equal protection," illuminated them by focusing on the pivotal justice:

> Justice Sandra Day O'Connor played a key role in the outcome of both cases—staking out middle ground on an issue that has divided the nation and often seemed to defy compromise.
>
> She wrote the majority opinion upholding the law school admissions program and provided a critical fifth vote while concurring in an opinion written by Chief Justice William Rehnquist striking down the undergraduate program.
>
> She explained the difference between the law school and undergraduate cases in her written concurrence in the undergraduate case. "The law school considers the various diversity qualifications of each applicant, including race, on a case-by-case basis," Justice O'Connor writes. "By contrast, the Office of Undergraduate Admissions relies on the selection index to assign every underrepresented minority applicant the same, automatic 20-point bonus without consideration of the particular background, experiences, and qualities of each individual applicant."[120]

The papers devoted equal effort to assessing the rulings' local impact. The *Atlanta Journal-Constitution* reported that "University of Georgia officials said Monday the U.S. Supreme Court's rulings on affirmative action could open the door for the university to again consider race as a factor in student admissions."[121] The *Columbus Dispatch:* "Ohio State University likely will have to modify its point-based admissions system, but university leaders nonetheless cheered the U.S. Supreme Court's decision yesterday that allows colleges to continue considering race in admissions."[122]

Editorials mushroomed immediately, most of them endorsing both of the Court's decisions. The *Boston Globe* stated, "Diversity is a societal good and must be upheld. The court took a big step yesterday in keeping the doors of higher education open for minority students."[123] The *Santa Fe New Mexican* ventured that the decisions "could be a blueprint for racial fairness on our college campuses and beyond."[124] But the *Wall Street Journal* bemoaned Justice O'Connor's "split-the-baby jurisprudence."[125]

DOES GOD HAVE RIGHTS?

A year later, in 2004, all eyes were on the Supreme Court as it decided whether "under God" should be constitutionally stricken from the Pledge of Allegiance. Or did it decide? An atheist named Michael A. Newdow, father of a public-school kindergarten student in California, claimed that required classroom recitation of the pledge violated his daughter's rights under the establishment clause and the free exercise clause of the First Amendment.[126] The girl's mother, with whom she lived, filed an opposing brief stating that she desired that her daughter continue reciting the pledge. The Court, in fact, did not decide the question, but sidestepped it, ruling that the father, who was never married to the mother but had joint custody of the daughter, did not have standing to sue on her behalf. Therefore the Court reversed an appellate court ruling that the father had standing and that "under God" was unconstitutional.[127] The ruling was confusing because, although all eight participating justices concurred in the judgment, three protested that the Court had improperly denied standing, and that, in any event, "under God" did not violate the First Amendment.[128]

A political science teacher, Alain L. Sanders, surveyed the *Newdow* coverage and found that several newspapers and one network incorrectly implied that the Court "had decided something about the legality of reciting 'under God.'"[129] His criticism was directed in part at headlines, citing these, among others: New York *Daily News:* "Supremes Keep God in Pledge"; *Dallas Morning News:* "High Court Allows Words 'Under God' to Stay in Pledge; Justices Rule on Basis of Man's Custody, Don't Tackle Constitutionality"; *Los Angeles Times:* "Justices Keep 'God' in Pledge of Allegiance."[130]

In some lead sentences Sanders found further inaccuracies. The *Los Angeles Times:*

> The Supreme Court, ruling on Flag Day, preserved the wording of "one nation, under God" in the Pledge of Allegiance and threw out a lawsuit Monday that had challenged it as a form of state-mandated religious indoctrination.

USA Today:

> The Supreme Court kept the words "under God" in the Pledge of Allegiance on Monday, by reversing a lower court's decision that said leading students in reciting those words was unconstitutional.

The *Washington Post:*

> A unanimous Supreme Court ruled yesterday that the phrase "under God" may remain in the Pledge of Allegiance as recited in public school classrooms.[131]

Sanders commented: "Unfortunately for the *Post,* the ruling was not unanimous" because the justices voted "for different reasons," and "the Court decided absolutely nothing concerning the phrase 'under God.'"

Sanders scorned Tom Brokaw's introduction to the story on *NBC Nightly News* as "bombastic, misleading, and confusing." Quoting Brokaw:

> In the nation's classrooms, just as in service club meetings, when Boy Scout troops gather and American Legion posts assemble, if the ceremony includes the Pledge of Allegiance, God stays in the picture. That's the ruling today from the Supreme Court. The decision came on Flag Day, and it struck down a lower court ruling that said public school teachers could not lead students in reciting the Pledge of Allegiance because it contained the phrase "under God."[132]

In fact, Brokaw promptly acknowledged, undoubtedly confusing viewers, that the Court had not decided the church-state issue. Similarly, several of the newspaper headlines that Sanders found misleading were followed, he said, by accurate stories about the decision. But some damage was done to public understanding.

THE TAKING OF PROPERTY

Questions of property law do not ordinarily excite public interest, but the Supreme Court's upholding of the eminent-domain acquisition of several private properties in New London, Connecticut, did. The Court ruled in 2005 that New London's plan for redeveloping its downtown and waterfront, intended to create jobs and enhance city revenues, satisfied the takings clause of the

Fifth Amendment, which states that private property may not "be taken for public use without just compensation." Susette Kelo, who had extensively improved her Victorian house, and several of her neighbors sued to block the "taking" on the ground that the plan contemplated for-profit development by private companies, and they won their trial. But a divided Connecticut Supreme Court ruled against them, and so did a divided U.S. Supreme Court.

Justice Stevens, writing for a majority of five, declared, "Because that plan unquestionably serves a public purpose, the takings challenged here satisfy the public use requirement of the Fifth Amendment." In a forceful dissent for herself and three others, Justice O'Connor protested, "Under the banner of economic development, all private property is now vulnerable to being taken and transferred to another private owner, so long as it might be upgraded—i.e., given to an owner who will use it in a way that the legislature deems more beneficial to the public—in the process."[133]

The media, giving short shrift to the constitutional analysis, did not take kindly to the decision. Applying it locally, the *Boston Herald* wrote: "The U.S. Supreme Court yesterday solidified the power of the Boston Redevelopment Authority and other government agencies to seize homes and businesses for economic projects ranging from glitzy offices to sports stadiums."[134] CNN anchorman Aaron Brown introduced the story this way: "In America your home, they say, is your castle, but if it lies in the path of a riverfront shopping mall, the government can take it away and knock it down. That's, in effect, what the U.S. Supreme Court decided today."[135] The *Bangor* (Maine) *Daily News* groused that the decision was "unmoored from its practical effect."[136] The *Daily Herald* in suburban Chicago called it "an aggressive intrusion into the hallowed American notion of private property rights."[137] "Homeowners now own their homes only if the government wants them to," ranted the *Washington Times.*[138] The *St. Petersburg Times* predicted, "The Kelo ruling will undoubtedly prove to be one of the court's worst mistakes in years."[139] But the *New York Times,* almost alone, came to the Court's defense, calling the ruling "a welcome vindication of cities' ability to act in the public interest."[140]

PUBLIC RELIGIOUS DISPLAYS

In 2005 the Rehnquist Court announced on the same day two superficially contradictory rulings on government displays of the Ten Commandments, barring them in Kentucky courthouses but permitting them on a monument on the Texas state capitol grounds. Both results turned on narrow interpretations of the establishment clause of the First Amendment. The votes were 5-4 and the dissents were fierce, protesting in the Kentucky case that acknowledgment of a Creator was not tantamount to the establishment of religion. In the Kentucky courthouses, the Court said, the displays were predominantly religious in purpose, in violation of the establishment clause.[141] But the Texas monument was described as just one among 17 monuments and 21 historical markers on the 22 acres of the capitol grounds, commemorating people, ideals, and events comprising Texan identity, all part of the state's political and legal history, so this rendering of the Ten Commandments was deemed different from prayers in public schools.[142]

Some newspaper stories, perhaps feigning exasperation, called it confusing hairsplitting rather than striving to reconcile the rulings. Stephen Henderson wrote in the *Philadelphia Inquirer:*

> Washington—In split rulings, the Supreme Court reached a Solomonic compromise yesterday on government displays of the Ten

Commandments that advocates on both sides of the issue decried as adding "mud to murky water."

The justices struck down displays in two Kentucky courthouses, saying the intent and purpose of those displays were explicitly religious and therefore at odds with constitutional protections against government-sponsored proselytizing.

But the court upheld a 44-year-old display on the Texas Capitol grounds, saying its history and context were sufficiently nonreligious to avoid conflict, no matter what its original purpose or intent.

The rulings, both 5-4 and accompanied by biting dissents, conform to the court's long history of confusing—and seemingly contradictory—rulings on church and state matters.[143]

Bill Adair of the *St. Petersburg Times* wrote that the Court "offered muddled and confusing answers" to the question of the Ten Commandments displays.[144] From Winder, Georgia, an Atlanta suburb, Larry Copeland and Toni Locy reported in *USA Today* that the rulings "confused the issue here where the Ten Commandments are at the center of a grueling and polarizing court battle."[145]

Editorial comments were few, but not perverse. The New York *Daily News* said the "Supreme Court proved itself supremely inconsistent, downright confusing and, practically speaking, right."[146] The *New York Times* proclaimed the rulings "an important reaffirmation of the nation's commitment to separation of church and state."[147] The *Christian Science Monitor* declared soberly, "The court took a moderate tack—not 'establishing' a religion, which is forbidden by the Constitution, but not stripping God from the public sphere either."[148] All three broadcast networks led their evening news broadcasts with the Court's rulings, and ABC's *Nightline* explored them further. CNN gave the story a generous six minutes and fifty seconds, but anchorman Aaron Brown's introduction made no mention of the First Amendment or the establishment clause and the rest of the time was devoted to his conversation with a conservative Christian and an activist rabbi, leaving viewers to discern for themselves what the constitutional issue was and why the rulings differed.[149]

Under newly installed Chief Justice John Roberts the Supreme Court in 2006 revisited the issue of assisted suicide, though in a limited way. The Court, 6–3, voided a drug regulation issued by then–Attorney General John Ashcroft intended to interfere with Oregon's Death with Dignity Act.[150] Ashcroft acted under the Controlled Substances Act, enacted in 1970 to combat drug abuse. The Oregon law exempts from liability Oregon-licensed physicians who dispense or prescribe a lethal dose of drugs requested by an Oregon resident with a terminal illness expected to cause death within six months. The Court ruled that the federal statute did not authorize the attorney general to prohibit physicians from prescribing drugs for suicide in accordance with state law. The chief justice and Justices Scalia and Thomas dissented, contending that the Controlled Substances Act's "public health and safety" clause did indeed authorize the attorney general's action.

The decision, reported Stephen Henderson of Knight Ridder, "makes clear that a court majority believes executive power cannot be expanded by a president beyond limits set by Congress in some cases."[151] The *Denver Post,* supporting the decision, took an editorial swipe at the dissenters: "Apparently it hasn't occurred to the new justice (nor colleagues Antonin Scalia and Clarence Thomas) that the people of Oregon have the right and wisdom to govern their medical affairs."[152] The *Boston Globe* said the Court "acted wisely. . . . Whatever one's view of this practice, Oregonians should be allowed to make this choice."[153]

The broadcast networks gave the story top position in their evening newscasts, and all misstated the Court's ruling. Wyatt Andrews of CBS reported, "The ruling legalizes the right of terminally ill Oregon patients ... to end their lives when they choose with a doctor-prescribed dose of barbiturates."[154] NBC's Pete Williams gave it the same erroneous twist, stating that the Court "upheld an Oregon law."[155] ABC, too, reported that the Supreme Court "upheld Oregon's doctor-assisted suicide law."[156] Were the networks copying each other? Did their reporters read the opinions? The validity of the state statute was not at issue, simply the U.S. attorney general's right to prevent physicians from utilizing it.

When the Environmental Protection Agency declined to regulate motor vehicle emissions that allegedly contributed to global warming, several state and local governments and environmental organizations challenged that determination, and the Supreme Court ruled against the agency. The vote was 5-4. Justice Stevens wrote for the majority that greenhouse gases from autos fit within the Clean Air Act's broad definition of "air pollutant" and therefore the EPA was required to consider regulating them, and to justify with scientific evidence any decision not to do so.[157] Justice Scalia's disagreement was so colorful that it was prominently quoted. "In a stinging dissent," wrote Jeff Nesmith of the *Austin American-Statesman,* "Justice Antonin Scalia said the decision was based on such a sweeping definition of air pollution that 'everything airborne, from Frisbees to flatulence, qualifies as an "air pollutant."'"[158]

Newspapers provided abundant coverage of the decision, and many immediately sounded off, not so much about the ruling as about the Bush administration's reluctance to respond to global warming. The *Salt Lake Tribune* rejoiced: "That ruling is important to Utahns because it eliminates another of the president's excuses for not taking action."[159] Papers in California, which had been bucking the administration on environmental regulations, were especially pleased. The *San Francisco Chronicle* proclaimed: "One of the great head-in-the-sand performances—the White House's refusal to act on global warming—is over, by legal decree."[160] Paul Rogers wrote in the *San Jose Mercury News* that "Monday's landmark U.S. Supreme Court ruling on global warming increases the chances that a new generation of fuel-efficient cars could begin hitting the roads as soon as next year."[161] The *Boston Globe*, too, saw the decision in a larger context: "[T]he most immediate effect of yesterday's ruling might be to strengthen the authority California has claimed to insist on strict emission limits in cars sold there. Ten other states, including Massachusetts, plan to adopt the same standards."[162] But the *Wall Street Journal* lambasted the decision as the work of "jolly green justices," saying global warming was something for Congress to decide on, as Chief Justice Roberts argued in his dissent.[163]

The networks provided extensive coverage on their evening newscasts, with NBC and CBS each running the story a full five minutes. NBC included a rundown on current environmental actions in California. CBS assessed the impact on the auto industry, Anthony Mason reporting from the New York Auto Show that "with the Supreme Court's ruling, the auto industry's campaign to fight off stricter emission rules may be running out of road."[164]

ABORTION, AGAIN

The volatile, never-ending quarrel over abortion rights returned to the Supreme Court in 2007, when it upheld the constitutionality of the Partial-Birth Abortion Ban Act of 2003. A criminal statute, it proscribes a rare procedure known medically as intact dilation and evacuation performed in the second trimester to abort a living fetus. The Court, sharply split 5-4, reversed two circuit courts of appeals, basing its ruling on its 1992 decision in *Planned Parenthood v. Casey,* which affirmed that the state has legitimate interests throughout pregnancy in protecting both the life of the fetus that may become a child and the health of the woman, thus recognizing that continuation of a pregnancy might threaten her well-being and so justify an abortion.[165] The Partial-Birth Act, however, did not provide an exception for the health of the mother.

On television the story was trumped by the revelations that the Virginia Tech killer of thirty-two people, months before he snapped in April 2007, had been adjudged in court an "imminent danger" to himself, and that he had left an angry videotape of himself made during a lull in his murderous rampage. The TV stories on this ran as long as eleven minutes. Nevertheless, the networks, always intently interested in the abortion issue, handled the decision remarkably well in limited time. On ABC's *World News with Charles Gibson,* Jan Crawford Greenburg reported that "today's decision represents a seismic shift for the first time since Roe versus Wade. The court said the government could ban a specific type of abortion procedure. And for the first time, it upheld an abortion law that did not contain an exception for a woman's health." After a scene of protesters at the Court and a short interview with one of them, Greenburg continued:

> At issue, a bipartisan federal law that banned one type of abortion performed in the second trimester. The law is called the Partial-Birth Abortion Act because the fetus is partially delivered from the womb before it is killed. Writing for the majority, Justice Anthony Kennedy said Congress found the procedure "gruesome" and

never medically necessary. Kennedy said the government has the right to pass laws that show its profound respect for the life within the woman. In court today, an angry Justice Ruth Bader Ginsburg took the unusual step of reading parts of her dissent aloud. She said that the decision was alarming and could jeopardize women's health. She said it cannot be understood as anything other than an effort to chip away at the right to an abortion. Conservatives agreed. They said the decision is a significant change that will lead to more restrictions on abortion.[166]

Wyatt Andrews reported on the *CBS Evening News* that "the ruling is huge because the ban is now the first abortion restriction ever approved with no exception for the health of the mother."[167] PBS's *NewsHour with Jim Lehrer,* eschewing pictures of protesters at the Court and interviews with partisans, covered the story quite differently. It emphasized the law rather than the politics, through a long interview by Judy Woodruff with Marcia Coyle of the *National Law Journal,* who explained briskly but clearly that in Justice Kennedy's majority opinion,

> the first point was that this statute was more precise than a state statute on partial-birth abortion that the court struck down seven years ago, so he felt the void for vagueness argument fell by the wayside. It offered clear guidance.
>
> But then he also said—and he addressed probably the central battle in this, under this law—he looked at whether this law was unconstitutional because it imposed an undue burden on a woman's right to choose, because it lacked a health exception.
>
> And here is where he said that the states, in the face of medical uncertainty as to whether there were health risks imposed by this procedure, had room to legislate. This was different from what the

court did seven years ago when it said, in the face of substantial uncertainty over health or medical risks, Congress must include a health exception.[168]

Newspapers, less preoccupied by the Virginia Tech disclosures, found room for the Court decision on the front page, and many wrote local-impact stories as well. Linda Greenhouse of the *New York Times* pointed out in her second paragraph, "The most important vote was that of the newest justice, Samuel A. Alito, Jr. In another 5-to-4 decision seven years ago, his predecessor, Justice Sandra Day O'Connor, voted to strike down a similar state law. Justice Alito's vote to uphold the federal law made the difference in the outcome announced Wednesday."[169] Tracy Wheeler reported in the *Akron Beacon Journal* that "in Ohio, the effect of Wednesday's Supreme Court ruling is that dilation and extraction (also known as D&X in medical circles, or partial-birth abortion by opponents) is illegal in all cases. The health of the mother will no longer be considered."[170] The *Albuquerque Journal* said, "Although opponents and supporters of the ban argued over the ruling and its impact, they agreed on one thing: It probably will intensify the politics surrounding abortion in New Mexico."[171]

Editorial opinion was profuse, mixed, and sharp. The *Augusta* (Georgia) *Chronicle* asserted: "Folks, even if your views on other abortion procedures are, shall we say, nuanced, partial-birth abortion is nothing but infanticide."[172] The *Tampa Tribune* celebrated "a victory for humanity."[173] But the *San Francisco Chronicle* called the decision "an outrage."[174] The *Boston Globe,* noting that the American College of Obstetricians and Gynecologists had found the procedure appropriate in some circumstances, a fact mentioned by Justice Ginsburg in her dissent, complained that "[t]he five justices of the court majority and the politicians who passed the law they approved have overruled the best judgment of the doctors who are most informed on this issue."[175]

FIREFIGHTERS FIGHT

A 2009 affirmative-action decision by the Supreme Court attracted special attention because it reversed a Second Circuit Court of Appeals holding in which Judge Sonia Sotomayor, just nominated by President Obama for the Supreme Court, had participated. The appellate court had summarily affirmed a ruling by a U.S. district court that the city of New Haven, Connecticut, acted correctly when it threw out the results of a firefighter promotion examination on which blacks scored poorly. White and Hispanic firefighters who had passed the examination but were denied promotions sued the city under the Civil Rights Act of 1964, alleging racial discrimination. The Supreme Court, 5-4, ruled that the contrasting examination results were insufficient to demonstrate a "disparate impact," a Civil Rights Act legal standard that would have justified junking the exam. Justice Kennedy wrote for the majority that "before an employer can engage in intentional discrimination for the asserted purpose of avoiding or remedying an unintentional disparate impact, the employer must have a strong basis in evidence to believe it will be subject to disparate-impact liability if it fails to take the race-conscious, discriminatory action." Justice Ginsburg, dissenting, argued that the majority ignored flaws in the New Haven test and the fact that "better tests" in other cities "yielded less racially skewed outcomes."[176] Kennedy's "strong-basis-in-evidence" standard was new, and more restrictive than the precedential standard that the Sotomayor court had been obliged to apply. Subtle, indeed.

Joan Biskupic of *USA Today* concisely stated the dilemma posed by the Civil Rights Act: "Justice Anthony Kennedy said the city violated a provision of Title VII of the Civil Rights Act that bars discriminatory treatment. New Haven officials had said they were trying to meet a separate Title VII rule that bars tests that cause a discriminatory impact."[177] Perceptively, Adam Liptak of the *New York Times* reported, "The new standards announced by the court will make it much harder for employers to discard the results of hiring and promotion tests once they are administered, even if they have a disproportionately negative impact on members of a given racial group."[178] But many papers played up the easy Sotomayor angle rather than the new legal standard enunciated by the Court. Michael Doyle of the *San Jose Mercury News* wrote in his second paragraph: "The court's much-anticipated 5-4 decision is guaranteed to become prime fodder for Sotomayor's Senate confirmation hearings."[179] The Associated Press: "A sharply divided Supreme Court ruled yesterday that white firefighters in New Haven, Conn., were unfairly denied promotions because of their race, reversing a decision that high court nominee Sonia Sotomayor endorsed as an appellate court judge."[180] But the *Baltimore Sun,* focusing on the Court's new interpretation of the statute, declared that Judge Sotomayor's "handling of the Ricci case shows that she is far more moderate than the five-member majority that overruled her. Instead of conjuring up a new legal standard, as the court contrived to do, she relied on precedent."[181]

Television coverage was seriously crimped by the networks' continuing massive attention to the recent sudden death of entertainer Michael Jackson, and by the sentencing of Wall Street swindler Bernard Madoff. CNN skipped the decision in its *AC360* broadcast, but the *CBS Evening News* managed to allocate three minutes to it, albeit with a Sotomayor twist.

We have surveyed here some of the most intense coverage ever given by the American news media to the Supreme Court. Abortion, affirmative action, school prayer, flag burning, religious displays by government, free expression, the environment. Americans care about these issues, and when they bubble up to the Supreme Court, the media pay attention. Though hampered by the Court's no-cameras rule, television, especially, ratchets up its coverage of such cases above that given to less inflammatory but often more profound questions of the extent of federal authority, antitrust and other economic conflicts, and even voting rights (with the notable exception of *Bush v. Gore*).

Has all this maximum effort succeeded in edifying the public about the work and impact of the Supreme Court of the United States? There is probably no clear answer. However, in a sense this intense coverage distorts the public view of the Court because its other cases are given proportionately less attention. Another downside is that, because these hot-button issues are political and social as well as legal, it is all too easy for reporters and editors, especially those unfamiliar with the Court and legal issues, to jump immediately to reaction, interpretation, and impact without first carefully explaining the legal reasoning of the justices. That was especially apparent in the New Haven firefighters' case. In covering many of these hot-button cases, NBC television, in particular, commonly ignored the constitutional and legal aspects of Court decisions, both the underlying law at issue and the Court's reasoning, to concentrate on the policy changes wrought, much like reporting actions by a legislative body.

Is there a perceived need by the news media, especially television, to hype these culture-wars decisions in order to capture audience attention? The decisions hardly need it, for they are intrinsically major news. But how else explain the errors that occasionally occur, notably in newspaper headlines and in newscasts, such as the glaring misstatement by all three broadcast networks of the Court's holding in *Gonzales v. Oregon,* the assisted-suicide case? The question before the Court was interpretation of a federal statute, not the constitutionality of the Oregon law. Another possible explanation is that the reporters, writers, and editors producing some Court stories simply did not understand the decisions. Either way, news organizations can hardly countenance such sloppiness.

That said, and striving to take a larger view, it could be argued that half a loaf is better than none, that some or even occasionally erroneous coverage is better than no coverage. For the Supreme Court's work is always important, always newsworthy to some extent, and it is journalism's task to bring to public attention news that is significant, explaining why. That is a more demanding challenge than simply reporting the winner and loser in a controversial case and then flying off to seek opposing opinions in lieu of understanding. Yes, half a loaf may be better, but it is hardly sufficient.

PART FOUR
CLOSING ARGUMENTS

TWELVE

THE NECESSARY FUTURE

No appraisal of media coverage of the Supreme Court and the relations between the two institutions finds them satisfactory. The media fall short in five respects: inaccuracy; failure to explain clearly the legal basis and reasoning of each decision; reporting decisions like the policy determinations of a legislative body; overemphasis on reaction and impact at the expense of the decision itself; and downplaying with inadequate space or time, or omitting altogether, newsworthy stories. For its part, the Court throughout its entire history has lagged behind the reasonable needs of the public and the press—read, the needs of democracy—to learn about and to understand its decisions. As always, the Court also lags behind the states in protecting freedom of the press, particularly now in regard to protection of journalists' confidential sources. More on the Court later.

We have seen numerous examples of media inaccuracy, notably in newspaper headlines and television reports of decisions. Justice Ruth Bader Ginsburg acknowledges, "It is indeed hard, under the pressure of publication deadlines, to describe judicial opinions with entire accuracy."[1] But that, of course, must be the media's goal. Some further examples of falling short: the *Chicago Sun-Times,* reporting the Court's 2001 decision on the Chicago suburbs' frustrated landfill proposal,[2] incorrectly stated that the villages "claimed that the U.S. Army Corps of Engineers lacks jurisdiction because the pools do not connect with any interstate waterway."[3] In fact, as the Court's opinion made clear, the case turned on the definition of "navigable waterways," long under the jurisdiction of the Corps of Engineers and always comprehending intrastate as well as interstate waterways. The *Florida Times-Union* stated erroneously in covering the two Ten Commandments decisions in 2005[4] that "[t]he First Amendment's establishment clause prohibits government promotion of religion," when, of course, it prohibits merely government establishment of a state religion.[5] It is not difficult for a reporter, or a copy editor, to check the Constitution.

Each Supreme Court decision interprets the Constitution or a statute, and a solid story should mention that underlying law and probably explain it. Then the decision itself requires a clear statement of the Court's interpretation, and an explanation of the legal reasoning as well. Dissenting opinions, especially those on behalf of three or four justices, should be quoted and their reasoning contrasted with the majority's.

Embracing all this can be tricky, particularly, as Justice Ginsburg notes, under time pressure. With their limited minutes and seconds, which are usually insufficient to convey complex stories with adequate clarity, the networks often fall short in this respect, but they need not shoulder the entire blame. The 2009 decision in the New Haven firefighters' reverse discrimination case, so closely covered because Judge Sotomayor had joined the Second Circuit's ruling against the firefighters, left the print media gasping for breath, too. Many newspaper stories, anxious to point out the reversal of her court, failed to mention that the justices moved the goalposts, changing the burden of proof they required under the Civil Rights Act of 1964 in the delicate balance between "discriminatory treatment" and "discriminatory impact."

A LEGAL BASIS FOR A LEGAL DECISION

An unfortunately common shortcoming of the media is mentioning no legal basis at all for a Supreme Court decision. For instance, the Baton Rouge *Advocate*'s story on a Guantanamo detainee ruling in 2004,[6] written with an appropriate local twist, started out with this suitable lead but neglected to mention at any point habeas corpus or due process, the legal essence of the rulings:

> The U.S. Supreme Court ruled Monday that the war on terrorism does not give the federal government a "blank check" to hold a U.S. citizen and foreign-born terrorist suspects in legal limbo in the case of Yaser Esam Hamdi, a Baton Rouge native captured as an enemy combatant in Afghanistan in 2002.[7]

A study of 1998–99 decisions coverage by forty-six newspapers and the three commercial television networks found that newspapers did better than television when it came to reporting the legal basis for the Court's ruling. "Newspapers can allocate more space, allowing for greater breadth and depth of coverage," declared two political scientists, Rorie L. Spill and Zoe M. Oxley. They said TV stories were more likely to be altered or cut "if they lack sufficient entertainment value," and "[t]he brevity of television stories coupled with this focus on entertainment likely results in presenting the Court's decisions without much attention to relevant legal issues and arguments." More broadly, looking at both network and newspaper stories, only two-thirds of them provided "justifications" such as citing the Constitution or a statute, the study found.[8]

This confirms what we have seen in this book: when it comes to characterizing Court decisions as policy pronouncements rather than legal determinations, the television networks are the most culpable. Spill and Oxley state that "the typical broadcast story . . . summarizes the content of the decisions, discusses its future implications, and states whether any person or group will be helped or harmed by the decision." In particular, they say, stories covered by "non-Court reporters," those not holding press passes for the full term, "focus more attention on the future and political implications of a decision, treating the Supreme Court like any other political institution."[9]

Charitably, we can attribute such shortcomings in broadcasters' coverage to their time limitations as well as to their need to catch viewers' attention with each story. But this glossy NBC lead on the Guantanamo detainee rulings simply evokes a power struggle rather than reporting a legal judgment: "In a stinging rebuke, the justices today say the Bush administration cannot expect the courts to stay on the sidelines in the war on terror." Neither habeas corpus nor due process, the legal issues decided by the Court, was mentioned at any point in the story.[10]

Unfortunately, newspapers, too, can play the political game. The Supreme Court ruled in 1995 that Georgia's congressional map, drawn in response to the Voting Rights Act of 1965 to create three majority-black districts, was so bizarre that it could be explained only on racial grounds, and compliance with the statute alone was not a compelling state interest that could justify such a racial preference. Therefore, the Court held, 5-4, that the map violated the Fourteenth Amendment's due process clause, whose "central mandate is racial neutrality in governmental decisionmaking."[11] But none of this reasoning, not even the Voting Rights Act or the Fourteenth Amendment, made it into the *Augusta* (Georgia) *Chronicle*'s lead story on the case, which focused instead on whether the federal district court or the legislature would now draw a new map:

> Georgia lawmakers may be heading back to the political drawing board after the U.S. Supreme Court threw out Rep. Cynthia McKinney's 11th Congressional District on Thursday.
>
> The Supreme Court's 5-4 ruling striking down the majority-black 11th could open all Georgia congressional districts to new legislative scrutiny, including that of U.S. House Speaker Newt Gingrich.[12]

Throughout the last several chapters we have seen many examples of reaction reporting, sometimes overriding the coverage of the Court's decision. This way of covering the Court is easier, indeed instinctive, for the average journalist, as opposed to the more laborious process of reading, comprehending, and summarizing succinctly the legal reasoning of the justices. This is not a recent phenomenon. It was noted nearly half a century ago by researcher Chester A. Newland in a study of how newspapers covered two groundbreaking 1962 decisions by the Warren Court, *Engel v. Vitale,* the first school prayer case,[13] and *Baker v. Carr,* the Tennessee legislative districts case.[14] He found that the papers reported more about the reaction, which of course was immense in those instances, than about the decisions themselves.[15] A California lawyer and sometime court journalist wrote in 1970 that "these public furor stories contribute little to the public's understanding (and probably much to its misunderstanding) of what the Court has decided."[16]

This journalistic temptation, or perversion, is greatest in cases like *Engel* and *Baker,* or the Georgia redistricting case mentioned above, or, to take the most extreme example of all, *Bush v. Gore,* where the ruling touches a sensitive public nerve or where the implications are great and immediate. In such instances the reporter covering the decision may feel a necessity to gather reaction and report it prominently in his story, almost inevitably at the expense of closer scrutiny of the opinion. Such were the Court's 2003 rulings in the two University of Michigan affirmative-action admissions cases.[17] The *St. Petersburg Times,* anxious to apply them locally, used "university admissions" in its lead sentence without clarifying that the Court ruled separately on undergraduate and law school admissions, with opposite results. Then the paper wrote this puzzling contradiction about the impact in Florida:

> In the most significant affirmative action decision in a generation, a split U.S. Supreme Court on Monday ruled that race can be used as a factor in university admissions but not the predominant one.
>
> The decision brought immediate pressure on Florida Gov. Jeb Bush, who outlawed the use of race in university admissions in his One Florida plan four years ago.
>
> "Gov. Bush made a mistake with One Florida, and he needs to correct that mistake," said U.S. Rep. Kendrick Meek, who along with state Sen. Tony Hill, staged a sit-in at the governor's office in 2000 protesting One Florida.
>
> The Supreme Court cases, both out of the University of Michi-

gan in Ann Arbor, are not expected to have any immediate impact on Florida universities.

Bush issued a statement Monday saying he will stick to his plan.[18]

The paper made no mention of the legal basis for the decisions until it tacked on to the bottom of its long, 2,000-word story several short quotations from the opinions, including a reference by Chief Justice Rehnquist to the Fourteenth Amendment. The Civil Rights Act under which the rejected applicants had sued was never cited.

CRITICS' CHOICE

Faulting the American media for a "less-than-stellar job when covering courts at all levels, including the Supreme Court," Catherine Crier of *Court TV,* who was a prosecutor and a judge in Texas before turning to journalism, cites the coverage of *Gonzales v. Raich,* a 2005 federal-state confrontation involving homegrown marijuana. The Supreme Court upheld, 6-3, federal agents' seizure under the Controlled Substances Act of marijuana plants grown by California residents suffering from serious medical conditions, a cultivation legal in that state. The Court reasoned that such production would have an impact on the interstate market for marijuana and thus was within Congress's authority under the commerce clause.[19] The case was "a fascinating debate over federalism, states' rights, and the limits of the constitution's Commerce Clause," Crier writes, but to many journalists it "was simply a battle between liberal advocates of medical marijuana and those conservatives who believe such use is a slippery slope to legalization. . . . Most of the coverage was no different than that analyzing congressional politics or sports."[20]

Among the well-informed critics of media coverage of the Court are at least a few justices and some reporters who have done the job. As early as 1875 Justice Samuel Freeman Miller wrote despairingly:

> The newspaper tyranny is the most oppressive now in existence, and the gravest problem of the age is to determine where relief shall come from. . . . [L]ately they have combined to bring the Courts and the administration of justice under their control, by their appeals to popular prejudice, accompanied by the usual amount of lying.[21]

A biographer of Chief Justice Stone, who presided from 1941 to 1946, quotes him as being highly distressed by newspaper errors in Supreme Court stories:

> What "really shocked" the Chief Justice was "the misleading, not to say completely inaccurate, statements" appearing in the press. And for this he had at least a partial explanation. It was "due to the fact that the Court is constantly dealing with more and more technical and complex questions than ever before in its history, and the layman who undertakes to comment on it is often undertaking to write about something which he does not understand."

While despairing, Stone had a solution: the papers should hire a professor of constitutional law to critique their stories before publication. "Lawyers and laymen alike," writes the biographer,

Alpheus T. Mason, "might then rely on press accounts as confidently as the British depend on the London *Times*."[22]

Washington Post Supreme Court reporter James E. Clayton wrote in 1968: "The press still does a poor job of covering the courts in general and the Supreme Court in particular."[23] David L. Grey of Stanford University studied media coverage of the headline-making Warren Court in the 1960s and concluded that

> the press is not providing enough perspective on the Supreme Court as the important governmental institution it really is. There is a general absence of penetrating coverage of long-term trends and legal developments, while much of the short-term news coverage that does exist ends up preoccupied with the drama of the "news event" or the persons and organizations involved and not enough with the why and the explanations of what it all *really means,* anyhow.[24]

In their 1998 study of Court coverage, Elliot Slotnick and Jennifer Segal found a "substantial distance between the amount and nature of the information about the Court made available to the mass public and the informational needs about the Court suggested by the dictates of classical democratic theory."[25] In chapter 1 we noted longtime Supreme Court reporter Tony Mauro's apologia for journalism's "inadequacies" in covering the courts.[26] And so it goes. No one is satisfied.

Journalists and justices—not to mention the public—simply need to recognize that Court coverage is not routine journalism. It is, as Chief Justice Stone observed, technical and complex, and considerably more so now than in the 1940s. In fact, it is quite different from other work that journalists do. As one law professor observes, Supreme Court reporters must have an appreciation for the subtleties of legal tradition, the nuances of legal argument, and the inherent humanity, for better and for worse, of our justice system. On the other hand, they must possess the sharpest of journalistic skills if they are to translate the peculiar archaisms of law into stories that convey to their audience the practical import of those rules and their results. The best of our court reporters are at once keen observers, logical thinkers, and master storytellers.[27]

Linda Greenhouse of the *New York Times* feels a Supreme Court reporter should produce a story that is "necessarily interpretive . . . more than an accurate statement of the holding. Readers also need to know the context of the decision, what the decision means, how the case got to the Court in the first place, what arguments were put to the Justices, what the decision tells us about the Court, and what happens next."[28]

To cover decisions well requires, first of all, a foreknowledge of the cases to be decided, which can be acquired through a careful reading of the lawyers' briefs available at the Court and online through the American Bar Association. Next, coverage of oral argument sharpens a reporter's insight into the legal nuances of a case, and what aspects of it will probably be influential in the justices' decision. Interviewing the lawyers in the case and other, uninvolved legal experts is useful. Then when a decision comes down, which happens without advance notice from the Court, accurate reporting requires a fast but careful reading of the opinion or opinions before commencing to write, which also must be done rapidly. Formerly only wire-service reporters felt this immediacy, but the Internet now puts them all under pressure. Even for a seasoned deadline reporter this is a challenge. As John P. MacKenzie, Supreme Court reporter for the *Washington Post,* wrote in 1968:

The Court's decisions are the start of an argument more often than they are the final, definitive word on a given subject. Opinions often are written in such a way that they mask the difficulties of a case rather than illuminate them. New decisions frequently cannot be reconciled with prior rulings.[29]

They are not easy reading, especially if a conscientious reporter intends to explain the justices' legal reasoning, citing constitutional provisions, statutes, and precedents, which are abundant in every opinion. Fortunately for the media, in recent years the Court is not increasing its output, holding the total number of decisions to about 80 per term, which is down sharply from historic highs of 170 or more. But in other respects the Court reporter's challenge may be on the rise. In the 2008–09 term the justices wrote a total of 191 opinions, including concurrences and dissents, 9 more than the average of the ten prior years; of these, 78 were dissenting opinions, 16 more than the ten-year average. The number of unanimous opinions in 2008–09 was only 15 (and just 11 in the year before that), well below the ten-year average of 24. The total number of opinions in the 2009–10 term was also well above average, 189.[30] These multiple opinions demand extra attention.

CAN LAW REPORTERS DO BETTER WITH LAW EDUCATION?

It is obvious that a Supreme Court correspondent must have mastered deadline reporting before venturing into those marble precincts, but it is equally clear that a reporter will have a greater chance of success if he or she has specialized knowledge, too. Tony Mauro puts his finger on it: "we are way behind on the things we can improve—notably preparation and training, and also the effort required to understand and then to summarize matters both subtle and complex."[31]

Education in the law greatly facilitates that effort—and consequently public understanding of what the Court ruled. This is hardly a new idea. As in recent decades, several current Court reporters have law degrees, including Joan Biskupic of *USA Today,* Jan Crawford Greenburg of ABC, Jess Bravin of the *Wall Street Journal,* Adam Liptak of the *New York Times,* and Greg Stohr of Bloomberg News.[32] Is it mere coincidence that they are among the best reporters there?

The *Times,* in fact, has insisted on legal training for its Court reporters ever since Justice Felix Frankfurter, who served from 1939 to 1962, pushed or perhaps shamed the paper into it. His biographer Liva Baker tells this delightful story:

> Beginning in 1933, Frankfurter barraged Arthur Hays Sulzberger, publisher of the *Times,* with letters in which he was outspokenly critical of its failings—and equally outspokenly congratulatory of its triumphs. Finally, in the mid-1950's, Frankfurter was instrumental in changing *Times* Supreme Court reportage. Sulzberger and Frankfurter lunched in Washington, and a young reporter and Pulitzer Prize winner named Anthony Lewis was sent to Harvard Law School for a year, then assigned to cover the Supreme Court. The *Times* expanded and deepened its court coverage.[33]

David L. Grey corroborated the story by interviewing the *Times*'s legendary Washington bureau chief of that era, James (Scotty) Reston: "Reston confirms that it was Justice Frankfurter who first urged the *Times* to train a man in the law. He recalls that the justice once remarked to him personally in the mid-1950s that the *Times* would not think of sending a sports reporter to Yankee Stadium who knew as little about baseball as *Times* reporters knew about the Court."[34] At the Court commencing in the mid-1950s Anthony Lewis distinguished himself by his thorough comprehension of its work and his lucid writing. He went on to win a Pulitzer Prize for his Court coverage and wrote a book describing the gripping human story behind a landmark criminal law case he covered in 1963, *Gideon v. Wainwright.* In *Gideon* the Warren Court held that the Sixth Amendment's right to counsel applied to the states through the Fourteenth Amendment, and thus an indigent charged in Florida with a capital crime was entitled to legal counsel at state expense.[35] Lewis also wrote a book about *New York Times v. Sullivan,* which he covered, too.[36]

Lewis was followed by a one-time Nashville reporter and trial lawyer hired from a legal post at the U.S. Department of Labor, Fred Graham.[37] After Graham moved to CBS in the 1970s the *Times* assigned a former prosecutor, Lesley Oelsner, and then another lawyer, Stuart Taylor, Jr. Looking ahead, the *Times* sent its Albany bureau chief, Linda Greenhouse, to Yale Law School for a year to prepare to cover the Court. On the job for twenty-seven years, she, too, was awarded a Pulitzer Prize, "for her consistently illuminating coverage of the United States Supreme Court." Seven of the nine justices attended a retirement party for her in 2008. The *Times* then appointed Adam Liptak, who first worked for the paper as an attorney but switched to reporting and wrote many law stories including court decisions before his full-time assignment to the Supreme Court. It is instructive that this line of law-educated reporters has provided the finest Supreme Court coverage of any media organization over the last half-century.

Is such expensive education feasible at a time when news organizations, especially newspapers, are under financial pressure? Yes. Both

Lewis and Greenhouse, as well as other Supreme Court reporters like John MacKenzie of the *Washington Post* and Michael McGough of the *Pittsburgh Post-Gazette,* attended law school for a year on journalism fellowships. These still are available. Another source of lawyer-reporters is young people who have put themselves through law school but find that the practice of law, or perhaps even the prospect of it, is not personally fulfilling. Some of these young lawyers turn naturally to journalism to capitalize on their knowledge and on their skills of fact-gathering, analysis, and clear expression, the basic tools of all journalists as well as all lawyers.

A news organization gains more than a well-grounded Supreme Court reporter when it assigns a law-trained journalist to that beat. Our society is enmeshed in law. Much of today's news, not just Supreme Court decisions, has legal implications that may be covered by such a skilled reporter, particularly during the Court's long summer recess. Moreover, the reporter's expertise can be tapped to guide other reporters, editors, and producers, and to establish best practices for covering courts and other legal stories. Perhaps most important, in connection with Supreme Court coverage, a law-trained reporter is better equipped from the outset to be the independent, authoritative journalist that the beat requires. Few producers and editors have covered the Supreme Court. They naturally look to the Court reporter to guide them in deciding which cases to cover and to develop other story ideas about the law. As Linda Greenhouse writes in the *Yale Law Journal,* more than in other beats,

> the reporters tend to make these calls because editors have no independent means for evaluating the importance of the dozens of discrete events that may constitute the Supreme Court's activities on a given day. While this circumstance offers an unusual amount

of freedom to the reporter, it also means there is unlikely to be
much informed discussion with colleagues and editors back at the
office.[38]

Whether it be in Washington or far away, "the desk" needs
reliable, trustworthy, and sometimes immediate guidance, to allocate space (or time) and perhaps to commit additional resources.
That would include, most importantly, assigning other journalists
to do the reaction stories while allowing the Court reporter to
work through the opinions and maximize the benefit of his or her
special knowledge. The Associated Press, the *New York Times,* the
Washington Post, and others often mobilize additional staff members in this fashion, but those decisions depend at least in part on
input from the Court reporter. He or she is an adviser as well as
a reporter.

It goes without saying that over the years and still today many
fine reporters have excelled at the Supreme Court without the
benefit of formal education in the law. Lyle Denniston of Scotus
blog.com, Nina Totenberg of National Public Radio, and Tony
Mauro of *Legal Times,* all fortified by long tenure at the Court,
come readily to mind. However, some years ago when the regular
Court reporters, some law-schooled and some not, were asked
what advice they would give to an aspiring reporter about the best
educational preparation for covering the Court and other legal
news, 11 out of 15 said law.[39] It makes sense.

To be sure, no matter how well qualified or capable a Supreme
Court reporter may be, the reporter's publication or other organization must make a commensurate commitment to convey news
of the Court. Over many years the *New York Times* and the *Washington Post* have consistently placed Court decision stories on page
one; no reader of the *Times* or the *Post* can be unaware of impor-

tant rulings the Court has handed down. Other papers and the broadcast networks are not so insistent that the audience needs to know what the Court did. In this time when newspapers, which cover far more cases than the networks, are shrinking, Court coverage will wither proportionately unless editors make decisions that enable Court stories to survive (and their headlines to be accurate), perhaps even to flourish. The likelihood of this happening is bound to be related to the qualifications and quality of the reporter covering the Court.

Given today's communications, that reporter need not be at the Supreme Court. More on this coming up after the break.

THE COURT CAN HELP ITSELF

If better training and higher priority are ways in which news organizations can improve their coverage of the Court, what can the Court itself do? First, however, it is appropriate to ask, do the justices care about how their decisions are communicated to the citizenry? To judge by their practices and some justices' comments, the answer is, not much. For more than a century the Court failed to provide as a regular practice printed copies of its opinions on the day those decisions were announced from the bench. Newspaper stories, therefore, had few quotations and almost no details, usually nothing of the legal reasoning leading to the decision. Not until the late 1920s did same-day distribution of printed opinions become standard practice, and not until 1935, after the Associated Press jumped the gun and reported an important decision incorrectly, did the Court decide to hand out its opinions to reporters at the commencement of the oral reading, which is the moment when the decisions become official and public, rather than afterward.[40]

Chief Justice Earl Warren, unusual among justices in that he had faced the electorate many times and was highly experienced in public communication, was nevertheless indifferent to the Court's reliance on the news media to tell the citizenry of its decisions. "As the figurehead and moving force behind a Court that was upsetting applecarts throughout the country," Fred Graham writes in his memoir, "Earl Warren made a point of being oblivious to the outcry that it created. He was the Rhett Butler of judicial public relations; frankly, he didn't give a damn."[41] On the other hand, Graham says, Earl Warren's successor, Warren Burger, "became an enthusiastic reformer of the *mechanics* of covering the Supreme Court."[42] He had the Court's press officer hand out opinions in the pressroom rather than blasting them down from the bench through pneumatic tubes. He ordered the printing of the official summary at the top of each opinion rather than reserving them for publication in official volumes much later. He spread out the inevitable end-of-term barrage of decisions by having the Court meet several days a week in June, and even occasionally stretched the Court's term into the early days of July to facilitate greater attention to important decisions.

However, Graham goes on, "Burger never conceded that there was a legitimate public interest in such matters as the justices' health, their finances, their reasons for disqualifying themselves from cases, their votes on deadlocked appeals, and their off-the-bench activities."[43] And Burger would not allow television cameras into the courtroom, a proposal that had been around for a number of years already but was steadfastly blocked by the justices. Graham writes:

Byron White once stated his objection to me this way: "I can't see why the Court should do anything to make CBS richer." White said he might consider permitting cameras if only the Public Broadcasting System was involved. When I tried to argue that newspapers had made money for years off their coverage of the Court, all I got was a stony stare.[44]

THE SUPREME COURT TAPES

For years, without informing the press or the public, the Court unobtrusively recorded its oral arguments and stashed the tapes away at the Court. At some point the Court decided instead to store them in a vault at the National Archives. The justices completely ignored the tapes' potential usefulness to both print and broadcast reporters seeking to improve Court coverage. In 1981 Fred Graham purloined a copy of the tape of an important oral argument, in the 1971 Pentagon Papers case, the First Amendment prior-restraint test involving the *New York Times* and the *Washington Post*,[45] and broadcast portions of it on the tenth anniversary of the decision, on both CBS radio and television. Graham writes that he thought "the Court would get the point" that electronic coverage "could be interesting and tasteful," but he was mistaken.

The chief justice went into orbit. Burger blamed the National Archives for the leak; nothing so wicked had happened so long as the recordings had been kept within the Court. After an unsuccessful hunt for the leaker, Burger decreed that no more recordings would go to the Archives—and for the next five years, none went.[46]

Linda Greenhouse of the *Times* deems the Court "quite blithely oblivious to the needs of those who convey its work to the outside world." Remembering a day in June 1988, "a journalistic nightmare" when the Court handed down nine decisions that ran nearly 450 pages, Greenhouse subsequently suggested to Chief Justice Rehnquist that the Court "make a greater effort to spread out the decision announcements in the last weeks of the Term." He responded, according to Greenhouse, "'Why don't you save some for the next day?' On one level, this was harmless, and cost-free, banter. On another, it offered a dramatic illustration of the gulf between us."[47] ABC's Court correspondent Tim O'Brien recounted to researchers Slotnick and Segal this exchange: "'Personally,' a justice tells me, 'personally, I sympathize with you. But I think it would be wrong to take your interest into consideration.'"[48]

Under Chief Justice Roberts, things have improved. The Court posts its opinions promptly on its Web site, makes written transcripts of its sessions available to the media shortly after it adjourns for the day, and on rare occasions releases an audio recording of an oral argument promptly after the session.[49] These practices have enhanced the accuracy of quotations by the media, and the quality of broadcast reports about those occasional audio-recording cases.

However, the Court continues to frown on a hoary proposal by the news media that they be granted advance reading time under secure conditions, a "lock-up," to prepare to report decisions as they are announced from the bench. This idea is seen as eminently sensible by the press, and beneficial to both the Court and the public. It would reduce errors and facilitate reporting of the legal reasoning of decisions rather than just calling a winner and seeking reaction. But the justices consistently ignore it.[50]

They cannot so easily ignore the other big potential enhancement of Court coverage: television. This is the overriding bone in the throat of the media, still stuck after decades of pleading and cajoling. Frank Stanton, the highly respected president of CBS from 1946 to 1971, felt television was unjustly denied the same access to the Supreme Court as the print media.[51] As one of many academic examinations of the idea of televising Court proceedings found in 1995, "It seems incongruous with democratic principles that the scope of a citizen's access to the process of momentous legal decision making should be dictated by the personal preferences of individual justices, rather than the needs and purposes of the judicial process itself."[52] The perceived benefits to the public, as stated in another journal article, are twofold: "first, the public, through their surrogate of the media, can act as an accountability check on the judicial branch; second, the expanded opportunity to view judicial workings through media coverage provides a valuable educational opportunity to all American citizens."[53]

At least one law professor has gone so far as to argue that because the First Amendment prohibits government regulation of the content of expression, and because cameras convey different content than words alone, the ban on cameras violates the First Amendment. "News-gathering by the technological methods appropriate to each medium of communication should be recognized as entitled to constitutional protection," writes Diane L. Zimmerman of New York University. "This expansion in the scope of the first amendment is necessary to ensure that news media may convey information without interference for capricious or insubstantial reasons."[54]

Americans want to know more, indeed *need* to know more, about the omnipotent institution in the imposing marble edifice on Capitol Hill, and they are entitled to. It is *their* Court, *their* Constitution. A public poll in 2006 found that 70 percent of the respondents thought it was a "good idea" to televise Supreme Court proceedings, a sharp increase from just 50 percent six years earlier.[55] Every day that the Supreme Court is in session tourists stand outside in long lines snaking down the street, hopeful of snaring one of the 200 public seats in the courtroom; only about 30,000 make the grade in the entire term, about equal to the number of spectators at a single major league baseball game.[56] Referring to a day in January 2008 when a high-profile voter registration case was being heard,[57] the *New York Times* editorialized:

> It was, like many legal showdowns in the court, something Americans would have been interested in observing firsthand. Yet, beyond a few hundred visitors, the public was denied that opportunity because members of the court, stubbornly clinging to their clubby ways, refuse to allow their proceedings to be televised. . . .
>
> Justice Clarence Thomas told a Senate hearing last year that televising the court would have a negative impact on its argument sessions and would raise security concerns "as members of the court who have some degree of anonymity would lose their anonymity." . . .
>
> Mr. Thomas's fears did not deter him from appearing on "60 Minutes" last fall to promote his book.[58]

Justice Scalia also has spoken out against television. "We don't want to become entertainment," he said on NBC's *Today* show in 2005. "I think there's something sick about making entertainment out of real people's legal problems. I don't like it in the lower courts, and I don't particularly like it in the Supreme Court."[59]

Although at least some of his colleagues are opposed to televising the Court's sessions, Chief Justice Roberts appears not to have dismissed the notion altogether. "The Court functions pretty well," he told a judges' meeting in 2006, and "oral argument is part of that. . . . We're going to look carefully at anything that might have an adverse impact on that." Roberts, acknowledging that the occasional release of audiotapes "has had a generally positive effect," did not suggest what that adverse impact might be.[60] Others have worried that television might encourage grandstanding by both judges and lawyers; experience indicates otherwise, as we shall see shortly.

Because the Court has not voluntarily opened its doors to television, Senator Arlen Specter of Pennsylvania, a longtime member of the Senate Judiciary Committee, repeatedly has introduced bills that would *require* the Court to allow TV coverage of its public sessions, "unless it decides by a vote of the majority of Justices that allowing such coverage in a particular case would violate the due process rights of one or more of the parties involved in the matter." When introducing his bill in 2005, Specter, then the chairman of the Judiciary Committee, told the Senate:

> The purpose of this legislation is to open the Supreme Court doors so that more Americans can see the process by which the Court reaches critical decisions of law that affect this country and everyday Americans. Because the Supreme Court of the United States holds power to decide cutting-edge questions on public policy, thereby effectively becoming a virtual "super legislature," the public has a right to know what the Supreme Court is doing. And that right would be substantially enhanced by televising the oral arguments of the Court so that the public can see and hear the issues presented to the Court.[61]

Senator Patrick Leahy of Vermont, now the chairman of the Judiciary Committee, joined Senator Specter as a cosponsor of the bill, stating, "This legislation springs from one of our most essential principles: A democracy works best when the people have all the information the security of the Nation permits."[62]

The bill was approved by the Senate Judiciary Committee in March 2006, as was a similar bill sponsored by Specter and Leahy in July 2008, but they went no further.[63] A bill that would *authorize* the presiding judge to allow televising or recording in all federal courts, including the Supreme Court, passed the House, 353 to 45, in November 2005.[64] It was not acted on by the Senate.

The subject of cameras in the Court came up in an unexpected and dramatic way when Justices Thomas and Breyer testified in 2009 before a House of Representatives subcommittee on the Court's annual appropriation request. Tony Mauro recounted the strange moment in the *National Law Journal:*

> The provocateur was conservative Rep. John Culberson, R-Tex. . . .
>
> "It's a very easy matter on the Internet," Culberson said, and to prove it, he took out a device, aimed at the justices and announced that at that very moment, their visages were being seen live on the Internet. . . .
>
> The justices were startled, but smiled for the camera. . . .
>
> "The next American revolution is going to come through the Internet," Culberson told the justices. "I encourage you to break down that wall. It's as easy as pushing this button." . . .
>
> As he often does, Breyer said the current members of the Court are just temporary stewards of a cherished institution who don't want to damage it in any way. . . .
>
> But [Thomas] did say that within the Court, "there has been quite a bit of discussion" about the issue, especially since legislation

that would require the Court to allow cameras was introduced in Congress.

Mauro commented, "If the Court eventually, finally, says yes sometime in this century, Thursday's hearing of the financial services and general government subcommittee of the House Appropriations Committee will have played a significant part."[65]

Representative Culberson's broadening of the argument to include the Internet was astute, for a study released in 2009 showed that computers climbed to second place in the amount of time that Americans devote to media each day, surpassing radio for the first time; print media came in fourth. Television remained number one, consuming eight-and-a-half hours per day for most age groups.[66]

CONSIDER THE FACTS

If the justices of the Supreme Court would seriously address the idea of admitting cameras, they would not do so in a vacuum. They can, and should, consider the experience of the state supreme courts, most of which permit at least some televising of their sessions, and the experience of the two U.S. circuit courts of appeals that do so.

Judge Diarmuid F. O'Scannlain of the Ninth Circuit, which from 1991 through 2005 granted 144 requests for camera access, or two-thirds of the requests presented, writes:

> as a general rule my colleagues and practitioners have acted with the civility and decorum appropriate to a federal appellate courtroom, by and large resisting the temptation to play to the television

audience.... My own experience with cameras in the courtroom has been overwhelmingly positive.[67]

Judge O'Scannlain acknowledges that cameras may give rise to security risks but contends that "appellate judges, no less than district judges or legislators, are public officials who must stand behind their decisions." He believes televising oral arguments "may increase the accuracy of reporting on the cases that we hear, thereby helping—I hope—to de-politicize the perception of the federal judiciary" that appellate courts are "results-oriented bodies." Specifically, he points to the Ninth Circuit's affirmation in 2003 of the voting procedure to be used to consider the recall of the California governor Gray Davis:[68] "The televising of oral arguments in that case may have helped to inform the public and the news media that these eleven judges were not partisan advocates, but were non-political actors attempting to reach the proper legal resolution to a difficult case in a very brief period of time." In addition, O'Scannlain declares, "I think there is a general benefit to showing America that our courts are open and our proceedings are not secretive."[69] He notes that the Ninth Circuit requires camera operators to wear proper attire, to avoid using lights or creating any distraction, and not to broadcast conversations between attorneys and clients.[70]

In the broadest experience of all, as of June 2009 two-thirds of the state supreme courts, thirty-four of them, permitted cameras in their courtrooms in some fashion—live or delayed transmission, public or commercial channels, cameras installed and operated by the state or simply admitted, all sessions recorded or on a case-by-case request basis. Some camera operations are carried on in conjunction with a state educational television network, a university, or a law school, and some videos are accessible on the court's Web site. Some states provide DVDs to the press and public for a nominal charge. As of June 2009 even more states, forty-two, provided or permitted live or delayed audio recordings. Among the states admitting cameras are all of the largest except Pennsylvania.[71] Like the U.S. Ninth Circuit, some state courts have allowed cameras for a decade or more. Iowa started in the 1980s. The states' experience has been very favorable.

As his court was considering cameras, Associate Justice Robert L. Brown of the Arkansas Supreme Court undertook his own survey and found that "state supreme courts have blazed a significant technological trail." He writes in a law journal: "The public's response, according to those state supreme courts that provide these video broadcasts, borders on the exuberant. . . . [N]o state that currently provides video of its oral arguments cites grandstanding as a problem."[72] Justice Brown quotes the chief justice of the California Supreme Court, Ronald M. George, as telling him in a phone call that its videos provide "the best P.R. you can imagine." Referring to the U.S. Supreme Court, Justice Brown concludes, "Access to videos of those important proceedings is long overdue, and the nation's highest court should not continue to lag behind the state supreme courts in this significant area of technological change."[73]

FLORIDA WAS READY FOR 2000

Justice Brown is especially complimentary about two of the pioneer video systems, Indiana's, which was started in 2001, and Florida's, begun in 1997. Both states have their own video systems, using four remotely operated, broadcast-quality cameras installed unobtrusively in the courtroom. According to Robert Craig Waters, public information director of the Florida Supreme Court (and its spokesman during the 2000 election appeals), each of its four cameras is "only a few inches in height, two recessed into the wall behind and above the bench and two placed atop half-pillars near the rear of the courtroom," looking "no different from standard closed-circuit security cameras."[74] The cameras are connected by fiber-optic cable to the communications center at Florida State University and are "controlled by FSU staff and communications students from inside an old electrical room at the top rear of the courtroom . . . converted into a control booth invisible to anyone on the bench or in the well or gallery."

Video and audio are fed via a state-owned satellite transponder "to anyone with a satellite downlink dish," including TV "news departments and local cable systems." The court's oral arguments became part of "the normal roster of programming fed statewide via this satellite to cable systems through the newly created Florida Channel, which rapidly became Florida's version of C-SPAN."[75]

The well-established system worked smoothly in the 2000 election cases leading up to and including *Gore v. Harris*[76] (which later became *Bush v. Gore* at the U.S. Supreme Court). Waters describes the day of oral argument:

> So, when the clock showed 10:00 A.M. on December 7, 2000, the test pattern flowing up to the satellite and on to the world dissolved. It was replaced by the live scene of the Marshal intoning the traditional oyez. Chief Justice Charles T. Wells then called the only case of the day, styled *Albert Gore, Jr. v. Katherine Harris.* With that, millions of viewers sat down to watch what would become only the second appellate oral argument in history to be broadcast live from start to finish on all the world's major networks. The first had occurred only days earlier, on November 20, 2000, in the

same courtroom in a separate appeal also arising from the 2000 presidential election dispute. [footnote omitted][77]

There were two benefits to public knowledge and understanding of the case. One was viewers' ability to see the court's decorum, dignity, and thoughtful process contrasting with the political hubbub outside. The second was the important enhancement of TV news stories that washed over the globe during and after the hearing, stories that were more graphically appealing and engaging than a correspondent's paraphrase or voice-over. For instance, the bulk of David Bloom's report from Tallahassee for the *NBC Nightly News* was excerpts from the court videotape, with sound cuts from both lawyers and three of the justices.[78]

What a pleasing vision to transmute to the U.S. Supreme Court. Instead of rushing off to get equally balanced interviews and pictures of political protagonists and antagonists, TV reporters and producers could concentrate on the legal controversy, the legal reasoning, the case itself. Going beyond the imposing but all-too-familiar Court facade, they could convey the essence of the Supreme Court of the United States—the give-and-take in oral argument between justices and advocates on the points of law that may well determine the decision, the demeanor and tone of the justices' reading of their opinions on decision day. Who can deny that this kind of coverage would enhance the citizenry's understanding of the Court and its decisions?

COVERING THE COURT FROM AFAR

Another benefit accrues to the Court by admitting cameras. It was little noticed at the time, but because of the Florida video service, reporters elsewhere, anywhere, could write the Florida Supreme Court story. Lyle Denniston did so. Without leaving his Washington office, Denniston, an old hand at covering oral arguments at the U.S. Supreme Court, adroitly captured the scene and the justices' body language for the *Baltimore Sun* and other papers:

> WASHINGTON—Lectured by the U.S. Supreme Court, blamed for "mischief" by three federal appeals judges and blindsided by lawyers, the Florida Supreme Court went looking Thursday for a graceful way out of the presidential election dispute.
>
> The seven justices explored for 68 minutes what to do in what might be their last act in the fight over Florida's decisive electoral votes—a fight over counting about 14,000 disputed ballots. They seemed tempted to take charge, as they had on Nov. 21. And yet they also appeared to sense that the temptation should be resisted.
>
> The target of criticism almost from the moment of their decision 17 days ago that set the ground rules for finishing the manual counting of presidential ballots, the state court did not look intimidated. But it did little to conceal its wounds.[79]

As this superb sketch demonstrates, a court providing camera access as well as opinion texts and oral-argument transcripts opens the door to another kind of reporter, perhaps one who knows the case better than any reporter at the Supreme Court. That would be the local reporter, at city hall or the courthouse or perhaps on the business beat, who covered the case from its inception, who knows the parties and their lawyers, who has seen the human side of the controversy, who is already familiar with the relevant law and the conflicting arguments, who has established quotable sources—law professors or other experts—to elucidate the matter as it progressed from trial court to appellate court to the petition for certiorari to the U.S. Supreme Court. At that point, ordinarily, this local reporter must step aside in favor of a Washington bureau or wire service reporter who then has to start from scratch, to learn the case from the lawyers' briefs in order to cover competently the oral argument and the decision. The local knowledge of the case, the institutional memory, if you will, is lost.

No newspaper or station, in any other situation, would turn its back on the experienced reporter who knows the story as it proceeds to its climax. With courtroom video it will no longer be necessary in covering a Supreme Court case, either. True, the local reporter will not have the Supreme Court reporter's acquired knowledge of the justices, their questioning styles, their voting records, and that expertise sometimes may determine that the assignment stays in Washington. But the justices' records, the most important background, can be learned readily from an abundance of public materials. This alternative way of covering at least some Court cases would free up resources to broaden coverage to more cases and especially to handle more decisions rapidly and accurately in the busy final weeks of the Court's annual term.

FINIS

This brings us to the end of our tour. It has been quite a ride. From John Marshall to John Roberts. From Capitol obscurity to architectural magnificence. From anonymity to authority. From discoursing to posting. From the *National Intelligencer* to the *New York Times,* the wires, TV, and the Web. From hearsay and happenstance to purpose and Pulitzers. As the Court and its decisions have become more important, more resonant in American life, to the point of deciding a presidential election, covering it well has become more demanding, more exacting.

Despite the financial pressures on the news business, it is simply unthinkable that responsible journalism would cut back coverage of the Supreme Court. Neither is it acceptable, from the standpoint of our democracy, merely to perpetuate the habitual coverage of the past. We have seen its shortcomings. Nor is it tolerable for journalists to be jailed for refusing to disclose confidential sources. The media should take to the Supreme Court an appropriate case to seek a new common-law testimonial privilege protecting such essential professional confidences.

We have heard the dissatisfaction of journalists and justices, scholars and savants, about Supreme Court coverage. If readers and viewers realized how shallow the coverage sometimes is, how many important cases are omitted or just sideswiped, how much legal reasoning and justification remain unexplained, how frequently uninformed reaction and commentary are substituted for the difficult aspects of an opinion, if people recognized such defects as readily as they would in a story about an important baseball game, they, too, would be disappointed. They, too, would demand better.

Law and journalism are ingrained, indeed intertwined, in the United States of America. Both are constitutional. Just as the country owes much to the practitioners of these professions, so they owe much to the nation. Our democracy relies on both. Nowhere do they converge more dramatically or more importantly than at the United States Supreme Court. Journalists and justices owe it to each other and to the country to strive incessantly to elevate their aspirations for their own work and for the nation. And to realize them.

NOTES

◈

CHAPTER ONE

1. *McCulloch v. Maryland,* 4 Wheat. (17 U.S.) 316 (1819).

2. This description is based on Jean Edward Smith, *John Marshall: Definer of a Nation* (New York: Owl Books, Henry Holt, 1996), 447–52.

3. *McCulloch,* 431.

4. U.S. Constitution, Article III, Section 1: "The judicial Power of the United States, shall be vested in one supreme Court, and in such inferior Courts as the Congress may from time to time ordain and establish."

5. *Marbury v. Madison,* 1 Cranch (5 U.S.) 137 (1803).

6. Linda Greenhouse, "Telling the Court's Story: Justice and Journalism at the Supreme Court," *Yale Law Journal* 105 (April 1996): 1537–61, 1538.

7. William J. Brennan, Jr., "Why Protect the Press?" *Columbia Journalism Review* 18, no. 5 (January–February 1980): 59–62, 59.

8. Greenhouse, "Telling the Court's Story," 1538.

9. Tony Mauro, "Five Ways Appellate Courts Can Help the News Media," *Journal of Appellate Practice and Process* 9, no. 2 (Fall 2007): 311–21. Mauro, a Supreme Court reporter for more than a quarter-century, stated that he was paraphrasing the chief justice.

10. John Helprin, Associated Press, "Scalia Sees Shift in Court's Role," *Washington Post,* October 23, 2006. (On the other hand, although the justices are not given to public praise of Supreme Court reporters, the Warren Court paid Anthony Lewis of the *New York Times* a high compliment by citing his law review article, "Legislative Apportionment and the Federal Courts," *Harvard Law Review* 71 (1958): 1071, in a landmark voting-rights decision, *Baker v. Carr,* 369 U.S. 186, 206 n. 27 (1962).

11. Mauro, "Five Ways," 312.

12. Greenhouse, "Telling the Court's Story," 1539.

13. Ibid., 1559.

14. "Color Line Case in Supreme Court: Federal Tribunal Decides It Has No Jurisdiction," *Atlanta Constitution,* May 29, 1906. The case was *Hodges v. United States,* 203 U.S. 1 (1906).

15. Fred Graham, *Happy Talk: Confessions of a TV Newsman* (New York and London: W.W. Norton, 1990), 119–20.

16. Sheryl Gay Stolberg, "Sonia Sotomayor: A Trailblazer and a Dreamer," *New York Times,* May 27, 2009, A1.

17. Adam Liptak, "A Careful Pen with No Broad Strokes," *New York Times,* May 27, 2009, A1.

18. Richard Sandomir, "A Baseball Ruling, Hailed Again," *New York Times,* May 27, 2009, B11.

19. Denise Grady, "Health Spotlight Is on Diabetes, Its Control and Its Complications," *New York Times,* May 27, 2009, A18.

20. "The New Justice," *New York Times,* May 27, 2009, A24.

21. Noah Feldman, "When Arrogance Takes the Bench," *New York Times,* June 11, 2009, A25.

22. *District Attorney's Office v. Osborne,* 129 S.Ct. 2308 (2009).

23. Nina Totenberg, "Court Weighs Convict's Right to Test DNA," *All Things Considered,* National Public Radio, March 2, 2009.

24. United Press International, "Black–Jackson Feud Flares Up Again in Court," *Los Angeles Times,* May 5, 1948.

25. Graham, *Happy Talk,* 107.

26. *Richmond v. J. A. Croson Co.,* 488 U.S. 469 (1989).

27. Rita Braver, "Affirmative Action/Richmond, Virginia, Case," *CBS Evening News,* January 23, 1989.

28. Graham, *Happy Talk,* 107.

29. "2 Supreme Court Justices in Fear of Live Burial," *Chicago Daily Tribune,* February 13, 1908. Perhaps coincidentally, Justice Moody that year was afflicted by crippling rheumatism so severe that it forced him to resign two years later.

30. *Pollock v. Farmers' Loan & Trust Co.,* 157 U.S. 429 (1895).

CHAPTER TWO

1. *Plessy v. Ferguson,* 163 U.S. 537 (1896).

2. *Williams v. Mississippi,* 170 U.S. 213, 225 (1898).

3. *Cumming v. Richmond County Board of Education,* 175 U.S. 528 (1899).

4. *Berea College v. Commonwealth of Kentucky,* 211 U.S. 45 (1908).

5. *Patterson v. Colorado,* 205 U.S. 454 (1907).

6. *Toledo Newspaper Company v. United States,* 247 U.S. 402, 419, 420 (1918). Not until 1941 did the Court, some years after stating that the First Amendment rights of free speech and free press were applicable to the states (*Gitlow v. New York,* 268 U.S. 652 [1925]), overturn a newspaper's conviction for contempt of court, in this case for publishing opinions about pending criminal cases. *Bridges v. California,* 314 U.S. 252 (1941).

7. *In re Rapier,* 143 U.S. 110 (1892).

8. *Lewis Publishing Company v. Morgan,* 229 U.S. 288, 316 (1913).

9. Geoffrey R. Stone, *Perilous Times: Free Speech in Wartime, from the Sedition Act of 1798 to the War on Terror* (New York and London: W.W. Norton, 2004), 192.

10. *Schenck v. United States,* 249 U.S. 47, 52 (1919).

11. As Stone, of the University of Chicago Law School, points out, Holmes's oft-quoted "clear and present danger" standard was "finally and unambiguously embraced" by the Supreme Court exactly fifty years after *Schenck,* in *Brandenburg v. Ohio,* 395 U.S. 444 (1969). Stone, *Perilous Times,* 522.

12. *Frohwerk v. United States,* 249 U.S. 204, 209 (1919).

13. *Debs v. United States,* 249 U.S. 211, 214–15 (1919). Other such cases: *Schaefer v. United States,* 251 U.S. 456 (1920), *Pierce v. United States,* 252 U.S. 239 (1920), and *Gilbert v. Minnesota,* 254 U.S. 325 (1920). In two later decisions upholding state laws that outlawed advocacy of the violent overthrow of the government, *Gitlow v. New York,* 268 U.S. 652 (1925) and *Whitney v. California,* 274 U.S. 357 (1927), the Court seriously considered the First Amendment but overrode it.

14. "Debs Loses Appeal; To Serve Ten Years," *New York Times,* March 11, 1919.

15. "The Case of Debs," *New York Times,* March 12, 1919.

16. "The Debs Decision," *Chicago Daily Tribune,* March 11, 1919.

17. "The Debs Decision," *Washington Post,* March 12, 1919. One press historian contends that the press typically stands up only for its own First Amendment rights and not those of unpopular speakers. John Lofton, *The Press as Guardian of the First Amendment* (Columbia: University of South Carolina Press, 1980), chapter 12.

18. Virginia adopted its constitution in 1776. The other early adopters: North Carolina, Pennsylvania, Maryland, and Delaware, 1776; Georgia, 1777; South Carolina, 1778; Massachusetts, 1779; New Hampshire, 1783. New York, which in 1777 adopted a constitution without a free-press guarantee, recommended that one be included in the federal Constitution when ratifying it in 1788. Connecticut and Rhode Island did not adopt constitutions until after Independence. All states' constitutions now guarantee freedom of the press.

19. Massachusetts Declaration of Rights XVI, quoted in Bernard Schwartz, *The Bill of Rights: A Documentary History* (New York: Chelsea House, 1971), 1:221.

20. See, for instance, Harold L. Nelson, "Seditious Libel in Colonial America," *American Journal of Legal History* 3 (1959): 165.

21. Letter from Thomas Jefferson to Thomas M. Coray, 1832, quoted in Louis Edward Ingelhart, comp., *Press and Speech Freedoms in America, 1619–1995, A Chronology* (Westport, Conn., and London: Greenwood, 1997), 74.

22. Letter from Thomas Jefferson to John Adams, 1788, quoted in Louis Edward Ingelhart, *Press Freedoms: A Descriptive Calendar of Concepts, Interpretations, Events* (Westport, Conn.: Greenwood, 1987), 131.

23. Geoffrey R. Stone explores the possible reasons for Holmes's volte-face (which he denied) in *Perilous Times,* 198–211.

24. *Abrams v. United States,* 250 U.S. 616, 630–31 (1919).

25. Ibid., 629.

26. *Milwaukee Social Democratic Pub. Co. v. Burleson,* 255 U.S. 407, 437 (1921).

27. *Near v. Minnesota,* 283 U.S. 697 (1931).

28. Ibid., 704, 710, 718.

29. Ibid., 720.

30. *Gitlow v. New York,* 268 U.S. 652 (1925).

31. *Bantam Books, Inc. v. Sullivan,* 372 U.S. 58 (1963). The Court cited *Near v. Minnesota* and several prior-restraint cases of the 1930s, '40s, and '50s involving not the press but religious or political expression, some of it in pamphlets or other publications, striking down local ordinances restricting expression in public places and in door-to-door calling: *Lovell v. Griffin,* 303 U.S. 444 (1938); *Schneider v. State,* 308 U.S. 147 (1939); *Cantwell v. Connecticut,* 310 U.S. 296 (1940); *Kunz v. New York,* 340 U.S. 290 (1951); *Staub v. City of Baxley,* 355 U.S. 313 (1958).

32. *Bantam Books,* 372 U.S. at 70, 72, Douglas, J., concurring.

33. *New York Times Co. v. Sullivan,* 376 U.S. 24 (1964).

34. Most notably the Agricultural Adjustment Act (*United States v. Butler,* 297 U.S. 1 [1936]), the National Industrial Recovery Act (*Schechter Poultry Corporation v. United States,* 295 U.S. 495 [1935]), the Bituminous Coal Conservation Act (*Carter v. Carter Coal Co.,* 293 U.S. 238 [1936]), and a Bankruptcy Act amendment that provided mortgage relief to farmers (*Louisville Joint Stock Land Bank v. Radford,* 295 U.S 555 [1935]).

35. *New York Times Co. v. Sullivan,* 376 U.S. at 293.

36. *New York Times Co. v. United States,* 403 U.S. 713 (1971).

37. Fred Graham, *Happy Talk: Confessions of a TV Newsman* (New York: W. W. Norton, 1990), 134–35.

38. *New York Times Co. v. United States,* 403 U.S. at 717, Black, J., concurring.

39. Ibid., 720, Douglas, J., concurring.

40. *Times-Picayune Publishing Corp. v. Schulingkamp,* 419 U.S. 1301, 1307 (1974). The publisher's subsequent appeal to the Supreme Court was dismissed eight months later as moot. *Times-Picayune Publishing Corp. v. Schulingkamp,* 420 U.S. 985 (1975).

41. *Grosjean v. American Press Company,* 297 U.S. 233 (1936).

42. *Branzburg v. Hayes,* 408 U.S. 665, 727 (1972).

43. *Nebraska Press Association. v. Stuart,* 427 U.S. 539 (1976).

44. Ibid., 569, 570.

45. Ibid., 613.

46. Ibid., 617.

47. 22 F.2d 234 (1975).

48. *Dow Jones & Company, Inc. v. Simon,* 488 U.S. 946, 948 (1988), White, J., dissenting.

49. *Cable News Network, Inc. v. Noriega,* 498 U.S. 976 (1990), Marshall, J., dissenting.

50. *Grosjean v. American Press Co.,* 297 U.S. 233, 238, 250 (1936).

51. *Minneapolis Star & Tribune Co. v. Minnesota Commissioner of Revenue,* 460 U.S. 575 (1983).

52. *Arkansas Writers' Project, Inc. v. Ragland,* 481 U.S. 221 (1987).

53. *Leathers v. Medlock,* 499 U.S. 439 (1991).

54. *Associated Press v. United States,* 326 U.S. 1 (1945).

55. Ibid., 20, n. 18.

56. *Chicago Joint Board, Amalgamated Clothing Workers of America v. Chicago Tribune,* 435 F.2d 470 (1970). It should be emphasized that when the Supreme Court denies a petition for certiorari, that is not tantamount to affirming or upholding the decision of the lower court, nor does it preclude the Court's accepting a similar case later. In accord with the Seventh Circuit decision, the Ninth Circuit Court of Appeals declined to order that the *Los Angeles Times* had a First Amendment obligation to publish movie advertisements without editing them, or even an obligation to publish them at all. *Associates & Aldrich v. Times Mirror,* 440 F.2d 133 (1971).

57. *Mills v. Alabama,* 374 U.S. 214 (1966).

58. Ibid., 218, 220.

59. Ibid., 220–21, Douglas, J., concurring.

60. *Miami Herald Publishing Co. v. Tornillo,* 418 U.S. 241, 258, 261 (1974).

61. *Landmark Communications, Inc. v. Virginia,* 435 U.S. 829, 845 (1978).

62. *Butterworth v. Smith,* 494 U.S. 624, 635–36 (1990).

63. *Milwaukee Social Democratic Pub. Co. v. Burleson,* 255 U.S. 407 (1921), over the dissents of Justices Holmes and Brandeis.

64. *Hannegan v. Esquire, Inc.,* 327 U.S. 146, 151, 158 (1946).

65. *City of Lakewood v. Plain Dealer Publishing Co.,* 486 U.S. 750, 758, 764 (1988). Chief Justice William Rehnquist and Justice Anthony Kennedy did not participate in the case.

66. *City of Cincinnati v. Discovery Network, Inc.,* 507 U.S. 410, 430 (1993). The principal precedents cited were *Central Hudson Gas & Electric Corp. v. Public Service Commission of New York,* 447 U.S. 557 (1980) and *Board of Trustees of State University of New York v. Fox,* 492 U.S. 469 (1989), both recognizing First Amendment protection for truthful, nonmisleading commercial speech.

67. *City of Cincinnati,* 507 U.S. at 445, Rehnquist, C. J., dissenting.

68. *Zurcher v. Stanford Daily,* 436 U.S. 547, 567 (1978).

69. P.L. 96–440, 94 Stat. 1879, 42 U.S.C.S. sec. 2000aa.

70. *Associated Press v. United States,* 326 U.S. 1, 9, 20 (1945).

71. *Mabee v. White Plains Publishing Co.,* 327 U.S. 178 (1946).

72. *Donaldson, Postmaster General v. Read Magazine, Inc.,* 333 U.S. 178 (1948).

73. *Pittsburgh Press Co. v. Pittsburgh Commission on Human Relations,* 413 U.S. 376 (1973).

74. *Seattle Times Co. v. Rhinehart,* 467 U.S. 20 (1984).

75. *Harper & Row, Publishers, Inc. v. Nation Enterprises,* 471 U.S. 539 (1985).

76. *Cohen v. Cowles Media Co.,* 501 U.S. 663 (1991).

CHAPTER THREE

1. *New York Times Co. v. Sullivan,* 376 U.S. 254 (1964).

2. Anthony Lewis, at the time a Pulitzer Prize–winning Supreme Court reporter for the *New York Times,* details the story of the case in *Make No Law: The Sullivan Case and the First Amendment* (New York: Vintage Books, 1992).

3. *New York Times Co.,* 376 U.S. at 257–58.

4. *Brown v. Board of Education,* 347 U.S. 483 (1954).

5. *New York Times Co. v. Sullivan,* 376 U.S. 254 (1964).

6. Ibid., 292.

7. Ibid., 270.

8. Ibid., 279–80. This American rule is unusually favorable to the press. In Canada, for instance, "politicians and other public figures have the same right to sue for defamation as any other citizen." Dean Jobb, *Media Law for Canadian Journalists* (Toronto: Emond Montgomery, 2006), 274.

9. *Rosenblatt v. Baer,* 383 U.S. 75, 85 (1966).

10. *Curtis Publishing Co. v. Butts,* 388 U.S. 130, 154–55 (1967), consolidating *Associated Press v. Walker,* 389 U.S. 28 (1967). In the other case the Court affirmed a libel judgment obtained by the University of Georgia athletic director Wally Butts, famous as a football coach and therefore

also deemed a "public figure" by the Court, against the Curtis Publishing Co., publisher of the *Saturday Evening Post,* which had run a story based solely on an unconfirmed tip from a known criminal that Butts had conspired to fix a 1962 football game between Georgia and archrival University of Alabama. The magazine's mishandling of the story met the new standard of "highly unreasonable conduct," the plurality stated, giving a clear warning to the press.

11. *Curtis Publishing Co.,* 388 U.S. at 163.

12. *Greenbelt Cooperative Publishing Association, Inc. v. Bresler,* 398 U.S. 6 (1970).

13. *Monitor Patriot Co. v. Roy,* 401 U.S. 265 (1971).

14. *Time, Inc. v. Pape,* 401 U.S. 279 (1971).

15. *Ocala Star-Banner Co. v. Damron,* 401 U.S. 295 (1971).

16. *Gertz v. Robert Welch, Inc.,* 418 U.S. 323 (1974).

17. Ibid., 350–52.

18. *Gertz v. Welch,* 680 F.2d 527 (1982).

19. *Gertz,* 418 U.S. at 355, Burger, C.J., dissenting; at 355–60, Douglas, J., dissenting; at 361, Brennan, J., dissenting; at 370, White, J., dissenting.

20. *Time, Inc. v. Firestone,* 424 U.S. 448 (1976).

21. *Hutchinson v. Proxmire,* 443 U.S. 111 (1979).

22. *Wolston v. Reader's Digest Association, Inc.,* 443 U.S. 157 (1979).

23. *Philadelphia Newspapers, Inc. v. Hepps,* 475 U.S. 767, 777 (1986).

24. Ibid., 780–81.

25. *Masson v. New Yorker Magazine, Inc.,* 501 U.S. 496, 517 (1991).

26. *Masson v. New Yorker Magazine, Inc.,* 83 F.3d 1394 (9th Cir., 1996).

27. *Curtis Publishing Co. v. Butts,* 388 U.S. 130 (1967).

28. *Harte-Hanks Communications, Inc. v. Connaughton,* 491 U.S. 657, 692, 693 (1989).

29. *Scott v. News-Herald,* 25 Ohio St.3d 243 (1986).

30. *Milkovich v. Lorain Journal,* 497 U.S. 1, 21 (1990).

31. *Milkovich,* 497 U.S. at 30, Brennan, J., dissenting.

32. New York Civil Rights Law, NY CLS Civ R secs. 50–51.

33. *Time, Inc. v. Hill,* 385 U.S. 374, 388 (1967).

34. Ibid., 410, Harlan, J., dissenting.

35. *Hustler Magazine v. Falwell,* 485 U.S. 46, 54 (1988).

36. *Cox Broadcasting Corp. v. Cohn,* 420 U.S. 469, 495 (1975).

37. *Smith, Judge v. Daily Mail Publishing Co.*, 443 U.S. 79 (1979).

38. *The Florida Star v. B.J.F.*, 491 U.S. 524 (1989).

39. *Time, Inc., v. Hill*, 385 U.S. 374 (1967).

40. *Cantrell v. Forest City Publishing Co.*, 419 U.S. 245, 253 (1974).

41. *Zacchini v. Scripps-Howard Broadcasting Co.*, 433 U.S. 562 (1977).

42. Ibid., 577.

CHAPTER FOUR

1. *Gideon v. Wainwright*, 372 U.S. 335 (1963).

2. *Miranda v. Arizona*, 384 U.S. 436 (1966).

3. *Mapp v. Ohio*, 367 U.S. 643 (1961).

4. *Marshall v. United States*, 360 U.S. 310, 312–13 (1959).

5. *Estes v. Texas*, 381 U.S. 532 (1965).

6. *Irvin v. Dowd*, 366 U.S. 717 (1961).

7. Ibid., 722.

8. *Sheppard v. Maxwell*, 384 U.S. 333 (1966).

9. Ibid., 355, 363 (1966).

10. *Nebraska Press Association v. Stuart*, 427 U.S. 539 (1976).

11. *Gannett Co. v. DePasquale*, 443 U.S. 368 (1979). The two suspects were seized, along with Clapp's truck and his sixteen-year-old wife, in Michigan. She was charged only with stealing the truck.

12. *Richmond Newspapers, Inc. v. Virginia*, 448 U.S. 555 (1980).

13. Ibid., 581.

14. *Globe Newspaper Co. v. Superior Court*, 457 U.S. 596 (1982).

15. Ibid., 608.

16. Ibid., 614, Burger, C. J., dissenting.

17. *Press-Enterprise Co. v. Superior Court*, 464 U.S. 501 (1984). This case became known as *Press-Enterprise I (P-E I)* when a second case brought by the same company against the same court emerged later.

18. Ibid., 512.

19. *Waller v. Georgia*, 467 U.S. 39 (1984).

20. Ibid., 46, 47, 48, 49.

21. *Press Enterprise Co. v. Superior Court (P-E II)*, 478 U.S. 1, 12 (1986).

22. Ibid., 12, 13, 14.

23. *El Vocero de Puerto Rico v. Puerto Rico,* 508 U.S. 147, 150–51 (1993).

24. "Pulling Out the Gag," *Los Angeles Times,* July 1, 1976.

25. "Freedom Triumphs," *Chicago Tribune,* July 1, 1976.

26. "Wiping the Graffiti Off the Courtroom," *New York Times,* July 3, 1980.

27. "On Behalf of Openness in Court," *Los Angeles Times,* July 1, 1986.

28. Section 2, Canadian Charter of Rights and Freedoms, Part I of the Constitution Act, 1982, which in turn is Schedule B of the Canada Act 1982 (U.K.), 1982, c. 11.

29. See, for instance, *Toronto Star Newsapers Ltd. v. Ontario,* 2 S.C.R. 188 (2005), in which the Supreme Court dismissed a government appeal from the media's successful challenge of a lower court order sealing certain search warrants and the information on which they were based.

30. Michael G. Crawford, *The Journalist's Legal Guide,* 5th ed. (Toronto: Thomson Carswell, 2008), 20.

31. Ibid., 220.

32. Ibid., 182–83.

33. *Nebraska Press Association,* 427 U.S. at 548.

CHAPTER FIVE

1. 5 U.S.C.S. sec. 552.

2. 47 U.S.C.S. sec. 301 *et seq.*

3. *Environmental Protection Agency v. Mink,* 410 U.S. 73, 94 (1973).

4. *Department of the Air Force v. Rose,* 425 U.S. 352 (1976).

5. *United States Department of Justice v. Tax Analysts,* 492 U.S. 136 (1989).

6. *United States Department of Justice v. Landano,* 508 U.S. 165 (1993).

7. *Department of the Interior v. Klamath Water Users Protective Association,* 532 U.S. 1 (2001).

8. *Kissinger v. Reporters Committee for Freedom of the Press,* 445 U.S. 136, 157 (1980).

9. *Central Intelligence Agency v. Sims,* 471 U.S. 159 (1985).

10. *Federal Bureau of Investigation v. Abramson,* 456 U.S. 615 (1982).

11. *United States Department of Justice v. Reporters Committee for Freedom of the Press,* 489 U.S. 749, 800 (1989).

12. *Bibles v. Oregon Natural Desert Association,* 519 U.S. 355 (1997).

13. *National Archives and Records Administration v. Favish,* 541 U.S. 157 (2004).

14. 5 U.S.C.S. sec. 706(2)(A).

15. In fact, this policy decision had been made much earlier, in the Radio Act of 1912, 37 Stat. 302, and the Radio Act of 1927, 44 Stat. 1156, 47 U.S.C. sec. 89, which empowered the Federal Radio Commission to grant broadcast licenses and regulate broadcasters, essentially the same authority later granted to the Federal Communications Commission. For Supreme Court interpretation of the Radio Act of 1927, see *Federal Radio Commission v. General Electric Co.,* 281 U.S. 464 (1930) and *Federal Radio Commission v. Nelson Brothers,* 289 U.S. 266 (1933).

16. *National Broadcasting Co. v. United States,* 319 U.S. 190, 227 (1943).

17. See *United States v. Southwestern Cable Co.,* 392 U.S. 157 (1968).

18. *Federal Communications Commission v. Beach Communications, Inc.,* 508 U.S. 307 (1993).

19. The Cable Television Consumer Protection and Competition Act of 1992, 47 U.S.C.S. sec. 534.

20. *Turner Broadcasting System, Inc. v. Federal Communications Commission,* 512 U.S. 622 (1994). In an unusual setback for the FCC, however, the Supreme Court sent the case back for determination of whether the must-carry rule was adequately supported by a factual showing of economic necessity. When the FCC, on reconsideration, handed down a finding of economic necessity, this was accepted by the Supreme Court, which ruled that the must-carry rule was indeed in compliance with the First Amendment. *Turner Broadcasting System, Inc. v. Federal Communications Commission,* 520 U.S. 180 (1997).

21. *Time Warner Entertainment Co. v. Federal Communications Commission,* 516 U.S. 1112 (1996). But rate regulation by the FCC was largely repealed in 1999 under provisions of the Telecommunications Act of 1996, 110 Stat. 56, 47 U.S.C.S. sec. 561.

22. *Time Warner Entertainment Co. v. Federal Communications Commission,* 531 U.S. 1183 (2001).

23. *Denver Area Educational Telecommunications Consortium, Inc. v. Federal Communications Commission,* 518 U.S. 727 (1996).

24. *Greater New Orleans Broadcasting Association, Inc. v. United States,* 527 U.S. 173 (1999).

25. Telecommunications Act of 1996, 47 U.S.C.S. sec. 561. Indecency regulation was a relatively minor part of the far-reaching act, which notably permitted broadcasters, cable operators, and telephone companies to enter each other's businesses.

26. *United States v. Playboy Entertainment Group, Inc.,* 529 U.S. 803 (2000).

27. *Federal Communications Commission v. Pottsville Broadcasting Co.,* 309 U.S. 134, 138 (1940).

28. *Federal Communications Commission v. Sanders Brothers Radio Station,* 309 U.S. 470, 475, 476 (1940).

29. *Federal Communications Commission v. WNCN Listeners Guild,* 450 U.S. 582, 596 (1981).

30. *RKO General, Inc. v. Federal Communications Commission,* 670 F.2d 215, 237 (D.C.Cir., 1981).

31. *RKO General, Inc. v. Federal Communications Commission,* 456 U.S. 927 (1982). In this bizarre case the Supreme Court, curiously, did not have the last word, for RKO General sought and obtained special legislation from Congress allowing it to sell the stations rather than just relinquish the licenses. The FCC later gave RKO the same favorable out in regard to other stations whose licenses the commission declined to renew.

32. *Radio Corporation of America v. United States,* 341 U.S. 412, 419–20 (1951).

33. Ibid., 426, Frankfurter, J., *dubitante.*

34. *United States v. Southwestern Cable Co.,* 392 U.S. 157 (1968).

35. *City of New York v. Federal Communications Commission,* 486 U.S. 57 (1988).

36. *Federal Communications Commission v. Brand X Internet Services,* 545 U.S. 967 (2005).

37. *Pappas Telecasting of Southern California, L.L.C. v. Federal Communications Commission,* 531 U.S. 1071 (2001).

38. *Grid Radio and Jerry Szoka v. Federal Communications Commission,* 537 U.S. 815 (2002).

39. *EMR Network v. Federal Communications Commission,* 545 U.S. 1116 (2005).

40. *Time Warner Entertainment Co., L.P. v. Federal Communications Commission,* 240 F.3d 1126 (2001).

41. *Consumer Federation of America v. Federal Communications Commission,* 534 U.S. 1054 (2001). After years of further study, and with the support of extensive statistical and economic documentation, the FCC in 2007 reiterated the 30 percent horizontal limit, but asked for further public comment on the vertical limit, in part because of the great increase of channel capacity since the original rule was formulated. FCC 07-219, December 18, 2007.

42. *Great Lakes Broadcasting Co.,* 3 F.R.C. Ann. Rep. 32 (1929).

43. Telecommunications Act of 1996, 47 U.S.C.S. sec 315.

44. *Red Lion Broadcasting v. Federal Communications Commission,* 395 U.S. 367 (1969).

45. See Wayne Overbeck, *Major Principles of Media Law,* 2005 ed. (Belmont, Calif.: Thomas Wadsworth, 2005), 460–65, for a succinct description of the life and death of the fairness doctrine.

46. *United States v. Midwest Video Corp.,* 406 U.S. 649 (1972). A few years later the Court reversed itself on public access, *Federal Communications Commission v. Midwest Video Corp.,* 440 U.S. 689 (1979), but the tradition of public access was established, and Congress codified some public access requirements in 1984: Public Law 98-549, 98 Stat. 2780, 47 U.S.C. 521.

47. *Columbia Broadcasting System, Inc. v. Democratic National Committee,* 412 U.S. 94 (1973).

48. *CBS, Inc. v. Federal Communications Commission,* 453 U.S. 367 (1981). But this decision, in the Court as in the FCC, was by a divided vote, with Justices White, Stevens, and Rehnquist dissenting.

49. *Capital Cities Cable, Inc. v. Crisp,* 467 U.S. 691 (1984). This was an early test of the must-carry rule, first promulgated by the FCC, later codified by Congress, and upheld by the Supreme Court in the *Turner Broadcasting* case described above.

50. 18 U.S.C. sec. 1464.

51. *Federal Communications Commission v. Pacifica Foundation,* 438 U.S. 726, 750–51 (1978).

52. *Prometheus Radio Project v. Federal Communications Commission,* 373 F.3d 372, 435 (2004).

53. *National Association of Broadcasters v. Federal Communications Commission,* 545 U.S. 1123 (2005). Although the Supreme Court did not accept this case, it had, years earlier, unanimously affirmed the FCC's then-novel cross-ownership ban. *Federal Communications Commission v. National Citizens Committee for Broadcasting,* 436 U.S. 775 (1978).

CHAPTER SIX

1. Maryland was the first, in 1896, the legislation now codified at A.C.Md. 9-112(c).

2. *Branzburg v. Hayes,* 408 U.S. 665 (1972).

3. Ibid., 696–97.

4. Ibid., 710, Powell, J., concurring.

5. Ibid., 743, Stewart, J., dissenting.

6. *Furman v. Georgia,* 408 U.S. 238 (1972).

7. "Press Loses Plea to Keep Data from Grand Juries," *New York Times,* June 30, 1972.

8. Ala. Code 12-21-142.

9. Mont.C.A. 26-1-902.

10. Neb.R.S. 20-146.

11. Nev.R.S. 49.275.

12. A.R.C.Wash. 5.68.010.

13. Most notably, the Second Circuit, *Baker v. F & F Investment,* 470 F. 2d 789 (1972), *United States v. Burke,* 700 F.2d 70 (1983), *Von Bulow v. von Bulow,* 811 F.2d 136, 142 (1987), *Gonzales v. NBC,* 194 F.3d 29, 35 (1998); and the District of Columbia Circuit, *Zerilli v. Smith,* 656 F.2d 705, 712 (1981).

14. *Vanessa Leggett v. United States,* docket no. 01-983 (5th.Cir. 2002).

15. *McKevitt v. Pallasch,* 393 F.3d 530 (7th Cir. 2003). The reporters decided to comply with the court's order.

16. *In re Special Proceedings,* 291 F.Supp.2d 44 (D.R.I. 2003), aff'd 373 F.3d 37 (1st Cir. 2004); Jack White, "Taricani Guilty of Contempt," *Providence Journal Bulletin,* November 29, 2004.

17. *In re: Grand Jury Subpoena, Judith Miller,* 397 F.3d 964 (D.C.Cir. 2005), cert. denied sub nom *Miller v. United States,* 545 U.S. 1150 (June 27, 2005). A parallel case against Matthew Cooper of *Time* magazine also brought a ruling of contempt, but he then testified and was not jailed.

18. *Wen Ho Lee v. Department of Justice,* 401 F.Supp.2d 123 (D.D.C. 2005). The scientist's related libel case was settled in June 2006.

19. Associated Press, "After 226 Days, Freelancer Joshua Wolf Released from Jail," April 4, 2007, www.firstamendmentcenter.org/news .aspx?id=18369&SearchString=joshua_wolf (accessed April 1, 2009).

20. On September 25, 2006, the reporters were sentenced to as much as eighteen months by U.S. District Court Judge Jeffrey S. White. *In re Grand Jury Subpoenas to Mark Fainaru-Wada and Lance Williams* (N.D.Cal. No. CR 06-90225 JSW), Order Holding Mark Fainaru-Wada and Lance Williams in Civil Contempt. Judge White stayed his order pending an appeal to the Ninth Circuit Court of Appeals. The case became moot when the source disclosed his role. Bob Egelko, "Lawyer Enters Guilty Plea as BALCO Leaker," *San Francisco Chronicle,* February 16, 2007.

21. *New York Times Co. v. Gonzales,* 459 F.3d 160 (2d Cir. 2006).

22. Kevin Johnson, "Judge Holds Reporter in Contempt in '01 Anthrax Case," *USA Today,* February 20, 2008.

23. Jesse J. Holland, Associated Press, "Judges Throw Out Contempt Order Against Reporter," November 18, 2008.

24. Fed.R.Evid. 501 (1975).

25. Federal Rules of Evidence, Notes to Rule 501; Notes of Committee on the Judiciary, House Report No. 93-650, posted by Legal Information Institute, www.law.cornell.edu/rules/fre/ACRule501.htm. F.R.Crim.P. 26 provides that the trial testimony of witnesses must be taken in open court, or in exceptional circumstances, by two-way video presentation in open court.

26. *Western Union Tel. Co. v. Call Pub. Co.,* 181 U.S. 92, 101–102 (1901). That definition has now been superseded in *Black's Law Dictionary,* in part by the following: "*American common law.* 1. The body of English law that was adopted as the law of the American colonies and supplemented with local enactments and judgments. 2. The body of judge-made law that developed during and after the United States' colonial period, esp. since Independence." *Black's Law Dictionary,* 8th ed. (St. Paul: West, 2004), 293.

27. *Riley v. City of Chester,* 612 F.2d 708 (3d Cir. 1979).

28. 42 Pa. Cons. Stat. Ann. 5942.

29. *United States v. Cuthbertson,* 630 F.2d 139 (3d Cir. 1980). The ruling covered nonconfidential information as well.

30. *United States v. Criden,* 633 F.2d 346, 356 (3d Cir. 1980). The court also found the privilege "deeply rooted in the first amendment" and termed it absolute "when no countervailing constitutional concerns are at stake." At 356.

31. Ibid., 357.

32. *In re Madden,* 151 F.3d 125, 128 (3d Cir. 1998). Nevertheless, the court of appeals reversed the district court's recognition of a reporter's privilege, on the grounds that the claimant was not a journalist at all but rather an entertainment publicist.

33. *In re: Grand Jury Subpoena, Judith Miller,* 397 F.3d 964, 986 (D.C. Cir. 2005), Tatel, J., concurring in the judgment.

34. Department of Justice, "Policy with Regard to Issuance of Subpoenas to Members of the News Media," 28 C.F.R. 50.

35. *Miller,* 397 F.3d at 986–87.

36. Ibid., 992.

37. Ibid., 995.

38. *Trammel v. United States,* 445 U.S. 40 (1980).

39. *United States v. Trammel,* 583 F.2d 1166 (1978).

40. *Hawkins v. United States,* 358 U.S. 74 (1958).

41. *Trammel,* 445 U.S. at 53.

42. *Upjohn Co. v. United States,* 449 U.S. 383 (10th Cir. 1981).

43. *Trammel,* 445 U.S. at 51, quoted 449 U.S. at 389.

44. *Upjohn Co.,* 449 U.S. at 396.

45. *Jaffee v. Redmond,* 518 U.S. 1 (1996).

46. *Jaffee v. Redmond,* 51 F.3d 1346 (7th Cir. 1995).

47. Ibid., 1355–56, 1357.

48. *Jaffee,* 518 U.S. at 12–13.

49. See discussions in *Trammel,* 445 U.S. at 50–53, and in *United States v. Nixon,* 418 U.S. 683, 709–10 (1974).

50. *Jaffee,* 518 U.S. at 35, 36, Scalia, J., dissenting.

51. *In re Madden,* 151 F.3d 125 (1988).

CHAPTER SEVEN

1. *Chisholm v. Georgia,* 2 Dall. (2 U.S.) 419 (1793). The Eleventh Amendment, ratified in 1798, removed jurisdiction in suits commenced against a state by citizens of another state, the *Chisholm* situation.

2. Jean Edward Smith, *John Marshall: Definer of a Nation* (New York: Owl Books, Henry Holt, 1996), 285, n. 32.

3. Quoted in William E. Ames, *A History of the National Intelligencer* (Chapel Hill: University of North Carolina Press, 1972), 28.

4. Ibid.

5. Ibid., 42.

6. *Marbury v. Madison,* 1 Cranch (5 U.S.) 137 (1803).

7. Ibid., 178.

8. "Mandamus," *Washington Federalist,* February 25, 1803.

9. "From the Virginia Argus," *National Intelligencer,* May 13, 1803.

10. *United States v. Peters,* 5 Cranch (9 U.S.) 115 (1809).

11. Ibid., 144.

12. *Fletcher v. Peck,* 6 Cranch (10 U.S.) 87 (1810).

13. Ibid., 134.

14. *New-England Palladium,* March 23, 1810.

15. Smith, *John Marshall,* 394.

16. "Supreme Court," *Salem Gazette,* March 24, 1818.

17. "Dartmouth College," *Columbian Centinel,* February 10, 1819.

18. *Dartmouth College v. Woodward,* 4 Wheat. (17 U.S.) 518, 636 (1819).

19. *Ogden v. Saunders,* 12 Wheat. (25 U.S.) 213 (1827). The case was closely watched because in a previous decision, *Sturges v. Crowninshield,* 4 Wheat. (17 U.S.) 122 (1819), the Court had voided an earlier New York insolvency statute because it discharged a previously existing debt, thus violating the contracts clause. *Sturges* was widely covered by the press and created considerable consternation.

20. "Important Intelligence," *Republican Star and General Advertiser,* May 20, 1827.

21. *Ogden,* 12 Wheat. (25 U.S.) at 269.

22. "Insolvent Laws," *Connecticut Courant,* Hartford, February 26, 1827.

23. *Clark v. Washington,* 12 Wheat. (25 U.S.) 40 (1827).

24. U.S. Constitution, Article I, Section 8: "The Congress shall have Power . . . To make all laws which shall be necessary and proper for carrying into Execution the foregoing Powers, and all other Powers vested by this Constitution in the Government of the United States, or in any Department or Officer thereof."

25. *McCulloch v. Maryland,* 4 Wheat. (17 U.S.) 316 (1819).

26. Charles Warren, *The Supreme Court in United States History,* (Boston: Little, Brown, 1924), 1:505.

27. *McCulloch,* 17 U.S. at 421.

28. Ibid., 431.

29. *Niles' Weekly Register* 16, no. 65 (March 20, 1819), quoted in Norval Neil Luxon, *Niles' Weekly Register: News Magazine of the Nineteenth Century* (Westport, Conn.: Greenwood, 1970), 120.

30. Smith, *John Marshall,* 446–47. The hostility in Virginia, much of it emanating from Marshall's old friends and neighbors, was noted in chapter 1.

31. *Nashville Clarion,* quoted in *Scioto Gazette,* April 16, 1819, and *Argus of Western America,* March 26, 1819, both quoted in Warren, *Supreme Court,* 1:513. Warren provides an extensive review of press reaction to *McCulloch* at 510–27.

32. "Washington," *National Intelligencer,* March 13, 1819.

33. *Gibbons v. Ogden,* 9 Wheat. (22 U.S.) 1 (1824).

34. Ibid., 221.

35. *Baltimore Patriot & Commercial Advertiser,* March 4, 1824.

36. Smith, *John Marshall,* 480 (footnote omitted).

37. *Scott v. Sandford,* 19 How. (60 U.S.) 393 (1857).

38. *Charles River Bridge v. Warren Bridge,* 11 Pet. (36 U.S.) 420 (1837).

39. "From Our Correspondent," *Mississippian,* Jackson, Mississippi, February 24, 1837.

40. *Charles River Bridge,* 11 Pet. (36 U.S.) at 553.

41. "The Warren Bridge," *New Hampshire Patriot and State Gazette,* Concord, New Hampshire, February 27, 1837.

42. "The Supreme Court," *Vermont Chronicle,* Bellows Falls, Vermont, March 21, 1838.

43. *New York v. Miln,* 11 Pet. (36 U.S.) 102 (1837), overruled in 1941 by *Edwards v. California,* 314 U.S. 160.

44. *Bank of Augusta v. Earle,* 38 US. 519 (1839).

45. *Swift v. Tyson,* 16 Pet. (41 U.S.) 1 (1842), overruled by *Erie Railroad Co. v. Tompkins,* 304 U.S. 64 (1938).

46. See, for instance, *License Cases: Thurlow v. Massachusetts, Fletcher v. Rhode Island, Peirce v. New Hampshire,* 5 How. (46 U.S.) 504 (1847); *Passenger Cases: Smith v. Turner, Norris v. Boston,* 7 How. (48 U.S.) 283 (1849).

47. *Cooley v. Board of Wardens of the Port of Philadelphia,* 12 How. (53 U.S.) 299 (1852).

48. *Texas v. White,* 74 U.S. 700 (1869).

49. "The Recent Supreme Court Decisions," *Chicago Daily Tribune,* April 14, 1869.

50. "The U.S. Supreme Court," *Weekly Georgia Telegraph,* Macon, Georgia, April 16, 1869.

51. *Legal Tender Cases: Hepburn v. Griswold,* 75 U.S. 603 (1870), and *Knox v. Lee* and *Parker v. Davis,* 79 U.S. 457 (1871). The cases were an early harbinger of the current justices' disagreements over whether the Constitution is to be interpreted according to its original meaning or intent, or in line with the legal precedents interpreting and applying it since it was adopted.

52. "The Legal-Tender Decision," *Atlanta Constitution,* April 28, 1871.

53. "United States Supreme Court. Constitutionality of the Legal-Tender Acts Affirmed—Important Decision Given Yesterday," *New York Times,* May 2, 1871.

54. *Slaughterhouse Cases,* 16 Wall (83 U.S.) 36 (1873).

55. "Washington. More Supreme Court Decisions," *Boston Daily Advertiser,* April 16, 1873.

56. "U.S. Supreme Court. The Decision in the Louisiana Slaughter-House Cases," *Daily Arkansas Gazette,* Little Rock, April 24, 1873.

57. "The New Orleans Abattoir Decision," *Chicago Daily Tribune,* April 19, 1873.

58. "The Scope of the Thirteenth and Fourteenth Amendments," *New York Times,* April 16, 1873.

59. "Washington. Important Decisions by the Supreme Court and Court of Claims," *Milwaukee Daily Sentinel*, April 29, 1873.

60. *Pollock v. Farmers' Loan & Trust Co.*, 157 U.S. 429 (1895).

61. *Springer v. United States*, 102 U.S. 586 (1881).

62. "'Beauties' of the Income Tax," *Washington Post*, March 7, 1895.

63. "Prominent Persons Sick with Grip. The Disease Still Raging," *New York Times*, March 10, 1895.

64. "Edmunds on Income. The Tax Characterized as an Act of Tyranny," *Washington Post*, March 12, 1895.

65. Associated Press Leased-Wire Service, "Income-Tax Cases. Atty.-Gen. Olney Argues for the Government," *Los Angeles Times*, March 13, 1895.

66. "Income Tax Law Dead," *New York Times*, May 21, 1895. Justice Harlan would later dissent from the infamous "separate but equal" ruling, *Plessy v. Ferguson*, 163 U.S. 537 (1896) and a number of other important decisions of the Fuller Court.

67. "Democratic Doctrine Destroys the Populist Income Tax," *New York Times*, May 21, 1895.

68. "No Income Tax," *Boston Daily Globe*, May 21, 1895.

69. "Death of the Income Tax," *Atlanta Constitution*, May 21, 1895.

70. *Champion v. Ames*, 188 U.S. 321 (1903).

71. Ibid., 357.

72. "Nation Can Rule Trusts," *Chicago Daily Tribune*, February 24, 1903.

73. *McCray v. United States*, 195 U.S. 27 (1904).

74. "Oleo Act Upheld; Plants May Shut," *Chicago Daily Tribune*, June 1, 1904.

75. *McCray v. United States*, 195 U.S. 27 (1904).

76. *United States v. Doremus*, 249 U.S. 86 (1919).

77. *Hoke v. United States*, 227 U.S. 308 (1913).

78. *Hammer v. Dagenhart*, 247 U.S. 251 (1918).

79. "The Child Labor Decision," *New York Times*, June 5, 1918.

80. "Chief Justice Taft," *Boston Daily Globe*, July 2, 1921.

81. "Chief Justice Taft," *Los Angeles Times*, July 2, 1921.

82. *Hill v. Williams*, 259 U.S. 44, 68 (1922).

83. *Board of Trade v. Olsen,* 262 U.S. 1 (1923).

84. "Grain Futures Act Found Constitutional," *Wall Street Journal,* April 17, 1923.

85. "Grain Futures Act Upheld by Highest Court," *Chicago Daily Tribune,* April 17, 1923.

86. *Home Building & Loan Association v. Blaisdell,* 290 U.S. 398 (1934).

87. *Nebbia v. New York,* 291 U.S. 502 (1934).

88. John Herrick, "Supreme Court Upholds Price Fixing by State," *Chicago Daily Tribune,* March 6, 1934.

89. "A Notable Decision," *New York Times,* March 6, 1934.

90. Arthur Krock, "In Washington," *New York Times,* March 6, 1934.

91. *Gold Clause Cases: Norman v. Baltimore & Ohio Railroad Co.,* 294 U.S. 240 (1935), *Nortz v. United States,* 294 U.S. 317 (1935), and *Perry v. United States,* 294 U.S. 330 (1935). In still another pro–New Deal decision, a year later the Court upheld the constitutionality of the Tennessee Valley Authority Act in *Ashwander v. Tennessee Valley Authority,* 197 U.S. 288 (1936).

92. *Louisville Joint Stock Land Bank v. Radford,* 295 U.S. 555 (1935).

93. *Humphrey's Executor v. United States,* 295 U.S. 602 (1935).

94. *Panama Refining Co. v. Ryan,* 293 U.S. 388 (1935) and *Schechter Poultry Corp. v. United States,* 295 U.S. 495 (1935).

95. *Butler v. United States,* 297 U.S. 1 (1936).

96. *Carter v. Carter Coal,* 298 U.S. 238 (1936).

97. *Morehead v. New York ex rel. Tipaldo,* 298 U.S. 587 (1936).

98. "Into the Limbo," *Wall Street Journal,* May 28, 1935.

99. "Time for a Showdown," *Washington Post,* February 6, 1937.

100. *National Labor Relations Board v. Jones & Laughlin Steel Corp.,* 301 U.S. 1 (1937).

101. *West Coast Hotel v. Parrish,* 300 U.S. 379 (1937).

102. Ibid., 391–92.

103. *Helvering v. Davis,* 301 U.S. 619 (1937). A year later the Court would uphold a federal milk-products control statute as within Congress's authority under the commerce clause. *United States v. Carolene Products Co.,* 304 U.S. 144 (1938). The last major piece of New Deal legislation, the Fair Labor Standards (Wages and Hours) Act of 1938, was

sustained by the Court in early 1941, again as a constitutional application of the commerce clause. *Darby Lumber Co. v. United States,* 312 U.S. 100 (1941).

104. *Hartford Courant,* quoted in "Press Comment on Wagner Act Ruling," *Chicago Daily Tribune,* April 13, 1937.

105. Arthur Krock, "In Washington," *New York Times,* April 13, 1937.

106. *Erie Railroad v. Tompkins,* 304 U.S. 64 (1938), overruling *Swift v. Tyson,* 16 Pet. (41 U.S.) 1 (1842).

107. Arthur Krock, "In the Nation: A Momentous Decision of the Supreme Court," *New York Times,* May 3, 1938.

108. *Cloverleaf Butter Co. v. Patterson,* 315 U.S. 148 (1942); *United States v. Wrightwood Dairy Co.,* 315 U.S. 110 (1942); and *United States v. Pink,* 315 U.S. 203 (1942). U.S. Constitution, Article VI, Section 2: "This Constitution, and the Laws of the United States which shall be made in Pursuance thereof; and all Treaties made, or which shall be made, under the Authority of the United States, shall be the supreme Law of the Land; and the Judges in every State shall be bound thereby, any Thing in the Constitution or Laws of any State to the Contrary notwithstanding."

109. *Wickard v. Filburn,* 317 U.S. 111 (1942).

110. "A Flexible Commerce Clause," *Wall Street Journal,* November 11, 1942.

111. "Power to Regulate," *New York Times,* November 13, 1942.

112. *National Broadcasting Co. v. Federal Communications Commission,* 319 U.S. 190 (1943).

113. Associated Press, "Radio Leaders Disagree on FCC Ruling's Effect," *Chicago Daily Tribune,* May 11, 1943.

114. "Broadcasting Industry Prepares to Comply with FCC Regulations," *Wall Street Journal,* May 12, 1943.

115. "Regulating the Radio," *Chicago Daily Tribune,* May 13, 1943.

116. *Youngstown Sheet & Tube Co. v. Sawyer,* 343 U.S. 579 (1952).

117. Stephen K. Galpin, "Justice Black Writes Opinion Holding That President Lacks 'Inherent Power,'" *Wall Street Journal,* June 3, 1952.

118. "Truman Gets His Severest Rebuff," *Los Angeles Times,* June 3, 1952.

119. "Steel: Theory and Practice," *New York Times,* June 3, 1952.

120. "Not Unlimited," *Washington Post,* June 3, 1952.

121. Similar to the Fourteenth Amendment, which applies to the states, the Fifth Amendment states in part: "No person shall be . . . deprived of life, liberty, or property, without due process of law."

122. *Watkins v. United States,* 354 U.S. 178 (1957). The defendant was a United Auto Workers official in Illinois who had declined to answer some questions of the House Un-American Activities Committee.

123. *Yates v. United States,* 354 U.S. 298 (1957).

124. *Service v. Dulles,* 354 U.S. 363 (1957).

125. James B. Reston, "Judiciary Seen as Setting Limit on Other Branches," *New York Times,* June 18, 1957.

126. Two exceptions, in contradiction: the Burger Court interpreted the commerce clause one way, then reversed itself, on whether federal regulation of wages and hours applied to municipalities. In 1976 the Court said no. *National League of Cities v. Usery,* 426 U.S. 833 (1976). Nine years later the Court, 5–4, said yes. *Garcia v. San Antonio Metropolitan Transit Authority,* 469 U.S. 528 (1985).

127. *United States v. Nixon,* 418 U.S. 683 (1974). The burglars of the Democratic Party headquarters were found to have connections with the White House and the Central Intelligence Agency.

128. "The Court and the President," *Los Angeles Times,* July 25, 1974. The huge story was temporarily shunted aside just a day later when the Court struck down a federal district court desegregation order requiring the busing of black students from Detroit into neighboring white suburbs. It, too, was extensively covered. *Milliken v. Bradley,* 418 U.S. 717 (1974).

129. *Solid Waste Agency of Northern Cook County v. Army Corps of Engineers,* 531 U.S. 159 (2001).

130. Ibid., 174.

131. Kris Axtman, "High Court Hands Blow to Wetlands," *Christian Science Monitor,* January 10, 2001.

132. "Welcome Limits on Water Rules," *Atlanta Journal and Constitution,* January 10, 2001.

133. "U.S. High Court Ruling Endangers State's Wetlands," *Capital Times,* Madison, Wisconsin, January 10, 2001.

134. *Cheney v. United States District Court,* 542 U.S. 367 (2004).

135. "Cheney's Energy Task Force," *CBS Evening News,* June 24, 2004.

136. "Court Declines to Make Cheney Energy Task Force Records Public," Gina Holland, Associated Press, *Aiken Standard,* Aiken, South Carolina, June 25, 2004.

137. "A Loss for Open Government," *New York Times,* June 25, 2004.

138. *Bush v. Gore,* 531 U.S. 98 (2000).

139. *Winter v. Natural Resources Defense Council,* 129 S.Ct. 365 (2008).

140. Ibid., 381, 382.

141. Ibid., 392, Ginsburg, J., dissenting.

142. *Pleasant Grove City v. Summum,* 129 S.Ct. 1125 (2009); the Court unanimously rejected a religious organization's request to place the monument in a city park in Utah.

143. Ray Suarez and Marcia Coyle, "Supreme Court," *NewsHour with Jim Lehrer,* November 12, 2008.

144. Bob Egelko, "Restrictions on Navy's Use of Sonar Eased," *San Francisco Chronicle,* November 13, 2008.

145. "The Supreme Court Strikes the Correct Balance," *Washington Post,* November 14, 2008.

CHAPTER EIGHT

1. Marshall once headed the Virginia branch of the American Colonization Society, which advocated the relocation of freed blacks to Liberia. Jean Edward Smith, *John Marshall: Definer of a Nation* (New York: Owl Books, Henry Holt, 1996), 290.

2. *Boyce v. Anderson,* 27 U.S. 150 (1829).

3. *Barron v. Baltimore,* 7 Pet. (32 U.S.) 243 (1833).

4. *Groves v. Slaughter,* 15 Pet. (40 U.S.) 449 (1841).

5. *Prigg v. Pennsylvania,* 16 Pet. (41 U.S.) 539 (1842).

6. *Jones v. Van Zandt,* 5 How. (46 U.S.) 215 (1847).

7. *Strader v. Graham,* 51 U.S. 82 (1851).

8. *The Amistad,* 40 U.S. 518 (1841). The leader in Supreme Court coverage, the *Daily National Intelligencer,* published the full opinion and other papers picked it up. "The Case of the Amistad," *Daily National Intelligencer,* March 15, 1841.

9. "The Supreme Court and the Subject of Slavery," *Hinds County Gazette,* Raymond, Mississippi, January 3, 1851.

10. "A Remarkable Decision in the Supreme Court," *Liberator,* Boston, January 31, 1851.

11. *Scott v. Sandford,* 19 How. (60 U.S.) 393 (1857).

12. "The Decision of the Supreme Court in the Dred Scott Case, and Its Tremendous Consequences," *Charleston Mercury,* March 16, 1857.

13. "The Case of Dred Scott," *Fayetteville Observer,* Fayetteville, North Carolina, March 12, 1857.

14. "The Decision of the Supreme Court," *Pittsfield Sun,* Pittsfield, Massachusetts, March 26, 1857.

15. Observer, "The Decision of the Supreme Court in the Case of Dred Scott," *New-York Daily Times,* March 10, 1857.

16. "From Our New York Correspondent," *Milwaukee Daily Sentinel,* March 16, 1857.

17. "Practical Effect of the Dred Scott Judgment," *New York Herald,* March 11, 1857.

18. "Decision of the Supreme Court in the Dred Scott Case," *Whig and Courier,* Bangor, Maine, March 11, 1857.

19. "Decision of the Dred Scott Case," *Lowell Daily Citizen and News,* Lowell, Massachusetts, March 7, 1857.

20. *Osborn v. Nicholson,* 80 U.S. 654 (1872); *Bradwell v. Illinois,* 16 Wall. (83 U.S.) 130 (1873).

21. "No state shall make or enforce any law which shall abridge the privileges or immunities of citizens of the United States." This is the same clause that the Court had construed narrowly just the day before in the *Slaughterhouse Cases,* 16 Wall (83 U.S.) 36, which sanctioned a New Orleans statutory monopoly.

22. "Washington. More Supreme Court Decisions—Mr. Justice Bradley's Views of Woman's Rights," *Boston Daily Advertiser,* April 16, 1873.

23. Charles Lane, a former Supreme Court reporter for the *Washington Post,* graphically describes the events and the prosecution in *The Day Freedom Died: The Colfax Massacre, the Supreme Court, and the Betrayal of Reconstruction* (New York: Henry Holt, 2008).

24. *United States v. Cruikshank,* 92 U.S. 542 (1876).

25. Editorial, *Galveston Daily News,* Houston, March 28, 1876.

26. *United States v. Reese,* 92 U.S. 214 (1876). We will see this case again in chapter 10 on voting rights.

27. "The Enforcement Act," *The Constitution,* Atlanta, March 30, 1876.

28. "The States Rights Question," *Boston Daily Globe,* March 30, 1876.

29. "The Supreme Court and the Enforcement Act," *New York Times,* March 29, 1876.

30. *Hall v. DeCuir,* 95 U.S. 485 (1878).

31. *Virginia v. Rives,* 100 U.S. 313 (1880).

32. *Civil Rights Cases,* 109 U.S. 3 (1883). On the other hand, the Waite Court held violative of the Fourteenth Amendment an all-white jury law, *Strauder v. West Virginia,* 100 U.S. 303 (1880); deliberate exclusion of Negroes from juries, *Ex parte Virginia,* 100 U.S. 339 (1880) and *Neal v. Delaware,* 103 U.S. 370 (1881); and a San Francisco business license ordinance written to discriminate against Chinese laundry operators, *Yick Wo v. Hopkins,* 118 U.S. 356 (1886).

33. "Harlan Dissents," *Los Angeles Times,* November 18, 1883. Justice Harlan apparently was not yet satisfied with his dissent as published in the *Times,* for his wording is somewhat different in the United States Reports, the Court's official record.

34. "Washington. A Supreme Court Decision that Causes a Sensation," *Milwaukee Daily Journal,* October 16, 1883.

35. "The Civil Rights Decision. No Change in the Condition of Colored People Involved," *New York Times,* October 16, 1883.

36. Editorial, *North American,* Philadelphia, October 16, 1883.

37. "A Righteous and Welcome Decision," *Atlanta Constitution,* October 16, 1883.

38. James W. Ely, Jr., *The Chief Justiceship of Melville W. Fuller 1888–1910* (Columbia: University of South Carolina Press, 1995), 150.

39. *Chae Chan Ping v. United States,* 130 U.S. 581 (1889).

40. *Fong Yue Ting v. United States,* 149 U.S. 698 (1893).

41. Associated Press, "Excited Chinamen," *Los Angeles Times,* May 16, 1893.

42. "Boston Chinaman Sullen" and "Plea for the Chinese," *Boston Daily Globe,* May 16, 1893.

43. "Now They Leave," *Galveston Daily News,* Houston, May 16, 1893.

44. "The Geary Chinese Law," *Chicago Daily Tribune,* May 16, 1893.

45. Editorial, *Milwaukee Journal,* May 18, 1893.

46. *Louisville, New Orleans & Texas Railway Co. v. Mississippi,* 133 U.S. 587 (1890). The Waite Court decision was *Hall v. DeCuir,* 95 U.S. 485 (1878).

47. *Plessy v. Ferguson,* 163 U.S. 537 (1896). Overturned by *Brown v. Board of Education,* 347 U.S. 483 (1954). The Fuller Court in effect did extend *Plessy* to schools three years later, holding unanimously that a Georgia school board did not violate the equal protection clause when it closed the state's only public high school for black students, allegedly to provide greater support to black primary education, while allowing a nearby whites-only high school to continue to operate without integration. *Cumming v. Richmond County Board of Education,* 175 U.S. 528 (1899).

48. *Plessy,* 163 U.S. at 559, Harlan, J., dissenting.

49. Editorial, *Atchison Daily Globe,* Atchison, Kansas, May 25, 1896.

50. "No Objection Is Raised by the Negro," *Atlanta Constitution,* May 22, 1896.

51. "Heated Hot. Supreme Court Decision Is Denounced," *Boston Daily Globe,* May 20, 1896.

52. *Hawaii v. Mankichi,* 190 U.S. 197, 218 (1903).

53. *Dorr v. United States,* 195 U.S. 138, 145 (1904).

54. Ibid., 156, 155, Harlan, J., dissenting.

55. "No Trial by Jury in the Philippines," *New York Times,* June 1, 1904.

56. "No Constitutional Rights," *Atlanta Constitution,* June 6, 1904.

57. *Frank v. Mangum,* 237 U.S. 309 (1915). Sentenced to death, Frank received a commutation to life imprisonment, but was taken from prison and lynched by a mob.

58. *McCabe v. Atchison, Topeka & Santa Fe Railway Co.,* 235 U.S. 151 (1914).

59. *Toledo Newspaper Co. v. United States,* 247 U.S. 402 (1918). This case also was mentioned in chapter 2.

60. *Schenck v. United States,* 249 U.S. 47 (1919); *Frohwerk v. United States,* 294 U.S. 204 (1919).

61. *Debs v. United States,* 249 U.S. 211 (1919); *Abrams v. United States,* 250 U.S. 616 (1919).

62. *Abrams,* 250 U.S. at 630.

63. The Court upheld the act. *National Prohibition Cases,* 253 U.S. 350 (1920). The Eighteenth Amendment, banning the production and sale of intoxicating liquors, took effect in January 1920.

64. *Gitlow v. New York,* 168 U.S. 652 (1925).

65. In a recent question of incorporation, the Second Amendment's right to bear arms, held previously by the Supreme Court to bar a District of Columbia gun-control law (*District of Columbia v. Heller,* 128 S.Ct. 2783 [2008]), was interpreted to strike down municipal bans on handgun ownership. *McDonald v. City of Chicago,* 2010 U.S. LEXIS 5523 (June 28, 2010).

66. *Gitlow,* 168 U.S. at 673.

67. Associated Press, "Plea to Revolt Is Not Granted by Free Speech," *Chicago Daily Tribune,* June 9, 1925.

68. "When Anarchy Is Criminal," *New York Times,* June 9, 1925.

69. "When Anarchy Is Criminal," *Carroll Times,* June 18, 1925.

70. *Whitney v. California,* 274 U.S. 357 (1927).

71. *Hirabayashi v. United States,* 320 U.S. 81 (1943).

72. *Korematsu v. United States,* 323 U.S. 214 (1944); *Ex parte Mitsuye Endo,* 323 U.S. 283 (1944). The release of Endo was ordered on the ground that the detention of loyal Americans was not intended by the program.

73. Geoffrey R. Stone, *Perilous Times: Free Speech in Wartime, from the Sedition Act of 1798 to the War on Terrorism* (New York and London: W. W. Norton, 2004), 302.

74. Warren B. Francis, "Supreme Court Rules Loyal Nips Held Illegally," *Los Angeles Times,* December 19, 1944.

75. *Tunstall v. Brotherhood of Locomotive Firemen & Enginemen,* 323 U.S. 210 (1944).

76. Willard Edwards, "Supreme Court Defines Rights of Race Groups," *Chicago Daily Tribune,* December 19, 1944. Geoffrey R. Stone says, "Over the years, *Korematsu* has become a constitutional pariah. The Supreme Court has never cited it with approval of its result." Stone, *Perilous Times,* 307.

77. *Everson v. Board of Education of Ewing Township,* 330 U.S. 1 (1947).

78. *Illinois ex rel. McCollum v. Board of Education District 71, Champaign County,* 333 U.S. 203 (1948).

79. *Shelley v. Kraemer,* 334 U.S. 1 (1948).

80. Dorothea Andrews and Robert T. Allan, "Supreme Court Ruling to Halt Montgomery Religious Classes," *Washington Post,* March 10, 1948.

81. Rev. John Evans, "Church Council Acts to Retain Bible Teaching," *Chicago Daily Tribune,* March 11, 1948.

82. *Hurd v. Hodge,* 334 U.S. 24 (1948).

83. "Anti-Negro Pacts on Realty Ruled Not Enforceable," *New York Times,* May 4, 1948.

84. Arthur Krock, "In the Nation: The Chief Justice Closes a Loophole," *New York Times,* May 4, 1948.

85. "Ruling Is Acclaimed Here," *New York Times,* May 4, 1948.

86. "A Victory for Democracy," *New York Amsterdam News,* May 8, 1948.

87. Frank Wilder, "Race Covenant Rule Disappoints Many," *Washington Post,* May 4, 1948.

88. "Judge Denies Order to Prevent Negroes Moving into Home," *Chicago Daily Tribune,* May 6, 1948.

89. "Restrictive Covenants," *Chicago Daily Tribune,* May 8, 1948.

90. Jim Newton, *Justice for All: Earl Warren and the Nation He Made* (New York: Riverhead Books, 2006), 517.

91. *Brown v. Board of Education,* 347 U.S. 483 (1954). The defendants were public schools in Kansas, Delaware, Virginia, and South Carolina.

92. *Plessy v. Ferguson,* 163 U.S. 537 (1896).

93. *Brown,* 347 U.S. at 493. The Court's historic admonition "with all deliberate speed" was not in that first *Brown* opinion, but in a subsequent opinion on implementation of the Court's ruling. It was addressed only to the school districts involved in the litigation. *Brown v. Board of Education,* 349 U.S. 294 (1955).

94. United Press, "School Segregation Outlawed," *Charleston Daily Mail,* Charleston, West Virginia, May 17, 1954.

95. "An Editorial: We Shall Continue to Live Under the Constitution," *Charleston Daily Mail,* May 17, 1954.

96. Clarence J. LaRoche, "Few S.A. Problems Seen in Ruling," *San Antonio Express,* May 18, 1954.

97. Associated Press, "Southern Leaders Vary in Reaction to Ruling," *Los Angeles Times,* May 18, 1954.

98. Decision Is Applauded by Savannah Rotarians," *New York Times,* May 17, 1954.

99. "Editorial Excerpts from the Nation's Press on Segregation Ruling," *New York Times,* May 18, 1954.

100. *Loving v. Virginia,* 388 U.S. 1 (1967).

101. United Press International, "Supreme Court Upholds Racially Mixed Marriages," *Albuquerque Journal,* June 13, 1967.

102. *Mapp v. Ohio,* 367 U.S. 643 (1961).

103. *Gitlow v. New York,* 268 U.S. 652 (1925).

104. *Gideon v. Wainwright,* 372 U.S. 335 (1963).

105. Quoted in Anthony Lewis, *Gideon's Trumpet* (New York: Vintage Books, 1989), 216. Lewis won a Pulitzer Prize (his second) in 1963, the year of the *Gideon* decision, for his coverage of the Supreme Court for the *New York Times.*

106. *Escobedo v. Illinois,* 378 U.S. 438 (1964).

107. *Miranda v. Arizona,* 384 U.S. 436 (1966).

108. United Press International, "Police Rap New Ruling," *Chicago Defender,* June 18, 1966.

109. Leonard Downie, Jr., "Police Move to Meet New Court Ruling," *Washington Post,* June 15, 1966.

110. "Law Enforcement Officials Assail Court Confession Ruling," *Fresno Bee,* June 14, 1966.

111. "Why Police Get Gray," *Chicago Tribune,* June 14, 1966.

112. Arthur Krock, "In the Nation: The Wall Between Crime and Punishment," *New York Times,* June 14, 1966.

113. Ronald J. Ostrow, "Old Issue Revived: U.S. Supreme Court vs. Public Opinion," *Los Angeles Times,* June 19, 1966.

114. "Restraining the Police," *Washington Post,* June 18, 1966.

115. *Tinker v. Des Moines Independent Community School District,* 393 U.S. 503 (1969).

116. *Brandenburg v. Ohio,* 395 U.S. 444, 447 (1969).

117. *Whitney v. California,* 274 U.S. 357 (1927).

118. United Press International, "Justice Black Explodes at Decision on Students," *Billings Gazette,* Billings, Montana, February 25, 1969.

119. "School Chiefs Wary of Armband Ruling," *Chicago Tribune,* February 25, 1969.

120. "Revolt Invited in the Romper Set," *Chicago Tribune,* February 26, 1969.

121. "Freedom of Expression in the Schools," *Washington Post,* February 26, 1969.

122. *Brandenburg v. Ohio,* 395 U.S. 444 (1969).

123. Associated Press, "Ted's Correction Causes Strom to Hit Senate Ceiling," *Salina Journal,* Salina, Kansas, June 10, 1969.

124. Philip Warden, "Senate OKs Burger to Be Chief Justice," *Chicago Tribune,* June 10, 1969.

125. United Press International, "Kennedy and Thurmond Clash in Angry Debate over Douglas," *New York Times,* June 10, 1969.

126. *Sniadach v. Family Finance Corp.,* 395 U.S. 337 (1969).

127. *Red Lion Broadcasting Co., Inc. v. Federal Communications Commission,* 395 U.S. 367 (1969).

128. Ethan Katsh, "The Supreme Court Beat: How Television Covers the U.S. Supreme Court," *Judicature* 67, no. 1 (June–July 1983): 8, 9, 10.

129. *Roe v. Wade,* 410 U.S. 113 (1973).

130. Katsh, "Supreme Court Beat," 10.

131. Tim O'Brien, "Yes, but . . . ," *Judicature* 67, no. 1 (June–July 1983): 12–15.

132. Ibid., 12.

133. *Swann v. Charlotte-Mecklenburg Board of Education,* 402 U.S. 1 (1971).

134. *Fullilove v. Klutznick,* 448 U.S. 448 (1980).

135. United Press International, "South Stirred by Busing Rule," *Chicago Tribune,* April 21, 1971.

136. "More Equal Than Others," *Wall Street Journal,* July 7, 1980.

137. *Penry v. Lynaugh,* 492 U.S. 302 (1989).

138. *Stanford v. Kentucky,* 492 U.S. 361 (1989).

139. *Richmond v. J. A. Croson Co.,* 488 U.S. 469 (1989).

140. *Ward's Cove Packing Co. v. Atonio,* 490 U.S. 642 (1989); *Patterson v. McLean Credit Union,* 491 U.S. 164 (1989); and *Will v. Michigan,* 491 U.S. 58 (1989).

141. *Martin v. Wilks,* 490 U.S. 755 (1989).

142. *Texas v. Johnson,* 491 U.S. 397 (1989). We will look at this case more closely in chapter 11.

143. Tony Mauro, "Rulings This Year Worry Civil Rights Community," *USA Today,* June 29, 1989.

144. Marshall Ingwerson, "Curbs on Anti-Bias Cases," *Christian Science Monitor,* June 16, 1989.

145. "Second Reconstruction Period Ended by Court," *St. Louis Post-Dispatch,* June 24, 1989.

146. "Searching for Ways to Turn Back the Clock," *Arkansas Democrat-Gazette,* Little Rock, Arkansas, June 18, 1989.

147. Elliott E. Slotnick and Jennifer A. Segal, *Television News and the Supreme Court: All the News That's Fit to Air?* (Cambridge, Eng.: Cambridge University Press, 1998). Table 5.3 on pages 171–72 details the network coverage, case by case.

148. *Rutan v. Republican Party of Illinois,* 492 U.S. 62 (1990).

149. *United States v. Eichman,* 496 U.S. 310 (1990).

150. *Board of Education of the Westside Community Schools v. Mergens,* 496 U.S. 226 (1990).

151. *Oregon Employment Division v. Smith,* 494 U.S. 872 (1990).

152. *Hodgson v. Minnesota,* 497 U.S. 417 (1990).

153. *Cruzan v. Director, Missouri Department of Health,* 497 U.S. 261 (1990).

154. *Michigan State Police v. Sitz,* 496 U.S. 444 (1990).

155. *Maryland v. Buie,* 494 U.S. 325 (1990).

156. Slotnick and Segal, *Television News,* 203–11.

157. Ibid., 205.

158. Ibid., 210.

159. Ruth Bader Ginsburg, "Communicating and Commenting on the Court's Work," *Georgetown Law Journal* 83 (July 1995): 2119–29, 2123.

160. Linda Greenhouse, "Telling the Court's Story: Justice and Journalism at the Supreme Court," *Yale Law Journal* 105 (April 1996): 1537–61, 1546. It was not a new kind of error, even at the *Times.* A 1962 story reporting that the Court "let stand unchanged a Federal Trade Commission order requiring Crown Zellerbach Corporation to divest itself of assets of St. Helena Pulp and Paper Company" carried this incorrect headline: "Divestiture Upheld by Supreme Court." Associated Press, "Divestiture Upheld by Supreme Court," *New York Times,* June 26, 1962.

161. *Oregon Department of Human Resources v. Smith,* 494 U.S. 872 (1990).

162. *Wisconsin v. Yoder,* 406 U.S. 205 (1972).

163. George Will, "Scalia Followed Founders' Wish to Subordinate Religion to Order," *Alton Telegraph,* Alton, Illinois, April 25, 1990.

164. *United States v. Lopez,* 514 U.S. 549 (1995).

165. *Chicago v. Morales,* 527 U.S. 41 (1999).

166. Associated Press, "Court Rejects Federal Law Establishing Gun-Free School Zones," *Daily Herald,* Chicago, Illinois, April 27, 1995.

167. Joan Biskupic, "Top Court Ruling on Guns Slams Brake on Congress," *Chicago Sun-Times,* April 28, 1995.

168. Jan Crawford Greenburg, "High Court Strikes Down City Anti-Loitering Ordinance," *Chicago Tribune,* June 10, 1999.

169. Slotnick and Segal, *Television News,* 175, 159. Table 5.4 on page 174 lists the networks' stories case by case. The authors attribute the decline in coverage to "the triumph of 'infotainment' in the broadcast news industry, aided and abetted by the Court's shrinking docket.... [T]he Supreme Court is not a subject matter that often meets the standards for newsworthiness in the commercially driven broadcast news industry." Slotnick and Segal, *Television News,* 187–88.

170. *Rosenberger v. University of Virginia,* 515 U.S. 819 (1995).

171. *Capitol Square Review and Advisory Board v. Pinette,* 515 U.S. 753 (1995).

172. *Hurley v. Irish-American Gay, Lesbian and Bisexual Group of Boston,* 515 U.S. 557 (1995).

173. *Vernonia School District v. Acton,* 515 U.S. 646 (1995).

174. *Miller v. Johnson,* 515 U.S. 900 (1995).

175. *Roper v. Simmons,* 543 U.S. 551 (2005). The previous ruling, upholding the death penalty for juveniles, was *Stanford v. Kentucky,* 492 U.S. 361 (1989).

176. Paige Akin, "Juvenile Petersburg Killer Spared Death After Ruling," *Richmond Times Dispatch,* March 2, 2005.

177. Staff and wire reports, "Supreme Court Death Penalty Ruling to Have Profound Effect in Texas," *Galveston County Daily News,* Galveston, Texas, March 2, 2005.

178. Rosanna Ruiz and Allan Turner, "The Supreme Court Ruling:

Families of Victims Attempt to Come to Grips with Ruling; They Voice Their Concern That the Killers Someday May Be Set Free," *Houston Chronicle,* March 2, 2005.

179. "A Welcome Reprieve That's Too Late for Some," *Austin American-Statesman,* March 2, 2005.

180. "A Proper Ruling on Death," *Milwaukee Journal Sentinel,* March 2, 2005.

181. "Young Killers," *Las Vegas Review-Journal,* March 2, 2005.

182. *Hamdi v. Rumsfeld,* 542 U.S. 507 (2004).

183. *Rasul v. Bush,* 542 U.S. 466 (2004).

184. Frank Davies, "Guantanamo Detainees Can Challenge Captivity, Supreme Court Rules," *Miami Herald,* June 29, 2004.

185. Joan Biskupic and Toni Locy, "Detainees Still Will Face Many Hurdles to Freedom," *USA Today,* June 29, 2004.

186. "Prudent Check on Detentions," *Christian Science Monitor,* June 30, 2004.

187. "Supreme Court Ruling on Detainees Helps Restore Important Checks and Balances," *Columbus Dispatch,* July 1, 2004.

188. "Detainees Win One: Court Ruling Is Setback for Commander in Prosecuting New Kind of War," *Omaha World-Herald,* July 3, 2004.

189. *Hamdan v. Rumsfeld,* 548 U.S. 557 (2006).

190. "Trying Terrorists by Military Rules," *Boston Herald,* June 30, 2006.

191. "Supreme Court Goes Overboard," *Daily News,* New York, June 30, 2006.

192. *Boumediene v. Bush,* 128 S.Ct. 2229, 2307, 2294, 553 U.S. 723 (2008), Scalia, J., dissenting.

193. Michael Abramowitz, "Administration Strategy for Detention Now in Disarray," *Washington Post,* June 13, 2008.

194. "Rule of Law Wins," *Seattle Post-Intelligencer,* June 13, 2008.

195. "Three Strikes: Supreme Court Rightly Affirms the Constitution," *Salt Lake Tribune,* Salt Lake City, Utah, June 13, 2008.

196. "Reason Prevails on Habeas Corpus," *Virginian-Pilot,* Norfolk, Virginia, June 13, 2008.

197. *Ledbetter v. Goodyear,* 550 U.S. 618 (2007). Congress subsequently overrode the decision with the Lily Ledbetter Fair Pay Act of 2009.

198. *Morse v. Frederick,* 551 U.S. 393 (2007).

199. *Baze v. Rees,* 128 S.Ct. 1520 (2008).

200. *District Attorney's Office v. Osborne,* 129 S.Ct. 2308 (2009).

201. "Court Right on Bias Law," *Contra Costa Times,* Contra Costa, California, May 30, 2007.

202. "Three Bad Rulings," *New York Times,* June 26, 2007.

203. "The Supreme Court Fine-Tunes Pain," *New York Times,* April 17, 2008.

204. "Unparalleled and Denied," *New York Times,* June 19, 2009, A20.

205. *District of Columbia v. Heller,* 128 S.Ct. 2783 (2008). The Second Amendment: "A well regulated Militia, being necessary to the security of a free State, the right of the people to keep and bear Arms, shall not be infringed."

206. "Supreme Court/Gun Ruling," *NBC Evening News,* June 26, 2008.

207. Linda Greenhouse, "Justices, Ruling 5-4, Endorse Personal Right to Own a Gun," *New York Times,* June 27, 2008.

208. "Saying the Obvious," *Arkansas Democrat-Gazette,* Little Rock, Arkansas, June 29, 2008.

209. "A Constitutionally Appropriate Gun Decision," *Capital Times,* Madison, Wisconsin, June 27, 2008.

210. "Locked and Loaded," *Oregonian,* Portland, Oregon, June 27, 2008.

211. "Court Shoots from the Hip," *Berkshire Eagle,* Pittsfield, Massachusetts, June 27, 2008.

212. "Gun Ruling Helps Only Criminals," *Chicago Sun-Times,* June 27, 2008.

213. "High Noon for Gun Control," *Boston Globe,* June 27, 2008.

CHAPTER NINE

1. *Fletcher v. Peck,* 6 Cranch (10 U.S.) 87 (1810).

2. *Dartmouth College v. Woodward,* 4 Wheat. (17 U.S.) 518 (1819).

3. *Sturges v. Crowninshield,* 4 Wheat. (17 U.S.) 122 (1819). State insolvency legislation was preempted by a national bankruptcy law in 1898.

4. *Ogden v. Saunders,* 12 Wheat. (25 U.S.) 213 (1827).

5. *Gibbons v. Ogden,* 9 Wheat. (22 U.S.) 1 (1824).

6. *Charles River Bridge v. Warren Bridge,* 11 Pet. (36 U.S.) 420 (1837).

7. *Pennsylvania v. Wheeling and Belmont Bridge Co.,* 13 How. (54 U.S.) 518 (1852).

8. *License Cases,* 5 How. (46 U.S.) 504 (1847), involving Massachusetts, Rhode Island, and New Hampshire statutes.

9. *Cooley v. Board of Wardens of the Port of Philadelphia,* 12 How. (53 U.S.) 299 (1852).

10. *O'Reilly v. Morse,* 56 U.S. 62 (1854).

11. *Slaughterhouse Cases,* 16 Wall. (83 U.S.) 36 (1873).

12. *Munn v. Illinois,* 94 U.S. 113 (1877).

13. *Yick Wo v. Hopkins,* 118 U.S. 356 (1886).

14. *Chicago, Milwaukee & St. Paul Railway Co. v. Minnesota,* 134 U.S. 418 (1890).

15. *Pollock v. Farmers' Loan & Trust Co.,* 157 U.S. 429 (1895).

16. *In re Debs,* 158 U.S. 564 (1895).

17. *Robertson v. Baldwin,* 165 U.S. 275 (1897).

18. *Clyatt v. United States,* 197 U.S. 207 (1905).

19. *Hodges v. United States,* 203 U.S. 1 (1906).

20. *Lochner v. New York,* 198 U.S. 45 (1905).

21. Ibid., 73.

22. "Ten-Hour Law Killed by Court," *Boston Daily Globe,* April 18, 1905.

23. *Bailey v. Alabama,* 211 U.S. 452 (1908). Three years later, under Chief Justice White, the Court reconsidered the case with new evidence and reversed the conviction. *Bailey v. Alabama,* 219 U.S. 219 (1911).

24. *Employers' Liability Cases,* 207 U.S. 463 (1908).

25. *Adair v. United States,* 208 U.S. 161 (1908).

26. *Loewe v. Lawlor,* 208 U.S. 274 (1908).

27. "Maritime Law," *Rocky Mountain News,* Denver, January 27, 1897.

28. "Color Line Case in Supreme Court: Federal Tribunal Decides It Has No Jurisdiction," *Atlanta Constitution,* May 29, 1906.

29. "Boycotts by Unions Under Court Ban," *New York Times,* February 4, 1908.

30. "Nation's First Jurist Restrains Unionists," *Los Angeles Times,* February 4, 1908.

31. "Blow to Labor Unions," *Wall Street Journal,* February 4, 1908.

32. "More Advice: Is After New Laws on Labor," *Los Angeles Times,* February 7, 1908.

33. "Plan Safeguard on Constitution," *Chicago Daily Tribune,* February 10, 1908.

34. "Respect for the Supreme Court," *Chicago Daily Tribune,* June 2, 1906.

35. *United States v. E. C. Knight Co.,* 156 U.S. 1 (1895).

36. *United States v. Trans-Missouri Freight Association,* 166 U.S. 290 (1897).

37. *United States v. Joint Traffic Association,* 171 U.S. 505 (1898).

38. "Hard Blow to the Railroads," *Chicago Daily Tribune,* October 25, 1898.

39. Associated Press, "Must Fit the Law: Railroad Reorganization May Be Necessary," *Los Angeles Times,* October 26, 1898.

40. "Joint Traffic Decision," *New York Times,* October 26, 1898.

41. "A Far-Reaching Decision," *Oregonian,* Portland, Oregon, October 26, 1898.

42. *Northern Securities Co. v. United States,* 193 U.S. 197 (1904).

43. "Northern Securities Company an Outlaw," *Boston Daily Globe,* March 15, 1904.

44. "The Merger Case," *Chicago Daily Tribune,* March 15, 1904.

45. "The Northern Securities Case," *Wall Street Journal,* March 15, 1904.

46. *Dr. Miles Medical Company v. John D. Park and Sons Company,* 220 U.S. 373 (1911).

47. *Standard Oil Company of New Jersey v. United States,* 221 U.S. 1 (1911).

48. *United States v. American Tobacco Company,* 221 U.S. 106, 192 (1911), Harlan, J., dissenting.

49. "Tobacco Trust Found Guilty and Must Dissolve; Court Is to Fix Legal Form of Big Business," *New York Times,* May 30, 1911.

50. "Justice Harlan Caustic," *New York Times,* May 30, 1911.

51. "The Tobacco Trust Decision," *Boston Daily Globe,* May 30, 1911.

52. "Two Anarchies and a Compromise," *Wall Street Journal,* June 1, 1911.

53. "The Tobacco Trust Decision," *Chicago Daily Tribune,* May 31, 1911.

54. Associated Press, "Cabinet Member's Opinion," *New York Times,* May 31, 1911.

55. *United States v. United States Steel Corporation,* 251 U.S. 417 (1920).

56. *United States v. General Electric Company,* 272 U.S. 476 (1926).

57. *United States v. International Harvester Company,* 274 U.S. 693 (1927).

58. *Cline v. Frank Dairy Company,* 274 U.S. 445 (1927).

59. *United States v. Trenton Potteries Company,* 273 U.S. 392 (1927).

60. *Bedford Cut Stone Company v. Journeymen Stone Cutters' Association,* 274 U.S. 37 (1927).

61. "Union Held Subject to Anti-Trust Law," *New York Times,* April 12, 1927, *Bedford,* 274 U.S. at 65, Brandeis, J., dissenting.

62. *Truax v. Corrigan,* 257 U.S. 13 (1921).

63. *Bailey v. Drexel Furniture Co.,* 259 U.S. 20 (1922).

64. *Adkins v. Children's Hospital,* 261 U.S. 525 (1923).

65. "Gompers Calls Decision 'Base,'" *Boston Daily Globe,* April 10, 1923.

66. "Won't Affect Bay State Law, Says Miss Johnson," *Boston Daily Globe,* April 10, 1923.

67. "Regrets Wage Law Ruling," *Los Angeles Times,* April 10, 1923.

68. "The Minimum Wage Decision," *Washington Post,* April 10, 1923.

69. *Standard Oil Company (Indiana) v. United States,* 283 U.S. 163 (1931).

70. *Appalachian Coals, Inc. v. United States,* 288 U.S. 344 (1933).

71. *United States v. Swift & Co.,* 286 U.S. 106 (1932).

72. "Packers Must Adhere to 1920 'Consent' Pact," *Chicago Daily Tribune,* May 3, 1932. "The Decision in the Packers' Case," *Chicago Daily Tribune,* May 4, 1932.

73. *National Broadcasting Co. v. United States,* 319 U.S. 190 (1943).

74. Associated Press, "Supreme Court Upholds Radio Networks Curb," *Los Angeles Times,* May 11, 1943.

75. Associated Press, "Radio Leaders Disagree on FCC Ruling's Effect," *Chicago Daily Tribune,* May 11, 1943.

76. David Lawrence, "Supreme Court's Decision in Radio Case Opens Way for Curb on Press—Lawrence," *Alton Evening Telegraph,* Alton, Illinois, May 11, 1943.

77. "The Radio Decision," *Wall Street Journal,* May 12, 1943.

78. *United States v. E. I. du Pont de Nemours & Co.,* 353 U.S. 586, 611 (1957), Burton, J., dissenting.

79. Philip Dodd, "Rules DuPont G.M. Holdings Violate Law," *Chicago Daily Tribune,* June 4, 1957.

80. Arthur Krock, "In the Nation: The Court Goes Beyond the New-Fair Deal," *New York Times,* June 4, 1957.

81. "The Du Pont Decision," *Wall Street Journal,* June 5, 1957.

82. *Textile Workers v. Lincoln Mills,* 353 U.S. 448 (1957).

83. *Brown Shoe Co. v. United States,* 370 U.S. 294 (1962).

84. Ibid., 343–44.

85. "High Court Says Kinney Acquisition by Brown Shoe Violated Trust Law," *Wall Street Journal,* June 26, 1962. "Clayton Act Is Given Wide Scope as Court Bars Shoe Firm Merger," *Washington Post,* June 26, 1962.

86. *Engel v. Vitale,* 370 U.S. 421 (1962).

87. "Summary of Actions Taken by the Supreme Court," *New York Times,* June 26, 1962.

88. *Federal Trade Commission v. Procter & Gamble Co.,* 386 U.S. 568 (1967).

89. *Utah Pie Co. v. Continental Baking Co.,* 386 U.S. 685 (1967).

90. Louis M. Kohlmeier, "Consumer Justice: Two Antitrust Rulings Point Up High Court's Clumsy Role," *Wall Street Journal,* June 13, 1967.

91. *United States v. Sealy, Inc.,* 388 U.S. 350 (1967); *United States v. Arnold, Schwinn & Co.,* 388 U.S. 365 (1967).

92. *National Labor Relations Board v. Allis-Chalmers Manufacturing Co.,* 388 U.S. 185 (1967).

93. *National Labor Relations Board v. Great Dane Trailers, Inc.,* 388 U.S. 912 (1967).

94. Associated Press, "Resale Curbs on Franchises Upset by Court," *Chicago Tribune,* June 13, 1967.

95. "High Court Rules Two Distribution Methods Violate U.S. Anti-trust Laws," *Washington Post,* June 13, 1967.

96. David R. Jones, "Non-Striker Fines by a Union Upheld," *New York Times,* June 13, 1967.

97. Eileen Shanahan, "High Court Cites Dealership Curbs," *New York Times,* June 13, 1967.

98. *Fogerty v. Fantasy, Inc.,* 510 U.S. 517 (1994).

99. *Campbell v. Acuff-Rose Music, Inc.,* 510 U.S. 569 (1994).

100. Aaron Epstein, "A Rap Ruling: Parody Is Protected," *Philadelphia Inquirer,* March 8, 1994.

101. Linda Greenhouse, "Ruling on Rap Song, High Court Frees Parody from Copyright Law," *New York Times,* March 8, 1994.

102. "The Supreme Form of Flattery," *New York Times,* March 9, 1994.

103. "'Pretty Woman' Meets Hip-Hop," *Washington Post,* March 8, 1994.

104. Linda Greenhouse, "Final Twist in 'Rear Window' Case," *New York Times,* April 25, 1990. *Stewart v. Abend,* 495 U.S. 207 (1990).

105. Stephen Wermeil and David J. Jefferson, "Film Industry Is Dealt Copyright Blow," *Wall Street Journal,* June 25, 1990.

106. *Qualitex Co. v. Jacobson Products Co.,* 514 U.S. 159 (1995).

107. Ibid., 211.

108. Lorrie Grant, "Ruling Sets New Standards on Unique Clothing Designs," *USA Today,* March 23, 2000.

109. Daniella Dean, "Wal-Mart Cleared of Stealing Designs; Knock-offs Legal, High Court Says," *Washington Post,* March 23, 2000.

110. *New York Times Co. v. Tasini,* 533 U.S. 483, 505 (2001).

111. *Federal Election Commission v. Colorado Republican Federal Campaign Committee,* 533 U.S. 431 (2001).

112. Warren Richey, "Publishers Lose Ground to Freelancers in Copyright Case," *Christian Science Monitor,* June 26, 2001.

113. David D. Kirkpatrick, "The Supreme Court: The Reaction; Publishers Set to Remove Older Articles from Files," *New York Times,* June 26, 2001.

114. *Eldred v. Ashcroft,* 537 U.S. 186 (2003).

115. Pamela McClintock, "Coveting the Classics," *Daily Variety,* January 16, 2003.

116. Bill Hillburg, "Supreme Court Delivers Victory to Disney in Copyright Extension Case," *Daily News,* Los Angeles, California, January 16, 2003. *Eldred,* 537 U.S. at 208.

117. Lyle Denniston, "Justices Uphold Copyright Extension: Media Firms Cheer Ruling on '98 Law Pushed by Disney," *Boston Globe,* January 16, 2003. *Eldred,* 537 U.S. at 223. Denniston, the respected dean of Supreme Court reporters, has been on the job for more than fifty years;

he is currently reporting for WBUR radio in Boston and writing for an authoritative Web site, Scotusblog.com.

118. Dan Gillmore, "Ruling a Ripoff of Consumers," *San Jose Mercury News,* January 16, 2003.

119. "The Supreme Court Docket: The Coming of Copyright Perpetuity," *New York Times,* January 16, 2003.

120. *Whitman v. American Trucking Associations, Inc.,* 531 U.S. 457 (2001).

121. U.S. Constitution Article I, Section 1: "All legislative Powers herein granted shall be vested in a Congress."

122. *Whitman,* 531 U.S. at 475.

123. "Wise Ruling," *Post-Standard,* Syracuse, New York, March 1, 2001.

124. "No Smog from Ruling," *Palm Beach Post,* March 1, 2001.

125. Linda Greenhouse, "E.P.A.'s Right to Set Air Rules Wins Supreme Court Backing," *New York Times,* February 28, 2001.

126. "A Victory for Cleaner Air," *New York Times,* February 28, 2001.

127. Joe Mathewson, "Economists and Antitrust," *Wall Street Journal,* January 14, 1964.

CHAPTER TEN

1. U.S. Constitution, Article IV, Section 4 (in part): "The United States shall guarantee to every State in this Union a Republican Form of Government."

2. *Luther v. Borden,* 7 How. (48 U.S.) 1 (1849).

3. *Farmers' Cabinet,* Amherst, New Hampshire, January 11, 1849.

4. E. B., "Dorrism in Law," *Semi-Weekly Eagle,* Brattleboro, Vermont, January 8, 1849.

5. U.S. Constitution, Amendment XIV, Section 1: "All persons born or naturalized in the United States and subject to the jurisdiction thereof, are citizens of the United States and of the State wherein they reside. No state shall make or enforce any law which shall abridge the privileges or immunities of citizens of the United States; nor shall any State deprive any person of life, liberty, or property, without due process of law; nor deny to any person within its jurisdiction the equal protection of the laws."

6. *Minor v. Happersett,* 21 Wall. (88 U.S.) 162, 177 (1875).

7. *United States v. Reese,* 92 U.S. 214 (1876).

8. *United States v. Cruikshank,* 92 U.S. 542 (1876).

9. "The Kentucky Election Case," *Boston Daily Advertiser,* March 28, 1876.

10. *Elk v. Wilkins,* 112 U.S. 94, 122–23 (1884), Harlan, J., dissenting.

11. "The Great Court," *Atchison Daily Globe,* Atchison, Kansas, November 4, 1884.

12. *Giles v. Harris,* 189 U.S. 475, 486, 488 504 (1903).

13. *Giles v. Teasley,* 193 U.S. 146 (1904).

14. "Can Disfranchise a Race," *Waterloo Daily Reporter,* Waterloo, Iowa, April 28, 1903.

15. "Negroes Lose Suffrage Case," *Atlanta Constitution,* April 28, 1903.

16. However, it must be noted that in 1927 the Court, by a unanimous vote, invoked the equal protection clause of the Fourteenth Amendment to void a Texas statute barring blacks from voting in the Democratic primary election. The Fifteenth Amendment was pleaded, too, but the Court did not rule on it. *Nixon v. Herndon,* 273 U.S. 536 (1927).

17. *Grovey v. Townsend,* 295 U.S. 45 (1935).

18. *Norris v. Alabama,* 293 U.S. 552 (1935).

19. "2d Scottsboro Death Penalty Upset by Court," *Chicago Daily Tribune,* April 2, 1935.

20. "Texas Negro Loses Primary Vote Plea," *New York Times,* April 2, 1935.

21. Associated Press, "Negro Vote Ban in Texas Upheld," *San Antonio Express,* April 2, 1935.

22. *Smith v. Allwright,* 321 U.S. 649 (1944).

23. Associated Press, "Primary Vote for Negro Denounced" and Associated Press, "Texans Review Decision and Outline Steps," *Amarillo Daily News,* April 4, 1944.

24. Arthur Krock, "In the Nation: Self-Reexamination Continues in the Supreme Court," *New York Times,* April 4, 1944.

25. "Open Primaries," *Washington Post,* April 4, 1944.

26. "No Racial Discrimination in State Primaries," *Los Angeles Times,* April 4, 1944.

27. *Colegrove v. Green,* 328 U.S. 549, 556 (1946).

28. "Feud Rips Supreme Court!" *Chicago Daily Tribune,* June 11, 1946.

29. Willard Edwards, "Jackson Denounces Black," *Chicago Daily Tribune,* June 11, 1946.

30. George Tagge, "Plea to Remap Illinois Loses in High Court," *Chicago Daily Tribune,* June 11, 1946.

31. "Redistricting Plea for Illinois Denied," *New York Times,* June 11, 1946.

32. *Baker v. Carr,* 369 U.S. 186 (1962).

33. "Supreme Court Gives U.S. Judges Voice in States' Reapportioning; Urban-Rural Struggle at Issue," *New York Times,* March 27, 1962.

34. James E. Clayton, "U.S. Courts to Accept Lawsuits by Voters on 'Unfair' Apportioning," *Washington Post,* March 27, 1962.

35. William Beecher, "Political Upheaval?" *Wall Street Journal,* March 27, 1962. The dissenting Justice Harlan was the grandson of the original Justice Harlan.

36. Associated Press, "High Court Ruling Boosts City Voters' Remap Hopes" and Associated Press, "Court Ruling May Bring a Political Chain Reaction," *Waterloo Daily Courier,* Waterloo, Iowa, March 27, 1962.

37. Associated Press, "Views Differ on Shifting House Seats," *Newport Daily News,* Newport, Rhode Island, March 27, 1962.

38. Associated Press, "Some Cheer Court Ruling in Mississippi," *Lake Charles American Press,* Lake Charles, Louisiana, March 23, 1962.

39. William S. White, "U.S. Constitution Starts to Topple," *Cedar Rapids Gazette,* Cedar Rapids, Iowa, March 30, 1962.

40. Roscoe Drummond, "Rights of States Aren't Threatened," *Cedar Rapids Gazette,* Cedar Rapids, Iowa, March 30, 1962.

41. David Lawrence, "A Break in the Clouds on Political Questions," *Charleston Daily Mail,* Charleston, West Virginia, March 31, 1962.

42. "A Gain for Majority Rule," *New York Times,* March 27, 1962.

43. "The Legislature's Obligation," *New York Times,* March 23, 1962.

44. "Apportionment Decision Sounds Needed Warning," *Charleston Gazette,* Charleston, West Virginia, March 30, 1962.

45. *Gray v. Sanders,* 372 U.S. 368 (1963).

46. *Wesberry v. Sanders,* 376 U.S. 1 (1964).

47. *Reapportionment Cases* (June 1964).

48. *Reynolds v. Sims,* 377 U.S. 533, 562 (1964).

49. *Lucas v. Forty-Fourth General Assembly of Colorado,* 377 U.S. 713 (1964); *WMCA v. Lomenzo,* 377 U.S. 633 (1964).

50. Anthony Lewis, "Supreme Court Holds States Must Apportion Legislatures on Basis of Equal Population," *New York Times,* June 16, 1964.

51. "Supreme Court Rules Both Houses of Legislatures Must Be Apportioned with Population Used as a Basis," *Wall Street Journal,* June 16, 1964.

52. Harry Kelly, Associated Press, "Reapportionment Ruling Rocks Many States, Opinions Differ," *Fresno Bee Republican,* Fresno, California, June 16, 1964.

53. *Reynolds,* 377 U.S. at 624, Harlan, J., dissenting.

54. James Marlow, Associated Press, "Why Court Made Decision on Representation," *Kokomo* (Indiana) *Tribune,* June 16, 1964. "Potential Power Shift Excites Clark Lawmakers," *Reno Evening Gazette,* June 16, 1964.

55. "Ruling Doesn't Make Sense, Says Senator Edgar Brown," *Aiken Standard and Review,* Aiken, South Carolina, June 16, 1964.

56. Associated Press, "Apportionment Order Reactions Are Noisy," *Corpus Christi Times,* Corpus Christi, Texas, June 16, 1964.

57. "Popular Sovereignty," *Washington Post,* June 17, 1964.

58. "Constitutional Revolution," *New York Times,* June 16, 1964.

59. "And Some Legal Questions," *Wall Street Journal,* June 18, 1964.

60. "The Supreme Court Usurps More Power," *Chicago Tribune,* June 16, 1964.

61. "'Daley Power Bid Aided by Court'—Scott," *Chicago Tribune,* June 17, 1964.

62. "Why Two Houses?" *New Mexican,* Santa Fe, New Mexico, June 17, 1964.

63. David Lawrence, "States on Short End," *Lowell Sun,* Lowell, Massachusetts, June 17, 1964.

64. "The Noose Draws Tighter," *Delta Democrat-Times,* Greenville, Mississippi, June 17, 1964.

65. *Avery v. Midland County,* 390 U.S. 474 (1968).

66. Ibid., 490–91, Harlan, J., dissenting.

67. William Kling, "Extend 1-Man, 1-Vote Rule," *Chicago Tribune,* April 2, 1968.

68. John P. MacKenzie, "Court Widens Vote Rule," *Washington Post,* April 2, 1968.

69. Associated Press, "County Reapportionment Will Result from Order," *Abilene Reporter-News,* Abilene, Texas, April 2, 1968.

70. Ronald J. Ostrow, "Supreme Court Applies 1-Man, 1-Vote Rule to Cities, Counties," *Los Angeles Times,* April 2, 1968.

71. Fred P. Graham, "Justices Extend Equal-Vote Rule to Local Bodies," *New York Times,* April 2, 1968. *Avery,* 390 U.S. at 494, Harlan, J., dissenting and 390 U.S. at 510, Stewart, J., dissenting.

72. Harley Dadswell, "Area Officials Assess 'One Man, One Vote' Ruling," *Middlesboro Daily News,* Middlesboro, Kentucky, April 2, 1968.

73. "Precinct Redistricting Should Await Legislature," *Abilene Reporter-News,* Abilene, Texas, April 4, 1968.

74. "1-Man, 1-Vote Applied to County," *Daily Herald,* Chicago, Illinois, April 5, 1968.

75. *USV Pharmaceutical Corp. v. Weinberger,* 412 U.S. 655 (1973).

76. "Court Allows Deviations in Apportioning," *Washington Post,* June 19, 1973. *White v. Regester,* 412 U.S. 755, 773, Brennan, J., dissenting.

77. Warren Weaver, Jr., "High Court, by 6 to 3, Reinstates Two Districting Plans," *New York Times,* June 19, 1973.

78. *Whitcomb v. Chavis,* 403 U.S. 124 (1971).

79. Associated Press, "Rulings May Reshape State Politics," *Abilene Reporter-News,* June 19, 1973.

80. Richard Rodda, "Court's Eased Reapportionment Rules May End State Battle," *Fresno Bee,* Fresno, California, June 19, 1973.

81. *City of Richmond v. United States,* 422 U.S. 358, 382 (1975), Brennan, J., dissenting.

82. "Annexations Approved by Top Court," *Syracuse Post-Standard,* June 25, 1976.

83. United Press International, "Supreme Court Eases Up on Annexation of Suburbs," *Pocono Record,* The Stroudsburgs, Pennsylvania, June 25, 1975.

84. United Press International, "Southern White Suburbs Win Partial Victory," *Argus,* Fremont, California, June 25, 1975.

85. United Press International, "OK City-Suburb Merger," *Chicago Defender,* June 25, 1975.

86. CDN, "Court Backs Richmond Annexation," *Kingsport Times,* Kingsport, Tennessee, June 25, 1975.

87. Warren Weaver, Jr., "High Court Backs Richmond's Annexation of White Suburb That Altered Racial Balance," *New York Times,* June 25, 1975.

88. John P. MacKenzie and Jay Mathews, "Annexation in Richmond Given Boost," *Washington Post,* June 25, 1975.

89. U.S. Constitution, Article I, Section 8: "The Congress shall have Power To . . . provide for the . . . general Welfare of the United States."

90. *Buckley v. Valeo,* 424 U.S. 1 (1976). The name plaintiff, James L. Buckley, was himself a member of Congress (a conservative senator from New York) when Congress passed the statute as well as when the Supreme Court ruled on it. The former Minnesota senator Eugene McCarthy, then a candidate for the Democratic Party's presidential nomination, was another of the bipartisan plaintiffs.

91. Associated Press, "Candidates Differ on Fund Ruling," *Oakland Tribune,* January 31, 1976.

92. Walter R. Mears, Associated Press, "Loophole for 'Fat Cats' in Campaign?" *Des Moines Register,* January 31, 1976.

93. Linda Mathews, "Justices Void Key Election Money Curbs," *Los Angeles Times,* January 31, 1976.

94. "Old Politics?" *El Paso Herald-Post,* January 31, 1976.

95. "The Half-Dead Monster," *Wall Street Journal,* February 2, 1976.

96. Warren Weaver, Jr., "Impact This Year," *New York Times,* January 31, 1976.

97. Linda Greenhouse, "State Campaign Fund Law Now Faces Sharp Revision," *New York Times,* January 31, 1976.

98. Stephen Isaacs, "End Seen Near for Commission," *Washington Post,* January 31, 1976.

99. "Campaign Finance: Second Thoughts," *Washington Post,* February 2, 1976.

100. *City of Mobile v. Bolden,* 446 U.S. 55 (1980).

101. *Rogers v. Lodge,* 458 U.S. 613 (1982).

102. *California Democratic Party v. Jones,* 530 U.S. 567 (2000).

103. Linda Greenhouse, "Court Strikes Down California Primary Placing All Parties on a Single Ballot," *New York Times,* June 27, 2000.

104. *Dickerson v. United States,* 530 U.S. 428 (2000).

105. *Apprendi v. New Jersey,* 530 U.S. 466 (2000).

106. Richard Carelli, Associated Press, "Gonzalez Case Hits Supreme Court," *Intelligencer,* Doylestown, Pennsylvania, June 27, 2000. Two days later the Court denied the application for a stay of the lower court order. *Gonzalez v. Reno,* 530 U.S. 1270 (2000). On that same day Elian flew to Cuba with his father, who had come to fetch him. His mother had drowned attempting to escape from Cuba with Elian.

107. *Bush v. Gore,* 531 U.S. 98 (2000).

108. Ibid., 111.

109. Peter Marks, "Contesting the Vote: The Media," *New York Times,* December 13, 2000.

110. For instance, Walter R. Mears, Associated Press, "Bush Must Now Prove to Be a Uniter: An AP News Analysis," and Miles Benson, Newhouse News Service, "The Real Struggle May Just Be Under Way," December 13, 2000.

111. Daily News Wire Services, "Divided Court Issues Dissenting Views," *Philadelphia Daily News,* December 13, 2000.

112. "Justice Stevens's Dissent," *Washington Post,* December 13, 2000. *Bush,* 531 U.S. at 128–29, Stevens, J., dissenting.

113. Joan Biskupic, "Ruling Reveals Depths of Divide on Court," *USA Today,* December 13, 2000.

114. Linda Greenhouse, "Bush Prevails," *New York Times,* December 13, 2000.

115. The Court said federal law "requires that any controversy or contest that is designed to lead to a conclusive selection of electors be completed by December 12." *Bush,* 531 U.S. at 110. The date is sometimes described as a "safe harbor" insulating the result from any challenge by Congress.

116. *Chronicle Telegram,* Elyria, Ohio, December 13, 2000.

117. "High Court Decision Properly Certifies Bush's Presidency," *Lancaster New Era,* Lancaster, Pennsylvania, December 13, 2000.

118. "'Supreme' Court?" *Denver Post,* December 13, 2008.

119. "An Ugly Ending," *San Jose Mercury News,* San Jose, California, December 13, 2000.

120. "The Court Decides," *St. Louis Post-Dispatch,* December 13, 2000.

121. David M. Shribman, "An Ordeal That Sullied All in Its Path," *Boston Globe,* December 13, 2000.

122. "The Court Rules for Mr. Bush," *New York Times,* December 13, 2000.

123. Laurie Asseo, Associated Press, "Will Decision Hurt the Top Court?" December 13, 2000.

124. *McConnell v. Federal Election Commission,* 540 U.S. 93 (2003).

125. Ibid., 264, 283, Thomas, J., dissenting.

126. Gina Holland, "Campaign Finance Law Clears Supreme Court, but Fight Not Over," Associated Press, December 11, 2000.

127. Julia Malone, "Cash Scramble Changes Focus; Outside Groups 'Major Players,'" *Atlanta Journal-Constitution,* December 11, 2003.

128. "Court Right in Upholding 'Soft Money' Regulations for Federal Campaigns," *Austin American-Statesman,* December 11, 2000.

129. "Court Puts Little Guy in the Political Game," *Boston Herald,* December 11, 2000.

130. *McConnell,* 540 U.S. at 248, Scalia, J., dissenting.

131. "Upholding McCain-Feingold," *Milwaukee Journal Sentinel,* December 11, 2003.

132. "Democracy in America," *St. Louis Post-Dispatch,* December 11, 2003.

133. "Our Views: Free Speech," *Charleston Daily Mail,* Charleston, West Virginia, December 11, 2003.

134. "A Futile and Stupid Gesture," *Las Vegas Review-Journal,* December 11, 2003.

135. "The Supreme Court Trashes the 1st Amendment," *New York Post,* December 11, 2003.

136. Tom Brokaw, Pete Williams, and David Gregory, "Supreme Court/Campaign Finance," *NBC Nightly News,* December 10, 2003.

137. Nina Totenberg, "Supreme Court Rules McCain-Feingold Campaign Finance Reform Law Is Constitutional," *All Things Considered,* National Public Radio, December 10, 2003.

138. *League of United Latin American Citizens v. Perry,* 548 U.S. 399, 423, 441 (2006). The decision was based on standards set forth in *Thornburg v. Gingles,* 478 U.S. 30 (1986), a case not discussed in this book.

139. Warren Richey, "'On Demand' Redistricting Upheld," *Christian Science Monitor,* June 29, 2006.

140. "Partisanship Is Big Winner in Court's Redistricting Ruling," *Austin American-Statesman,* June 29, 2006.

141. "Texas Massacre," *Boston Globe,* June 29, 2006.

142. "U.S. Supreme Court: Opening the Floodgates?" *Milwaukee Journal Sentinel,* June 29, 2006.

143. "The Thicket's Dangers: Supreme Court Is Right to Proceed Carefully in Judging 'Partisan Gerrymandering,'" *Omaha World-Herald,* June 29, 2006.

144. *Federal Election Commission v. Wisconsin Right to Life,* 551 U.S. 449, 469–70, 127 S.Ct. 2652, 2667 (2007).

145. Ibid., 2686, Scalia, J., concurring.

146. Robert Barnes, "Supreme Courts Weakens Curbs on Pre-Election TV Ads; Ruling on McCain-Feingold Law Opens Door for Interest Groups in '08," *Washington Post,* June 26, 2007.

147. Jim Angle, "Political Headlines," *Fox Special Report with Brit Hume,* June 25, 2007.

148. *Northwest Austin Municipal Utility District Number One v. Holder,* 129 S.Ct. 2504 (No. 08-322, June 22, 2009).

149. Jess Bravin, "Court Upholds Voting Rights Act," *Wall Street Journal,* June 23, 2009, A3.

150. Mark Sherman, Associated Press, "Voting Rights Act Upheld, Big Question Ignored," *San Francisco Chronicle,* June 23, 2009; and Robert Barnes, "Voting Rights Act Upheld, but Court Hints at Change," *Washington Post,* June 23, 2009.

151. Chuck Lindell, "Supreme Court Lets Voting Right Act Stand in Austin Case," *Austin American-Statesman,* June 23, 2009.

152. Associated Press, "Supreme Court Exempts Texas District in Voting Rights Case," www.dallasnews.com, June 22, 2009 (accessed August 4, 2009).

153. See, for instance, Associated Press, "Voting Rights Act Survives Court Challenge," *Boston Globe,* June 23, 2009.

154. "Voting Rights Victory," *Washington Post,* June 23, 2009.

155. "The Voting Rights Act Survives," *New York Times,* June 23, 2009, A22.

156. *Citizens United v. Federal Election Commission,* 130 S.Ct. 876 (2010).

157. "The Court's Aggressive Term," *New York Times,* July 5, 2010, A14.

158. David Lightman, Margaret Talev, and Michael Doyle, "Ruling Could Magnify Special Interests' Role in U.S. Politics," McClatchy Newspapers, January 22, 2010.

159. "Major Victory for Free Speech: A Decision by the Supreme Court Reverses Decades of Laws That Only Served to Drive Campaign Finance Underground," *Denver Post,* January 22, 2010.

160. *Colegrove v. Green,* 328 U.S. 549 (1946).

CHAPTER ELEVEN

1. U.S. Constitution, First Amendment (in part): "Congress shall make no law respecting an establishment of religion."

2. *Engel v. Vitale,* 370 U.S. 421, 424, 435, 442 (1962).

3. Anthony Lewis, "Supreme Court Outlaws Official School Prayers in Regents Case Decision," *New York Times,* June 26, 1962.

4. Joseph Hearst, "Supreme Court Bans School Prayers," *Chicago Daily Tribune,* June 26, 1962.

5. James E. Clayton, "High Court Rules Out Public School Prayers in Six-to-One Decision," *Washington Post,* June 26, 1962.

6. "In Behalf of Religion," *Washington Post,* June 26, 1962.

7. Harry Kelly, Associated Press, "Limits Feared in Court Rule," *Lake Charles American Press,* Lake Charles, Louisiana, June 26, 1962.

8. Associated Press, "Amendment Offered to Permit Prayers," *Emporia Gazette,* Emporia, Kansas, June 26, 1962.

9. Associated Press, "Prayer Decision Protest Mounts," *Brazosport Facts,* Freeport, Texas, June 26, 1962.

10. Robert J. Donovan, HTNS, "Court Has Bear by Tail in Prayer Ruling," *Chronicle-Telegram,* Elyria, Ohio, June 27, 1962.

11. "Most Area Ministers, Parents Oppose Prayer Decision," *Southern Illinoisan,* Carbondale, Illinois, June 26, 1962.

12. Westbrook Pegler, "Fair Enough," *Bridgeport Post,* Bridgeport, Connecticut, July 6, 1962.

13. David Lawrence, "The Girard Case," *Portsmouth Times,* Portsmouth, Ohio, July 2, 1962.

14. See, for instance, *Abington School District v. Schempp,* 374 U.S. 203

(1963), Bible reading and Lord's Prayer prohibited; *Stone v. Graham,* 449 U.S. 39 (1980), state-required posting of Ten Commandments not allowed; *Widmar v. Vincent,* 454 U.S. 263 (1981), equal access to public-university facilities; *Wallace v. Jaffree,* 472 U.S. 38 (1985), state-mandated moment of silence unconstitutional; *Board of Education v. Mergens,* 496 U.S. 226 (1990), federal statute on equal access to secondary school facilities upheld; and *Santa Fe Independent School District v. Doe,* 530 U.S. 290 (2000), student-led pregame prayer over loudspeaker disallowed. We will look at some of these cases. Numerous constitutional amendment proposals to allow school prayer have been introduced in Congress but failed.

15. *Griswold v. Connecticut,* 381 U.S. 479, 484, 486, 510, 530 (1965).

16. *Estes v. Texas,* 381 U.S. 532 (1965).

17. *Amalgamated Meat Cutters v. Jewel Tea Co., Inc.,* 381 U.S. 676 (1965); *United Mine Workers v. Pennington,* 381 U.S. 657 (1965); *United States v. Brown,* 381 U.S. 437 (1965).

18. *Linkletter v. Walker,* 381 U.S. 618 (1965).

19. Fred P. Graham, "7-2 Ruling Establishes Marriage Privileges—Stirs Debate," *New York Times,* June 8, 1965.

20. "Marital Privacy," *Washington Post,* June 8, 1965.

21. *Swann v. Charlotte-Mecklenburg Board of Education,* 402 U.S. 1, 24 (1971).

22. United Press International, "Supreme Court 'Lays It On Line' Again About U.S. School Integration," *Provo Daily Herald,* Provo, Utah, April 21, 1971.

23. Associated Press, "Massive School Busing Given Court Approval," *Florence Morning News,* Florence, South Carolina, April 21, 1971.

24. Ibid.

25. Associated Press, "White House Bows to Rule on Busing," *Santa Fe New Mexican,* April 21, 1971.

26. "Supreme Court's Ruling on Busing Should Make Integration a Reality," *Fresno Bee Republican,* April 21, 1971.

27. "Fear Teacher Job Loss: Sizemore, Charles Hit U.S. High Court Ruling on Busing," *Chicago Daily Defender,* April 21, 1971.

28. "Expects No Effects Here," *Chicago Tribune,* April 21, 1971.

29. In 1980 the Chicago Board of Education and the U.S. Justice Department agreed in U.S. district court on a school desegregation plan that

contemplated busing. Casey Banas and Jay Branegan, "School Board, U.S. Set Integration Guidelines," *Chicago Tribune,* September 25, 1980.

30. "The Court's Integration Decision," *Los Angeles Times,* April 22, 1971. The Supreme Court later rejected, 5-4, a city-suburb desegregation plan that called for busing between two different school districts in and around Detroit. *Milliken v. Bradley,* 418 U.S. 717 (1974).

31. *Roe v. Wade,* 410 U.S. 113, 152, 153, 155 (1973).

32. Ibid., 222, White, J., dissenting.

33. "Abortion," *NBC Nightly News,* January 22, 1973.

34. Associated Press, "Assembly to Fill Abortion Law Gap," *Newport Daily News,* Newport, Rhode Island, January 23, 1973.

35. Associated Press, "Court Abortion Ruling Gets Mixed Reaction," *Morning Herald,* Hagerstown, Maryland, January 23, 1973.

36. Mark Henckel and Carol Saboe, "No Abortions Likely in Billings Soon," *Billings Gazette,* Billings, Montana, January 23, 1973.

37. Jerry Szumski, "Introduce Bill to Revise Iowa's Abortion Law," *Des Moines Register,* January 23, 1973.

38. "Abortions and the Right of Privacy," *Los Angeles Times,* January 23, 1973.

39. Warren Weaver, Jr., "National Guidelines Set by 7-to-2 Vote," *New York Times,* January 23, 1973.

40. "Indecision on Abortion," *Chicago Tribune,* January 23, 1973.

41. *Bakke v. Regents of the University of California,* 28 Cal.3d 34 (1976).

42. *Regents of the University of California v. Bakke,* 429 U.S. 1090 (1977).

43. *Regents of the University of California v. Bakke,* 438 U.S. 265 (1978).

44. Elliot E. Slotnick and Jennifer A. Segal, *Television News and the Supreme Court: All the News That's Fit to Air?* (Cambridge, Eng.: Cambridge University Press, 1998).

45. Ibid., 102.

46. Ibid., 105.

47. Ibid., 106.

48. Ibid., 109.

49. Ibid., 92.

50. *Newsweek,* July 10, 1978, quoted in Slotnick and Segal, *Television News,* 93.

51. Philip Hager, "Bakke Wins but Justices Uphold Affirmative Action," *Los Angeles Times,* June 29, 1978.

52. Glen Elsasser and Jack Fuller, "Wins Reverse Bias Case," *Chicago Tribune,* June 29, 1978.

53. Warren Weaver, Jr., "Guidance Is Provided," *New York Times,* June 29, 1978.

54. Carol H. Falk and Urban C. Lehner, "The Bakke Ruling: Supreme Court Gives Qualified Approval to Affirmative Action," *Wall Street Journal,* June 29, 1978.

55. "A Calm, Reasoned Opinion," *Los Angeles Times,* June 29, 1978.

56. "The Bakke Decision," *Washington Post,* June 29, 1978.

57. Laurel Saiz, "Bakke's Victory Unlikely to Affect SU," *Post-Standard,* Syracuse, New York, June 29, 1978.

58. Pat O'Conner, "'Not Much Change' Expected at UNI," *Waterloo Courier,* Waterloo, Iowa, June 29, 1978.

59. Robert Lindsey, "Focus of Historic Battle in Civil Rights Law," *New York Times,* June 29, 1978.

60. *United Steelworkers of America v. Weber,* 443 U.S. 193 (1979).

61. *Fullilove v. Klutznick,* 448 U.S. 448 (1980).

62. Ibid., 482.

63. Linda Greenhouse, "Congress's Power to Give Benefits Based on Race Is Supported by 6 to 3," *New York Times,* July 3, 1980.

64. Associated Press, "Court Endorses Business Minority Quotas," *Daily Intelligencer,* Doylestown, Pennsylvania, July 3, 1980.

65. *Richmond Newspapers v. Virginia,* 448 U.S. 555 (1980).

66. *AFL-CIO v. American Petroleum Institute,* 448 U.S. 607 (1980).

67. *Wallace v. Jaffree,* 472 U.S. 38, 56 (1985).

68. Tim O'Brien, "Supreme Court Strikes Down Alabama School Prayer Law," *World News Tonight,* ABC, June 4, 1985.

69. Philip Hager, "Court Voids Silent Prayer, May Allow School Meditation," *Los Angeles Times,* June 5, 1985.

70. "Plaintiff in Prayer Suit Says the Case Hurt His Children," *New York Times,* June 5, 1985.

71. Harry Rosenthal, Associated Press, "Prayer Ruling Stirs Emotional Issue," *Gettysburg Times,* Gettysburg, Pennsylvania, June 5, 1985.

72. Associated Press, "School Silence Can't Promote Prayer," *Santa Fe New Mexican,* Santa Fe, New Mexico, June 5, 1985.

73. Staff and United Press International, "Prayer Ruling to Have No Effect in State," *Pharos-Tribune,* Logansport, Indiana, June 5, 1985.

74. Dave Urbanek, "State's Verse on Prayer May Be Unconstitutional," *Daily Herald,* Chicago, Illinois, June 5, 1985.

75. "Ruling Consistent, but Perhaps Not Necessary," *Syracuse Herald-Journal,* Syracuse, New York, June 5, 1985.

76. *Fullilove v. Klutznick,* 448 U.S. 448 (1980).

77. *Richmond v. J. A. Croson Co.,* 488 U.S. 469, 499, 552–53 (1989).

78. Linda Greenhouse, "Court Bars a Plan Set Up to Provide Jobs to Minorities," *New York Times,* January 24, 1989.

79. *Texas v. Johnson,* 491 U.S. 397 (1989).

80. Ibid., 419.

81. Ibid., 424, Rehnquist, C. J., dissenting.

82. Carl Stern, "Supreme Court/Freedom of Speech/Flag Burning," *NBC Evening News,* June 21, 1989.

83. Tony Mauro, "Vets See Flag Ruling as a 'Slap,' " *USA Today,* June 22, 1989.

84. Frank Green, "World War II Veteran Incensed at Flag Ruling," *San Diego Union-Tribune,* June 22, 1989.

85. United Press International, "DJs Call for Day of Mourning for Flag," June 22, 1989.

86. Associated Press, "Veteran Who Retrieved Ashes of Burned Flag Grieves over Ruling," *Syracuse Herald Journal,* Syracuse, New York, June 22, 1989.

87. "New Glory for Old Glory," *New York Times,* June 23, 1989.

88. "Burning Flags," *Washington Post,* June 24, 1989.

89. "Flag-Burning," *Post-Standard,* Syracuse, New York, June 22, 1989.

90. *Webster v. Reproductive Health Services,* 492 U.S. 490 (1989).

91. *Roe v. Wade,* 410 U.S. 113 (1973).

92. Slotnick and Segal, *Television News,* 116, 127.

93. Ibid., 114–16.

94. Linda Greenhouse, "Supreme Court, 5-4, Narrowing Roe v. Wade, Upholds Sharp State Limits on Abortions," *New York Times,* July 4, 1989.

95. Ethan Bronner, "Split Supreme Court Allows States to Restrict and Regulate Abortions," *Boston Globe,* July 4, 1989.

96. Karen L. Koman, "Both Sides Vow: Fight Will Move to Clinics, Legislatures," *St. Louis Post-Dispatch,* July 4, 1989.

97. Ellen Goodman, "Counting the Votes," *Washington Post,* July 4, 1989.

98. George Will, "Now, Let's Have a 50-State Row over Abortion," *Orlando Sentinel,* July 5, 1989.

99. Slotnick and Segal, *Television News,* 149, 150, 154.

100. *Romer v. Evans,* 517 U.S. 620 (1996).

101. Associated Press, "Supreme Court Hands Gay Advocates Biggest Victory," *Daily Herald,* Tyrone, Pennsylvania, May 21, 1996.

102. "Supreme Court Rejects Anti-Gay Initiative," *Santa Fe New Mexican,* May 21, 1996.

103. Tom Brokaw and Pete Williams, "Supreme Court/Gay Rights," *NBC Nightly News,* May 20, 1996.

104. *BMW of North America v. Gore,* 517 U.S. 559 (1996).

105. *Washington v. Glucksberg,* 521 U.S. 702 (1997).

106. William Goldschlag, "Suicide's Not a Right, Justices Say," *Daily News,* New York, June 27, 1997.

107. Basil Talbott, "No Right to Suicide Help; Supreme Court Upholds State Bans," *Chicago Sun-Times,* June 27, 1997.

108. Judy Wiessler, "Landmark Court Ruling; 'Right to Die' Ban Is Upheld," *Houston Chronicle,* June 27, 1997.

109. Linda Greenhouse, "Court, 9-0, Upholds State Laws Prohibiting Assisted Suicide," *New York Times,* June 27, 1997.

110. Richard Carelli, Associated Press, "Justices Rule Against Assisted Suicide 'Right,'" *Daily Sentinel,* Sitka, Alaska, June 26, 1997.

111. Anthony Collings, "Doctor-Assisted Suicide," *CNN World View,* June 26, 1997; Pete Williams, "Doctor-Assisted Suicide," *NBC Nightly News,* June 26, 1997.

112. *Grutter v. Bollinger,* 539 U.S. 306 (2003).

113. *Gratz v. Bollinger,* 539 U.S. 244 (2003).

114. *Adarand Constructors v. Pena,* 515 U.S. 200 (1995).

115. *Richmond v. J. A. Croson Co.,* 488 U.S. 469 (1989).

116. *Fullilove v. Klutznick,* 448 U.S. 448 (1980).

117. *Regents of the University of California v. Bakke,* 438 U.S. 265, 317 (1978).

118. Bob Franken, "Affirmative Action," *CNN NewsNight,* June 23, 2003.

119. John Aloysius Farrell, "Court Backs Diversity in College Admissions," *Denver Post,* June 24, 2003.

120. Warren Richey, "Race in Admissions Revised," *Christian Science Monitor,* June 24, 2003. *Gratz,* 539 U.S. at 276–77.

121. Kelly Simmons and Andrea Jones, "Supreme Court: Affirmative Action: UGA May Rethink Its Policy," *Atlanta Journal-Constitution,* June 24, 2003.

122. Alice Thomas, "OSU Likely to Adjust Admissions Process," *Columbus Dispatch,* June 24, 2003.

123. "Back to Bakke," *Boston Globe,* June 24, 2003.

124. "Racial Fairness Upheld in Double Decision," *Santa Fe New Mexican,* June 24, 2003.

125. "Supreme Court Quotas," *Wall Street Journal,* June 24, 2003.

126. U.S. Constitution, First Amendment (in part): "Congress shall make no law respecting an establishment of religion, or prohibiting the free exercise thereof."

127. *Newdow v. United States Congress,* 328 F.3d 466 (9th Cir., 2002).

128. *Elk Grove Unified School District v. Newdow,* 542 U.S. 1 (2004).

129. Alain L. Sanders, "How the Media Reported the Supreme Court Ruling on the Pledge of Allegiance and Its Reference to God," *Judicature* 88, no. 5 (March–April 2005): 202–8, 203.

130. Ibid., 204.

131. Ibid., 205.

132. Ibid., 206.

133. *Kelo v. City of New London,* 545 U.S. 469, 484, 494 (2005).

134. Jay Fitzgerald, "High Court Bolsters Municipal Land Grabs," *Boston Herald,* June 24, 2005.

135. Aaron Brown, "Home Seizures," *CNN NewsNight,* June 23, 2005.

136. "Takings Advantage," *Bangor Daily News,* Bangor, Maine, June 24, 2005.

137. "Keep Land Acquisition Protection Intact," *Daily Herald,* Chicago, Illinois, June 24, 2005.

138. "A Win for Big Government," *Washington Times,* June 24, 2005.

139. "Eminent Mistake," *St. Petersburg Times,* St. Petersburg, Florida, June 24, 2005.

140. "The Limits of Property Rights," *New York Times,* June 24, 2005.

141. *McCreary County v. American Civil Liberties Union of Kentucky,* 545 U.S. 844 (2005).

142. *Van Orden v. Perry,* 545 U.S. 677 (2005).

143. Stephen Henderson, "Split on Ten Commandments; High Court Only Confused the Issue, Both Sides Argue," *Philadelphia Inquirer,* June 28, 2005.

144. Bill Adair, "Supreme Court: No Clear Rule on Religious Displays," *St. Petersburg Times,* June 23, 2005.

145. Larry Copeland and Toni Locy, "Decisions Leave Some Confused," *USA Today,* June 28, 2005.

146. "Thou Shalt & Thou Shalt Not," *Daily News,* New York, June 28, 2005.

147. "The Court Affirms Separation of Church and State," *New York Times,* June 28, 2005.

148. "Limits of Religion in Public Life," *Christian Science Monitor,* June 28, 2005.

149. Aaron Brown, "Ten Commandments," *CNN NewsNight,* June 27, 2005.

150. *Gonzales v. Oregon,* 546 U.S. 243 (2006).

151. Stephen Henderson, "Justices Uphold Assisted Suicide," *Augusta Chronicle,* Augusta, Georgia, January 18, 2006.

152. "Right to Die Law Is Upheld," *Denver Post,* January 18, 2006.

153. "Oregon's Assistants," *Boston Globe,* January 18, 2006.

154. Wyatt Andrews, "U.S. Supreme Court Rejects Bush Administration's Attempt to Stop Doctor-Assisted Suicide," *CBS Evening News,* January 17, 2006.

155. Pete Williams, "Doctor-Assisted Suicide," *NBC Nightly News,* January 17, 2006.

156. Elizabeth Vargas, "Right to Die; Supreme Court Upholds Oregon's Assisted Suicide Law," *ABC World News Tonight,* January 17, 2006.

157. *Massachusetts v. Environmental Protection Agency,* 549 U.S. 497 (2007).

158. Jeff Nesmith, "Justices OK Rules on Global Warming," *Austin American-Statesman,* April 3, 2007. *Massachusetts,* 549 U.S. at 558, Scalia, J., dissenting.

159. "Gassing the EPA: Supreme Court Crushes Bush Dodge on Global Warming," *Salt Lake Tribune,* April 3, 2007.

160. "A Clear Ruling on Clean Air Laws," *San Francisco Chronicle,* April 3, 2007.

161. Paul Rogers, "Supreme Court Ruling Backs Up State Law Requiring Eco-Friendly Cars," *San Jose Mercury News,* April 3, 2007.

162. "Court Tells Bush to Cool It," *Boston Globe,* April 3, 2007.

163. "Jolly Green Justices," *Wall Street Journal,* April 3, 2007.

164. Wyatt Andrews and Anthony Mason, "Supreme Court Rules Environmental Protection Agency Has Statutory Obligation to Regulate Auto Emissions," *CBS Evening News,* April 2, 2007.

165. *Gonzales v. Planned Parenthood Federation,* 550 U.S. 124 (2007). *Planned Parenthood of Southeast Pennsylvania v. Casey,* 505 U.S. 833 (1992).

166. Jan Crawford Greenburg, *World News with Charles Gibson,* ABC, April 18, 2007.

167. Wyatt Andrews, "Supreme Court Ruling on Abortion," *CBS Evening News,* April 18, 2007.

168. Judy Woodruff, "U. S. Supreme Court's Abortion Decision," *NewsHour with Jim Lehrer,* Public Broadcasting System, April 18, 2007.

169. Linda Greenhouse, "In Reversal of Course, Justices, 5-4, Back Ban on Abortion Method," *New York Times,* April 19, 2007. The prior case was *Stenberg v. Carhart,* 530 U.S. 914 (2000), which held unconstitutional a similar Nebraska statute. The Court differentiated the federal law as more specific and more precise.

170. Tracy Wheeler, "Procedure in Ohio Now Illegal; State Law Considered Health Risk to Women," *Akron Beacon Journal,* April 19, 2007.

171. Trip Jennings and Gabriela C. Guzman, "Abortion Ruling Fuels Debate in N. M.," *Albuquerque Journal,* April 19, 2007.

172. "Standing Against Infanticide; Abortion—in All Its Murderous Forms—Is Not a Right," *Augusta Chronicle,* Augusta, Georgia, April 19, 2007.

173. "Partial-Birth Abortion Ruling Is a Victory for Humanity," *Tampa Tribune,* April 19, 2007.

174. "Abortion Rights Under Assault," *San Francisco Chronicle*, April 19, 2007.

175. "An Erosion of Abortion Rights," *Boston Globe*, April 19, 2007.

176. *Ricci v. DeStefano*, 129 S.Ct. 2658 (2009).

177. Joan Biskupic, "Ruling's Impact on Hiring Weighed; High Court Reverses Sotomayor's Panel," *USA Today*, June 30, 2009.

178. Adam Liptak, "Supreme Court Finds Bias Against White Firefighters," *New York Times*, June 30, 2009.

179. Michael Doyle, "Supreme Court Rules for White Firefighters in Bias Case," *San Jose Mercury News*, San Jose, California, June 30, 2009.

180. Mark Sherman, Associated Press, "U.S. Justices Back White Firefighters and Overturn a Sotomayor Decision," *Star-Ledger*, Newark, New Jersey, June 30, 2009.

181. "Judicial Overreaching," *Baltimore Sun*, June 30, 2009.

CHAPTER TWELVE

1. Ruth Bader Ginsburg, "Communicating and Commenting on the Court's Work," *Georgetown Law Journal* 83 (July 1995): 2119–29, 2128.

2. *Solid Waste Agency of Northern Cook County v. Army Corps of Engineers*, 531 U.S. 159 (2001).

3. Gary Wisby, "Court Says No to Birds," *Chicago Sun-Times*, January 10, 2001.

4. *McCreary County v. American Civil Liberties Union of Kentucky*, 545 U.S. 844 (2005); *Van Orden v. Perry*, 545 U.S. 677 (2005).

5. Jeff Brumley, "The Ten Commandments: A High Court Split Decision; Decisions Open Door to Future Religious Suits," *Florida Times-Union*, June 28, 2005.

6. *Hamdi v. Rumsfeld*, 542 U.S. 507 (2004).

7. Gerard Shields, "High Court: War No 'Blank Check' in Detainees Cases," *Advocate*, Baton Rouge, Louisiana, June 29, 2004.

8. Rorie L. Spill and Zoe M. Oxley, "How the Media Portray the Supreme Court," *Judicature* 87, no. 1 (July–August 2003): 22–29, 24, 27.

9. Ibid., 28–29.

10. Pete Williams, "Supreme Court Hands Down Major Rulings

Against Bush Administration and Its Handling of Prisoners in War on Terror," *NBC Nightly News,* June 28, 2004.

11. *Miller v. Johnson,* 515 U.S. 900, 904 (1995).

12. James Salzer, "Ruling May Affect Entire State," *Augusta Chronicle,* Augusta, Georgia, June 30, 1995.

13. *Engel v. Vitale,* 370 U.S. 421 (1962).

14. *Baker v. Carr,* 369 U.S. 186 (1962).

15. Chester A. Newland, "Press Coverage of the United States Supreme Court," *Western Political Quarterly* 17 (1964): 15–36.

16. Lionel S. Sobel, "News Coverage of the Supreme Court," *American Bar Association Journal* 56 (June 1970): 547–50, 548.

17. *Grutter v. Bollinger,* 539 U.S. 306 (2003); *Gratz v. Bollinger,* 539 U.S. 244 (2003).

18. Stephen Hagen and Anita Kumar, "Race Preferences Okay—to a Point," *St. Petersburg Times,* June 24, 2003.

19. *Gonzales v. Raich,* 545 U.S. 1 (2005).

20. Catherine Crier, "Bridging the Great Divide: A Symposium on the State of Legal Journalism: Journalism and the Law," *Syracuse Law Review* 56 (2006): 387–99, 392.

21. Charles Fairman, *Mr. Justice Miller and the Supreme Court 1862–1890* (Cambridge, Mass.: Harvard University Press, 1939), 279.

22. Alpheus T. Mason, *Harlan Fiske Stone, Pillar of the Law* (New York: Viking, 1956), 626, quoting from Stone's letter to Ernest Kirschten, April 17, 1944.

23. James E. Clayton, "Interpreting the Court," book review, *Columbia Journalism Review* 7, no. 2 (Summer 1968): 47–48.

24. David L. Grey, *The Supreme Court and the News Media* (Evanston, Ill.: Northwestern University Press, 1968), 120.

25. Elliott E. Slotnick and Jennifer A. Segal, *Television News and the Supreme Court: All the News That's Fit to Air?* (Cambridge, Eng.: Cambridge University Press, 1998), 12.

26. Tony Mauro, "Five Ways Appellate Courts Can Help," *Journal of Appellate Practice and Process* 9, no. 2 (Fall 2007): 311–21.

27. Richard J. Peltz, "Preface: Bringing Light to the Halls of Shadow," *Journal of Appellate Practice and Process* 9, no. 2 (Fall 2007): 291–98, 296–97.

28. Linda Greenhouse, "Telling the Court's Story: Justice and Journalism at the Supreme Court," *Yale Law Journal* 105 (April 1996): 1545.

29. John P. MacKenzie, "The Supreme Court and the Press," *Michigan Law Review* 67 (December 1968): 303–16, 304.

30. Totals and averages are derived from annual Supreme Court statistics compiled by Tom Goldstein, Scotusblog and Akin, Gump, Strauss, Hauer, and Feld LLP, posted at http://scotuswiki.com/index.

31. Mauro, "Five Ways," 312.

32. Not to mention others who write about legal affairs including the Court: Dahlia Lithwick of *Slate* and Jeffrey Toobin of the *New Yorker* and CNN, author of *The Nine: Inside the Secret World of the Supreme Court* (New York: Doubleday, 2007). Greg Stohr of Bloomberg, a graduate of Harvard Law School, won the 2001 New York Press Club spot news award for his coverage of *Bush v. Gore,* and is the author of a book about the University of Michigan admissions disputes, *A Black and White Case: How Affirmative Action Survived Its Greatest Legal Challenge* (Princeton, N.J.: Bloomberg, 2004).

33. Liva Baker, *Felix Frankfurter* (New York: Coward-McCann, 1969), 218.

34. Grey, *Supreme Court,* 52.

35. *Gideon v. Wainwright,* 372 U.S. 335 (1963). With legal representation Clarence Earl Gideon was tried again and acquitted. The book is *Gideon's Trumpet* (New York: Vintage Books, 1989).

36. Anthony Lewis, *Make No Law: The Sullivan Case and the First Amendment* (New York: Vintage Books, 1992).

37. Graham believes a legal affairs reporter should prepare by more than just the study of the law: "I go farther than that—I think they can benefit from practicing law for a while before turning to journalism. My reason is that there is a legal culture that is just as important as the textbook law in reporting on the law." E-mail to the author, August 27, 2009.

38. Greenhouse, "Telling the Court's Story," 1541–42.

39. Everette E. Dennis, "Another Look at Press Coverage of the Supreme Court," *Villanova Law Review* 20, no. 4 (1974–75): 765–99, 792.

40. The error was on the Gold Clause cases, including *Norman v. Baltimore & Ohio Railroad Co.,* 294 U.S. 240 (1935), in which the Court upheld Congress's abrogation of contract clauses stipulating payment in

gold. David L. Grey quotes the AP bureau chief, Byron Price, as admitting in a letter to Grey that the AP "made a serious error as a result of too much haste." Price appealed personally to Chief Justice Hughes to advance the release of the printed opinions, and it was done. Grey, *Supreme Court,* 37.

41. Fred Graham, *Happy Talk: Confessions of a TV Newsman* (New York and London: W.W. Norton, 1990), 98.

42. Ibid., 100.

43. Ibid.

44. Ibid., 101–2.

45. *New York Times v. United States,* 403 U.S. 713 (1971).

46. Graham, *Happy Talk,* 96.

47. Greenhouse, "Telling the Court's Story," 1558.

48. Quoted in Slotnick and Segal, *Television News,* 50.

49. Only one such prompt release of an audio recording occurred in the 2008–2009 term, according to the Court's Public Information office. Patricia McCabe Estrada, deputy public information officer, e-mail to the author, July 20, 2009.

50. When in Albany, Linda Greenhouse of the *New York Times* participated in such an advance reading at the New York Court of Appeals, New York state's highest court, the accommodation enhanced further by an off-the-record availability of one judge to help explain the decision, which was an especially complex and sensitive one with potential impact on the financial markets. "To my knowledge, none of the reporters who took part in this episode broke the rules or betrayed the court's confidence." Greenhouse, "Telling the Court's Story," 1544.

51. Jack Gould, "Stanton Scores TV on Ruby Trial," *New York Times,* March 27, 1964, 49, reporting on a speech by Stanton at the University of Pennsylvania.

52. Elizabeth M. Hodgkins, "Court System Panel: Throwing Open a Window on the Nation's Courts by Lifting the Ban on Federal Courtroom Television," *Kansas Journal of Law and Public Policy* 4 (Spring 1995): 89–100, 97.

53. Audrey Maness, "Does the First Amendment's 'Right of Access' Require Court Proceedings to Be Televised? A Constitutional and Practical Discussion," *Pepperdine Law Review* 34 (2006): 123–85, 159.

54. Diane L. Zimmerman, "Overcoming Future Shock: *Estes* Revisited, or a Modest Proposal for the Constitutional Protection of the News-Gathering Process," *Duke Law Journal,* no. 4 (September 1980): 641–708, 708.

55. Fox News/Opinion Dynamics (2006 poll); the Gallup Organization, survey sponsors Cable News Network, *USA Today* (2000 poll); source for both: Roper Center at the University of Connecticut; cited in Lorraine H. Tong, "Televising Supreme Court and Other Federal Court Proceedings: Legislation and Issues," Congressional Research Service, updated November 8, 2006.

56. In the 2008–09 term the precise number admitted was 29,253. The Court maintains no count of thousands of other tourists who are allowed in for just three to five minutes ("I went to the Supreme Court!"); they wait in a separate long line. Patricia McCabe Estrada, deputy public information officer, e-mail to the author, July 20, 2009.

57. *Crawford v. Marion County Election Board,* 128 S.Ct. 1610 (2008). The Court affirmed Indiana's requirement that voters present a government-issued photo identification.

58. "The Supreme Court Club," *New York Times,* January 16, 2008, A22. Justice Thomas's book is *My Grandfather's Son: A Memoir* (New York: Harper, 2007). He also sat for nearly seven hours of interviews about his book and his life with Jan Crawford Greenburg of ABC News, which produced a seven-part series in fall 2007 called "Clarence Thomas: A Silent Justice Speaks Out," http://www.abcnews.go.com/TheLaw/story?id=3664143&page=1 (accessed August 20, 2009).

59. Associated Press, "Scalia Says He's Against Cameras in Supreme Court, Wouldn't Want to Go Through Senate Confirmation," October 10, 2005.

60. "A Conversation with U.S. Supreme Court Chief Justice John G. Roberts," 2006 Ninth Circuit Judicial Conference, Huntington Beach, California, July 13, 2006, Washington State Public Affairs TV Network, http://www.tvw.org/media/mediaplayer.cfm?evid=2006070110&TYPE =V&CFID=610960&CFTOKEN=18275594&bhcp=1 (accessed August 20, 2009).

61. 151 *Congressional Record* S10426, September 26, 2005.

62. Ibid.

63. S. 344, reported by the Senate Judiciary Committee, July 29, 2008, 154 *Congressional Record* S8130.

64. Tong, "Televising Supreme Court," p. 7. The bill was H.R. 1751.

65. Tony Mauro, "House Members Push Supreme Court Toward Transparency," *National Law Journal,* April 24, 2009, http://www.law.com/jsp/nlj/PubArticleNLJ.jsp?id=1202430151661. Representative Culberson's video is at http://qik.com/video/1530156 (accessed August 21, 2009).

66. Ball State University, "Most Detailed Study Yet of Consumer Video Viewing Suggests Some Rethinking Is in Order," March 26, 2009, http://www.bsu.edu/news/article/0,1370,7273-850-61579,00.html (accessed August 21, 2009). Consumers age 45 to 54 watched television even more, nine and a half hours per day. The yearlong study was conducted by Ball State University's Center for Media Design and Sequent Partners LLC, a consulting firm, for the Council for Research Excellence, an audience-measurement research group funded by the Nielsen Company.

67. Diarmuid F. O'Scannlain, "Some Reflections on Cameras in the Appellate Courtroom," *Journal of Appellate Practice and Process* 9, no. 2 (Fall 2007): 323–30, 327, 330.

68. *Southwest Voter Registration Education Project v. Shelley,* 344 F.3d 914, en banc (2003).

69. O'Scannlain, "Some Reflections," 328, 329.

70. Ibid., 324.

71. As of mid-2009, the states admitting or providing cameras were Alaska, Arizona, California, Connecticut, Florida, Georgia, Idaho, Illinois, Indiana, Iowa, Kentucky, Louisiana, Maryland, Massachusetts, Michigan, Minnesota, Mississippi, Missouri, Montana, Nebraska, Nevada, New Hampshire, New Jersey, New Mexico, New York, North Carolina, Ohio, Oklahoma, Oregon, Texas, Utah, Vermont, Washington, and West Virginia. Leslie Patton, Northwestern University, telephone and e-mail survey for this book, March–June 2009.

72. Robert L. Brown, "Essay: Just a Matter of Time? Video Cameras at the United States Supreme Court and the State Supreme Courts," *Journal of Appellate Practice and Process* 9, no. 1 (Spring 2007): 1–13, 9, 13.

73. Ibid., 9, 13. In 2010 the Arkansas Supreme Court became the thirty-fifth to admit TV cameras.

74. Robert Craig Waters, "Technological Transparency: Appellate Court and Media Relations After *Bush v. Gore," Journal of Appellate Practice and Process* 9, no. 2 (Fall 2007): 331–86, 337–38, 354. Waters is a member of the Florida Bar and a former Tallahassee statehouse reporter.

75. Ibid., 354, 356.

76. *Gore v. Harris,* 772 So.2d 1243 (Fla. 2000).

77. Waters, "Technological Transparency," 338.

78. David Bloom, "Bush v. Gore: Florida Recount," *NBC Nightly News,* December 7, 2000.

79. Lyle Denniston, "Barbs from the Bench; Wounded State Supreme Court Has Choice Words," *Milwaukee Journal Sentinel,* December 8, 2000.

SELECTED BIBLIOGRAPHY

◈

Ames, William E. *A History of the National Intelligencer.* Chapel Hill: University of North Carolina Press, 1972.

Belsky, Martin H., ed. *The Rehnquist Court: A Retrospective.* Oxford and New York: Oxford University Press, 2002.

Bork, Robert H. *The Antitrust Paradox: A Policy at War with Itself.* New York: Free, 1983.

Brigham, John. *The Cult of the Court.* Philadelphia: Temple University Press, 1987.

Chamberlain, Bill F., and Charlene J. Brown, eds. *The First Amendment Reconsidered: New Perspectives on the Meaning of Freedom of Speech and Press.* New York and London: Longman, 1982.

Chemerinsky, Erwin. "The Supreme Court, Public Opinion, and the Role of the Academic Commentator." *South Texas Law Review* 40 (Fall 1999): 943.

Clayton, James E. "Interpreting the Court." *Columbia Journalism Review* 7, no. 2 (Summer 1968): 47–48.

Crier, Catherine. "Bridging the Great Divide: A Symposium on the State of Legal Journalism: Journalism and the Law." *Syracuse Law Review* 56 (2006): 387.

Davis, Richard. *Decisions and Images: The Supreme Court and the Press.* Englewood Cliffs, N. J.: Prentice Hall, 1994.

Dennis, Everette E. "Another Look at Press Coverage of the Supreme Court." *Villanova Law Review* 20, no. 4 (1974–75): 765–99.

Denniston, Lyle. "Horse-and-Buggy Dockets in the Internet Age, and the Travails of a Courthouse Reporter." *Journal of Appellate Practice and Process* 9, no. 2 (Fall 2007): 299–309.

Devol, Kenneth S., ed. *Mass Media and the Supreme Court: The Legacy of the Warren Years.* New York: Hastings House, 1982.

Ely, James W., Jr. *The Chief Justiceship of Melville W. Fuller, 1888–1910.* Columbia: University of South Carolina Press, 1995.

Fiss, Owen. *The Irony of Free Speech.* Cambridge, Mass., and London: Harvard University Press, 1996.

Friedman, Lawrence M. "The Rehnquist Court: Some More or Less Historical Comments." In *The Rehnquist Court: A Retrospective,* ed. Martin H. Belsky. Oxford and New York: Oxford University Press, 2002.

Garbus, Martin. *The Next 25 Years: The New Supreme Court and What It Means for Americans.* New York and Toronto: Seven Stories, 2007.

Gillman, Howard, and Cornell Clayton, eds. *The Supreme Court in American Politics: New Institutionalist Interpretations.* Lawrence: University Press of Kansas, 1999.

Ginsburg, Ruth Bader. "Communicating and Commenting on the Court's Work." *Georgetown Law Journal* 83 (July 1995): 2119–29.

Graham, Fred. *Happy Talk: Confessions of a TV Newsman.* New York and London: W. W. Norton, 1990.

Greenburg, Jan Crawford. *Supreme Conflict: The Inside Story of the Struggle for Control of the United States Supreme Court.* New York: Penguin, 2007.

Greenhouse, Linda. "Telling the Court's Story: Justice and Journalism at the Supreme Court." *Yale Law Journal* 105 (April 1996): 1537–61.

Grey, David L. *The Supreme Court and the News Media.* Evanston, Ill.: Northwestern University Press, 1968.

Hall, Kermit L., ed. *The Oxford Companion to the Supreme Court of the United States.* Oxford and New York: Oxford University Press, 1992.

———, ed. *The Oxford Guide to United States Supreme Court Decisions.* Oxford and New York: Oxford University Press, 1999.

Hasen, Richard L. *The Supreme Court and Election Law: Judging Equality from Baker v. Carr to Bush v. Gore.* New York and London: New York University Press, 2003.

Hibbing, John R., and Elizabeth Theiss-Morse. *Congress as Public Enemy.* Cambridge, Eng., and New York: Cambridge University Press, 1995.

Hindman, Elizabeth Blanks. *Rights vs. Responsibilities: The Supreme Court and the Media.* Westport, Conn., and London: Greenwood, 1997.

Hodgkins, Elizabeth M. "Court System Panel: Throwing Open a Window on the Nation's Courts by Lifting the Ban on Federal Courtroom Television." *Kansas Journal of Law and Public Policy* 4 (Spring 1995): 89–100.

Hoekstra, Valerie J. *Public Reaction to Supreme Court Decisions.* Cambridge, Eng., and New York: Cambridge University Press, 2003.

Ingelhart, Louis Edward, comp. *Press and Speech Freedoms in America, 1619–1995: A Chronology.* Westport, Conn., and London: Greenwood, 1997.

———. *Press Freedoms: A Descriptive Calendar of Concepts, Interpretations, Events.* Westport, Conn.: Greenwood, 1987.

Irons, Peter. *A People's History of the Supreme Court.* New York: Penguin Books, 1999.

Iyengar, Shanto. *Is Anyone Responsible? How Television Frames Political Issues.* Chicago and London: University of Chicago Press, 1991.

Katsh, Ethan. "The Supreme Court Beat: How Television Covers the Supreme Court." *Judicature* 67, no. 1 (June–July 1983): 6–12.

Keith, Linda Camp. "The United States Supreme Court and Judicial Review of Congress, 1803–2001." *Judicature* 90, no. 4 (January–February 2007): 166–73.

Kerr, Robert L. "Considering the Meaning of *Wisconsin Right to Life* for the Corporate Free-Speech Movement." *Communication Law and Policy* 14, no. 2 (Spring 2009): 105–52.

Landes, William M., and Richard A. Posner. *The Economic Structure of Intellectual Property Law.* Cambridge, Mass., and London: Belknap Press of Harvard University Press, 2003.

Lane, Charles. *The Day Freedom Died: The Colfax Massacre, the Supreme Court, and the Betrayal of Reconstruction.* New York: Henry Holt, 2008.

Lewis, Anthony. *Freedom for the Thought We Hate: A Biography of the First Amendment.* New York: Basic Books, 2007.

———. *Gideon's Trumpet.* New York: Vintage Books, 1964.

———. *Make No Law: The Sullivan Case and the First Amendment.* New York: Vintage Books, 1992.

———. "Problems of a Washington Correspondent." *Connecticut Bar Journal* 32, no. 4 (December 1959): 363–71.

Lofton, John. *The Press as Guardian of the First Amendment.* Columbia: University of South Carolina Press, 1980.

Luxon, Norval Neil. *Niles Weekly Register: News Magazine of the Nineteenth Century.* Westport, Conn.: Greenwood, 1947.

MacKenzie, John P. "The Supreme Court and the Press." *Michigan Law Review* 67 (December 1968): 303–16.

Manness, Audrey. "Does the First Amendment 'Right of Access' Require Court Proceedings to Be Televised? A Constitutional and Practical Discussion." *Pepperdine Law Review* 34 (2006): 123.

Marshall, Thomas R. *Public Opinion and the Supreme Court.* Boston: Unwin Hyman, 1989.

Mauro, Tony. "Bridging the Great Divide: A Symposium on the State of Legal Journalism: The Chief and Us: Chief Justice William Rehnquist, the News Media, and the Need for Dialogue Between Judges and Journalists." *Syracuse Law Review* 56 (2006): 407.

McGough, Michael. "Bridging the Great Divide: A Symposium on the State of Legal Journalism: Journalism's Legal Fiction: The Cult of Objectivity and Deference in Supreme Court Coverage." *Syracuse Law Review* 56 (2006): 401.

Mott, Frank Luther. *American Journalism, A History, 1690–1960.* New York: Macmillan, 1962.

National Opinion Research Center, University of Chicago. *General Social Surveys, 1972–1996: Cumulative Codebook.* Storrs: Roper Center for Public Opinion Research, University of Connecticut, 1996.

Newman, Roger K. *Hugo Black: A Biography.* New York: Fordham University Press, 1994.

Newton, Jim. *Justice for All: Earl Warren and the Nation He Made.* New York: Riverhead Books, 2006.

Pacelle, Richard L., Jr. *The Role of the Supreme Court in American Politics: The Least Dangerous Branch?* Boulder, Colo.: Westview, 2002.

Perry, Barbara A. *The Priestly Tribe: The Supreme Court's Image in the American Mind.* Westport, Conn., and London: Praeger, 1999.

Pether, Penelope. "Regarding the Miller Girls: Daisy, Judith, and the Seeming Paradox of In re Grand Jury Subpoena, Judith Miller." *Cardozo Studies in Law and Literature* 19 (Summer 2007): 187.

Posner, Richard A., ed. *The Essential Holmes: Selections from the Letters, Speeches, Judicial Opinions, and Other Writings of Oliver Wendell Holmes, Jr.* Chicago and London: University of Chicago Press, 1992.

Rehnquist, William H. *The Supreme Court.* New York: Vintage Books, 1987.

Roosevelt, Kermit, III. *The Myth of Judicial Activism: Making Sense of Supreme Court Decisions.* New Haven, Conn., and London: Yale University Press, 2006.

Rosen, Jeffrey. *The Supreme Court: The Personalities and Rivalries That Defined America.* New York: Times Books/Henry Holt, 2007.

Sanders, Alain L. "The Press and the Pledge Case." *Judicature* 88, no. 5 (March–April 2005): 202–8.

Schwartz, Bernard. *A History of the Supreme Court.* New York and Oxford: Oxford University Press, 1993.

Scott, Douglas Gerber. *The Jurisprudence of Clarence Thomas.* New York and London: New York University Press, 1999.

Segal, Jeffrey A., and Harold J. Spaeth. *The Supreme Court and the Attitudinal Model Revisited.* Cambridge, Eng.: Cambridge University Press, 2002.

Semonche, John E. *Keeping the Faith: A Cultural History of the U. S. Supreme Court.* Lanham, Md.: Rowman and Littlefield, 1998.

Slotnick, Elliot E., and Jennifer A. Segal. *Television News and the Supreme Court: All the News That's Fit to Air?* New York: Cambridge University Press, 1998.

Smith, Jean Edward. *John Marshall: Definer of a Nation.* New York: Owl Books, Henry Holt, 1996.

Sobel, Lionel S. "News Coverage of the Supreme Court." *American Bar Association Journal* 56 (June 1970): 547–50.

Spill, Rorie L., and Zoe M. Oxley. "How the Media Portray the Supreme Court." *Judicature* 87, no. 1 (July–August 2003): 23–29.

Stone, Geoffrey R. *Perilous Times: Free Speech in Wartime, from the Sedition Act of 1789 to the War on Terrorism.* New York and London: W. W. Norton, 2004.

Toobin, Jeffrey. *The Nine: Inside the Secret World of the Supreme Court.* New York and London: Doubleday, 2007.

Wermiel, Stephen J. "Conference: News Media Coverage of the United States Supreme Court." *St. Louis Law Journal* 42 (Fall 1998): 1059.

Woodward, Bob, and Scott Armstrong. *The Brethren: Inside the Supreme Court.* New York: Simon and Schuster, 1979.

INDEX

◈

ABC, 171, 173, 201, 206, 216, 281, 286, 307, 318, 333, 335, 358, 365, 441n58
ABC World News Tonight, 312, 313, 318, 431n68, 435n156
Abilene (Texas), 423n69
Abilene Reporter-News, 271, 423n69, 423n73, 423n79
abortion, 17, 201, 205, 304, 320–23, 336–39, 432n94, 433n95, 433n98
Abrahamson, David, xvi
Abrams, Jacob, 28
Abrams v. United States, 250 U.S. 616 (1919), 29, 188, 382n24, 405n61, 405n62
"actual malice," 54–55, 57, 58, 59, 62, 63
AC360, 341
Adair, Bill, 333, 435n144
Adair v. United States, 208 U.S. 161 (1908), 414n25
Adams, John, 26, 27, 124, 125, 179, 382n22
Adarand Constructors v. Pena, 515 U.S. 200 (1995), 326, 433n114
Adkins v. Children's Hospital, 261 U.S. 525 (1923), 416n64
Advocate, 349, 437n7
affirmative action, 204, 306–8, 311, 315, 325–28, 352

Afghanistan, 212, 349
AFL-CIO v. American Petroleum Institute, 448 U.S. 607 (1980), 431n66
Agricultural Adjustment Act of 1933, 155, 157, 383n34
Agricultural Adjustment Administration (AAA), 156
Aiken (South Carolina), 402n136, 422n55
Aiken Standard (and Review), 402n136, 422n55
Air Force Academy. *See under* United States
Akin, Gump, Strauss, Hauer, and Feld LLP, 439n30
Akin, Paige, 411n176
Akron Beacon Journal, 339, 436n170
Alabama, 22–23, 33, 43–44, 203, 214, 223, 258, 259, 266, 278, 312, 324
Alabama shield law, 109, 392n8
Alabama State College, 52
Alabama Supreme Court, 53
Alaska, 204, 214, 215, 433n110, 442n71
Albany (New York), 359, 440n50
Albuquerque Journal, 197, 300, 339, 408n101, 436n171
Alito, Samuel A., Jr., 9, 14, 114, 119, 213, 289, 339

451

Joe Mathewson is a lecturer at Northwestern University's Medill School of Journalism, a former Supreme Court reporter for the *Wall Street Journal*, the author of *Up Against Daley*, and a contributor to the *Chicago Tribune, BusinessWeek Online, Editor & Publisher Online*, and the *Chicago Sun-Times*. He is a graduate of the University of Chicago Law School and practiced law in Chicago.

Fred Graham was the chief anchor and managing editor of CNN's *In Session* (formerly *Court TV*) when it launched in 1991. A former legal reporter for the *New York Times* (1965–1972) and law correspondent for CBS News (1972–1987), he is the author of *The Self-Inflicted Wound, Press Freedom Under Pressure, The Alias Program*, and *Happy Talk: Confessions of a TV Newsman*.